Navigators
Forging a Culture and
Founding a Nation: Volume I

Navigators Forging a Matriarchal Culture in Polynesia

Dedication

THIS BOOK IS DEDICATED TO THE FIRST FEMALE PRIME MINISTER OF THE INDEPENDENT ISLAND NATION OF SAMOA:

HON. FIAME NAOMI MATA'AFA.

Fata Ariu Levi

Navigators Forging a Culture and Founding a Nation Volume I:
    Navigators Forging a Matriarchal Culture in Polynesia
First edition 2021
Published by Ariu Levi

ISBN: 978-1-954076-06-8

Cover image by Faigā Tapusone Asiata

Cover design by Sheila Deeth

Edited by Sheila Deeth

Praise for *Navigators Quest for a Kingdom in Polynesia* by Ariu Levi

A Samoan Orator Chief, Levi is tasked with keeping and propagating the history, laws, language, genealogy, customs, and mythology of his people. The volume augments that traditional knowledge with historical accounts from other cultures—both ancient and modern—as well as scientific studies into the archaeology, genetics, and linguistics of Polynesia. The result is what the author refers to as an "aerial survey," a bird's-eye view that attempts to present a broad picture by taking all possible knowledge into account. (When discussing tiny islands surrounded by a vast expanse of ocean, it's really the only view that makes sense.) The story that emerges is one of human movement: migration that did not end 3,000 years ago but rather continues among Samoans to this day... Levi's prose is balanced and engaging, as one might expect from a professional orator... He adeptly weaves together various threads of information... Levi is the perfect teller of this tale, and it is a story worth hearing... A captivating trove of ideas about the mysterious settlers of Samoa.

Kirkus Book Reviews, Nov 9, 2020

Expertly written and presented by an Orator Chief and native Samoan, an experienced teacher of the Island Nation's history, culture, genealogy, religious rituals, and language, with a passion for research... With the guidance of Orator Chief, Fata Ariu Levi, "Navigators Quest For A Kingdom In Polynesia" reveals the timeline of the Polynesian Navigators' migration, with waves of voyages following that first migration out of Africa around 60,000 years ago—journeys into the Asiatic Archipelago, Indonesia, and the Malay Archipelago before the last Glacial Maximum, when the Sahul Shelf was part of Australian continent. As well as how the Austronesian-speaking people were an amalgamation of migrants into the Asiatic Archipelago. Meet the Seafaring population of the coastal line from Taiwan to Madagascar off the coast of East Africa. And follow the Navigators to Polynesia—the land of Mythology... An eloquent and impressively informative study, "Navigators Quest For A Kingdom In Polynesia" will have a very special value for personal, professional, community, college, and university library Cultural Anthropology collections in general, and Polynesian History supplemental curriculum studies lists in particular.

Midwest Book Reviews
Redefining Possible
Ron Alford & Dustin Hillis
Southwestern Publishing Group

Fata Ariu Levi's version of human origins and expansion is rooted in Sāmoa's ways of thinking; he is both our modern Pili and Leatiogie, respectively casting a wide net and wielding the power of the "pen/keyboard" primarily to produce an exegesis of how and where today's Polynesians fit into world history, a group commonly marginalized in diaspora in spite of its critical contribution in world and regional development; secondarily, to mend the hearts and minds of young generations of Samoans and Manuans in diaspora, motivating them to leave behind the insecurities and fears of being different and to stand tall as movers and shakers in the landscaping and peopling of the globe since the beginning of the human race (the homo sapiens sapiens).

M. Luafata Simanu-Klutz

Navigators
Forging a Culture and
Founding a Nation: Volume I

Navigators Forging a Matriarchal Culture in Polynesia

By Fata Ariu Levi

With a forward by
Tuiloma Loau Luafata Simanu-Klutz, Ph.D.
Retired Associate Professor,
University of Hawai'i at Mānoa

Acknowledgements

To my late brothers Faigā Asiata and Taliaoa Fa'alepo Vaotu'ua who both passed away this past May, 2021, due to complications in their diabetic illnesses. They are dearly missed.

To my late cousin High Chief Lealaifuaneva Pete Reid Jr. and his wife Julie Reid. His guidance and wisdom allowed me to build a network of relationships across the American Samoan leadership community.

To my sisters Selaina Miller Levi and Avasā Kitty Levi for their unwavering support of my work and our family.

Orator Chief Moemai Joseph and Shirley Kleis have been my reliable sources of encouragement and support. Chief Moemai has and will always be a mentor to me. His has been a reliable source of ancient cultural legends and references throughout my Orator career and I thank them both.

To Le Sūsūga Fa'amatuainu Jones Iakopo Tu'ufuli for his much-needed assistance in our Dialogue seminar.

To Reverend Henry and Katie Yandall for sponsoring the Church Youth Dialog seminar.

To my friends out in Newport Beach California, Guy and Trish Johnson; I can always count on their support. And to James Edwards for his wisdom and guidance in business and in the cultural diversity of Southern California and the country of Mexico.

My many thanks and gratitude to my friend and business partner Tony Wong for his support and assistance for the last twenty years.

To Tuiloma Loau Luafata Simanu-Klutz, Ph.D. Retired Associate Professor, University of Hawai'i at Mānoa, Hawai'i. Fa'afetai lava mo lau faivamanaia i le Foreword.

And a special thanks to Sheila Deeth for wisdom and expertise in guiding this effort to fulfillment.

This book is also dedicated to my daughter,
Manaia Launoa (Iliganoa) Levi

as a reminder
of her mother's undying love and care for her
and as a token of her father's love.

Disclaimer

Samoan and Manu'an history belongs to the people. So everyone has their own version of it. It's based on personal experience and knowledge of local events in history, as chronicled by local and island historians and by the chieftain system.

There are Samoan and Manu'an writers who have recorded events in the history of the archipelago, in the vernacular of the islands. I have aggressively collected and acquired many written works, in both the English and the Samoan languages, as foundations to my research efforts. Many of these works are included in the reference section of this book. I'm not able to list them all, due to limited space, but I am indebted to them all nevertheless.

I have relied on several writings because of their comprehensive coverage of history, and the independence of their sources.

- *O le Mavaega i le Tai* by Lafai Sauoāiga Apemoemanatunatu, of Apia, Samoa, 1988, is an effort that resulted from the collaboration of in excess of thirty chiefs across the Samoan and Manu'an Archipelago. It was reviewed and approved by the Congregational Church of Samoa, E.F.K.S. (Old LMS Mission Church). Their collaborative effort is not diminished by the fragmentation of tales of events in the history of the archipelago.
- *Palefuiono* by S. P. Mailo of Tutuila, American Samoa, likewise represents the collaboration of in excess of fifteen chiefs across the archipelago.
- Fuimaono Na'oia Tupua's *O le Suaga a le Va'atele* was the result of his research done under the Department of Tourism of the Government of Samoa, of which he was one of the directors and manager. This effort required Fuimaono Na'oia Tupua to visit every village in Upolu, Savai'i, Apolima, and Manono Islands, gathering his research data.
- Ali'i Felela Fred Henry's (Marist Brothers) *Talafa'asolopitoo Samoa* was reviewed by K.R. Lambie, the Director of the

Department of Education of the Western Samoa Government, in 1958.

- *Lagaga: A Short History of Western Samoa* by Malama Meleisa was a collaborative effort with over thirteen co-authors at the Institute of Pacific Studies, University of the South Pacific, Apia, Samoa. Again, this effort was sanctioned by the University of the South Pacific at Apia, Samoa.
- *Samoa Ne'i Galo* is a collective effort by the Ministry for Youth, Sports, and Cultural Affairs, Youth of the Government of Samoa, 1994. Hon. Pule Lameko was the final editor, and approval is under his signature. The taskforce collectively performed research and documented the myths, and also translated the results into English. The English language translation was invaluable in my effort. And the important issue is the wide range of collective opinions that were incorporated into the work, that gives measure to the writing.

Referencing these works allowed me to rely on the vetting process these authors had already gone through.

Moreover, there is Dr. Augustin Krämer's monograph which stands erect and uncontested. This is an heirloom of the archipelago. While some Samoans and Manu'ans might have complaints about specific details of Dr. Krämer's *The Samoa Islands*, their complaints are usually at a local or village level and cannot minimize the impact and value of the work to Samoan culture, history, and people.

Foreword

Tuiloma Loau Luafata Simanu-Klutz, Ph.D.
Retired Associate Professor,
University of Hawai'i at Mānoa

Our Fa'asāmoa (Sāmoan Way) has been an existential path of tautua (service) for both the author, Paramount Orator Fata Ariu Levi (henceforth Orator Fata), and me. We have been traversing this road for at least fifty to sixty years for our families and nation, returning to Samoa frequently as the need for personal or physical presence presents itself. We have been both blessed, through faith and hard work, with the power to achieve cultural, academic, and professional goals and the confidence that our tautua is perpetual because we are Samoan. It is what defines our Samoanness. Thus, Orator Fata's quest to "exercise the responsibility of being an orator chief," as custodian of culture, history, and praxis in diaspora is evident of his laser-like focus on the settling of the archipelago by navigators who (re)imagined an identity of being Samoan and Manu'an. His primary audience is clearly the Samoan, particularly those of the younger generations—the Ys, Zs, and Millennials, themselves descendants; they are hungry for a Samoanness that transcends the brawn of the athletics and the sanitation of customs and traditions in rituals and symbolism. This volume is autobiographical in nature. It is a history about Samoa's and Manu'a's past with Orator Fata's 'Āiga Sā Malietoa' anchor and guiding star illuminating and leading us to and from familial and political constellations and connections. In his own words, *"[I]t's a history that is as long as the ancient development of diversity in culture, and as deep as the unfathomable cradle of the Pacific Ocean, creating an holistic vision of that epic migration"* (italics mine).

Forging a Culture is a cartography of crisscrossing gafa (genealogies), tuā'oi (boundaries), and fāiā (relationships). The popular maxim "knowledge is power" is what one will feel after an immersion, if not submersion, in a network of roots and routes which the ancestors planted and stretched respectively beyond the shoreline. This is about a culture that has spiraled from a matrilinearity to being both matrilineal and patriarchal and in which women have remained both anchors and sails alongside their men. It is not about deboning a fish, but a reboning that reflects how and why Fa'asāmoa has survived multiple invasions and colonization. Our illustrious orator believes that... *[k]nowledge of history is power. And a prerequisite of eloquence in Samoan oratory is knowledge of these historical events. While the stories are fragmented, in view of the long history of Samoa, they represent pieces of the puzzle, stones in the mosaic tapestry of Samoa's history. The more pieces of the mosaic we have, collected into a cohesive storyline or in a book, the better will be our focus on the beauty of Samoa's history* (Documenting the Oral History, page 134) (Italics mine).

I have lived in the United States for more than thirty years, and I suspect it has been longer for the Orator, but our involvement in the upkeep of our families and villages in Sāmoa and the States has not waned, even in retirement; this is also true of our sense of obligation to help the younger generations of Samoans understand that being Samoan is so much more than wearing a tattoo, playing football, or dancing the siva on the streets of Waikiki to protest a mask mandate during the COVID-19 pandemic. If I may, I wish to illustrate what I mean by the previous statement.

One day, one of my daughters who lives in New Zealand called that she wanted to have a malu, the female tattoo, since she felt this would make her feel more Samoan. My immediate response was, "Absolutely not!" We left it at that. She ended up with the tattoo on the back of the hand which is an appropriation for Samoa's women.

One day, a student was concerned that non-Samoans were getting the Samoan tattoo; another one, yet, on a different day, emphatically expressed her disgust that non-Samoan tattooists were stealing Samoan motifs. My response: "If this is how you feel about others owning a bit of our Samoan culture, then imagine them asking the same about you wearing their clothes and eating their food." I found myself repeating this throughout the years as my Samoan students were learning about and finding courage to speak up against colonialism's cultures while publicly displaying the same behavior and mentality for which they have despised the palagi. Interestingly, such a response was often followed by complete silence, and then it was time to settle down into an hour and fifteen minutes of Samoan oral traditions and literature which had implications for how to forge, build, and develop an identity and empathy for others.

I share these to illustrate a conundrum plaguing Samoa's diasporic millennials—those born and raised outside of Samoa, and those leaving Samoa at an early age. They have been concerned with not quite knowing who or what they are, either in the singularity of being ethnically Samoan, or as hyphenated ethnic nationals, the Samoan American. In a way, there is a hint here of a Dr. Jekyll and Mr. Hyde bipolar ethos which I know has been perpetuated by the media and research, and by a ritualization of Fa'asāmoa by community organizations, family, and church. I believe that what has been missing, however, in any attempt to model a balancing of competing cultural and social priorities and identities, is a comprehensive grounding of theory and practice *in history*, in what Orator Fata deems the "deep well of the past," which he defines in *Navigators: Quest for a Kingdom in Polynesia*—the first book in a trilogy that traces the origins and migration for thousands of years, of the ancestors of Samoans and Manu'ans out of Africa and later Southeast Asia, and their eventual settling of an archipelago of volcanic islands which Jerome Grey sings about as "green, blue, and lush with beauty..." These islands are the roots of a Samoan identity, of a culture shaped by knowledge and skills internalized for survival in the long durée of a search for a place to call our own.

The Samoan word for identity is fa'asinomaga—fa'asino is to point; the noun-forming suffix, maga, makes it a referent for one's point of origin—Samoa and Manu'a—from whence one spirals to and fro, syncretizing and reshaping multiple identities to meet the exigencies of a particular time and place. In the process, what is sustainable over time becomes a standard, a value, a tradition; what does not make sense is retired. The millennials' passion, if not insistence, on understanding what being Samoan means can now be strengthened and satisfied by

Orator Fata's trilogy about the Navigators: the ancestors of the Samoans and Manu'ans. Specifically, *Forging a Culture* is about praxis—the application of thoughts and practice from the past onto the present. It is the how-to and the why-fore of a culture that is like a fish: full of bones but each bone has a function. A missing or broken bone is detrimental to the health of the fish.

Forging a Culture is richly sourced with archival records and Orator Fata's lived experiences. He is both source and teller of oral traditions scented by the tōfā and fa'autaga—knowledge and wisdom—of the ancestors and memorialized and recited in oratory each time there is an obligatory event, or fa'alavelave, such as a funeral (maliu), wedding (fa'aipoipoga), or title investiture (sāofa'i). It is our orality as the product and process of our pasts, reconstituted and/or reshaped by the written records in the chiefs' and elders' 'api (tablets), ethnologies, and ethnographies by both Samoan and non-Samoan scholars, in the lagi soifua or vavau (material evidence in the environment and language, i.e. names), and the whispers in the wind during late-night faigāfāgogo (bedtime storytelling). For the diasporic, the struggle to feel Samoan is mitigated by this narrative, it is presented in accessible prose and with rich examples of how and why certain traditions such as the sua (gifting of food), ava ceremony, tattooing, gender relations, boundaries, and respect system, were forged and sustained. To a large extent, Orator Fata's text is not about a single past or one history, but many, where the weavings are not so much about accuracy of where and when an event happened (the "stuff" of an academically driven history), but about the teller's and reader's mosaic of interpretations or meaning making—simply, their truths.

Forging a Culture aptly illustrates what the late Greg Dening called a "poetic of histories."[1] He was not talking about a poem, but a historiography of the past manipulated in the present which it transforms in order to fit the idiosyncratic nature of its cultural and social reality. In this way, the teller or historian makes sense

---

[1] Greg Dening, Poetic of Histories: Transformations that Present the Past. In Clio in Oceania: Toward a Historical Anthropology, edited by Aletta Biersack, Washington and London: Smithsonian Institution Press, 1991: 347-380.

of the present by recalling the past and in turn making history. In his effort to urge a better understanding of how history and anthropology can be two sides of the same coin, Dening is set on privileging Pacific ways of knowing and knowledge of the past which had been long subjugated by colonialism and which he sees as credible sources of history and as sites of investigation. The historian is therefore both a participant and observer doing ethnographic history. The prefix "ethno" is a colonial problematic for those of us studying our own people—how can our own people be our "other?" What's in a label?

I have not met Paramount Orator Fata Ariu Levi in person, but we have developed an author-reader relationship through emailing and since his request for a review of *Book I Navigators: Quest for a Kingdom in Polynesia*, for Amazon Kindle. After that, I could not wait for more of his erudite and entertaining storytelling; but, remember the saying, "Be careful of what you wish for?" Well, I literally got what I had wished for, and then some.

I must admit that when Orator Fata asked me to write the foreword for this book, I balked and emailed back that I had never written a foreword before, therefore I did not think I would be the right person to do it. I signed the email with my nickname, Fata. I did not hear back from him for a while, but just when I thought that the lengthy gap in our emails meant that I could now enjoy retirement, a message arrived in which he called me Luafata, my given name in full, and wrote that he still hoped that I would contribute a foreword. I am rarely called by my full name these days, but by "Fata," which is a nickname necessitated by my New Zealand professors' wish for a more pronounceable identity. For palagi convenience, many of us from the islands chopped our names to four letter words. Nonetheless, after agreeing to write a foreword, I have made a conscious effort to sign off as Luafata when emailing with Orator Fata. What's in a name, one may ask. What is an identity? As demonstrated in this oratory, names are history books, critical for sustaining tuā'oi or boundaries, and above all, they are identity markers. The meanings attached to a name can be derived from the name itself. Needless to say, attached in his email was the first draft of Book II, Volume I.

A quick surf on the internet revealed that forewords were mostly written by celebrities or experts, but a glance through the Contents page left me with no other choice, but to accept the challenge. At the risk of being self-effacing, I am neither a celebrity nor an "expert" in Samoan and Manu'an culture, but I am a Samoan historian who has studied and taught Samoan respect and ceremonial language and culture, literature, and Pacific histories at the University of Hawai'i since the turn of the millennium and until retirement at the end of 2020. I also hold the orator (tulāfale) title, Tuiloma, from one of my ancestral villages (Sāpunaoa, Faleālili), and a high chief's (ali'i) title, Loau, from another one (Sāoluafata). The latter, according to Orator Fata in his introductory email, is how he and I may find a genealogical connection. Like our illustrious author, my primary years growing up in Samoa have also come to bear on what I know about Fa'asāmoa and how I interpret and share it. The merging of both personal and professional/scholarly interests in the study of changes and continuities in gender relations in Sāmoan society vis a vis Le Nu'u o Teine o Sāoluafata, makes me an eligible choice to write this foreword. It is indeed a privilege to do so.

Ma lo'u ava tele!
Soifua!

CONTENTS

Preface

This book, when both volumes have been released, will be the second of three works in my *Navigators* series:

- Navigators: Quest for a Kingdom in Polynesia (released in 2020)
- Navigators: Forging a Culture and Founding a Nation
- Navigators Return: God's "Charge of the Light Brigade" Missionaries

My first book, *Navigators Quest for a Kingdom in Polynesia*, looked at where we came from and how the many sciences of the modern world help us trace our migration path to this place.

Now, in my second book, I am looking at who we became as a people when we arrived here, and how we became who we are. Space considerations compel me to release the book in two volumes, so this volume, *Forging a Matriarchal Culture in Polynesia,* will focus on the culture of Manu'a and Samoa, how that culture was formed, both in isolation and on the arrival of Western influences, and how it continues to be formed. In Volume II, *Founding a Christian Nation in Polynesia,* I will look more closely at the history of the Island Nations and how that history was affected by and affects our culture and cultural identity.

The third book in the series, *God's "Charge of the Light Brigade" Missionaries*, will explore what we have done with God's great gift to us and where we have taken it.

God's grand design is evidenced at latitude minus 13 degrees 48 minutes and 26 seconds South, and longitude minus 171 degrees 46 minutes 30 seconds West, where lies Samoa; and at latitude minus 14 degrees 18 minutes 23 seconds South, and longitude minus 170 degrees 41 minutes 42 seconds West, where lie Manu'a and American Samoa. These islands stand erected by

God, some 2.3 million years and 1.6 million years ago respectively, out of the core of the Pacific "Ring of Fire" hotspots in the belly of the Pacific Ocean. This is the kingdom of the Navigators of the Archipelago, the "land of mythology."

The history of these people is the history of Polynesia and of those indigenous peoples who first discovered and colonized it, people called Polynesians. It's a history that is as ancient as the human evolutionary journey across Africa, the Levant, Pontic Steppe, Eurasian Steppe, across the continent of Asia and the Asiatic Archipelago, and finally crossing the Pacific Ocean during the Neolithic period. It's a history that is as long as the ancient development of diversity in culture, and as deep as the unfathomable cradle of the Pacific Ocean, creating an holistic vision of that epic migration.

Our origin is a family tree that grew into a forest across Polynesia in the South Pacific Ocean. The tree is formed of clans and tribes of people of the same blood (or DNA).[i] And a mosaic image of their mythology lies on the bed of the East Pacific Ocean, colorful and emblematic of their migrational quest to find freedom.

This is the history of humankind's evolutionary journey through the challenges of survival. It's a story of "survival of the fittest," to borrow from the sage Darwin's observations and posits. For Samoan and Manu'an culture is as ancient as their migrational timeline, with peoples tied together by a language that is one of the world's oldest languages—one whose ancestors include Sanskrit, Dravidian, Tamil, and the Indo-Aryan and Indo-European languages.

The celestial knowledge, that is the basis for long-distance navigational skills to cross oceans, gives evidence of a cognitive development that was far more advanced than Western sages had been willing to accept, recognize, or call civilized. The chasm separating civilized and so-called "savage primitive" minds was bridged by use of the compromising idiom "noble savage," which offers "noble" at one end and "savage" at the other. But what began as "savage" has now evolved into "sage." For, as we continue to unravel the mystery of the Polynesians and the Navigators of the archipelago's ancient history and culture, we find more evidence of their sage nobility than their savagery.

A civil society is defined by its cultural norms and customs, and the tenets that secure freedom, responsibility, security, and sustainability, both at a personal level and at a collective level within the family, clan, and national brand. And the degree of sophistication of a culture is dependent, first, on its language. The Navigators had to hone their language, while simultaneously determining how to make a living and build a community. Their language innovations and development form the glue which ties the cultural norms and tenets together. For language development stimulates development of the brain, and well-honed oration leads the culture-building process.

Chronicling the Navigators' history, after their arrival, requires a study in human evolutionary development in isolation for a considerable period of time—even thousands of years. Thus, understanding the ethnology of the Navigators, prior to and during their migration, is a prerequisite to understanding the historical development of their kingdom after arrival.

We elaborated extensively on the amalgamation of fragmented DNA-sequencing studies of Polynesians in general, and Samoans and Manu'ans in particular, in my previous book. But, as I labored to point out in *Navigators Quest for a Kingdom in Polynesia*, genetics by itself does not paint a complete picture of the Navigators. A combination of ethnological, anthropological, and archeological findings, of climatic changes and changes in geographical patterns over time, of oceanography, astronomy (particularly the movement patterns of celestial bodies), and of economic development, all must be woven together to create a clear and realistic tapestry bearing the image of the Samoan and Manu'an people.

As we move forward in search of similar clarity on the Navigators' history in the archipelago, we should be consistent in our methodology, again looking for an aerial (or holistic) view of their history, from arrival to the present day. Today's conventional knowledge is based on fragmented and scarce studies by early European social scientists looking at Manu'an and Samoan archaeology. Their initial findings could, in a conventional way, give evidence of the degree of isolation of these islands in the middle of this very large Pacific Ocean for over 3,000 years. However, while there are no monuments as would be found in "high-culture" areas, the existence of this highly developed culture, evidenced by its profound oral history and mythology, makes the case that there must have been an inter-island network of commercial trading and exchange of cultural collateral. This offers a counterargument to the conventional assumption of island "isolationism."

I am not writing a history of the region, so I will defer the technical aspects of its history to the class of experts already abundant throughout Oceania and beyond. But the current dogma concerning the Pacific Ocean region is that its indigenous peoples, Melanesian, Polynesian, or Micronesian, were long interconnected in a network of economic trading systems and inter-island explorations.

That said, there is no clear evidence of "high culture" exchanges or infusion with other oceanic cultures for a significantly larger period of time. This compels me to conclude that the Manu'an Archipelago has indeed been in a traditional state of isolation for over 3,000 years. Thus my focus in this writing is the Samoan and Manu'an Archipelago and their cultural development, history, and building of a country.

So yes, this is a history that covers over three thousand years in isolation. And its record has been entirely orally based, with the exception of the last 200 years after the arrival of missionaries in 1830—the people who first began the documentation of this culture and history. So an overwhelming emphasis on oration should be obvious. And the honing of oral skills, exploiting innovations and technology, as applied to achieving proficiency of language, has long been the strategy and focus.

Historians chronicle the ages by selecting statistical samplings of events in a timeline to examine the environment, people, cultures, economies, sciences, organizations, and the ethnological makeup of a society. Depending on the size of the statistical sampling, they determine how comprehensive their overall view might be of the culture and country's history at a given period in time. The events are like interlocking pieces of a jigsaw puzzle that produce a picture, or diagram, of a culture and country within a given timeline. But the picture depends on how many pieces or events are being identified and examined, and getting a pictorial view is not enough; an ethnological point of view is needed to gain quality insights into the character of a culture and the society of a people.

The Navigators' migrational journey tested their constitutional fortifications, but now they had to turn their attention to building a sustainable society and country. Here, the role of a matriarchal organization and structure, in early social development, nurtured the building blocks of the cultural norms and rituals, as well as the economic development.

A close examination of the transition, whether deliberate or otherwise, from the original matriarchal cultural structure into the current patriarchal nature of Samoan and Manu'an society is an important focus. It appears the transition or transformation took place on the island in an evolving process, during the early dawn of their culture and society-building process. The struggle to build a family, clan, and homestead in a new land would have been harsh, physically, and would have caused much tribulation due to the unknown, with their environment in the largest ocean in the world. As we have learned from many other human migrations across the globe, risk-reward is a reality of entrepreneurship, and forging settlements in a new land, in the middle of a large ocean and far from other lands, must have been a trying experience. We don't have to strain the imagination to understand the toils and tribulations involved in settling in a harsh, new environment.

Because of the distance between islands and peoples among the Pacific Islands, the rate of incoming migrant populations from other islands—primarily from Fiji, Toga, and outlying islands of the northwest region of the Eastern Pacific—would have been a slow drift, referenced in what they remembered in tales and myths from Southeast Asia, and in what they experienced in the Fiji Archipelago for about 800 years.

A major shift in the society's culture was induced by the (deliberate) curtailment (as settlement grew) of the role of the male population in active seafaring exploration. The males of the population now became "home-bodies," performing domestic labor, and this created a major shift in the structure of family leadership and organization. This sudden change was rapid and disruptive at the local, family level, and profound and revolutionary at the cultural level. This shift propelled the transformation of the culture into a patriarchal society rather than matriarchal, which had profound implications on de-emphasizing the role of women vis-a-vis the original culture and society. It represented a major disruption in Samoan and Manu'an society.

In attempting to understand the anatomy of this cultural transition, we will shed light on the source of our current present-day situation. While the world struggles with women's plight and their fight to gain personal freedom, identity, equality, and justice, unrestrained and free from abuse, as recognized members of family, community, and society, Samoa is not exempt from the same struggle. This has been a conundrum to me, and I knew, in the course of my journey as a member of the custodian class of the culture, that the "see something say something" ethos would offer a timely opportunity for change. Now is my opportunity. I will not only shed light, but I will offer several challenges for the culture to ruminate on.

As well, the paradigm shift in how Samoans internalize God's message of peace and salvation, delivered to them by the heroic missionaries from the London Missionary Society (LMS) of England in 1830, is a treasure that must be retold in a new narrative. For we should not minimize the missionaries' gallantry in crossing the western and eastern continents of the world's geography, and the largest ocean in the world, to deliver God's message of love and peace to Polynesians. This will deserve greater enumeration in Volume II of this work, *Navigators Founding a Christian Nation in Polynesia*. For the plethora of detailed evidence there yields an added perspective that changes the narrative.

Most of the current literature has been written by, from, and for the writers, all of whom were European missionaries, with their own specific point of view. Even subsequent Samoan versions were based on the original European missionaries' writing, thus reinforcing the same narrative. And, as we have learned through history, the more we repeat a narrative, the more we memorialize it as the truth. To properly account for the teaching and missionary work that Samoans carried out in Melanesia from 1846 to 1970, in the most inhospitable land and circumstances in the history of proselytizing Christianity around the globe, we have to get clarity on how and why Samoans became so proficient in the practice of adherence to the word of God.

Christian colonization came with a price. It was a double-edged sword where one side offered enlightenment to Christianity's views and way of life, and the other brought the ways of the outside world—"the good, the bad, and the ugly" to use a familiar idiom. So Samoa was given a major cultural infusion that changed Samoan lives forever.

Cultural infusion up to this point in Samoa's ethnological development had been limited to the influences of other Polynesians, mainly Tongans and the Melanesian Fijians. This was the extent of diversity in the Samoan population, and the reality of its isolated geographical location.

Now, when the outside world of Europe descended on the island, the Navigators of the Archipelago would go through a cultural transformation that would add more diversity, new paradigms in knowledge, learning, technology, tools, and weaponry, and a whole new way of life. The 70-year period from 1830 to 1900 was the time of the Samoa Condominium, the partitioning amongst the United States of America, Great Britain, and Germany. In this period, Samoans would manage to absorb all these cultural changes in a compressed, fast-forward acceleration, to catch up with over 3,000 years of technological advancement in civilized cultures of the outside world. So the concern of my chronicle, limned in Volume II of this book and published separately as *Navigators Founding a Nation*, will be the rate of absorption, adoption, comprehension, recursion, retention, and assimilation.

As is the nature of science, changes can take place continuously, or in quantum steps, or in a giant leap. But the important issue is the rate and nature of change. Whether looking at culture, history, or genetics, a microscopic view of these changes in Samoan ethnography in the 70 years since the arrival of Christianity will illuminate and clarify the challenges posed by their new cultural diversity.

What they came up with is evidenced in the period of the following 62 years, up to finally achieving self-governance as an

Independent Island Nation in 1962. It took the Navigators several thousands of years to search for a kingdom in the Asian continent, and they found it in the East Pacific Ocean. They settled and developed it for over 3,000 years. But they had only 70 years to accept, embrace, and assimilate new changes from the outside world intruding into Samoan culture, or into the *Fa'aSamoa*, while building a sustainable modern nation for the future.

So that is the challenge of chronicling the history of Samoans. Not only are the events in time and the cultural development of its long history salient to this effort, but equally important is the anatomy of human psychology through the cultural infusion of the last 132 years (1830-1962).

Thus, *Forging a Culture* will focus more on cultural development, and *Founding a Nation* more on the historical events that led to the development of a Nation.

<u>Introduction</u>

What is a Culture?

The forging of a culture begins with human migration. Initially, there are just hunters and gatherers tracking across the globe, either on land or on river or ocean waters, but they eventually become a formalized group. As the group begins to recognize its organization, its members begin to recognize and define standard tasks, and a standard way of life.

One might also say that the origin of a culture lies in the collaboration of those magical functions of the brain, coming from the cerebrum that performs higher functions, like interpreting touch, vision, and hearing, as well as speech, reasoning, emotions, learning, and fine control of movement. The interactions and collaboration of different combinations of these various brain functions lead to the envisioning of images and symbols, and of objects that are interpreted into myths.

Mythology, then, is as much a part of culture as are the standard tasks of daily life. Mythology is a creation of human imagination. It becomes a culture's story. And then there is the "sounding" of the image, symbol, or sign, which is so foundational to the beginning of language and culture.[ii]

So, as a migrating group or family begins to develop habits and practices that are turned into repetitive procedures, then into standard protocols, and, finally, into customs and formalities, this is the beginning of a culture. Thus, we shall see, the culture of the Navigators originated with and developed from the beginning of their migration. Their culture's foundation is built on the layers of the Navigators' migrational path. Their experiences, negotiating the perils of navigating through thousands of miles of ocean water, helped shaped the foundation of their culture.

Culture is defined as describing the social behavior and norms of a human society. Cultural universals are found in all human societies; these include expressive forms such as art, music, dance, ritual, and religion, and technologies such as tool usage, cooking, shelter, and clothing.[iii]

History, Geography, and Sociology

When did Polynesian Culture Begin?

Inherent in all research studies on the Navigators' culture, from the early 1800s, was an attitude or belief about the Polynesian migration—a belief that everything in Polynesian cultural development and history "began after they colonized" the South Pacific Ocean and islands, and that these developments took place in isolation. But here's the news flash! It's not so. Polynesian culture started before they arrived and inhibited the islands.

While the 1800s' notion makes for an exciting and incredible story, the reality is the opposite. We have to go back and retrace the migration path, all the way back to its beginning, to clearly understand the evolutionary development of Polynesian culture and history. We have to appreciate the previous thousands of years, prior to their launching that "leap of faith" journey into the eastern South Pacific Ocean that led to the discovery of their new home. Hence, my approach and methodology are to show that the Polynesian Navigators had, long before, acquired the tools and skills that led to the development of their culture *along* the migration path.

For example: the family-centric social system, and the role of chiefdom defining the head of a family, was established long ago, during the "Out of Africa," "Out of India," and "Out of the Pontic Steppes" points of departure along the Navigators' migration. Further cultural development was gradually established and acquired along the migration route.

My idea in this series of books has been to retrace the migration steps backward, one by one, and examine each geographical area for cultural similarities with the Polynesians. By reviewing this multitude of cultures and comparing the similarities of customs, religious rituals, organizational structure, and tools and weapons along the long migration path, we can see clearly how Polynesian culture was influenced by these cultures and ethnicities along the route.

Where did Polynesian Culture begin?

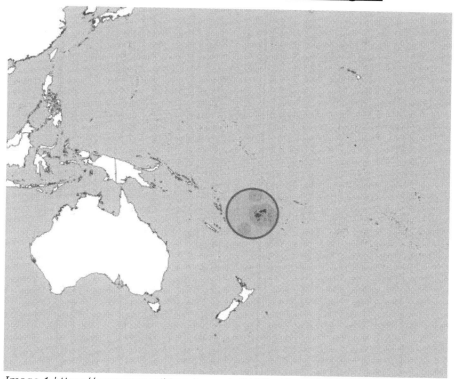

Image 1 https://commons.wikimedia.org/wiki/File:Map_of_Fiji.png licensed under the Creative Commons Attribution-Share Alike 3.0 Unported license

We start with the last point of departure on the Navigators' migration, with Fiji Island. The next geographical area from which they launched is Northeast Asia, around Maluku and Halmahera where the Molucca Sea joins the Celebes Sea and the Banda Sea to the South of the Indonesian Archipelago. Prior to arriving in the Northeast Indonesian islands, they traveled from mainland Sumatra eastward to the Islands of Java and Borneo.

Image 2 https://commons.wikimedia.org/wiki/File:Celebes_See.jpg Public Domain adapted from CIA World Factbook

Clearly, the whole notion that the entirety of the Navigators' cultural development took place in the South Pacific assumes we can ignore the cultural diffusion process that is found along this migration path. But this is where the culture began, on a path that begins in Africa.

Findings in genetics support a starting point in Africa. And it is generally believed that the whole world's human population traces its genetics back to a couple in North Africa that the scientific world called "scientific Adam and Eve." Y-chromosomes can be traced back to Adam, and mitochondrial DNA is traced back to Eve, as described in my earlier book, *Navigators Quest for a Kingdom in Polynesia.* Additionally, findings in comparative mythology, anthropology, ethnology, linguistics, and archeology from around the world also confirm that human migration began in Africa and nowhere else.[iv]

So a major migration was undertaken. If the tools and mental capacity to launch such an incredibly arduous voyage were lacking, this would imply the success of this migration was accidental, an action performed by people of rather primitive thinking. But the plethora of evidence shows the contrary, that the Polynesians were armed with the necessary tools and wherewithal to take these kinds of life-or-death risks.

As the Samoan Orator's mantra would say, "There is a source and reason for everything"—*E leai se mea e leai se mafuaaga*.

Who Are the Polynesians?

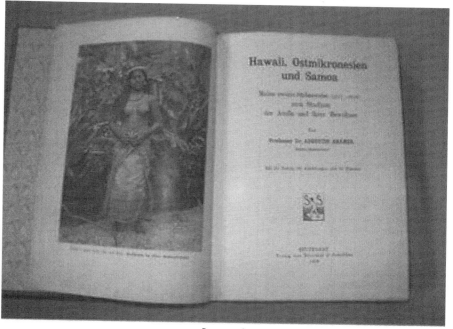

Image 3
https://commons.wikimedia.org/wiki/File:KramerHawaiiOstmikronesiaSamoa.jpg
Unknown author, Public domain, via Wikimedia Commons

Who are the Polynesians? 'O ai tagata o Motu Pasifita? Dr. Augustin Krämer authored a book called *The Samoa Islands*, published in 1902. He was a doctor specializing in studying the foundation of reefs that begin throughout South America, and his interest in expanding his field work in Samoa caused him to come to Samoa.

According to R.P. Gilson,[v] prior to the arrival of missionaries, the only European settlers in Samoa were mainly of the refugee classes—escaped convicts and deserting seamen who, for one reason or another, were desperate enough to try their luck among a reputedly hostile people. Thus they came from the poor and illiterate classes, and often the dissolute and violent. And it is from them that Samoans began to acquire a more intimate, if incomplete, knowledge of Western civilization.

The missionaries, in contrast, were organized European settlers, coming to Samoa in 1830 with a very specific mission, to teach the Christian way of life to the Samoans. However, shortly afterward, a group of merchant entrepreneurs also arrived, with a plan to explore business opportunities in Samoa. These were, for the most part, ethnic Germans from South America. They became the core group that established the German expatriate community at the Sogi property at Apia town.

Dr. Krämer, a German native born in Chile in South America, set out for Samoa on his schooner to continue his study of island reef formations. Studying the reefs helped him to demonstrate the existence of the entire landmass forming the Samoa Island chain. And he instantly fell in love with the island.

Prior to Dr. Krämer's arrival in 1898 and the commencement of his work in Samoa, LMS Missionaries had been gathering data about the Samoans from mission stations at village and district levels, and this resulted in the illustrious Rev. Pratt's *Grammar and Dictionary of the Samoan Language*, first released in 1862. Thus, Dr. Krämer had access to over 70 years of data accumulated by the missionaries. Even though fragmented and not formally organized into a single body of work with a deliberate scientific investigation of the Navigator's ethnology, this was nevertheless a great help to Dr. Krämer.

Dr. Krämer's major contribution, among many others, is seen in the gathering of family genealogical data and the reconciliation of that data to approximate generations. This affords the possibility of determining a timeline for the generational data. Dr. Krämer took this as a grand opportunity to influence, impact, and save the culture and history of the people of Samoa. He decided to switch his studies from researching reefs to documenting the way of life of this undiscovered culture.

Dr. Krämer wrote a proposal to the king (to use the European form of titling), asking permission to document all the villages throughout Samoa and Manu'a. The seal of Paramount High Chief Tupua Mata'afa evidences his approval for Dr. Krämer's research.

So, Paramount High Chief Tupua Mata'afa sent messengers to all the leaders of each village and district in Samoa, including the TuiManu'a, to notify them that he had approved this German doctor's proposal to document their individual village cultural practices and genealogies, and it would be good if they would receive Dr. Krämer in full cooperation and hospitality.

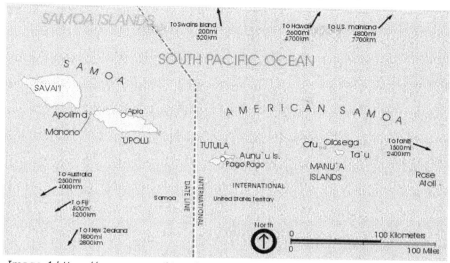

Image 4 https://commons.wikimedia.org/wiki/File:Samoa_islands_2002.gif From US National Park Service circa 2002, Public domain, via Wikimedia Commons

Dr. Krämer traveled throughout Upolu, Savai'i, Manono, Apolima, Tutuila and Manu'a to conduct his study, village after village, until it was completed. In each village he personally interviewed the chief leaders and senior orators. He questioned them about their genealogy, the collective salutation of the village, the Chief Titles Salutation, and the daily functions, activities, and way of life of the village. He even labored to cross-check the connections between title names and to reconcile the genealogies up to about 15 generations.

Today, the judges that preside over the Land and Titles Court of Samoa must be proficient in *The Samoa Islands: Volume I,* to the point of memorizing genealogies of various major families and connecting their relationships to other families. The judges reconcile the respective family genealogies of petition parties to Dr. Krämer's documented version.

Although not all the families of Samoa and Manu'a are included in Dr. Krämer's *The Samoa Islands,* it is nevertheless true that about 80% of major family genealogies have been documented up to 31 generations back from 1832.

Throughout the volumes of Dr. Krämer's writings we can find documentation of 15 major foundational families that were found to be the most prominent among the villages.

What the Sciences say

Through archaeological findings, we are able to date the human settlement of Samoa to between 1300 B.C. and 907 B.C. Such findings include human bones, axes made of rocks, and arrowheads.

Archaeologists have also found what seems to be a trading route, called Lapita, connecting Fiji, Tonga, Samoa, Marquesas, Papua New Guinea, and, of course, at the center of it all, Vanuatu. This particular trade route necessitated the use of a boat. You can learn more about this in my first book, *Navigators Quest for a Kingdom in Polynesia*.

As is usually the case, science is many years delayed in confirming oral history. But now geneticists have finally come through with a genetic study that unravels the mystery of Polynesian discovery and colonization of the East Pacific Ocean region. Genomic data from 430 modern-day people from 21 Pacific islands populations has helped unravel the mystery of Polynesia's genetic history and confirm their expansion migration across Eastern Polynesia, as noted by the lead author of the study, Alexander Ioannidis, a Stanford University computational geneticist.[vi] As I was preparing the publication of this second book, I caught the press release published by REUTERS: "Genetic study reveals ancient seafarers settled vast Polynesia" by Will Dunham, September 22, 2021. So, of course, I feel compelled to document it in this book.

The samples for this project were collected by the University of Oxford, Stanford University, and the University of Chile as part of their different studies.

Their reconstruction of the branching Polynesian migration sequence reveals a serial "founder expansion," characterized by directional loss of variants, that originated in Samoa and spread first through the Cook Islands (Rarotonga), then to the Society Islands (Totaiete mā) in the 11th century, the western Austral Islands (Tuha'a Pae) and the Tuāmotu Archipelago in the 12th century, and finally to the widely separated but genetically connected megalithic statue-building cultures of the Marquesas Islands (Te Henua 'Enana) in the north, Raivavae in the south, and Ester Island (Rapa Nui) the easternmost part of the Polynesian Islands, settled around A.D1200 via Mangareva. The study notes that Samoa was settled around 800 B.C.

In this "meeting of the minds, we find the sciences—genetics, archeology, anthropology, and linguistics—are finally in agreement with Samoan and Manu'an oral history and mythology. The timeline of Samoan and Manu'an history is now seen to be consistent with scientific evidence and findings to within plus-or-minus 150 years of its in excess of 3,000 years total history.

In linguistics, we see the phonetic relationship in the Lapita trading route to the Spanish words, but the name has no real connection to Spanish. However, archaeologists have also studied our language and found evidence of a language that contains variations of Malayan, Indonesian, Tagalog, and Polynesian; this combination is commonly referred to as Oceanic.

It is assumed the Oceanic language was the prevailing language used by the service providers or trading partners in the Lapita network. By this period, the Polynesian people had long prepared all they needed: the means of transportation, navigation via the constellations, weaponry, tools, shelter, agriculture, food preparation, religious rituals, and spirituality. And they continued honing their language skills in the development of the language they brought with them to the South Pacific. The Polynesian language may very well be the only surviving specimen of the ancient Proto-Austronesian language left on earth.

Also, while the study of mythology may not sound like a science, myths are important to archeologists. They form a fragmented account of human experiences during and after the migration journey of the Navigators. We can imagine how it might have been, but few real tales of the migrants' everyday experience are known. So, for over a thousand years before their arrival and colonization of the archipelago, the legends and tales that would give us a closer look at the real characters of the original migrants remain sketchy, until the time they landed and began the colonization process in Samoa. There we have an abundance of tales and legends from oral history to decipher, so we can gain insights into the human psychology of the Navigators.

A more in-depth discussion of the related sciences is available in my first book, *Navigators Quest for a Kingdom in Polynesia*.

Social Structures and Leadership

As we learn more, we can see how excitement and euphoria filled the early phases of settlement in the archipelago. It was excitement together with a shadow of fear and uncertainty about an unfamiliar environment. For this was the nature of immigration and human migration. The period of building a new life and acclimating into a new environment is always one of trials and tribulation. But there was a new thing called freedom that was quenching that internal thirst and motivating people to work hard to build the new life. And a new life required new, more evolved, social structures to govern and guide these new settlers.

The period of leadership emerges immediately, to guide the development and organization of the small, ambitious group of settlers. It starts with the challenges of a small family group and extends to a family clan.

The chieftain family organization was already integral to building and maintaining a sound community. The division of labor and assignment of responsibility further facilitated cultivating the new land for agriculture and raising crops. The learning curve covered the lifespan of these early settlers. Harvesting edible plants and roots, as well as medicinal plants and fruits, was a priority for the women. And their familiarity with the natural vegetation of tropical rainforests across the Southeast Asian archipelagos helped them quickly settle the land.

Shamanism, totemism, and religious rituals were all incorporated into the chieftain system of management and control. And the chieftain system was reinforced through promoting the warrior designation. Throughout the period of Samoa and Manu'a's colonization, primitive history is defined by the challenges of building a new way of life in early, basic settlements. Conquering land, and the acquisition of territory through marriages, expanded the family and clan. Then consolidation of family and clan developed into districts.

Government organization began to be developed at the clan and district level and was centered in their respective sacred meeting properties. The first idea of a national brand or a unified Samoa emerged during the preparation for the repulsion of the Tongans out of Samoa. And the beginning of a national brand was solidified in the Tongan defeat.

Chaos and Violence

As a natural, evolutionary process in ancient, virgin settlements, extreme chaos and violence were a way of life. Fighting for property rights, and for personal and family identity, always leads to warring conflicts and chaos. There were actors in leadership roles that legends note for cruelty and implications of cannibalism. And cruelty and violence were the common "modus operandi" in leadership positions and in rulers.

Violence and chaos form a standard phase in the development of early primitive societies, the epitome of "survival of the fittest" in human evolution. The food chain in primitive society was very basic; you find the next meal, or you become the meal. You learn how to kill or be killed. It's ugly. It's atrocious. But the reality is that, in a primitive, evolving society, it is the way of life, and Joseph Campbell quoted Professor Jensen about this way in which killing holds a special place in the way of life of animals and of men.[vii] So I shall not avoid or eschew the chronicling of the true anatomy of history.

The Navigators managed to avoid being a victim of the violent behavior they encountered in Melanesia, where the practice of cannibalism was a way of life, perpetuated by elite warriors. This unwelcome behavior of the Melanesians reconfirmed the Navigators' determination to push forward to find unconquered islands.

Their pause in the Fiji Archipelago, for about 800 years, allowed Samoans and Manu'ans to acclimate to the region, and they began to explore the adjacent archipelagos—at the same time flirting with the Fijian population. It was during this period that the mixture with Fijian blood began, though this appears to be an exception rather than the rule. For in such practices,

Samoans and Manu'ans were very much aloof from open-armed intermarriage with Melanesian Fijians.

This attitude of insisting on preserving their genealogy prevailed throughout their journey and settlement in the Samoa/Manu'a Archipelago. And oral legends tell stories of how the Navigators feared the Melanesian Fijians even more than the Tongans. The Tongans were kin, and the Fijians were of a different ethnicity. Everything about the Fijian culture and behavior was different from Samoan and Manu'an practice.

Settlement and Boundaries

So, after the excitement and euphoria of arrival in a new land to be called home, settlement activities and exploration began immediately. The environment was as predicted, based on knowledge accumulated over the period of their sojourn in the Fiji Archipelago. The landscape was familiar, and the richness of the soil provided an excellent prospect for planting agricultural food crops, making territorial claims and land acquisition a priority.

Drawing boundaries provided security, identification, ownership, and economic and social responsibility to the family and clan. The Navigators were experienced in this type of initial settlement and "startup mode," to borrow from the lexicon of modern entrepreneurship. They had long honed these skills during their long-term migration journey from the Western Pacific or Indonesia and the Bismarck Archipelagos.

Conflicts leading to outbursts of violence and warring engagements were necessary evils in the pioneering way of life in a new homeland, leading to a balancing act between excitement, euphoria, fear, insecurity, ambition, and determination to conquer the land. Humanity across the globe has gone through this migration phenomenon, ever since man began to follow or chase their prospects for food. Thus, all human experience has the same structure and characteristics, as to how we endure these physical and psychological challenges. But chronicling the anatomy of the Navigators' settlement of the archipelago is to peek into the experience, so we can better understand current cultural norms, rituals, and behavior.

The Role of Women

As noted in the title of this book, my emphasis is on the matriarchal cultural organization, or structure, that has been a foundation of Navigators' society. I pointed out in my earlier book, *Navigators Quest for a Kingdom in Polynesia*, that matriarchal societies are prevalent with the "seafaring" groups of people in the whole of the Indonesian and Malay Archipelagos. By their very nature, frequent movement and traveling on the vast body of ocean water requires that the women must anchor the family at home. The men lead the exploration efforts and ambition toward kingdom, and the women must ensure the safety and wellbeing of the family and home front. Then, in the early dawn of settlement in the Samoan Archipelago, the male role made a major shift from "seafaring" professions to local, home-building responsibility. I shall look at this change in this book.

Structure of This Book

Samoan culture originated with the development of human society through family organization, just as other ancient cultures did—this, according to social scientists who have labored 250 years in the study of humans and this society, since Louis Antoine Bougainville (who named the Island Navigator) landed and traded with the Manu'ans in 1768. (We should note, Jacob Roggeveen, who sighted the island in 1722, by contrast did not land or engage with the people.)

I say again, the Navigators brought their culture with them on their intrepid journey. For a people cannot leave home without taking their culture. It would be equivalent to leaving home naked, without clothing. Culture is the human skin, metaphorically speaking, that protects the body of a whole society. "Culture is critical" to family organization, planning and management, and control, in the impending, perilous journey, to use the lexicon modern business.

In describing the Forging of the Polynesian Culture, I intend to cover the following topics. For reasons of space, the resulting work will be released in two volumes, *Navigators Forging a Matriarchal Culture in Polynesia* and *Navigators Founding a Christian Nation in Polynesia*:

Part I: Forging a Culture: A Matriarchal Society

This volume, *Navigators Forging a Matriarchal Culture in Polynesia,* includes Part I of this study.

1. A summary of the culture and social structure the Navigators brought with them, leading to a matriarchal culture, and the history of matriarchal leaders in Samoan and Manu'an society.
2. The combination of matriarchal and patriarchal culture in tribes or clans, loosely scattered across the island chain, leads to the forging of a family-centric society and a chiefdom culture.
3. The cultural glue, binding history and governance, is seen in its titles and salutations.

4. Orators arise as custodians of history, genealogy, and culture.
5. The culture's mythology, legends, and folklore are preserved in the Mornings (*Taeao*) and retold by the orators.
6. Growth via expanding family genealogies through intermarriage leads to customs, protocols, and rituals for meetings, including the building of meeting houses and assignment of house-post seating protocols.
7. The ava ritual is central to the meeting protocol, and it has a rich history of its own.
8. Modern organizations and laws grew out of the history and culture of the island nation, first in isolation, and then in response to the influence of Western cultures.
9. Meanwhile cultural skills in language, navigation, house-building, mat-weaving, tattooing and agriculture continue to be maintained.

This volume ends with an analysis of where the culture could or should go in the future.

Part II: Building a Nation

Part II of this book will be released as a separate volume, *Navigators Founding a Christian Nation in Polynesia,* in which we will see how mythology and the written records of history combine to give a timeline of Samoan and Manu'an history that led to the culture and modern government of the Island Nation.

The timelines of history will cover several periods, recorded in oral or documented history. These can be viewed as eight overlapping periods:

1. The Navigators' migration to the archipelago, and the legend of Pulotu and PapaAtea.
2. The period of Tagaloalagi, and the decrees to delegate authority to human leaders.
3. The children of Tagaloalagi, and the move from myth to genealogy.
4. The period of TuiManu'a, TuiAtua, and TuiA'ana
5. The beginning of the consolidated ruling authority in Samoa.
   a. Major families
   b. The Warrior Queen Nafanua period

      c. The women of the matriarchal families organizing the consolidated ruling authority.

      d. Decrees delegating authority, responsibility, and salutations

      e. The wars for consolidation of ruling authority with Warrior Queen Nafanua's warrior troops

6. The beginning of the modern history of Samoa.

      a. TuiA'ana Tamālelagi and the first Tafa'ifa Salamasina, ruler of all Samoa.

      b. The growth of major families' authority and prominence.

      c. The first civil war of Samoa—peace and decrees establishing the modern royal houses of Samoa and paramount chiefs to lead the country.

7. The dawn of the arrival of Christianity

      a. Christianizing the Samoans and Manu'ans

      b. Establishing mission stations across Samoa and Manu'a

8. Forging a modern, parliamentary form of government.

      a. The arrival of Europeans and the development of trading enterprises

      b. The introduction of European common laws and parliamentary rules and organizations

      c. Major families dispute the single ruling authority, leading to tribal warfare.

      d. Peace agreements with the Americans, Germans, and British form a path to independence.

Part I
Forging a Culture

Matriarchal Culture and History

Samoan and Manu'an societies combine matriarchal and patriarchal aspects, but their foundation lies in an ancient matriarchal family structure that they brought with them on their ancestral journey. The mother and grandmother are the cornerstones of the family. It is the female genealogy that carries the lineage in the family tree. And the male carries the titles, such as Chief.

Matriarchal, Matrilineal, and Matrilocal

There is a difference between how anthropologists define "matriarchy" versus "matrilineal" and "matrilocal." The standard definition of a matriarchy is a family, group, or state, governed by a matriarch—i.e. by a woman who is head of the family or tribe. Social anthropologist A.R. Radcliffe-Brown (1881-1955) defined matrilineal society, also called "matriliny," as a group adhering to a kingship system in which ancestral descent is traced through maternal (female) instead of paternal (male) lines.[viii] In contrast to both terms, matrilocal refers to a custom or culture where the husband goes to live with the wife's family.

There are many cultural societies structured organizationally as matriarchies. Several North American native tribes and almost all South America's Amazon tribes are matriarchal. Many remote African countries and tribes—such as the Bamenda, Bijagos, Nubian, Ovambo, and others—are matrilineal and matrilocal societies. Jewish culture in the kibbutzim, and North American

Creek societies—Muskogean-speaking North American Indians who originally occupied the Georgia and Alabama flatlands—are both matrilineal and matrilocal. Almost all of Papua New Guinea's Austronesian-speaking independent nations are matriarchal or matrilineal societies. And, of the 52 countries listed as matrilineal and matrilocal on Wikipedia, over 50% are Asian countries.[ix] Tai or Siamese society is matriarchal. And the countries of the Amis and Puyuma, on the isolated eastern coast of Taiwan, are structured as matriarchal, matrilineal, and matrilocal societies.

In fact, as an observation, the closer we move toward the east of the island of Taiwan, closer to the island of Formosa and southeast toward the Bismarck Archipelago, the more we encounter matriarchal, matrilineal, and matrilocal cultural societies. Jeff Marck, of the Australian National University, writing in 1986 in *The Journal of the Polynesian Society*, cited many social scientists such as Per Hage, W. Divale, M. Allen, R. Blust, M. Ross, A. Pawley and M. Osmond, all experts in Melanesian and Proto-Oceanic cultures, who all confirmed that the Lapita and Proto-Oceanic cultures were matrilineal and matrilocal.[x] In fact, as far back as 1914, anthropologist W.H.R. Rivers originally proposed that Proto-Oceanic and Lapita society were matrilineal and matrilocal cultures.[xi]

These experts also agreed there was a slow erosion of the matrilineal structure over time in Proto-Oceanic societies. But matriarchal, matrilineal, and matrilocal social structures are as old as the beginning of family. The culture may be primitive in its ancient origin, but the human species continues to refine and evolve it as a way of survival.

Ancient Samoan Society

It should be no "sudden surprise" to find that ancient Samoan society was matriarchal, matrilineal, and matrilocal. We just have to go back far enough to where the people came from, and we see a common social structure in those societies along their migration path. The Navigators brought this culture with them to their new homeland, with a clear balance between matriarchal, matrilineal, and matrilocal forms of organization woven into the floor-mat of the family structure. The result is a system that then shares with a patrilineal structure (where descent is traced through males from a founding male ancestor).

There are classifications of chief titles that are designated to address the dignity of the female descendants in family and village. The special salutation of *Ma'oupū* or *Ma o upu i le feagaiga*, is attached to any title that is carried by a descendant from the female line, to acknowledge the honorable dignity of the female side of the family. It is said by the chiefs that the whole island of Tutuila (American Samoa) is the residence of *Ma'oupū* title chiefs. This is because many paramount chiefs throughout history visited Tutuila or were ostracized there after being defeated by their enemies, or were banished there by their collective families. These chiefs married women on the island and built families there. Their high chief titles, sometimes the same title as held by the father, were now bestowed on their offspring. So, to differentiate between two holders of the same title, one is referred to as a *Ma'oupū*. This could also be a different title name, but it's still designated as a *Ma'oupū* with a separate salutation. In this way reverence and honor are given to the numerous paramount chiefs, from the various islands of Samoa and Manu'a, who married females of these families in Tutuila.

Famous Ladies in Samoan History

Threading the biographies of key people and actors into the timelines of history allows us a multi-dimensional perspective, to better understand the motivation behind actions and events. And so I will give here a glimpse at the history of Samoans and Manu'ans, through the lives of their most famous ladies.

Six famous ladies in Samoan history are illustrated on the cover of this book. But they are not the only ladies we should look at, and not the only famous ladies.

The history of Samoa evidences six major kingdoms that were ruled by matriarchs:

1. First was the Warrior *Nafanua*, half-human, half-spirit
2. Then *Gatoa'itele*, a royal "Crown" and ruler of the district of Sagaga. The English title "Crown" is equivalent to the official title PāPā, which signifies that the head of the

27

holder has been anointed or crowned. *Gatoa'itele* is progenitor of...

3. *Vaetamasoaali'i*, a royal Crown and ruler of the district of Safata, and her children...
4. *Tamālelagi*, *Valasi*, *LeAtougaugaatuitoga* (or *Atougaugaatuitoga*), and *Salamasina* (first to unify authority over all Samoa)
5. *Fofoaivao'ese* is the daughter of *Salamasina*, and her daughter...
6. *Taufau* decreed the two Crowns (TuiA'ana PāPā of the A'ana clan monarch, and TuiAtua PāPā of the Atua clan monarch) to her nephew, Paramount High Chief *Faumuinā*, thus ending the reigns of the female rulers.

The combined timeline for these female rulers is in excess of 450 years. But there was an older matriarchal district ruler, *LeTelesā*, in the district of Faleata around A.D.1000-1180 *LeTelesā* is the progenitor of the Ufi clan, ancestors of the Malietoa dynasty. Her adopted son, *Faumuinā*, was named *Telesā*, and *LeTelesā*'s reign was feared by all.

We should note here, the usage of *Le* (the) before the name denotes the name of a Paramount Chief ruler, as in LeTuiManu'a, LeTagaloa, etc. Similarly, the *Sa* in front of the title refers to the Paramount family or clan name as in SaMalietoa, SaTupua, SaMoeleoi, etc....

Princess *LeTelesā* of Faleata District

Lady *LeTelesā* was born around A.D.1100, from the union between TuiA'ana *Pilisosolo* of A'ana district and a lady *Manavafea'a* of Faleata. *Manavafea'a* gave birth to a boy named *'Ata'atanoa* and a girl named *LeTelesā*.

LeTelesā's brother

'Ata'atanoa married *Tofili*, daughter of *Patauave*, who was the son of *Ata* from the daughter of the TuiToga. *'Ata'atanoa* and *Tofili* produced a girl *Fa'aulimaumi* (or just *Ulimaumi*), a son *Fa'auli,* and the boy *Umi* who would later be adopted by *LeTelesā*. Their daughter, *Fa'aulimaumi* married *Ata*—his second marriage—and bore *Si'ufe'ai* and *Tafa'igata*.

Si'ufe'ai's genealogy is found in the ancestry of the Malietoa dynasty. *Tafa'igata's* genealogy would eventually produce the Mata'afa royal crown of Faleata district. And *Patauave* (grandfather to *Si'ufe'ai* and *Tafa'igata*) was the father of Paramount Chief *Matai'a* and his sister *Tofili* (the mother of *Si'ufe'ai* and *Tafa'igata*).

LeTelesā's son

Back to the Lady *LeTelesā*. There is no mention of *LeTelesā* ever marrying, but fragmented information about her notes that she desired a son. So one day she went to her brother *'Ata'atanoa* and said to him, "I want to have one of your sons to be my son."

'Ata'atanoa replied, "Go, take that boy that is preparing the *umu* there, in the kitchen hut." The *umu* is the cooking oven. He added, "And let that be his name—preparing the umu there." So his name was *Fai-umu-i-na* or *Faumuinā*. So *Faumuinā* inherited *LeTelesā's* paramountcy crown and all her real estate property in all of Faleata.

LeTelesā's reputation

LeTelesā's reputation was one of fearsome cruelty to those who crossed the boundaries of her district. Local legend in the district of Faleata describes her as a demonic spirit, one that often transformed herself into a beautiful lady, and traveled across Tuamasaga district to guard and protect the Malietoa dynasty.

All the villages across Tuamasaga have their own legends of *LeTelesā*. For they are all descendants of *Ata,* the progenitor all their families (*Si'ufe'ai*, *Tafa'igata*, and *Patauave*).

LeTelesā's authority over a major district, like Faleata, is the only known matriarchal authority in early Samoan history. And while there are very few details known about her life, other than her being a demonic spirit with a streak of cruelty, her Faleata dynasty was real. Her real-estate holdings, that her son *Faumuinā* inherited, form one of the largest in Samoa, giving clear evidence of a matriarchal society.

The name *LeTelesā* is memorialized in the "princess name" of *Faumuinā's* daughter. There is no mention of her mother's name, only that she was the daughter of *Faumuinā,* well-known son of *LeTelesā*.

People tend to confuse *LeTelesā*, the founder of the matriarchal Faleata dynasty, and *LeTelesā*, princess of the Paramount Chief Faumuinā. LeTelesā, the princess title of Faumuinā, began with one of the most popular ladies in all Samoa. Stories about the number of chiefs calling on *LeTelesā* in Faleata go back to the late 1300s, and my ancestor *Saenafaigā's* mother was LeTelesā Faumuinā in the mid-1500s.

Tafa'ifa *Salamasina*

Image 5 Salamasina by the author's brother

The most famous of Samoan and Manu'an ladies must surely be the Tafa'ifa *Salamasina*. But a life story of *Salamasina* will not be complete, nor will we realize its profundity, if we don't first tell how her father was stolen from his parents, and how her parents met and consummated their marriage.

Tamālelagi

TuiA'ana *Tamālelagi's* mother was *Vaetamasoaali'i*, and his father, *Selaginatõ*, was the son of LeTagaloa. For the LeTagaloa and his clan, the birth this grandchild was the birth of someone very special—was royalty. But the baby *Tamālelagi* was stolen at birth by the two warrior Chiefs *Ape* and *Tutuila* and brought to A'ana to be raised as their Paramount Chief.

Orator Chiefs *Ape* and *Tutuila* had made their plans with Elder Chief *Ta'elegalolo'o* of the village Sa'anapu, Safata. They would have to undertake, and endure, the huge responsibility of midwifery in order to steal this baby. So this would not be easy, but they were very much prepared for it. They had inquired about it from their mother and uncle and aunt, before they set out to do this incredible task.

The village was full of people from all over the district of Tuamasaga, together with a large contingent from Savai'i consisting of the Tagaloa Fa'aofonu'u clan, to celebrate the birth. There was a fleet of fifteen to twenty vessels anchored at Lotofagā and Sa'anapu Bay. For this child was royalty. So the people brought all the gifts and made all the preparations

31

required by customs and formalities in celebration of this special child.

Gifts included different types of "fine mats"—Samoan "*'ie from toga*," or *'ietoga* (*'ie* means a very fine clothing material, but is also used as a short form to refer to the fine mat). These included, for example, a mat for the baby's arrival, a mat for rocking him to sleep, a mat for the night, a mat for daytime, a mat of the firstborn, a mat of welcoming decree, a mat for the unification of paramount families, a mat of farewell for when they would return home to Savai'i, a mat for the boundary between the boy and his mother, and finally the mat of all mats, of farewell between LeTagaloa and *LeSanalāla* and *Vaetamasoaali'i*.

Image 6 A Fine Mat lying on grass. Image owned by author

This large crowd may very well have helped disguise *Ape* and *Tutuila* and what they were about to do—they were about to steal this child, all because they wanted a Paramount Chief for themselves and their family clan.

The intimate details of midwives carrying out their tasks in the birth of the baby were no different from the procedures for any other mother giving birth. It's the ultimate pain of love. It's a gift that is received by enduring pain, by the mother and not by the father. And it's at the point when the baby "drops out," and is still in the placenta, that two midwives, one on each side of the mother, have to tear the placenta off to bring out the baby with the umbilical cord. The second midwife has to suck out the membrane from the baby's nose so the baby can breathe.

Once this was done, *Ape* and *Tutuila* (disguised in midwives' clothing) immediately asked the midwife holding the baby to give them the child, as they were ready to perform the next task, of cutting the umbilical cord with a sharp bamboo knife. It was at this time that *Ape* and *Tutuila* slowly backed off, cut the umbilical cord, and went to bathe the baby at the spring where Orator *Ta'elegalolo'o* was waiting. And that's how *Ape* and *Tutuila* got away with the baby boy. For that was their plan.

Ape and *Tutuila* knew there would be challenges in feeding the baby, because of a lack of mother's milk. But they knew that ripe coconut meat, when chewed and spat out onto a banana leaf or ti-plant leaf, can be squeezed so that the juice is a substitute for milk. Likewise the juice of the unripe coconut fruit is very good for feeding a baby. So this procedure is what *Ape* and *Tutuila* had to go through, to procure their paramount chief.

At this point the baby still had no name. They brought the baby to their orator chief *Alipia,* and when he asked them where the baby came from, the two warriors responded, "It's the boy from heaven," hence the name *Tamā* (boy) from heaven (*Lagi*), *Tamālelagi*. (I mention this fact because history has a funny way of repeating itself.)

The Tenth Wife

So later, when the illustrious Paramount Chief TuiA'ana *Tamālelagi* was already married many times—his eighth and ninth wives respectively were the two sisters, *Siotafasi* and *Siotamea*, daughters of a senior orator chief named *Puni* of Samatau village—this is when *Tamālelagi* first laid eyes on *Vaetoeifaga*, the beautiful princess and daughter of the Tongan king. For *Vaetoeifaga* and her father were travelling from Toga on their way to Savai'i. They stopped to sojourn in the village of Samatau, Upolu, to visit her father's relative *Fiame*. There, Chief TuiA'ana *Tamālelagi* was living with his two wives.

TuiA'ana *Tamālelagi* was advanced in age, around his mid-60s, and he had already fathered ten known children with nine wives. Princess *Vaetoeifaga* was a teenager, around fifteen to seventeen years old.

When Senior Orator Chiefs *Galu* and *Mana* saw the beauty of Princess *Vaetoeifaga*, they immediately entered their deal-making (or king-making) mode and began to sell the idea that a union between the Tongan princess and the TuiA'ana could help alleviate war and conflicts between the island kingdoms. Obviously, they didn't have to push the idea very hard to TuiA'ana *Tamālelagi,* once the TuiA'ana first laid eyes on *Vaetoeifaga*. But to sell the idea completely, they had to convince Orator *Puni*, father of the TuiA'ana's eighth and ninth wives.

Convincing Chief *Puni* was a lot harder than they expected. *Puni* loved his girls and his grandchildren. So Orators *Galu* and *Mana* orchestrated a deal to persuade Chief Orator *Puni* to come around to the idea. *Galu* and *Mana* decided to divide their paramount authority of the A'ana district with *Puni*; in that culture, this was analogous to designating half of the district's sacred meeting house to Orator Chief *Puni,* while the other half remained theirs.

Once Orator *Puni* agreed, the two orator chiefs turned their sales skills to convincing the princess and her father, the king of Tonga. It was not easy with the princess, because of the age difference, and because TuiA'ana *Tamālelagi* was already married—let alone the fact that he still had all those other wives. But, as was customary in arranged marriages, it was the wisdom of the parents or, in the cases of paramount chiefs, the wisdom of the chief that in the end prevailed.

The wedding was beautiful and a major national celebration, a national project for both the kingdoms.

The Birth of *Salamasina*

Vaetoeifaga began to sense a lot of jealousy coming from the other wives of TuiA'ana *Tamālelagi,* because of the attention given to her by husband. And so, in fear for her life, she told her husband she was pregnant and that she would like to travel to her mother in Toga, so her mother could take care of her. TuiA'ana *Tamālelagi* prepared the fleet of vessels to take her to Toga.

Legend has it that *Vaetoeifaga* gave birth to *Salamasina* in Toga. Then, when *Vaetoeifaga* and *Salamasina* came back from Toga, they lived in Leulumoega. But some historians have said she gave birth to *Salamasina* in Leulumoega, the seat of government of A'ana.

TuiA'ana *Tamālelagi* requested his cousin *LeValasi* to come and help take care of *Salamasina* with *Vaetoeifaga*. *LeValasi's* mother was *LeAtougaugaatuitoga,* sister of *Vaetamasoaali'i,* who was the mother of TuiA'ana *Tamālelagi*. And this is how the bonding between *Salamasina* and *LeValasi* came about.

The training of *Salamasina* in all aspects of cultural protocols and language, as well as in the etiquette and formalities of royalty, was now the responsibility of *LeValasi* and *Vaetoeifaga*. *LeValasi* was given the TuiA'ana Tamālelagi's princess title, So'oa'emalelagi, to ensure that the village Chiefs Council of Leulumoega would understand the importance of the role she played in TuiA'ana *Tamālelagi's* family circle.

Salamasina receives the crowns

At this time the Warrior Queen *Nafanua* had gathered all four (crown) titles; TuiA'ana, Gatoa'itele, TuiAtua, and Vaetamasoaali'i. And *Tamālelagi* decreed that his last born, *Salamasina*, would obtain a royal title and succeed him as TuiA'ana. But eventually *Salamasina* obtained a title far greater than TuiA'ana, for she became the consolidated Tafa'ifa, Queen of all Samoa. It happened this way:

Nafanua sent *LeValasi's* brother *Tupa'i* to present her with the royal titles. And during this ceremonial meeting, *Valasi* allowed *Salamasina* to play with her hair and run around. *Tupa'i* asked *Valasi* if she wanted *Salamasina* to receive the titles instead. And *Valasi,* noting the illustrious genealogy of *Salamasina,* agreed.

And so *Salamasina* became the Tafa'ifa, Queen of all Samoa.

Salamasina's First Love

Being a Tafa'ifa (or a queen in the English language) does not exactly give you your own free will. There were, of course, many servants to cater to *Salamasina's* needs and wants. So, during her outings to the forest or her ocean excursions, there were many people preparing the destinations before her and accompanying her when she traveled there. There were young men, friends of the Tafa'ifa, that helped with fishing and pigeon-catching games, out at sea or out in the bushes of the lush tropical rainforests. But still, the Tafa'ifa often expressed feelings of loneliness to her female servants.

Tafa'ifa *Salamasina* was approaching her eighteenth birthday when her "adoptive mother" *LeValasi* (So'oa'emalelagi) began to talk with her about governing the country. At this time, the Tafa'ifa had many friends, male and female, and was also going through a critical developmental period in her adolescence. But *LeValasi* told her she might be at the age to find a suitor who she desired to marry.

In another camp, the "Orator group of Nine" chiefs and Senior Orator *Alipia* were already up to their usual game of matchmaking, to find the right and appropriate suitor for Tafa'ifa *Salamasina*. So, before *Salamasina* turned nineteen years of age, she was visited by *Alipia* and the Group of Nine to inform her that a son of Paramount Chief Tonumaipe'a *Saumaipe'a*, named *Tapumanaia*, might be an excellent candidate to be her suitor because of his pedigree, and also because he was a descendant of *Nafanua's* genealogy.

This didn't come as a surprise to Tafa'ifa *Salamasina*, as she knew of the lush orchestrations by Orator Chiefs *Galu* and *Mana* in her mom and dad's marriage. So this marriage was inevitable, except that she didn't like *Tapumanaia*. There was nothing attractive about him, nothing to her liking. But still her ruling majesty Tafa'ifa responded with honor and humility to the orator authority and said, "Your honor *Alipia* and the Council Group of Nine, your wisdom is a gift from the god and cannot be denied, but if it's wisdom that is sourced in love, then let me give some thought and consideration before we meet again."

Alipia was impressed with the response of the young royal, Tafa'ifa *Salamasina*, to their proposition. But the Tafa'ifa's heart was full of deep sadness and pain, because her heart was not inclined toward *Tapumanaia*.

A week or so later, *Salamasina* asked her servants to organize a pigeon-catching excursion out into the bush. These excursions could take a few days, and she required a few young, strong men to carry the apparatus and build traps on the trees to catch the pigeons. *Salamasina* picked only four young men, and so, early in the morning, they made their way to the forest, up toward the mountains bordering the A'ana district and the south side of the Tuamasaga district, at the Siumu Village property.

At about noon, with the sun at the peak of its heat, the Tafa'ifa wanted to rest and perhaps prepare for lunch. She requested that some of the young men should go gather the stuff to prepare food, and that one might stay behind to keep her safe. The four young men decided that the young man named *Alapepe*, the son of an orator chief in the village of Satupa'itea, which was the same village where *Tapumanaia* lived, should stay behind.

The young men already knew the Tafa'ifa was quite fond of *Alapepe*. She found him smart, eloquent with the ancient language, and hospitable. He was considered extremely handsome, and so it seems her heart was already pierced with Cupid's arrow. But *Salamasina* was saddened after the meeting with *Alipia* and the Council of Nine. So, in the time she spent with *Alapepe*, while the other young men were out gathering and preparing the food, she confided in him about what was being orchestrated by *Alipia* and the Group of Nine orators about the future of the kingdom.

Alapepe was very sad, but he hid his feelings from the Tafa'ifa and insisted he should counsel her to be strong and to try to savor the moment of the outing. And it was at this moment— when *Salamasina* was so extremely happy and comfortable with *Alapepe,* that she embraced and hugged him with passion—at this moment emotion took over, and love consumed them both.

Before the young men came to get lunch prepared, *Salamasina* said to *Alapepe*, "We did not do anything wrong, for we both know our hearts were committed to each other. But my dear friend, life ahead will not be kind to us. *Alipia* and the government are set on their path to forge a kingdom and, while I didn't choose this life, my father did. I have given an oath as the Tafa'ifa of Samoa. My heart will bleed for you every day that I live. You must be careful and protect yourself from the Tonumaipe'a clan, for they will most likely seek to kill you when they find out about us."

Tafa'ifa *Salamasina* knew at this point that she would never see her friend and lover again, and that this unsanctioned act and outburst of emotional love would forever alter the course of her life, and perhaps of the government.

This profound love of these pure, innocent hearts did pivot the course of Tafa'ifa *Salamasina's* reign. She finally acquiesced to *Alipia* and the Council of Nine orators by marrying *Tapumanaia* Tonumaipe'a *Saumaipe'a*. She was found to be pregnant shortly after the marriage, and thus *Tapumanaia* discovered her love affair with *Alapepe*; he immediately instructed the young warriors to seek and kill *Alapepe*. *Salamasina* found out about this, and so she orchestrated an escape for *Alapepe* to her family in Tonga. Unfortunately, *Tapumanaia* sent a warrior to kill *Alapepe* in Tonga and he was successful, and *Alapepe* was buried there in Tonga at the land of her father's residence.

History Repeats Itself

Tafa'ifa *Salamasina* gave birth to a beautiful girl, and she named her *Fofoaivao'ese* (to heal by consoling the painful heart at the forest—*my translation*). Then she gave birth to a son and named him after his father, *Tapumanaia*-II. Well...

The moment that boy came out the womb, while the ladies were preparing him, two orator chiefs from Falealili (*Talo* and *Ofoia*) came and stole the baby—just as *Tamālelagi* had been kidnapped in the past—and took him to Falealili to be raised as their paramount chief, because of his royal genealogy. When they arrived at Falealili, they changed the baby's name to *Tapumanaia*-II *Le Satele*, hence the paramount title Satele in the district of Falealili, Atua.

As the villagers were preparing to search for and kill the people responsible for this kidnapping, *Salamasina* declared that they should not go to war because of this, for her father had been kidnapped as well and had become Paramount Chief TuiA'ana. *Salamasina* decreed, that day, that the villagers must remember, going forward, where the stolen boy *Le Satele* was, because he carried the genealogy of the crown.

It took 150 to 200 years to bring Paramount High Chief Tafa'ifa (Queen) *Salamasina's* decree to fulfilment. *Fofoaivao'ese* succeeded her mother, not as Tafa'ifa but as the TuiA'ana TuiAtua PāPā. TuiA'ana TuiAtua *Fofoaivao'ese* married Paramount Chief *Tauatamainiulaita* from Satupa'itea and gave birth to two girls, *Sina* and *Taufau*, and a boy named *Asomualemalama*.

Taufau succeeded her mother to the TuiA'ana TuiAtua PāPā titles. She reigned until her son *Tupuivao* was disinherited from the titles. Then she bestowed the TuiA'ana TuiAtua titles on her sister *Sina's* son, *Faumuinā*.

This lineage continued down through to Tafa'ifa *Fonotī* (victorious in the civil war) and his son Tafa'ifa *Muagututi'a*. Then it shifted to the male descendants of *Salamasina*, to the lineage of *Tapumanaia*-I, *Tapumanaia*-II (the son that was stolen at birth by Orators *Talo* and *Ofoia* of Falealili village), and *Tapumanaia*-III.

This Tafa'ifa *Tupua Fuiavalili* was followed by his son *Galumalemana* and then his by his son Tafa'ifa *I'amafana*, who bequeathed the Tafa'ifa title to Malietoa *Vaiinupõ*, who was ruler when Christianity arrived in the Island Nation.

The Reign of *Salamasina*

The reign of Tafa'ifa *Salamasina* was peaceful, and the only violence planned, but defused, was orchestrated by her Tongan cousin *Ulualofaigā*, son of her mother's uncle (Tuitoga *Fa'aulufanua*, the brother of *Salamasina's* grandfather). His ill-advised, blind ambition, pure bloodthirst for power, and greed for material wealth, led to a plan to kidnap and assassinate Tafa'ifa *Salamasina*.

This evil plan was fostered by none other than the two orator chiefs *Leifi* and *Tautoloitua* of Aleipata, in the Atua district. These are the same two orator chiefs who came up with a culturally (and genetically) bad marriage proposal, to have two cousins wed each other, So'oa'emalelagi *Valasi* and her cousin TuiAtua *Mata'utia Fa'atulou*. They prevailed in this embarrassment of a marriage, which resulted in the miscarriage of *Tuimavave*, the name given to the "blood clot." And this name has survived through the TuiAtua genealogy via *Taua'a*, *Tago*, and Princess *Suluo'o,* granddaughter of Tafa'ifa *Salamasina*. *Suluo'o* married *Togafau* of Safotulafai, in Savai'i, connecting with TuiA'ana TuiAtua *Taufau's* lineage.

These two orator chiefs clearly poisoned High Chief *Ulualofaigā's* thinking. They thought they would lure the Tafa'ifa onto a fleet of Tongan vessels and trap her, saying they would take her to her mother who was supposedly dying from long and persistent illnesses. Then they would assassinate the queen, to wrest away the Tafa'ifa title, or at least the TuiAtua and TuiA'ana titles.

It was quite an ambitious effort. But So'oa'emalelagi *Valasi* had a premonition about the two orators, because she had long been suspicious that these two orators were intimately involved in the assassination of TuiA'ana *Tamālelagi* and her husband TuiAtua *Mata'utia Fa'atulou,* but she could not find concrete proof. However, she had never forgotten it, and she somehow had the feeling that she would eventually avenge her uncle's and husband's murders.

In around A.D.1570, while spending much of her time in Leulumoega tending to government affairs with the House of Nine Council and the Elder *Alipia*, Tafa'ifa *Salamasina* received a request from Tafa'i *Ta'inau* and *Tupa'i*, on behalf of the Tumua *Lufilufi*, for the queen to come for a visit, for they hadn't visited with her for quite some time. The queen immediately asked So'oa'emalelagi *Valasi* if she wanted to accompany her to visit the Tumua *Lufilufi*, as per their request. And she consulted her Tafa'i *Umaga* and *Pasesē*, *Fata* and *Maulolo*, and *Fuga* and *Mauava* about the proposed visit to the Tumua *Lufilufi*, the residence of the TuiAtua.

There were protocols to be arranged, as well as logistical boundaries to be considered, and harbingers to be dispatched to the districts so they would be better prepared to expect the unexpected. The Tafa'ifa's government structure and protocols required that each of the PāPā's pairs of Tafa'i would inform their respective Tumua or Faleupolu (their orators and their aumaga organizations). Under these structures, the Tumua and Faleupolu would organize and orchestrate the details of the plans and provide the necessary resources; the Faleupolu would organize the village aumaga and population. For this was the hierarchical structure of the Samoan Tafa'ifa government.

Within the main structure were the families of Samoa, directed by their Tumua or Pule and Faleupolu, authorities of the major families of Samoa. Hence the Island Salutations: "Tumua and Laumua and Pule Authorities, families and their princes and princesses together with their respective families, Faleupolu who served and protected the Vessel of Samoa and Manu'a" (this is a brief version). This all came about during the organization of the structure of the Tafa'ifa government.

Of course, *Valasi* was the chief coordinator of the journey, further bonding her relationship with the first Tafa'ifa. And so it was decided that *Alipia* and the Tumua *Leulumoega* would provide the crew and the full entourage of the trip, including the war warriors to guard both the fleet and the members of the queen's court and officials. All other authorities were to stand ready for any request that needed to be fulfilled.

When they arrived at the Malae (meeting place) of Lalogafu'afu'a, they were directed to Mulinu'ū in Fogaoloula, the residence of the TuiAtua. Tafa'i *Tupa'i* and *Ta'inau* were anxiously awaiting the arrival of Queen Tafa'ifa *Salamasina*. And the protocol was for the Tafa'i to provide coordination between the Tafa'ifa and her court officials and the Tumua *Lufilufi* and the twelve orators of their Chiefs Council.

The seating arrangement was different, of course, with the Tafa'ifa and her court officials: The Queen Tafa'ifa would sit at the *Sa'o* Paramount Chief's post, with the eight Tafa'i seated to her right and her left. To her right were *Umaga* and *Pasesē* (of the TuiA'ana PāPā) and *Tupa'i* and *Ta'inau* (of the TuiAtua PāPā). On her left were *Fata* and *Maulolo* (the *Gatoa'itele* PāPā) and *Fuga* and *Mauava* (for the *Vaetamasoaali'i* PāPā). The rest of the seats were only for the Tumua inside the maota in the presence of the Tafa'ifa. Only the paramount chief heads of monarch families (Malietoa, Tonumaipe'a, Liliomaiava, Leutelelei'ite and a few others) could be allowed to sit facing the Tafa'ifa. The rest of the high chiefs and orator chiefs were all seated outside, facing away from the maota, with only their backs to the Tafa'ifa. (So, for example, in Lufilufi only Tafa'i *Tupa'i* and *Ta'inau* and one or two representatives of the Tumua, usually *Fa'amatuainu* or *Manuõ* would be seated in the maota. In Afega, only *Fata* and *Maulolo* would have seats in the maota. And in Leulumoega it would be *Umaga* and *Pasesē* and *Alipia* or *Galu* and *Mana*.)

The greeting remarks were delivered by Tafa'i *Tupa'i* and were reciprocated by Tafa'i *Umaga* of Leulumoega, on behalf of the Tafa'ifa and her court. The welcoming oration was delivered by Elder Orator Chief Sūsūga *Fa'amatuainu* on behalf of the Tumua Lufilufi. And the response to the eloquence of the Tumua

Fa'amatuainu was delivered by *Fata* and *Maulolo* of Afega—even though only one spoke their salutation, it was required to call both names. The Tafa'ifa Queen's royal ava ceremony was prepared by SaLelesi (*Valasi's* adopted parents from Savai'i who were living in Saluafata), waiting for High Chief *Leota* to commence the serving of ava, which would be followed by a royal feast, gift-giving, and celebration.

During the course of the celebration, So'oa'emalelagi *Valasi* noticed the unusually high numbers of Tongans in the village. And she asked, "Who are these Tongans?" The answer came back that the rather big vessel from Toga came, a week before Queen Tafa'ifa arrived. This alarmed *Valasi* and filled her with suspicion.

The next morning, Tafa'ifa *Salamasina* took a short boat trip to Faleapuna, for a brief celebration with the village. The village knew that *Fata* and *Maulolo* were among the Tafa'i on the trip. Since they were members of the Malietoa family clan, it would be customary to show kinship with the presentation of food and gifts.

The next day brought another short trip, around the eastern corner of the Atua district, to Fagaloa Bay and the village of Musumusu, at Foganiutea, the sacred residence of TuiAtua *Togiai*. During the village presentation of foods and gifts to Tafa'ifa *Salamasina* and her entourage, a messenger came from the Tongan High Chief *Ulualofaigā*, who lived in Lona village. He was married to a Samoan lady of Chief *Leota's* family, daughter of Paramount Chief *Leutelelei'ite* of Falefa district. He was also the brother of *Vaetoeifaga's* father, TuiToga *Fa'aulufanua*. The message was to ask if the Tafa'ifa would be so gracious as to come to his village of Lona, for he had a message from her mother, from Toga, and he could not come to Musumusu village because of his severe illness.

So'oa'emalelagi *Valasi* had already determined that the Tongan guests in the bay area were friends of the two orator chiefs *Leifi* and *Tautoloitua,* as well as of High Chief *Ulualofaigā*. It appeared that her suspicions were coming to fruition, and so she was prepared for it. The So'oa'emalelagi and the Tafa'i had orchestrated the sailing of several fleets: from the northeast, from Falealili district, and from the Safata and Siumu sub-districts of Tuamasaga in Upolu; and in the southwest, from

Vaimauga district of Tuamasaga, upward and including Luatuanu'u, Saluafata, and Solosolo of Atua district. These fleets were to move rapidly in the direction of Lona and the Aleipata district.

Image 7 https://commons.wikimedia.org/wiki/File:Samoa_upolu.jpg Falefa Valley, looking north from Le Mafa pass at the east end of Upolu Island. licensed under the Creative Commons Attribution-Share Alike 2.5 Generic license.

The wisdom of So'oa'emalelagi *Valasi* was rewarded with a successful campaign, without a war even getting started. The only two people whose lives expired were the two orator chiefs *Leifi* and *Tautoloitua* of Aleipata. So'oa'emalelagi *Valasi* got her revenge for the murder of her husband and her cousin TuiA'ana *Tamālelagi*, for the punishment was to burn them both alive on top of her husband TuiAtua *Mata'utia Fa'atulou's* gravesite. Also their names would be changed forever, not to be used again, to *Tafua* and *Fuataga*. *Ulualofaigā* was given a light sentence, after he gifted all two hundred of the fine mats he had on board his fleet, including the famous ancient state mat, *Lagava'a*.[xii]

So'oa'emalelagi *Valasi's* service, or *Tautua* in Samoan, gives evidence of her undying love for her adopted daughter Tafa'ifa *Salamasina,* from the start all the way to the end. Tafa'ifa *Salamasina's* reign was made possible by the faithful servanthood of her "mother" So'oa'emalelagi *Valasi*. This is why Tafa'ifa *Muagututi'a* decreed only one Pious Family of Samoa, The *Aiga SaLeValasi*.

43

SaLeValasi

Image 8 SaLeValasi by the author's brother

The biography of Princess *Valasi* (*SaLeValasi*, *LeValasi*, *Levalasi*, or *So'oa'emalelagi*) is covered extensively in the details of her ancestors' stories and legends: That is, the genealogy and tales of her mother *Vaetamasoaali'i*, her grandmother *Gatoa'itele*, and her husband's genealogy with *Leutogitupa'itea*, her cousin *Tamālelagi*, and, of course, the iconic Warrior Queen *Nafanua*.

LeValasi's parents were decreed—from the ancient past, by *Nafanua's* great-great-grandparents—a decree that big and powerful families of Samoa would be born from them, and that the connections of all these families would lead to great and powerful leadership in Samoa. Princess *Valasi* was the heir apparent in fulfilling all these decrees and proclamations, for the future of the Island Nation in the Archipelago.

History and Fate

The twists and turns of history favor the appointed ones, but fate has its own mind, meaning one cannot definitively predict an outcome. Was *Valasi* destined to choose the first Tafa'ifa, which turned out to be Tafa'ifa *Salamasina*? Or was fate kinder, in sustaining the matriarchal principal and recognizing its need for a strong woman to chaperone it into the modern epoch of the Island Nation? After all, the Island Nation was already (around A.D.1500) over 2,500 years old.

What was fate's answer to the egregious marriage, against her will, between *Valasi* and her first cousin, *Mata'utia Fa'atulou*? Was this destiny, to fulfill the establishing of the first Tafa'ifa?

History records, orally, that *Valasi's* family would be known as Aiga Sa Levalasi. This stands as the only Aiga that has a Salutation of Pa'ia "the Sacred Family" of Samoa, a veneration given to a god or deity, as decreed by Tafa'ifa *Muagututi'a*.

Customs and Protocols

TuiA'ana *Tamālelagi* was *Valasi's* cousin. He had no siblings. And now, after nine wives, he had a young queen wife, *Vaetoeifaga,* from a different Island Nation, which, of course, compounded the reality that he was old. The jealousy his former wives and their respective families had for this new, young wife posed a real threat to *Vaetoeifaga*. Thus, *Tamālelagi* needed help to care for her, especially when she was pregnant. So TuiA'ana *Tamālelagi* sent his messenger, the Atamaiali'i, to his aunt, Lady *LeAtougaugaatuitoga*, to ask if she could honor his request to have *Valasi* come to help *Vaetoeifaga* in her pregnancy.

Lady *LeAtougaugaatuitoga* received the Atamaiali'i's message and spoke immediately to her husband Tonumaipe'a *Sauoāiga* to ask if he had any concerns about her nephew's request for *Valasi* to help out with Queen *Vaetoeifaga*. Tonumaipe'a *Sauoāiga* was more than ready to give support. He believed this was a special opportunity to support TuiA'ana *Tamālelagi*. And so Lady *LeAtougaugaatuitoga* instructed the family servants to prepare *Valasi* for the trip.

LeAtougaugaatuitoga discussed the trip with her son, who was now Paramount Chief *Tauiliili*, and with his brother, the ambassador *Tupa'ivaililigi (Tupa'i)*. It was decided that *Tupa'i* would chaperone the trip to Leulumoega, which was the seat of government of the A'ana district and the residence of *Tamālelagi*.

It is customary in royal protocols that the inclusion of a paramountcy member in a traveling party must be carefully orchestrated; you cannot just go empty-handed or with just a few suitcases. And *Valasi* was a princess, heir-apparent to fulfill the decrees of her ancient ancestors. Also, the protocol governing the boundary between a brother and sister had to be adhered to, and that is why *Tupa'i* had to lead the royal trip.

Customs and formalities were expected in the ceremony at Leulumoega. In anticipation of these, TuiA'ana *Tamālelagi* conferred with his adopted father Paramount Orator Chief *Alipia* and with the House of Nine orator chiefs about *Valasi*'s impending arrival. And, after quick deliberation, *Alipia* delivered an eloquent message to TuiA'ana *Tamālelagi*, that centered on the need to bestow the princess title So'oa'emalelagi on *Valasi*, in order to appropriately show, to the district of A'ana and the four major families of the TuiA'ana, that a sister of *Tamālelagi* with royal pedigree was here to serve Queen *Vaetoeifaga*. TuiA'ana *Tamālelagi* was extremely pleased with the wisdom of *Alipia* and the House of Nine orator chiefs, and totally accepted their recommendation.

Then came the protocols for the bestowment and royal investiture. This was expected by *LeAtougaugaatuitoga* and *Tupa'i,* and they were prepared for all the protocols before they departed Satupa'itea for Leulumoega.

A Queen and a Princess

It only took two days' travel, before *Tupa'i* and the fleet of vessels pulled up on the shore of Ma'auga and Nu'uausala, the sacred meeting place and residence of the TuiA'ana at Leulumoega, in A'ana. The people of the district of A'ana were filled with excitement, and some were wondering about how the relationship between *Vaetoeifaga* and the So'oa'emalelagi was going to work out. The two royal subjects—a queen and a princess—were both, independently, accustomed to their own way of life. But now they had to work together as partners.

So'oa'emalelagi *LeValasi* immediately took control of domestic affairs. She was also overly protective of *Vaetoeifaga*, because *Vaetoeifaga* was born and raised on her home island of Toga. The So'oa'emalelagi knew *Vaetoeifaga* was not fully accustomed to Samoan culture and language, and thus she needed help as well as needing the friendship of a sister.

Birth of the Child

Vaetoeifaga's pregnancy neared the delivery date for the baby. The evening of the delivery, So'oa'emalelagi *Valasi* sent the Atamaiali'i with a message to *Tamālelagi* that *Vaetoeifaga* was about to give birth to a baby. The Atamaiali'i returned with a message from *Tamālelagi* that he should be informed when the

46

baby was born. The baby girl was born, and *Valasi* sent word through the Atamaiali'i. Once TuiA'ana *Tamālelagi* received word of a baby girl, he said to name her *Salamasina*.

No definite information about the origin of the name *Salamasina* has been found, but there are rumors and a variety of tales about it. Some say the night of her birth there was a bright (*sāsala*) full moon (*masina*), hence *Sāsala le masina* or *Salamasina*.

So'oa'emalelagi went into her "midwife-and-mother" modus operandi, to ensure *Salamasina's* life was secure and one of complete health and wellbeing. *Salamasina* grew up rapidly and with all the training of a royal subject, with good manners and clarity on the cultural norms and practices.

Bestowing the PāPā

Salamasina was about ten or twelve when Ambassador *Tupa'i* came to speak with So'oa'emalelagi about Warrior Queen *Nafanua's* command—the command for the PāPā to be bestowed upon So'oa'emalelagi *Valasi*. It is this meeting that *Salamasina* kept interrupting, so that *Tupa'i* asked *Valasi* several times if she wished to "bestow the titles on the girl playing there," referring to *Salamasina.*

Valasi said, "Why not?"

Tupa'i said, "I have to go back to *Nafanua* and ask."

And the story has it that *Nafanua* said, "If that's *Valasi's* will, then so be it." For Warrior Queen *Nafanua* was well aware that *Salamasina* was, for all practical purposes, *Valasi's* adopted daughter. Certainly, that was how she had been raised—she *was* her daughter.

The Courtship of *Valasi*

At this point the people were well aware that the royal pedigrees—of *Salamasina*, heir apparent to TuiA'ana *Tamālelagi's* throne, and of *Valasi*—would merge into a combined royal family. So then, the two Paramount Orator Chiefs *Leifi* and *Tautoloitua*, later known as *Tafua* and *Fuataga*, came calling on *Alipia* and the House of Nine in Leulumoega, to discuss a courtship campaign for *Mata'utia Fa'atulou* with *Valasi*.

This proposed courtship situation was a major problem, because of the close family connections between So'oa'emalelagi *Valasi* and her first cousin, *Mata'utia Fa'atulou*. So this took time and several iterations.

When *Alipia* first introduced the idea to So'oa'emalelagi *Valasi,* she disapproved violently and went into depression for some time. But *Leifi* and *Tautoloitua* worked on the psyche of *Alipia* and the House of Nine. They talked about the concept of linking the TuiAtua and TuiA'ana titles together with the warring machine of Tonumaipe'a and *Nafanua's* spirit and demonic power—all this, let alone the Malietoa connection.

TuiA'ana *Tamālelagi's* health was declining rapidly, and so he called the family together with *Alipia*, so he could proclaim his last will and testament. TuiA'ana *Tamālelagi* bequeathed *Salamasina* to succeed him as TuiA'ana when the time came.

This didn't sit well with some of his children, but in particular not with *Tuala Tamālelagi*, the oldest and firstborn—his mother was *Namoaitele* (or *Namoa'itele*), daughter of *Folasāitu* of Faleata. But under TuiA'ana *Tamālelagi's* decree, *Tuala* was to serve *Salamasina's* TuiA'ana reign—this before she became the Tafa'ifa. Still, he was obedient to the decree.

It took some time to convince So'oa'emalelagi *Valasi Tonumaipe'a* to marry her cousin *Mata'utia Fa'atulou*, son of her uncle *Lalovimāmā*. Then *Valasi* had a miscarriage, and she did not bear any more children. This helped make the case for the adoption of *Salamasina*.

As can be seen from the beginning: when *LeValasi* became the caretaker of *Salamasina,* from birth through to the Tafa'ifa reign, she became a consummately devoted mother to Tafa'ifa *Salamasina* to the end of her life. This was the main reason why Tafa'ifa *Salamasina* moved to Lotofaga, in Atua district, to be with her mother *LeValasi* and her son *Tapumanaia*-II, who was in the nearby village of Falealili. Hence the illustrious name of the Aiga Sa Levalasi.

This is also where Tafa'ifa *Salamasina* is buried, at Lotofaga: "What a devoted mother to Tafa'ifa *Salamasina*" the fulfillment of the ancient ancestor's decrees.

Leutogitupa'itea

Image 9 Leutogitupa'itea by the author's brother

Leutogitupa'itea is the pride and progenitor of the Tonumaipe'a dynasty. The *Leutogitupa'itea* pedigree stems from *LeFa'asau's* union with *Le'unu'unu* around A.D.1200, which produced a girl named *Sevelefatafata*. She married Paramount Chief *Seali'imatafaga* (a name which means "high chief standing on the beach") and bore a girl, *Sagataetunga*. *Sagataetunga* married *LeTuiAsau*, orator chief of LeTagaloa *Funefe'ai* in Asau village, Savai'i, and bore *Poulifataiatagaloa*. *Poulifataiatagaloa* became the mother, with the ubiquitous Paramount Chief *LeMuliaga* (progenitor of SaMuliaga or SaLeMuliaga clan), of *Leutogitupa'itea* and her brother *Lafaitaulupo'o*

The union of *Poulifataiatagaloa* and *LeMuliaga* reunited the genealogy of the two warrior brothers, *Laifai* or (*Lafai*) and *Funefe'ai* (who was now known as Tagaloa *Funefe'ai*). *Laifai* and *Funefe'ai* are commonly referred to as the modern founders of Savai'i society. This reunification of the brothers' genealogies is the reason that the *Leutogitupa'itea* pedigree is paramount.

Crime and Punishment

From here, *Leutogitupa'itea's* genealogy snakes onward to reveal her as the ancestor of the Tonumaipe'a dynasty. Her legend is well-known, because of her punishment for a cruel action. She killed a baby boy, son of TuiToga *Manaia* from his second wife, out of envy and jealousy, and that led to the founding of the powerful dynasty, Tonumaipe'a.

The baby boy was the heir apparent to the Tongan Kingdom. One day *Leutogitupa'itea* invited the Tongan mother to go for a bath with her at the pool of a nearby waterfall, and so they went. When they arrived at the waterfall, the Tongan woman suggested she wanted to bathe first and *Leutogitupa'itea* could hold her baby while she bathed. *Leutogitupa'itea* agreed, "Let me hold onto the baby boy." And so, while the Tongan woman was in the water, *Leutogitupa'itea,* holding the boy in her arms, took the rib of the coconut leaf (which is like a toothpick) and thrust it into the boy's head.

The little one began to scream and wouldn't stop, so the mother took him back to the house, but the baby would not stop crying until, at last, the crying waned and finally ended. He died.

TuiToga *Manaia* started to investigate what had happened and how the baby boy's injury occurred. The mother of the child was convincing as she accused *Leutogitupa'itea* of murdering her son, and TuiToga *Manaia* believed her. He then ordered the execution of *Leutogitupa'itea* by tying her to a branch (*maga*) of the *fetau* tree (a tree of the Calophyllum type) and burning her to death. He instructed his servants to build a pyre under her, and lit it up with fire.

Just as the fire was beginning to burn ferociously, *Leutogitupa'itea* was calling out to her brother *Lafaitaulupo'o* for help, and then, in the midst of the burning fire, a swarm of white bats or foxes (*pe'a*) descended upon the pyre and dropped their water-waste. Incredibly the fire died. But how did this happen?

Leutogitupa'itea's brother *Lafaitaulupo'o* heard his sister calling for help and commanded (*fa'atonu* or *tonu*) the white foxes to fly out and "look over" (*tilotilo mai*) how they might help *Leutogitupa'itea*. Thus the white foxes (*pe'a*) flew over and saw (*tilotilo*) what the fire was about to do to *Leutogitupa'itea* and decided to urinate on the fire to put it out.

TuiToga *Manaia* and the people were dumbfounded and immediately suspicious about *Leutogitupa'itea*, wondering if she might possibly be a demonic half-human half-spirit being, as was common with Samoans. But the white foxes were a whole other thing, because this species is not indigenous in the Southeast Pacific region. And, as one can imagine, the fleet of flying foxes that it would take to produce that much water waste, to put out a fire of this magnitude, was, in itself, incredible.

With much superstition, TuiToga *Manaia* immediately ordered the servant to take *Leutogitupa'itea* and maroon her on a deserted island in the Toga Archipelago, to let her die there. So the servant took her, as instructed.

A New Start

The island was a desert, with absolutely no vegetation, just sand and ocean and a population of one—a demonic spirit from Samoa and Manu'a by the name of *Losi*. *Losi, Lefolasā, Lefanoga* and others had, in legend, orchestrated a war with *Tagaloalagi* in which they were victorious, and brought taro, fish, and many other foods, and the ava down to earth.

The Samoan version of the *Losi* legend tell it that *Losi* helped with the flying white foxes and, in addition, helped *Leutogitupa'itea* in providing and preparing food (breadfruit, taro, bananas, etc.) and finding water. Because there was no vegetation whatsoever, not even leaves to use as a cover for the *umu* (the Samoan cooking oven), she covered her oven with sand pebbles (*iliili* in Samoan).

After a short time had passed, a paramount chief of the island of Uēa or Wallis Island, west of Savai'i, came by on a dugout canoe. He saw a human being on the desert island and, when he pulled up on shore, to his surprise he met this Samoan princess *Leutogitupa'itea*. The paramount chief, the TuiUēa, said to *Leutogitupa'itea* that he would like to take her to his island kingdom, but he also wanted her to be his wife. And so *Leutogitupa'itea* agreed and married the TuiUēa. *Leutogitupa'itea* gave birth to a son named *Fa'asega*.

Throughout his teenage years *Fa'asega* was always curious about his mother's family in Samoa. He constantly made inquiries about it. So *Leutogitupa'itea* told *Fa'asega* all about her family genealogy in Samoa and about her dear brother *Lafaitaulupo'o*.

Farewell Decree

The day came when *Fa'asega* had to quench his thirst for more information about his mother's family in Samoa. He prepared to travel to Samoa to find the family. And *Leutogitupa'itea* agreed with *Fa'asega* that it was time for him to go to Savai'i to visit them. Hence (as we shall see in the Mornings section of this book, The Edict at the Motu Tu'ufua, page 163) the parting words of farewell were decreed between *Leutogitupa'itea* and her son *Fa'asega*: "Come my son; go to Savai'i Island and find my brother *Lafaitaulupo'o* and give the following titles for the family and in memory of me." The titles and proclamations are:

❖ The phrase: *Tonu* (a command) *mai* (from) *pe'a* (flying foxes), which makes Tonumaipe'a—*my translation*. This records the command from *Lafaitaulupo'o* to the white flying foxes to go see what help they could give to save his sister, and proclaims this title to be the name of the new dynasty. Tonumaipe'a *Saumaipe'a* was the first titleholder.

❖ The instructions to *Leutogitupa'itea* from the flying foxes as to how to perform various domestic activities for her well-being.

❖ Another phrase: *Tilo* (look on) *mai* (so, look from or on me), which makes *Tilomai—my translation*. This name was proclaimed as a title for the Sa'o Aualuma, the council of princesses for the Tonumaipe'a title and dynasty.

❖ *Tau* (the covers of the *umu* cooking oven) *iliili* (the sand pebbles that *Leutogitupa'itea* used to cover the umu oven), which makes *Tauiliili—my translation*. This name was proclaimed be a title of the firstborn (Ali'ioāiga) of Tonumaipe'a *Sauoāiga*. His son was named *Tauiliili*, and this name would define the genealogy connecting the monarchs of Samoa and Manu'a. The first Tonumaipe'a *Sauoāiga* married *LeAtougaugaatuitoga*, daughter of Gatoa'itele, who bore *Tauiliili*.

And so *Fa'asega* went to Savai'i and delivered the proclamations to his uncle *Lafaitaulupo'o* who was the great-grandfather of the first Tonumaipe'a *Sauoāiga*. *Fa'asega* married *Leutogitui*, daughter of Paramount Chief *LeFolasā* of Falelima, Savai'i, who bore a daughter *Finetele*. *Finetele* would be the ancestor of the princess *Tuaetali*, daughter of La'ulu *Nofovaleane*.

Tuaetali married the second Tonumaipe'a named *Saumaipe'a* (Tonumaipe'a *Saumaipe'a*, the son of *Tauiliili*) and begat *Tapumanaia*. Hence the reunification of *Leutogitupa'itea's* genealogy and that of her brother *Lafaitaulupo'o*.[xiii]

LeAtougaugaatuitoga

LeAtougaugaatuitoga was the second daughter of *Gatoa'itele* and *LeSanalāla*. *LeSanalāla* was the son of *Samoanagalo* (also known as *LeSanalāla*) and *Tunaifitimaupologa* (daughter of the TuiToga from a Samoan lady, *Paitoitogamau*, who was the daughter of Orator Chief *LeManu'aiseuga* of Mulivai village in southern Tuamasaga district, Upolu). This *LeSanalāla's* full name was *LeManu'a-LeSanalāla.* He became a TuiToga, and he came to Samoa to visit his grandmother's family in Mulivai. There he married *Gatoa'itele* and also, later, her sister *Gasoloaiaolelagi* who came to live with them. From this marriage issued a boy named *Lalovimāmā*, and two girls, *Vaetamasoaali'i* and *LeAtougaugaatuitoga*.

Samoanagalo (father of *LeSanalāla*) was a "forgotten" Samoan boy, left on Tongan vessels that were sojourning in Palauli, Savai'i. For a visiting couple (*Taumataū* and his wife *Mūaolepuso*) had been on the vessel, and their son was sleeping in the bilge of the double-hulled canoe. The fleet left, with the boy in a dead sleep, and when the sailing troops discovered him, they had gone too far to turn around. So the TuiToga took the boy with them to Toga, and the young boy's son was named after his father, the original *Samoanagalo* or *Sanalāla*.

So we see: *LeAtougaugaatuitoga's* genealogy combines TuiToga, Malietoa, TuiSamoa son of TuiFiti, TuiTele of Tutuila, and TuiManu'a.

The Courting of *LeAtougaugaatuitoga*

Tonumaipe'a *Sauoāiga* was very well aware of the royal genealogy of the lady *LeAtougaugaatuitoga*, let alone he was also very well aware of her beauty. Thus, he prepared his aumaga and orator chiefs to organize the *Fale Tautū*—a house to be built at the lady's property, to serve (*tautua*) the courting process, which could take any amount of time before she might accept his marriage proposal. He came with traveling vessels to Lotofagā village, Tuamasaga, Upolu, where *LeAtougaugaatuitoga* lived with her parents, to ask for marriage. This was accepted by her and her parents, *Gatoa'itele* and *LeManu'a-LeSanalāla*. Then the consummation of this marriage brought together the

Tonumaipe'a dynasty and the illustrious genealogy of *LeAtougaugaatuitoga* mentioned above.

The Warrior Queen *Nafanua*

This is a good time and place to remind readers that this is also the point of unification of the Warrior Queen *Nafanua*'s genealogy and the Malietoa dynasty, obtained through this marriage, keeping in mind that the origin of the Tonumaipe'a genealogy begins with *Nafanua*.

We should remember the decree pronounced at sea between the brothers *Saveasi'uleo* and *Ulufanuasese'e* (see The Morning (*Taeao*) of the Farewell at Sea in Alataua, Savai'i, page 148 in the Mornings section of this book) that they will meet again at the tail end of their respective future generations. And thus, *Saveasi'uleo* married his own niece *Tilafaigā* (one of the Siamese twins who were daughters of *Ulufanuasese'e* and his wife *Sinalalofutu*). *Tilafaigā* bore *Nafanua* (or *Suaifanua*). Then *Nafanua* married the same TuiToga *Manaia* who also married *Leutogitupa'itea*.

Nafanua gave birth to a son *Latuivai*. *Latuivai* married *Mimisapu'a* from Fai'a'ai, Savai'i, giving birth to a son *Faletapa'au* and a daughter *Taigalugalu*. Lady *Taigalugalu*'s genealogy would eventually produce a lady named *Mo'oui* who married *Lafainatau* of Palauli, great-grandson of *Lafaitaulupo'o* (the brother of *Leutogitupa'itea*). This marriage produced the first Tonumaipe'a *Sauoāiga*.

There are local historians who would argue that the first Tonumaipe'a was *Lafaitaulupo'o* himself, but, according to Dr. Krämer, the first is Tonumaipe'a *Sauoāiga*. And so the winding genealogy comes into focus, to better explain various decisions about the conundrum of the first consolidated ruler of Samoa, Tafa'ifa *Salamasina*.

Tonumaipe'a's Descendants

Mo'oui, descendant of *Nafanua*, married *Lafainatau*, descendant of *Lafaitaulupo'o* (brother of *Leutogitupa'itea*), giving birth to the first Tonumaipe'a *Sauoāiga,* and so the genealogy continues. Tonumaipe'a *Sauoāiga*'s union with *LeAtougaugaatuitoga* gave birth to:

❖ *Tauiliili* (firstborn, therefore decreed Ali'ioāiga)
❖ *Tupa'ivaililigi* (*Nafanua's* ambassador, *Tupa'i*)
❖ *Valasi* (also known as *LeValasi* or Princess So'oa'emalelagi of TuiA'ana *Tamālelagi*

At this point it should become obvious why the Warrior Queen *Nafanua* favored *Valasi*. Thus this Tonumaipe'a clan was now the most powerful warring machine in all of Samoa. Recognition of the "dynasty" came gradually, from victories in the various wars where they assisted, particularly in the wars for the Tafa'ifa PāPā.

The War Machine

The war machine was led by Tonumaipe'a *Sauoāiga*, as directed by Queen *Nafanua*, and was delivered by *Tupa'i*. Paramount Chief *Tonumaipe'a* may not have participated on the war front, but it was orchestrated between him, *Nafanua* and *Tupa'i*, and the clan.

It's estimated that the elapsed time of all these wars, fought intermittently to accumulate the PāPā titles, was about six years. That time-period turned out to cause some fatigue in *LeAtougaugaatuitoga* and Tonumaipe'a *Sauoāiga's* marriage. *LeAtougaugaatuitoga* had expressed concern about the excesses of wars and their impact on families. For her children were spread out to cater to all the major families fighting for power.

She saw her daughter *Valasi* leave to cater to cousin TuiA'ana *Tamālelagi's* babysitting needs, caring for the young *Salamasina* at Leulumoega (seat of government for the A'ana district). Her son *Tupa'i* was canvassing all over Samoa to orchestrate assistance in war for the respective PāPā families. And the firstborn Paramount Chief *Tauiliili* was anchoring the family with his father Tonumaipe'a *Sauoāiga*.

There were rumors about Tonumaipe'a *Sauoāiga's* strong and powerful leadership, even to the point of cruelty, and this too became a source of *LeAtougaugaatuitoga's* unhappiness in their relationship. It was not one, two, or three but rather many times she expressed her dismay about this warring behavior, but to no avail.

As seen in the history of warrior paramount chiefs, cruelty is almost a prerequisite to the sustainability of a chief's rule. This pushes leaders to show power and authority, sometimes through the practice of cannibalism—of which there was the belief that, by consuming an enemy's heart, a leader would be given the enemy's warrior power. Samoans have always vehemently denied that they are, nor ever were, cannibals. And in their defense, almost all the warrior leaders and chiefs who ever practiced cannibalism were successfully converted by their own people, eliminating this horrendous habit, or they faced being ostracized out of the clan, which often meant banishment to Tutuila. This disdain for cannibalism is evidenced throughout the Navigators' migration journey from the Western Pacific, as I stated in my first book: *Navigators Quest for a Kingdom in Polynesia*.

End of a Marriage

The "straw that broke the camel's back" in Tonumaipe'a *Sauoāiga* and *LeAtougaugaatuitoga's* marriage, to use a familiar idiom, came when Tonumaipe'a *Sauoāiga*, in the euphoric adrenalin from a victorious battle, followed the custom in war that the head of the defeated warrior must be severed and taken home as evidence—part of the celebration of victory. This practice goes as far back as Near-East Neolithic societies, such as the Greeks, Babylonians, Romans, and others.

This overzealous enthusiasm continued when *Tupa'i* brought with him the severed head of *Sagaate*, the one-time pretender to the TuiA'ana title who had just been defeated by *Tamālelagi*. He threw it into the water in the spring pool where *LeAtougaugaatuitoga* and her daughter, Princess So'oa'emalelagi *LeValasi,* were taking their baths! But this was a violation of the boundary between Paramount Chief Tonumaipe'a *Sauoāiga* and the matriarch *LeAtougaugaatuitoga* and Princess So'oa'emalelagi *LeValasi*. It was a most disgraceful act to commit against the family matriarch.

Lady *LeAtougaugaatuitoga* was extremely sad, disappointed, and angry at the lack of respect given to her dignity. After all, she was the queen of the decreed family of Warrior Queen *Nafanua*, and her daughter held the princess title in honor of the

TuiA'ana *Tamālelagi* government—let alone, this was her cousin. It's said she was distraught and ashamed of her husband's extreme disrespect to her and her daughter and family. As much respect as she had for her husband's newly founded dynasty and the mighty Warrior Queen *Nafanua's* power and well-known pedigree, she was offended. After all, she was of the Malietoa dynasty, from its founding, which had the only salutation: "the Malietoa, he who all Samoan listened to"—the first warrior chief dynasty to rule over all Samoa for well over 350 years.

It was at this point that *LeAtougaugaatuitoga* wanted to leave immediately, to go home to her family, for she was so embarrassed that she just wanted to hide herself there. So in the middle of the night, she instructed her maidservants to prepare the vessel for immediate travel. In the early morning, with a broken heart, *LeAtougaugaatuitoga* was on the double-hulled canoe with her servants, on their way to Upolu. So when Tonumaipe'a *Sauoāiga* woke up, *LeAtougaugaatuitoga* was nowhere in sight. Her vessel's sails were picking up the wind of the morning high tide to take her back home.

Tonumaipe'a *Sauoāiga* asked the servants where *LeAtougaugaatuitoga* was, and the answer returned was, "She is gone, on her way to Upolu." He was upset and worried about his wife's well-being, and he began searching for her by looking out offshore to see if he could see her vessels. And, in fact, he could see the vessel, but he could also see the wind picking up momentum, and he could see waves breaking on the side of the vessel, which was making a speedy getaway. And so he began to run after her vessel, in parallel along the shore on the beach. He waved out to *LeAtougaugaatuitoga's* vessel, but no one saw him.

The mighty paramount chief kept running, in parallel with the vessel, which was traveling slightly ahead of him. And he saw ahead the last beach shore, Fagalilo, before the vessel would completely disappear from his sight. And so he ran and ran toward Fagalilo, hoping his waving hands could be seen by the people on the vessel. But, unfortunately for Paramount Chief Tonumaipe'a *Sauoāiga*, his mighty strength and power could not demand that Cupid fire an arrow off to perform a miracle, allowing *LeAtougaugaatuitoga's* eyes to see him there, waving his hands to get her attention so he could humble himself in front of her, in an apology for the insidiousness of the act he had committed. The vessel and fleet disappeared from his sight.

The local family historian, author Lafai Sauoāiga Apemoemanatunatu, wrote in *O Le Mavaega I Le Tai*[xiv] that *LeAtougaugaatuitoga* was, in fact, told by one the sailors that someone was waving to them from the shore. It looked like someone wanted them to stop. But *LeAtougaugaatuitoga* said, "Do not stop, but continue sailing and rowing." Also, Lafai Sauoāiga Apemoemanatunatu confirmed that the Paramount Chief, crying profusely, stood at the Cape of Fagalilo; today there's a spot marked at the cape where he stood.

Lafai Sauoāiga continues his account by stating that Tonumaipe'a *Sauoāiga* never married again, inferring that this is evidence of his love for his wife *LeAtougaugaatuitoga*. Likewise, *LeAtougaugaatuitoga* never married again. And, as we have already seen the legend of *LeValasi*, we know now that this is where it all began.

Warrior Queen *Nafanua*

Image 10 Nafanua by the author's brother

The Warrior Queen *Nafanua* was born under the Acrux Constellation, commonly referred to as the Southern Cross. It consists of the stars Acrux (Alpha Crucis), Gacrux, Ginan, Imae, Mimosa, and Tupã. Acrux is the 12th brightest star in the night sky, so it's a very visible constellation.

Warrior Queen *Nafanua* was born around A.D.1170-1230. This is just about the period when the war began between Tongans and Samoans, to end the subjugation of Samoa by the king of Tonga, the TuiToga—the time of the birth of the Malietoa dynasty.

Warrior Queen *Nafanua's* parents were *Tilafaigā* (one of the famous conjoined twins) and *Saveasi'uleo* (also known as Savea Si'uleo). *Saveasi'uleo* was *Tilafaigā's* uncle, the brother of her father *Ulufanuasese'e*. *Tilafaigā* herself was originally referred to as *Nafanua* by name, before her daughter was named *Nafanua* and *Suaifanua*.

The Journey of the Conjoined Twins

The framing of *Nafanua's* life is the journey across the archipelago by her mother and her mother's (conjoined) twin sister, *Taemāmā* (or just *Taemā*). The twins were "demigods" with exceptional, supernatural strength that they showed on many occasions in their journey. The twins' genealogy had been decreed by their ancestors, their mother *Taufailematagi* and their father *Alao*. The well-known legend of the brothers *Saveasi'uleo* (the cruel sea-eel creature) and *Ulufanuasese'e* ended in a

59

decree at the Alataua sea in Savai'i where they parted ways. It was decreed that *Saveasi'uleo* would go toward the east of the archipelago, to Manu'a Island, and prepare the foundation of the prophesied government from there; *Ulufanuasese'e* would stay in Upolu to build the family and populate Upolu and Savai'i.

So, when *Nafanua* was a young lady in her teens, TuiToga *Manaia*-I dropped anchor in Safotulafai, Savai'i, to begin building a Tongan village as a basecamp in Savai'i. TuiToga *Manaia*-I (known as the handsome) remembered that his aunt *Laufafaetoga* had heard of the handsome (*manaia*) Samoan boys, *Tupa'imatuna*, *Tupa'ilelei* and *Tupa'isiva*. These boys were the sons of *Lealali* and *Malelegaaleto'elau*, progenitors of Savai'i's ancient population. Thus TuiToga *Manaia*-I had a familiarity with Savai'i's people and families. TuiToga *Manaia*-I wanted to wed *Nafanua Suaifanua,* and *Tilafaigā* and *Saveasi'uleo* gave their approval. The wedding ceremony and celebration was quick and proficient.

This was the first TuiToga *Manaia,* not to be confused with TuiToga *Manaia*-II who married *Leutogitupa'itea* around A.D.1300-1360. This couple produced one son, named *Latuivai*. He married a Samoan lady named *Mimisapu'a* from Fai'a'ai, sister of Paramount Chief *Folasā*, who was a descendant of *Tagaloalagi* through his daughter *Sinalagilagi*. They had a son, *Faletapa'au*, and a daughter, *Taigalugalu*. *Taigalugalu* would become the ancestor of the lady *Mo'oui* who, with *Lafainatau* (grandson of *Lafaitaulupo'o*, who was *Leutogitupa'itea's* brother) produced *Le Sauoāiga*, the first Tonumaipe'a *Sauoāiga*.

Summarizing the Legend of *Nafanua*

The legend of *Nafanua* as the great warrior heroine is covered in my first book: *Navigators Quest for a Kingdom in Polynesia*. But it is very important to our understanding of the role of women in Samoa, and, as that is a focus of this book, I will include a summary of stories of *Nafanua's* smartness and wisdom which orchestrated the foundation of Samoa's modern history.

Nafanua's mother and aunt, *Tilafaigā* and her twin sister *Taemā*, traveled to the land in the east to look for their father's brother, *Saveasi'uleo*. He lived in the place called Sauā, in Fitiuta, Manu'a. This where he had gone by decree, to prepare the foundation and path for the new government. And the twins' journey to find their uncle was to fulfill the decree that their genealogies would meet in a later generation.

This is where they finally met *Saveasi'uleo,* and he realized these girls were his brother's daughters. And so he turned human (as opposed to being a sea-eel) and decided to take *Tilafaigā* as a wife. Hence, the promise of the brothers' genealogical connection was fulfilled. But the promise to build a kingdom was, so far, a nebulous idea. It seemed particularly farfetched when their district of Alataua was, for all practical purposes, subjugated to Paramount Chief *Lilomaiava* and his clan.

So, a destiny to lead and build a paramount family dynasty, even a whole-island government, is what lay in store for *Nafanua*. The cry for a warrior leader echoed across Savai'i and Upolu. And then *Saveasi'uleo* said to *Nafanua,* "You must answer the call for help. The people's suffering is unbearable, and you must defeat *Lilomaiava* and his clan warriors.

"You have the war clubs—*Tafesilafa'i, Ulimasao,* and *Fa'auliulito*—given to you by the spirit warriors. The gods will guide your path, and the gods have ordained your mission, through your warring skills and strength."

This was the challenge that lay in her path, its fulfilment unbeknownst to *Nafanua*. And history bears out that in the end it was *LeValasi, Nafanua's* chosen one, who solidified the first Tafa'ifa for *Salamasina*.

Gatoa'itele

Image 11 Gatoa'itele by the author's brother

The biographical story of Lady *Gatoa'itele* (Royal Queen *Gatoa'itele*) begins with the fact she was a child decreed before birth to be a royal PāPā (Crown) of the first national matriarchy over all of Samoa, by her grandfather Malietoa *Uitualagi* in A.D.1410. It is also the fascinating story of her parents Malietoa *La'auli* and his wife *Gauifaleai.*

La'auli and *Gauifaleai*

Gauifaleai was the daughter of Paramount Chief TuiSamoa *Nonumaifele* of Falealili village, Atua. And *La'auli* was the adopted son of Malietoa *Uitualagi*, who was the son of Malietoa *Uilamatūtū*, according to Dr. Krämer.

La'auli unintentionally attracted the two sisters *Gauifaleai* and *Totogata*, the daughters of TuiSamoa *Nonumaifele*, while his younger brother *Fuaoleto'elau* was trying to woo the young ladies, hoping for a wife. For when *Gauifaleai*, the older girl, saw *La'auli* bathing in the water pool, she fell in love with him at first sight. And so, when *La'auli* returned home to Malie, *Gauifaleai* followed him to live with him.

La'auli was concerned about his brother, for *Fuaoleto'elau* wanted *Gauifaleai* as a wife. But *Gauifaleai* would not have it any other way; she wanted La'auli as her husband.

A few weeks later *Gauifaleai's* sister *Totogata* arrived from Falealili to be with her sister. She missed her so much that she had decided to come to live with her and her husband. This was quite common with Samoan sisters and siblings, because of their close upbringing. Samoan culture was such that, even though the husband had two wives, the original married partner would always be referred to as the wife and mother of the family.

Thus *La'auli* married *Gauifaleai*, giving birth to the two sisters *Gatoa'itele* and *Gasoloaiaolelagi*.

La'auli and Malietoa *Uitualagi*

La'auli loved his father, Malietoa *Uitualagi*, so much that he asked *Gauifaleai* and *Totogata* to periodically go over to visit and massage his father's feet and legs, for Malietoa *Uitualagi* was getting on in age. This really made his father extremely happy and appreciative. He was very touched by *La'auli's* gesture and his wives' kindness in caring for him.

There are rumors about Malietoa *Uitualagi's* womanizing habits, and rumors that *La'auli* actually asked *Totogata* to go and "care" for Malietoa *Uitualagi*. Hence, *Uitualagi's* fondness toward *Gauifaleai* and *Totogata*. Still, as a result, Malietoa *Uitualagi* made a decree to *Gauifaleai* and *Totogata* and *La'auli*. He decreed that:

- *La'auli* would follow him as heir to the Malietoa title.
- Their firstborn would have a PāPā crown title.
- To proclaim the birth of the royal child, a *ususū* (a long, extend sound or yell like "chooooo") must be sounded.
- The second-born son (or child) would also have a PāPā title.
- The PāPā titles would be equal to the TuiAtua PāPā title. At this period, TuiAtua was the prominent rival to the Malietoa dynasty. TuiA'ana prominence began with TuiA'ana *Tamālelagi*, father of *Salamasina*.
- Paramount Orator Chiefs *Fata* and *Maulolo* would be the authority and custodians of the PāPā. This decree did not come to fruition until the period of Warrior Queen *Nafanua*.

Origin of *Gatoa'itele's* Name

Malietoa *La'auli* and his daughter, not yet given a name, were seated out in the late afternoon, catching the cool breeze, when *Fata* and *Maulolo* came to visit Malietoa *La'auli* and brought a good-sized, fat, freshwater fish called an *'igato*, very much like a freshwater white bass, as a food gift to the paramount chief.

La'auli asked, "What is this that you bring?"

And the two orators said, "It's an *'igato* fish for your meal."

Malietoa *La'auli* said, "What a big, fat, fresh fish, a well-fed fish." Hence the name—*'igato-ai*, meaning eat; *tele*, meaning much or large; i.e. eat well or well-fed. Malietoa *La'auli* was pleased and touched by the generous gesture of the two orator chiefs. And so he proclaimed that his daughter's name would be *Gatoa'itele*. Then, he pronounced to *Fata* and *Maulolo* that they should take his daughter *Gatoa'itele*, and take good care of her, and she would be their paramount chief.

Henceforth, from that day forward, *Gatoa'itele* became *Fata* and *Maulolo's* royal paramount chief. But this title did not become a PāPā title until *Nafanua* proclaimed it to *Salamasina* and thus fulfilled Malietoa *Uitualagi's* decree.

The Wooing of *Gatoa'itele*

Stories, news, and rumors, about the beauty and royalty of these princesses of the Malietoa dynasty, were voracious, carried and spread by the wind across the Archipelago of the Navigators. And so the wooers began to arrive, weekly, at Faleula village, the residence of the Malietoa. But none caught the eyes of the sisters. Until *LeManu'a-LeSanalāla* (son of a Tongan father and Samoan mother) arrived from Lotofagā village. Almost simultaneously, *Folasāitu* or *Folasa-le-aitu* (*Folasa* the demonic spirit) also arrived from Faleata.

Immediately *Gatoa'itele* was taken by surprise, by the witty nature and handsome looks of *LeSanalāla*. And so she wanted to spend time visiting with him. The two young princes were very engaging and entertaining, and they kept the sisters very interested.

The sisters and the young princes were carrying on in the late evening. Then one early dawn, the aualuma of the girls saw that there were more than four feet showing at the bottom of the bedsheets! The ladies of the Aualuma were suspicious, given the numerous feet showing under the bedsheets, and one of aualuma said, "At least the feet appear to be of high chiefs"—*O vae* (feet) *o tama* (young man or warrior) *soā* (servants of the wooing chiefs) *Ali'i* (high chief), hence the origin of the name, *vae-tama-soa-ali'i* shortened to *Vaetamasoa*, *Tamasoāli'i*, or *Vaetamasoaali'i*. It looked as though the young princes had spent the evening there.

One day *Gatoa'itele* said to her sister *Gasoloaiaolelagi*, "Come, my dear sister. I am attracted to *LeSanalāla*, and I want to go with him. However, you go and wed *Folasāitu*. But if he mistreats you or is or cruel with you, come and be with me and *LeSanalāla*. Likewise, if *LeSanalāla* mistreats or is cruel to me, I will come and live with you and *Folasāitu*."

And thus *Gatoa'itele* married *LeSanalāla,* and they went to live in Lotofagā, in the Southern Tuamasaga district. *Gasoloaiaolelagi* married *Folasāitu*, and they went to live in Tuana'i, a village of Tuamasaga.

Before long, *Gasoloaiaolelagi* was being poorly mistreated by her husband *Folasāitu*. And she remembered the parting words of farewell with her sister *Gatoa'itele,* that if either one of them was being mistreated by her husband, she could go to live with the other sister. So *Gasoloaiaolelagi* left her husband and went to live with *Gatoa'itele* and *LeManu'a-LeSanalāla*.

The official oral legend has it that *Gatoa'itele* gave birth to:

- A son, *Lalovimāmā*,
- A daughter, *Vaetamasoaali'i*,
- And another daughter, *LeAtougaugaatuitoga*.

The War against Malietoa *Sagagaimuli*

After the children were grown and married, *Gatoa'itele* relocated back to her residence in Afega village, to better organize her government. This was the period of Malietoa *Sagagaimuli*, son of Malietoa *Falefatu*, son of Malietoa *La'auli*.

Malietoa *Sagagaimuli* was putting a lot of pressure on *Fata* and *Maulolo* to abandon their service and oath to *Gatoa'itele*, as their paramount chief, and come to serve him, the Malietoa, instead. But *Fata* and *Maulolo* refused.

Malietoa *Sagagaimuli* was well aware of Malietoa *Uitualagi's* decree that the PāPā titles should be equal to the TuiAtua and TuiA'ana titles. This became the reason *Gatoa'itele*, *Fata* and *Maulolo*, and the orator group Tuisamau went to war against

Malietoa *Sagagaimuli* and the orator group Auimatagi. This is also known as the war of the PāPā of *Gatoa'itele*, where *Nafanua* sent *Tupa'i* with warriors for assistance.

The Malietoa Title

As a footnote to Malietoa *Uitualagi's* decree, we should note that, from the founding of the Malietoa dynasty, the Island Nation had been ruled by successive Malietoa titleholders, but the Malietoa title is a warrior paramount chief title, with no royalty. There is no crown PāPā like there is for TuiAtua, TuiA'ana, Tuimanu'a, TuiToga, TuiFiti, TuiUeā and others across Polynesia. Some historians believe this is the reason the Malietoa clan orchestrated this creation of the PāPā titles to be equal to the TuiA'ana and TuiAtua.

Vaetamasoaali'i

Image 12 Vaetamasoaali'i by the author's brother

Royal Queen *Vaetamasoaali'i's* royal PāPā title was decreed by Malietoa *Uitualagi* before her mother *Gatoa'itele* and *Vaetamasoaali'i* were even born.

Vaetamasoaali'i was the firstborn of *Gatoa'itele* with *LeManu'a-LeSanalāla* of Lotofagā, in the Safata district of southern Tuamasaga, though Dr. Krämer noted *Gasoloaiaolelagi* as the biological mother. Hence, she was the firstborn of the "decree," as *Gatoa'itele* was firstborn of *Gauifaleai* and Malietoa *La'auli*. And so Gatoa'itele and *LeManu'a-LeSanalāla* carried out the fulfillment of Malietoa *Uitualagi's* decree, with *Vaetamasoaali'i* decreed to be the royal paramount chief of the Safata district of the southern Tuamasaga district. Safata district was the "Vanguard" district, working together with the "Rearguard" Faleata district in the war of the Tuamasaga district of the Malietoa monarchy.

Word spread rapidly about this beautiful royal princess, descendant of the TuiToga and Malietoa matriarchs, named *Vaetamasoaali'i*. And paramount chiefs came calling for her hand in marriage. But none fit the bill for this special young lady.

The TuiFiti came and quickly returned home defeated. Then TuiA'ana *Vaemā* had to get a Samoan chief *tatau*, or tattoo, to make a winning impression with *Vaetamasoaali'i*. Unfortunately for TuiA'ana *Vaemā*, he was in a hurry and the *tatau* had not completely healed. It turned into sores all over his lower body.

And aside from the ugliness of it, the smell was unbearable, so he too was rejected.

The Warrior Orators, *Ape* and *Tutuila*

The two warrior orators, *Ape* and *Tutuila* from Fasito'o village in A'ana district, heard how TuiA'ana *Vaemā's* courtship campaign had been declined by *Vaetamasoaali'i*. The two orators were in Savai'i at a celebration, but they found out the hard way that they didn't merit a gift from the ceremony, because they did not have a paramount chief to showcase as a paramountcy representative. Thus they immediately went searching for a chief with a paramountcy pedigree.

The two orators met up with Orator *Puleleu'u* of SaLeMuliaga, who told the orators to go to the Tagaloa clan nearby and ask for the son of Tagaloa *Fa'aofonu'u* and *Fitimaula*, daughter of Orator Chief *LeTufuga* of Safotulafai, and tell them "Your son will be our paramount chief." So the orators traveled to Safotulafai village, where Tagaloa *Fa'aofonu'u* and *Fitimaula* were, and they asked the couple for their son to be their high chief. *Fitimaula's* mother was the daughter of TuiA'ana *Uotele*, and her father was Orator Chief *LeTufuga* of Safotulafai.

Tagaloa *Fa'aofonu'u* and *Fitimaula* agreed and gave their son, named *Selaginatõ* but also known as Tagaloa *Tualafa*, to the two warrior orators. The orators were elated that they had found a paramount chief with an excellent pedigree, consisting of Tagaloa, TuiA'ana, LeTufuga of the Safotulafai authority, and few other significant family connections.

Ape and *Tutuila* immediately and rapidly journeyed to Upolu, to prepare *Selaginatõ* Tagaloa to court *Vaetamasoaali'i*. Once they were ready for their courtship campaign, they left for Safata district and, to their excitement, *Vaetamasoaali'i* seemed happy to entertain the idea of *Selaginatõ* Tagaloa *Fa'aofonu'u's* candidacy as a possible marriage partner.

After a period of two weeks, *LeSanalāla* asked *Vaetamasoaali'i* if she had any good feelings about Tagaloa *Tualafa* (*Selaginatõ* Tagaloa *Fa'aofonu'u*). And *Vaetamasoaali'i* said yes, she liked him. But she also asked her parents if they would like *Selaginatõ* Tagaloa as a son-in-law.

Gatoa'itele and Gasoloaiaolelagi and LeSanalāla were all in agreement about Selaginatõ Tagaloa. And so Vaetamasoaali'i accepted Selaginatõ Tagaloa to be her husband.

We should note, it is respectful etiquette, when a paramount chief's son marries a princess of a royal crown such as Vaetamasoaali'i, for the chiefs to refer to the husband with his father's title, hence his being called Tagaloa Selaginatõ. This is common practice with the sons of the Malietoa: wherever a son resided, that village would most likely call him Malietoa. This became a major point of confusion in the Malietoa genealogy, because there appeared to be too many Malietoas in the same generation, since each son was referred to as Malietoa. But really, the correct salutation was, Sūsū mai lau Sūsūga, Alo (son) o Malietoa, Seiuli.

Taking the Child

And now we come to the story we have hinted at earlier: Ape and Tutuila were full of excitement, and so, as they prepared to return to Fasito'o, A'ana, they met with Senior Elder Orator Chief Ta'elegalolo'o of the LeSanalāla family clan, asking him to please let them know once Lady Vaetamasoaali'i should get pregnant with a baby heir-apparent. Ta'elegalolo'o agreed, and Ape and Tutuila were pleased and ready to say goodbye with the new couple.

Ape and Tutuila waited patiently at their home in Fasito'o. They kept counting the days, weeks, and months since the couple married. And shortly after the marriage, Orator Chief Ta'elegalolo'o sent a message to Ape and Tutuila saying that Vaetamasoaali'i was pregnant.

During the next ninth months, Ape and Tutuila stayed always prepared to travel up the mountainous path, ready to cross over to Safata district, and to go to Lotofagā village where Vaetamasoaali'i's residence was. Then they decided to camp by the river, close to the village, and it was here that they orchestrated their plan, with some assistance from Orator Ta'elegalolo'o.

The plan was that, when the time came for the baby's delivery, Ta'elegalolo'o would notify Ape and Tutuila, so they could dress up in midwives' clothing and sneak up to the delivery house, where they would wait until the baby was fully born. And so the two orators, dressed up like midwives, were standing right by the real midwives assisting in the delivery process. And the baby came out.

Vaetamasoaaliʻi asked the midwives, "Is the baby a boy or a girl?"

One of the lady midwives said, "It's a boy."

And then, immediately, the two midwives standing right behind said, "Here, let us clean him up and get a fresh clean cloth to wrap him with." And the baby was passed to *Ape* and *Tutuila,* in midwives' clothing.

Immediately they took the baby and cleaned him up at the river. They thanked Orator Chief *Taʻelegaloloʻo,* and they told him they were on their way to Fasitoʻo.

The journey took a few days, because they had to stop and nurse the fragile baby. At the first campsite, *Ape* told *Tutuila* to take care of the baby while he rushed to get help from their uncle at Fasitoʻo. But first *Ape* had to climb up the coconut tree to pick unripe coconut fruits to feed the baby.

Ape and *Tutuila* knew that war warriors from the LeSanalāla family clan would be coming to chase them down, and this clearly would mean immediate death for them both. And they were correct; LeSanalāla warriors were determined to capture *Ape* and *Tutuila,* but more importantly they needed to retrieve the baby boy.

Later, *Tutuila* and Uncle *Liʻo* arrived with war warriors from their village to battle *LeSanalāla's* good number of warring warriors. Uncle *Liʻo* and a good number of warriors, in battle formations, began engaging the Safata warriors. It took several days of intermittent battle engagements, then Safata decided to call it an impasse and return home.

Naming the Child

While Uncle *Liʻo* and the vanguard warriors of Fasitoʻo village were fighting, *Ape* and *Tutuila* arrived at the promontory place called Sagameauta (later called Sagameatai). They needed a more stable person to take care of the baby and they both immediately thought of Paramount Orator Chief *Alipia* of

Leulumoega village. And so they journeyed to Leulumoega, to Orator Chief *Alipia's* residence.

When they arrived, *Alipia* asked, "What brought you two here?"

Ape immediately said, "We want you to care for our paramount baby."

Alipia was shocked and curious. "Let's see your paramount baby." And when he saw the baby boy he asked, "Where did you get your baby chief?"

And so Ape responded with, "It's from heaven." Hence the name, "boy from heaven"—*Tama* (boy) *a le* (of the) *lagi* (heaven) or *Tamālelagi*.

Ape continued speaking with *Alipia*. "We want you to care for our baby chief." And *Alipia* agreed to care for the baby boy, now named *Tamālelagi*.

Alipia immediately acknowledged the boy's royal pedigree; he said he had royalty in his veins. So *Alipia* was now officially the boy's adopted father, together with *Ape* and *Tutuila*.

It's this legend that also tells how *Ape* received the addition to his name, *moe manatunatu*, meaning light sleeper; hence *Apemoemanatunatu*. For *Ape* always worried about the baby, and thus he was a light sleeper.

Tutuila obtained the addition to his name, *le matemate*, which means lacking inquisitiveness or ambition; hence *Tutuilalematemate*. For he was always late getting the baby's food prepared.

And here, we have wound our way back to the beginning of the legend of TuiA'ana *Tamālelagi* and Tafa'ifa *Salamasina*.

71

Matriarchal Responsibility

In a matriarchal society, the female is the custodian of the family heirlooms and genealogy. She is responsible for maintaining the culture and customs, and for the organization and operation of daily activity in the family, including (if she is unmarried) the preparation of the ava for the ava ceremony. Everything about the culture is defined through the female lineage.

The female anchors the family to its homeland as designated by real-estate. She anchors the family and directs and advises its members. And she can become chief (chieftess) if no one on the male side is available or competent to carry out the responsibilities of the title. Within the Circle of Sitting Chiefs, the paramount chieftess shares equal authority with the family's paramount chief.

Many families have defaulted to the female side carrying the titles of the family. The children can inherit any of the titles and lands of both mother and father. The father's title might go first to the elder son and so on, but the children can also claim the titles and lands on their mother's side. However, inheritance of the title is decided on by the collective family. While it's customary to look to the sons, a son will only inherit if one is competent to carry the title. Titles are not automatically inherited by the sons—unlike in European monarchies.

This matriarchal family structure turns out to be crucial to understanding the organization of the Navigators' journey in migration. The male was always expected to travel and seek opportunity, to hunt and go on fishing exhibitions. Meanwhile the female was expected to stay home and take care of domestic chores and the home front. This nurturing type of family structure led to the development of a strong family foundation, hence the birth of the family-centric culture of the Navigators, a collective culture based, since its foundation, in motherly nurture—a foundation that reinforces collectivism as opposed to individualism.

In America, many people have to deal with problems of gender issues, but, in Samoan culture, the way we look at women is more respectful and more beautiful. There are individuals who mistreat people, regardless of whether male or female, but Samoan culture itself is steeped in respect. I've seen nothing in Western civilization that's comparable to the *feagaiga* between Samoan brothers and sisters.

Some people do not know that women can have titles in Samoa. But yes, our women can and do. Our women are part of the elders; our women take part in decision-making within the family. They're not relegated just to doing the *feau* in the back— or doing the chores in the kitchen.

One thing that always touches me about Samoan culture is that no matter where in the world you go, the moment a female and a male Samoan meet, they treat each other with respect. The *feagaiga* is applied right away. It doesn't matter whether they are *aiga* (family) or not, they will address each other as sister and brother. My hope is that we never lose sight of that.

Samoan women are strong, and Samoan men are humble.

The Sa'o Tama'ita'i

The role of women in Samoan and Manu'an societies should be kept very clear throughout any investigation: it is foundational in anchoring the family. It reveals the profound meaning of the African phrase, "It takes a village to care for a child," made famous by Margaret Mead in her book *The Coming of Age in Samoa*.[xv] It is the matrilineal and matrilocal focus of the Samoan extended family that led to the idea of de-emphasizing individual family kinship names beyond immediate family members. Instead, the emphasis is on the center or core of the family that anchors it.

We give to women the highest respect: For example, the *Sa'o* is the Paramount Chief. But the *Sa'o Tama'ita'i*—a female title as, for example, the Sa'o Tama'ita'i *Falenaoti*—is both *Tama'ita'i* and *Sa'o*. When a male (a brother for example) is a paramount chief and there is a *Sa'o Tama'ita'i* sitting titleholder, she sits opposite from the paramount chief in meetings. At this point she shares the responsibility of head of the family and villages. She can lobby her brother (or paramount family chief) to reduce the penalty for a crime or give total forgiveness. If the penalty is death, she can lobby to reduce it, and she must be taken seriously. Respect for protocol must be paramount—the dignity of the family demands that it must be adhered to. So, the *Sa'o Tama'ita'i*, a woman, is the only one who can change the decision of the *Sa'o*. She is equal and has equal responsibility in the life of the whole village. Which is pretty balanced if you think about it. The Navigators were wise people to structure and balance out this process for the people to practice.

The Aualuma

The *Aualuma* organization of women, in the village ruling authority structure, is an integral component of the village's management system. This evidences the role of women in the matriarchal structure of Samoan culture. The *Aualuma* structure mirrors, exactly, the structure of the men's Chiefs Council organization. The seating arrangements, titles, officers, the management and leadership responsibilities, all very much replicate the village Chiefs Council structure. Each member represents their family chief titleholder. And most are the wives of the family chief or the representative, usually the princess, of the family chief.

For example, in my case I'm a commuter from the U.S., and I don't have a wife, so my "resident princess" (the *Tafa'i Fata Fa'aususū-Manumaisialoa* title) represents me and my family in our village of Afega *Aualuma*. This would work the same way with lady chiefs (or chieftesses)—their respective family princess would represent them in the village *Aualuma*.

Performance is measured by attendance records and active participation in *Aualuma* activities. It's a fact that a well-organized and well-managed *Aualuma* is a source of blessing and wealth and wellbeing to the village. There is much evidence to show that the *Aualuma* wields much influence and authority in the village. It's the *Aualuma* that organizes and maintains arts and crafts for the women in the village. The weaving of fine mats and maintenance of heirlooms of the family are the domain of the *Aualuma,* which oversees these production activities. Organizing healthcare with sustainable infrastructure—such as health clinics, the teaching and training of personal hygiene and dietary instructions, and guidelines and maintenance procedures—all this has been the focus of many village *Aualuma*.

In our village of Afega, the *Aualuma* built one of the first village healthcare clinics to service not only our village but residents of nearby villages. The healthcare committee of the *Aualuma* works with the government healthcare agency and the hospital to teach and train housewives, mothers, and young girls in the science of healthcare. This has been and is a continuing focus of the *Aualuma,* to maintain wellbeing and wellness at the village level.

Education is also a major priority of the *Aualuma*. When literacy drops in a village, it is usually evidence of the *Aualuma's* performance being below par. The *Aualuma* has to encourage the family parents and elders to ensure the children are attending school. And school at the village is a commitment for which the Chiefs Council and the *Aualuma* both hold responsibility. Our village has maintained a public-school building, land, playgrounds, and maintenance facilities, since the village schools initiative started in the early 1900s.

The protocols are such that the *Aualuma* have a direct line to the village Chiefs Council. They can propose any program and make requests such as requesting funding for, or approval of, a particular program that impacts village ordinances.

The role of *Aualuma* organizations in the wellbeing and wellness of Samoan culture is crucial, particularly with the challenges we face today of domestic violence against women and justice for women. The *Aualuma* has been a formal women's organization from the beginning of the 3,000-year-old Samoan culture, and its existence evidences the continuation of the matriarchal culture of the Navigators.

When Paramount Chief La'ulu *Nofovaleane* (A.D.1470) of SaLeMuliaga, Savai'i, decreed his grandsons to be the princes of the royal *Aualuma* of Samoa, Samoa and Manu'a had already established the organization called *Aualuma*. Thus *Tapumanaia* was decreed to Leulumoega to serve there, and he was Prince *Toleafoa*; *Pesefeamanaia* was decreed to Palauli, Safotu, and Sagafili villages, so the *Aualuma* of *Vae* (leg) *o le Nofoafia*—the three-legged chair consisting of Palauli, Safotu and Sagafili—was served by him and he was Prince *Liliomaiava*; and *Le Aumoana* was decreed to be serve the *Aualuma* of SaLeMuliaga, and he was Prince *LeAumoana*.

The foundation of the development and reaffirmation of the *Aualuma* organization structure evidences the warrior spirit of the paramount chieftess, the spirit that helped build the Island Nation.

The Taupou

In formal meetings, in the maota, the village chief (*Sa'o*) sits at a post to the right of the house, and the post directly opposite is allocated to the *Sa'o Tama'ita'i*. And the *Taupou* has responsibility to serve the ava. The *Taupou* of the Malietoa title is *To'oa,* and in Sapapali'i she is known as the *Sa'o Galua*—a title which means she is the second head of the family.

When the *Sa'o Galua* title is bestowed on the *Taupou*, she removes herself from her ava task; the family will, therefore, designate a new *Taupou* to take on the responsibility of the ava.

Image 13
https://commons.wikimedia.org/wiki/File:3_Samoan_girls_making_ava_1909.jpg
Bartlett Tripp (1842-1911)Publisher: Cedar Rapids IA : Torch Press uploaded by
Teinesavaii, Public domain, via Wikimedia Commons

The role of the virgin

I should point out here that, contrary to what some people believe, we never sacrificed virgins in Samoa. That would have been idol worship, and Samoans did not worship idols. But Samoans have "offered" a virgin in order to save a village: In ancient times, the virgin daughter might be a kind of "sacrificial lamb" for war—a human sacrifice as it were, for the sins of the defeated village in war—in the sense that the paramount chief would offer her to the victorious warrior for sparing the chief and family; she would become the savior of the family by marrying the victorious warrior, and that is the whole extent of her being a "sacrifice." An example of this can be found in the story of *Lufasiaitu*, where Princess *Lagituaiva's* brave sacrifice pays for the sins of *Sa Tagaloalagi* (the household of *Tagaloalagi*).

The union of enemy children would produce offspring that would prevent future wars from occurring. If they produced a son, he would carry the titles of both families and would join the two families together. This is the way the Samoans negotiated wars. So, if women were "used" as these "sacrificial lambs," then why wouldn't they receive high honors within the family?

This is very similar to how things worked with Europeans. Kings and warriors would offer their sisters or daughters in marriage for the sake of peace. In Samoan it's called *togiola mo le aiga*, and we should think about that word, *Togiola* (sacrificial lamb): she is given to the winning warrior so that she can save the whole family.

In the same way in the Bible, when David went up against Goliath, Saul put up rewards, and one of the rewards was the hand of his daughter in marriage. David had his eyes on the reward, which was the daughter of the king.

Family-Centric Chiefdom and Responsibilities

Combining Matriarchal and Patriarchal Structures

Samoan matriarchal structures transitioned to a combination of matriarchal and patriarchal societal structures—a balancing act that evolved and developed in isolation after settlement of the islands—and we can clearly see evidence of this. It's a change that provides reason for the practice of memorizing and reciting family genealogies not only of your own family, but also of all the major foundational families of Samoa and Manu'a.

The combination of matriarchal, matrilineal, matrilocal, and patrilineal structures is uniquely challenged, of course, by the issue of property rights. The growth in size of extended families puts much pressure on the fair and equitable distribution of land held in common by the family. The system, where a single chief or small group of family chiefs makes decisions on the use of family land, is being challenged by the younger and more aggressive, educated members of the family, because it is counter-intuitive to their sense of individual freedom. As we all know, the important economic factors—relating to production and building economic freedom and personal wealth—are land, labor, and capital. The demand to stimulate the island economy drives the issue, requiring the deployment of large unproductive family lands and estates into more business production. And to do this, the sacred governance of the family and their property rights must somehow be changed. While the chorus of public protest is currently pianissimo, I have sensed a choir of protests ahead, producing a growing crescendo of impending pandemonium, and I will address some of these issues in the second volume of this book.

The Family Fishing Net

The web of family structure—like a large fishing net—is paramount to the culture. To know and to understand the

79

connecting points of family relationships—like the knots of that large fishing net—is powerful, especially for an orator chief. Understanding the relationships, origins, and generations allows the orator to use this knowledge to his advantage.

For example in my family: The major family began around A.D.1600 with the warrior hero who won the war and gave birth to a new major family. That warrior was the son of the man whose title I carry today. Thus my title is an Elder (Mātua) Orator Chief title of the Tuisamau Orator authority of the Tuamasaga district of the Malietoa dynasty. So among several salutations are those referring to Fata and Maulolo being the Mātua (Elder) Orators of Tuamasaga, evidencing authority, seniority, Fathers of the district, and Fathers of the Malietoa dynasty and of all Tuamasaga. It's also evidence of the progenitor genealogy of the district, inextricably linked to the Malietoa dynasty.

Similarly, in the Bible, Abraham is the "Elder" and "Father" to all Israel. Moses is the elder and senior chief, the leader who led the children of Israel out of Egypt. Then King Saul and King David would be given the royal salutations and the glory of the kingdom but, if a chief called Moses, a descendant of Moses' genealogy, were to appear in front of the king, Chief Moses would be referred to as the Elder and Father to all who came after him. His honor and salutations would reflect that he is the head—the father, elder, or senior—of the original family.

Family Terms and Structures

The Samoan and Manu'an idea of kinship is dictated by the structure of the family organization. The emphasis is on the parents and the elders, the Mātua(s) of the family. The lexicon is limited, with mother, father, sister, brother, cousin, grandfather, grandmother, uncle, and all the elders being described as Mātua. Parents (tinā, mother, and tamā, father) are terms used generically to refer to all parents. Brother (uso) is a generic term for all male friends and male family relatives. Sister is commonly referred to as a tuafafine (and, we should note, the boundaries between brother and sister are numerous and sacred. Violating these customs is tabu).

Other formal terminologies used to refer to a princess include Taupou, Feagaiga, Sa'o Nalua (or Galua), Sa'o Tama'ita'i,

Tausala, Aualuma, and *Se'eitalaluma,* depending on family protocol. "Cousin" is used generally throughout the family at large, through village or clan relationships. "Uncle" is used to refer to all older male members of the family, and to refer to male relationships within the village and clan.

The central theme is matriarchal and matrilineal, with the female as the source and anchor of the family. Meanwhile the *Mātua*(s)—the elders—are clearly understood to be the source of the family genealogy. So the extent of the radius of the family circle can be visibly understood. The genealogies and the chronological order of past generations are traced back through the sisters' or daughters' lineages.

Current culture is often concerned with the side that inherits the chief title, which can be either patrilineal or matrilineal. Many family chief titles are passed down through the sister's or daughter's lineage, but the common cultural practice is for the genealogy of the family to be traced through the female line, while the chief title is bestowed on the male heir.

All this is another remnant of the ancient matrilineal cultural structure. The current culture stands as the result of an elaborate and powerful patriarchal structure combined with an historical matriarchal structure that anchors the family in domestic affairs and duties, thus adding subtlety to the Navigators' motif. It evidences a happy balancing act between the old matrilineal and the newer patrilineal culture, leading to a truly family-centric society.

Division of Labor

The Samoan family-centric organizational structure leads naturally to an orderly division of labor to ensure the family's survival and security.

The 14th century philosopher and historian Ibn Khaldun was an expert in the ancient history of Bedouin society. Some would argue he was one of the greatest philosophers of the Middle Ages and a forerunner of the modern disciplines of sociology and demography.[xvi] Ibn Khaldun described the family-centric nature of nomadic society, dependent on the division of labor, with extended families and a chief or sheikh leading either the family or a larger social unit such as the tribe. He described a social network based on and maintained by deeply ingrained values and expectations, forming a system that governs the behavior and relationships of the society's members. Key values, he concluded, are harmony, kinship solidarity, and hierarchy."[xvii]

The process involves determining a family member's skillset and desires, assessing the family member's strength to perform certain tasks, and steering family members away from other tasks that they may not feel competent in. Talents begin to emerge—the enjoyment of fishing, success as a good farmer, articulate speech in the conduct of cultural etiquette and custom and formality, etc. Thus the assignment of responsibility can be well-guided.

For example: Having a good command of customs and formality, and knowing the family genealogy, are critical attributes that lead to a leadership role—to an orator chief title. Also, putting the family's needs above individual desires and goals is clearly a sign of someone with potential to fill a leadership role. But it becomes obvious that leadership titles are too few to go around as a family grows. Thus selecting those to lead the family is not easy; it often involves political canvassing throughout the family at large. Honing the performance of the family unit into harmonious unison is a source of both strength and economic and political power in the larger organization of the village and district.

Family-Centric Law

In the family-centric structure, inheritance means not only assets, but also authority. The Samoan legal family structure is such that the family is the sole authority. The paramount chief gets his or her authority from the family. This is why the Island Salutation starts with the honorifics or salutations of the family. And this is why Samoa does not have someone in absolute authority, like the King of Tonga.

In Samoa, the family can in fact banish a head of the family, a chief, and they have done so many times in the past. In this way Samoans are able to protect their land, because the paramount chief cannot sell or give away the family landholding, as the Hawaiians did—there, paramount chiefs inherit through marriage, and they outright sold the land without the family's consent; that's the sad story of about 75% of the land in Hawaii.

To Samoans, your authority is really a permission from the family. In Samoa, all you have to do is show evidence of your family genealogy, connected to the main family tree, and you can rebut any heirloom-like land decision made by the chief or chiefs.

The Origins of Chiefdom

In his famous *Muqaddimah*[xviii] Ibn Khaldun (A.D.1332-1406) details Bedouin tribal society, culture, clan hierarchy, organizational structure, and way of life in the Arabian deserts. He describes the transition from the title of "Chief" to "Sheikh" (in pre-Islamic antiquity) as head of the family and tribe.

This practice of chiefdom originated in the family structure, as the family would assign certain responsibilities to each member to benefit the family as a system. Chiefdom is not a Polynesian invention. It is as old as the early migrations—from Out of Africa I, II, III; Out of India; Out of the Eurasian Steppes; Out of Mainland Asia; and throughout the Malay and Indonesian Archipelagos.[xix] Although some social scientists have concluded that chiefdom originated in Vanuatu,[xx] I would remind them to look back at the path of human migration and see if they encounter chiefdom titles and organization in any of those ancient societies.

The chief's titles and responsibilities were honed all along the migration path. The fact that the male frequently spent time seafaring on the mighty Pacific Ocean meant the female, the wife, was left caring for the family, creating a matriarchal structure. Then the declining frequency of male seafaring journeys led to the erosion and downgrading of that matriarchal structure, combining it with a patriarchal structure within Polynesian societies.

Studies in Chiefdom

Studies by M. Kayser and S. Brauer (2006) and others[xxi] found anthropological and ethnological evidence that the first development of a hierarchical chiefdom and family structure, so foundational to the development of culture, occurred in around

2,000 B.C. on the Melanesian Island of Vanuatu (see above). Then in 2016, Pontus Skoglund revealed how this structure spread further down to Polynesia, as Polynesian migration continued down to the islands in the East Pacific.[xxii] This occurred during the initial establishment of the Lapita trading network, around 1,000-1,200 B.C.

At the same time many other countries—such as those in the Levant area, the Near East cultures, the Pontic Steppe cultures, India's Harappan and Mohenjo-Daro, cultures in Asia Minor, and many ancient "barbarian cultures" such as the Gauls, the Germanic cultures, the Vikings, ancient Celtic cultures, and African cultures—all had already long-established chiefdom-type structures to lead their family clans. This development became formalized at the dawn of the agricultural era, as described in National Geographic's *Concise History of the World an Illustrated Timeline,*[xxiii] and by Joseph Campbell.

So Vanuatu's "creation" of the chiefdom family structure might have been the first for the indigenous people of Vanuatu, but it wasn't its first instance for Polynesians, because the command organization of the Navigators' very organized vessels was itself based on the organizational structure of chiefdom and family. This would have been a prerequisite to the sort of long, extended voyage critical to this entrepreneurial venture.

Historical Chiefdom

A chief's responsibility in this system would have included:

- who is in charge of the ocean for fishing
- who is in charge of the plantation, for planting and harvesting the crops and bringing them home
- who are the food preparers
- who is in charge of ava—its preparation and ceremony,
- who is the orator to command communication between the family head and family members
- who are messengers to the village and to the regional and district councils

This was the beginning of what is known as an agricultural family organizational structure. For example, the person responsible for fishing studied the ocean tides and flying patterns of different seagulls and other birds to predict where it was more likely that fish could be caught. Likewise, the ocean navigator would study ocean currents; wind directions; seasonal, cyclical, and irregular patterns; ocean swells; and the moving patterns of moon, sun, and stars. These were learned through past anecdotal experiences that were transmitted from parents and ancestors orally.

We begin to see a legitimate society developing. During this period, Samoan society had discovered the organization of agricultural activities and knew how to optimally use the land. They had a working family system, with knowledge of arts, language, culture, economics, transportation, navigation, and weaponry, and a spiritual sense of belonging and creation. With such fast developments, rules were put in place to protect each family member. Eventually, a form of government was developed within the family system, and later extended to the village and subsequently the district. Interestingly, homes were built, displaying a metaphorical chiefdom structure, around the responsibilities of each family member—for example, cooks lived near the kitchen or *umu*.

The refinement of the chiefdom organizational structure, induced by the reduced frequency of extended seafaring voyages for the males, resulted in the male becoming, effectively, a homebody. And further participation of males in the daily affairs of the family led to males taking on the position of family leader.

Chief Titles and responsibilities

Leadership is fundamental in chieftain DNA, so to speak. It is very important for a chief to obtain trust and respect from the family and clan, in order to lead and expect the clan to follow. I am not writing a book on leadership here, of course—the libraries of the world are full of such books. But intuitively we have to accept the fact that these Polynesians could not have navigated across the largest ocean in the world and colonized these islands without sound planning, organization, culture, and, most important of all, leadership to guide them to the destination of their "promised land."

Chiefs must be able to bring family and clan members together, so they work together in a cohesive manner. To do this, a cultural dogma must be developed and established, and adequate training must be done repetitively, to ensure competence is achieved in all responsibilities and activities. Effective communication among the people must be constantly practiced.

Collective and collaborative efforts are very important in the conduct of everyday life. Tasks and responsibilities must be delegated, not only to achieve the desired objective, but also for training. Where performance is consistent, it becomes a form of reward. And the ultimate reward for undying service is to be a chief.

Orator Chiefs

Because of the fast growth of the Navigators' families, which eventually became villages, an orator was needed to send the high chief's message to the village people. During this time a written language had not yet been created. This necessitated the skills of an eloquent orator to bring accurate accounts from the high chief as well as to negotiate peace between two parties. The orator acts as a liaison between the high chief and village people.

This idea is found also in Greek mythology. Zeus wasn't going to talk to just anybody; he had the oracles—his designated messengers. Requests went from the people to the gods, and the oracle was needed to translate the message. Samoan orator chiefs demonstrate that Samoans had already established this process of delegation.

The people of the Navigators believed two things were very important for orators: knowledge of the "old wisdom" of the old high chiefs; and "experience and expertise" of the orator chief. Reasoning and logic are very important both in communicating with the high chiefs—'O le Tofā ma le Fa'autaga—and in interpreting the high chief's wisdom and messages to family members so they can understand and execute instructions—Tofā fa'atamali'i. The gift of "reasoning and logic," or of 'Ole Tofā ma le Fa'autaga, is foundational to the chieftain structure.

In an oral-based culture, it is important for those with the rank of orator chief to have eloquence, wisdom, and leadership, in order to give an accurate account of the high chief's wisdom, messages, and decrees to the family or clan. Orator chiefs are heralds, harbingers, and liaisons between the high chiefs and the family members and village people. So the orator must have leadership skills—the orator must perform well in all responsibilities, and in maintaining peace and harmony among family members and clan. The appointment of the orator is closely wound into Samoan culture.

Orators have to know their respective position, relative both to the occasion when they speak and to family relationships, and they have to use the appropriate language and words in their orations. Oration is an attribute of a leader. It is the most visible criterion for measuring leadership in the family. The orators would say, once you stand up to deliver your oration, you are facing your judgement day as an orator. An orator's reputation is almost always dependent on the delivery of the oration, its contents, structure, completeness, language (using ancient historical metaphors and vocabulary), knowledge of genealogies, and protocol for the occasion.

A Servant Culture

Samoan family structure allows the development of these skills to maintain efficiency and hone the art of serving the family. Becoming a good servant, of the family and the chief, is a prerequisite to enjoying an independent life. Samoans would say, *'O le ala i le Pule o le Tautua*—the path to authority lies in being a great servant. In the chief's wisdom, effective leadership can only be achieved through humility and service. This is the reason I practice the simple idea of the upside-down pyramid in my management approach to leading our family. I have to be the single point at the bottom to serve and support the rest of the pyramid above.

A chief must have command of the oral tradition of speech-making in the formal chieftain language and a detailed knowledge of family history and genealogy, and culture, custom, and formality. Armed with these tools of the trade, a chief can begin to exercise authority. It is the culture that commands the family and village organizations to operate in unison. This is the "fishing net," or the Samoan mat or carpet, woven neatly, tightly, and robustly, that makes the whole of the family organization work effectively. A chief's credibility is dependent on mastering all the culture, oration, history, and genealogy, and on people skills.

For example, the head of the family, chief or not, would designate family meetings and conduct worship in the evening. This would give the family leader an opportunity to discuss the day's work and status. The head of the family would assign responsibilities based on the need for completion of a task. This process helps us understand and practice these customs and formalities. Within these meetings the development of the family genealogy is spoken.

It was always important for the elders of the family to pass these things on to the next generation, especially in the days before a written language was established. So the family genealogy is very sacred in Samoan culture. In this purely oral fashion, the genealogy was maintained until the German explorer, Krämer, felt it necessary to document the information.

Titles and Salutations

Titles

One should never confuse a name with the chief title that a person takes. As Samoans would say, "When you're gone, you're gone," and your name passes on. Then after you, your *title* goes right back to the family. The title returns into the structure, and the structure goes on forever and ever. People will come and go, but this structure will stay. This is how our ancestors developed the village structure, so that it would be here forever—well, unless an earthquake or tsunami clears out the village.

If somebody passes on, so will their name pass to the *Lagi* (the heavens). This is very similar to the traditions of the Greeks, Mesopotamians, and Egyptians, where they also describe this process. The whole idea of building the pyramid was because the pharaohs were looking for a way to move up to the 10th heaven. And they had different salutations for them.

The first "outside-world, cultural model" that Samoans identified with was the Bible. They learned about European culture from missionaries and expatriates anecdotally, but formal education in the Bible was taken as an intellectual discipline. Everything the Scriptures said was taken as a "blueprint" that the indigenous population used, as a comparative culture, to reconcile with their own established culture and belief. Thus, their profound understanding of the Scriptures, which helped them accept the Bible without much recalcitrance.

Here again though, we might ask how Samoans ever figured this out on their own. They understood they came from *Tagaloalagi*. He was in the 10th heaven. Then the *Tagaloa* family began from the ninth heaven down to the first heaven. So that's how they understood the concept of different heavens. When the soul leaves this earth, their belief was that it was going up to these heavens, and, much like the Greeks and the Egyptians, Samoans described a place in the earth, where the high chief, after passing, goes one way and all the ordinary people go another way. It's called Pulotu.

These ideas were very much intact, and they were crucial in defining a sophisticated society.[xxiv] All this, of course, was before Christianity arrived. And while the description of this process might seem parallel to the Bible, we did not get this from the Bible. We invented it ourselves.[xxv]

Negotiation of Titles

Samoan titles are not inherited, as in the Western tradition. Samoan families decide who to give the family title to, whether it be to a female or a male, married into the family or of the bloodline. The family decides, based on who can best carry out the genealogy, maintain the land, and protect the family title. During such a complex process of negotiation, an orator's abilities to bring peace and mediation among family members are highly favored. After all, with a large family, it can become easy to forget about someone.

This reinforces the Samoan tradition of memorizing one's genealogy to protect one's stance. In the early 1800s, German travelers realized the importance of genealogy to the Samoan people and began documenting it to aid future generations. As we shall see, they were also able to document Samoan mythology, folktales, and the history of the islands dating back to 1,400 B.C.

Importance of Genealogy

An ancient Samoan proverb describes Samoan genealogy: it states that there are more roots than there are branches. And according to the official salutations of both Samoa and Tutuila (or American Samoa) and Manu'a: there eight foundational families of the Archipelago. The Official Salutations by Consensus Decree Families are:

1. Sa TuiManu'a
2. Sa TuiAtua
3. Sa TuiA'ana
4. Sa Tagaloa

5. Sa Malietoa
6. Sa Tonumaipe'a
7. Sa Levalasi
8. Sa Tuala

And a consensus of the Chiefs adds

9. Sa Lilomaiava, making eight plus one families of Samoa and Manu'a.

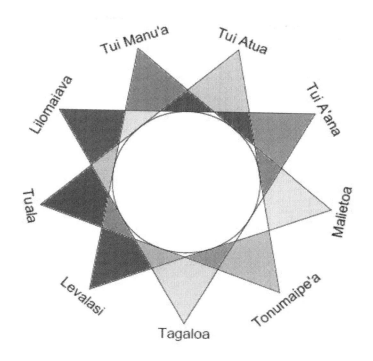

Image 14 owned by author

Many chiefs would argue there are other families which have grown in size and significance in the country genealogies, besides the eight plus one listed above: These additional families are really descendants of the eight or nine foundational families:

1. Sa Tunumafono
2. Sa Amituana'i
3. Sa Fenunuivao
4. Sa Tupua
5. Sa Mavaega
6. Sa Le'iataua
7. Sa Moeleoi

These are families of significance in the structure of Samoan culture and in the nation, for purposes of recognition and respect, but they are all sub-families of these seven: TuiAtua, TuiA'ana, Tagaloa, Malietoa, Tonumaipe'a, Sa Levalasi, and Sa Tuala.

Genealogy and Salutations

The official National Salutations must include the four families of PāPā:

- TuiAtua
- TuiA'ana
- Gatoa'itele
- Vaetamasoaali'i

This is very important because it evidences a very clever provision to ensure the balance of power: a paramount chief of a monarch may have the chief title(s), but without the PāPā they are not recognized as a royal monarch because they have not acquired and bestowed the corresponding PāPā. So, legally without the four PāPā families, the Navigators' nation has no king. And a country without a king has no kingdom.

To summarize, the salutations include:

- Honorific Families
- Aiga o Nofo (seat of foundation)
- Aiga o Fale (king)
- Aiga o PāPā.

In the official Salutations of the Archipelago there are three Royal Families:

- Sa Tuimanu'a (relinquished to the U.S. Constitution, thus the PāPā of Tuimanu'a is no longer bestowed. as per the partition agreement with the three world powers, Great Britain, Germany, and the United States of America.)
- Sa Malietoa
- Sa Tupua

When speaking in front of the Independent Nation of Samoa, you would refer only to the families that are in Samoa, not including Manu'a, keeping in mind that Manu'a was an independent Island Kingdom with their Tuimanu'a as king. So, when referring to only Samoa and Tutuila (or American Samoa) there only two active Royal Families today—Sa Malietoa and Sa Tupua. They are the ones that held the Tafa'ifa (the four royal crowns or PāPās—TuiAtua, TuiA'ana, Gatoa'itele and

Vaetamasoaali'i). Thus a chief, in oration, might address the Archipelago as they please, as long as they understand the structure.

Remembering there are two "types of families" in the salutations of Samoa—families of paramountcy (foundational to specific families) and families of monarchs or PāPās (SaTupua and SaMalietoa)—all families combine together into one or the other of these categories. So it is often asked, to which royal monarch do you belong? To one of them or to both? The TuiManu'a Kingdom of Manu'a is no longer recognized, abolished by the U.S. Constitution, but this keeps it simple and correct. The seven families I have mentioned above illustrate, as an example, the recognition of these ancient families.

In all, we see there are ten major families. Samoan genealogies connect through the intermarriages of these families. But it all begins with a very simple circle of ten families. The numerous generations and inter-marriages make an orator's task that much more important, for an orator must memorize the family's genealogy to protect it from becoming lost. Samoan culture is family-centric; therefore it is important to protect the genealogy.

Genealogy and Cooperation

Another Samoan metaphor is the fish skeleton metaphor: "The fish has many bones, and sometimes too many to count, but each bone performs a function critical to the life and survival of the fish. The major parts of the fish—such as the head, gills, backbone, rib bones, and tail fin or caudal fin—must all work in unison to allow the fish to swim."

Fish swim by flexing their bodies and tails back and forth. They stretch or expand their muscles on one side of the body, while relaxing the muscles on the other side. This motion moves the fish forward through the water. The back fin is used to help push the fish through the water.[xxvi]

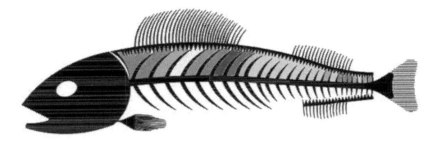

Image 15 owned by author

The Samoan analogy continues, whereby the head of the fish represents the major families of the island, the major "backbone and rib bones" are the princes and their families, and the tail fin is the vanguards and rearguards of the family, village, district, and country. The fish bones cover, metaphorically, each and every responsibility that is critical to carrying out the affairs of the family, village, and district. The fish, of course, cannot swim without all parts of its anatomy moving and working in concert, hence the apt metaphor.

The fish analogy is evoked by events in ancient time when a royal or paramount chief was insulted and was deliberating over going to war. The chief might want the warriors and sitting chiefs to avenge the insult by going to war. But all parts of clan must be in agreement, particularly the vanguard and rearguard families.

Disagreements over the various royal titles often called for war if they couldn't be resolved through peaceful means. But then the period after Christianity arrived. Europeans were promoting the concept of single "King" or monarch to rule the island, and this became a period of turmoil, with clans warring throughout most of the 1800s.

The Importance of Service and Other Qualities

Service in *Fa'aSamoa* (Samoan customs and cultural etiquette) is called *tautua*. This provides a very broad perspective on the idea of service; for example, *tautua* includes the completion of one's daily chores, caring for a relative, or the earning of an academic degree. *Tautua* is taught from birth, and it is expected of all titleholder candidates.

The *tautua* of relationship is another reason one may be granted a title, perhaps for the service one's parents have done for the family, service that has not been shown appreciation for otherwise. For example, one's mother may have raised her 8 younger siblings, and now her child or grandchild has a great potential to become a titleholder. The underlying point in this is the mother's' undying service and sacrifice for her family. It is one's *tautua* that gives authority and title.

Some families have given titles to people based on how much wealth they have acquired. However, this is not true of ancient customs, and *tautua* remains of greater importance than wealth and riches. *Le tautua musumusu mai le tautua e tautala fua le galuega* is a proverb which states that the fruit of your work will speak volumes for itself. There is also another proverb, *e le valea le fagau*, which means that the children are not forgetful. This proverb works well in this instance, for example, where the child remembers their grandmother's caring for their brother, which will give the child a great chance to receive a title.

A concern that I have seen surfacing recently is the question of whether a person can receive a title despite that person's geographic location and emotional distance from the family. The simple answer to this is yes, this person can still receive the title. Titles are in no way limited to immediate family members living in Samoa, or to the identification of belonging to only the Samoan culture. Title eligibility is based solely on *tautua*; no matter where one lives, or who one is. Then the person who receives the title carries the family.

Among other qualities a titleholder might possess, fearlessness and courage might be detrimental in making informed decisions regarding a large group of people. It is inevitable that opposition will arise, concerning one's decisions, and every wise leader needs to understand how to deal with such opposition. A titleholder is strategic and keeps track of all variables and possible outcomes.

Above all these character traits and capabilities, a person's faith and standing in their church is also given great consideration. This is so because Samoan people believe Jesus Christ is the way and the truth, leading to eternal life. A leader who shares this belief will guide the family closer to Jesus.

Women's titles

Samoan women have very specific titles and responsibilities. There is also a designated female who can sit in family meetings opposite from the family chief. Young and unmarried women also have designated responsibility for the ava.

Among Samoan women's titles are *Taupou*, *Sa'o Tama'ita'i*, and *Sa'o Galua*, which signify titles held by the sister and the brother. There are many more titles given to women by family and clan; these titles may be particular to a family and clan. For example, in Manu'a, the *Aufaoa* is the same title as the *Taupou* of the *Sa'o*, like *Samalaulu* for TuiManu'a. Malietoa *Ae'o'ainu'ū's* sister *To'oā*, named *Sa'o Tama'ita'i* of Malietoa, had the salutation *Sa'o Nalua* or *Sa'o Galua* (the second *Sa'o*).

The titles given to women are as follows:
1. *Aufaoa* (Manu'an equivalent of *Taupou*)
2. *Aualuma* (as we have already seen)
3. *Ali'i o le Ao*
4. *TamaSǎ*
5. *Faletua* (the title of a high chief's or pastor's wife)
6. *Tausi* (the title of an orator chief's wife)
7. *Masiofo* (a monarch titleholder's wife[xxvii])
8. *Augafa'apae*
9. *Māfine* (term of respect for a woman[xxviii])
10. *Taupou*
11. *Sa'o Tama'ita'i*
12. *Sa'o Galua*
13. *Feagaiga*
14. *Se'etalaluma*
15. *Tama'ita'i*
16. *Launatausala*

Marriage titles–Ma'oupū [xxix]

Some marriages are a direct result of a peace offering to end a war. The warrior who is to marry the chief's daughter can either return to his home village or become a part of the chief's village. The latter is much more difficult than the former, as in this case the warrior, as well as the chief, must go through a very complex process.

If the chief decides to bring his son-in-law to live in his village, this will be either because the chief feels his son-in-law can protect his family, or it will be for the sake of economic growth. The son-in-law is then given the *Ma'oupū* title. This title is negotiated between the warrior's home village and new village. If the warrior accepts it, he will then be granted the right to become a part of the chief's village.

In this way *Mauga*, the young mountain boy (we will meet him in Volume II), later became Paramount *Ma'oupūTasi*, meaning "The Number One (*tasi*) in Seniority *Ma'oupū*," decreed by Paramount Princess *Tapusalaia* Malietoa *Fuaoleto'elau*. Hence the address, *Afio mai lau Afioga le Ma'oupūTasi Mauga*.

Chief Titles and Responsibilities

The responsibilities of a chief are numerous and differ based on the chief's level and title. In general, the foremost responsibility is that of leadership in directing the various functions and activities of the family and village organizations; with senior-level titles, this includes district and national ceremonial roles. The chief class has the responsibility of being custodians of culture, language, family heirlooms, customs and ceremonies, genealogies of island families, history of the country, security of the people, and protection of the religious environment, land holdings, family titles, and physical environment. The paramount chief and most of the high chief titles carry with them a leadership role in senior management.

So, a chief title comes with a multitude of responsibilities, so the decision of who will obtain the title and lead the family is not taken lightly. There are various reasons one might be given a chief title, including:

- the family feels this person can protect the family; this person is a mighty warrior
- the family feels this person can expand the family's wealth or gain prestige for the family; this is typically done through marrying into a paramount family.

But outward appearances are not the only thing looked at in this choice; so too are inward qualities such as:

- service or *tautua*
- leadership skills
- knowledge of Samoan language, customs, and traditions
- family genealogy, and knowledge of family genealogy
- and the possession of wisdom and intellect beyond the person's years.

In fact, in Samoa, it takes nearly 40 years to train to serve food to the high chief, because the server must know how to appropriately address the high chief in regard to mannerisms and such.

Salutations

Village Salutations

Village Salutations identify the originating family and the village structure. They evidence how one family has grown into a good-sized village. It is here, at the village structure, that we can see the evolution of the family structure, the delegation of responsibility and authority, and the operations of daily life.

The village organization is fundamental to Samoan and Manu'an culture. It mirrors the family-centric foundation, functioning within the cultural dogmas and the specific village ordinances and *tapus* (taboos). Enforcement of these cultural customs and ordinances is carried out by the Village Council. And the salutations are the honorific titles, delineating the organizational structure of the village through the use of titles, designations, and responsibilities.

Each village has its founding paramount chiefs and families, and their princes—sons of the chiefs. The honorific titles indicate the rank or position:

- High Chief (*Ali'i*)
- Orator Chiefs (*Tu'ua*—elder in seniority, leader of the council; *Tamamātua*—orator elders in Tutuila; with particular salutation title words for them—*fetalaiga*, *tofā*, *fofoga*, *Sūsūga*—which all mean speaker)
- Senior (*Tu'ua*)
- Elder (*Mātua*)

- or member of the class of sitting orator chiefs and "dignities" designation (which catches all honorific salutations).

The village salutation details the following:

- the sacred meeting ground of the village,
- the chiefs' respective residences,
- and the "maidens" of the various chiefs and families,
- as well as the village protocols
- and the genealogies connecting to other families on the island.

Maidens are the chief's princess together with the sitting maidens of the village. They are a counterpart to the young warriors of the chiefs who cater to the chief's affairs. The respective princesses and their staff of currently sitting maidens cater to the various ceremonies of the Village Council and Chiefs Council, as well as teaching and taking custodianship of the village heirlooms and ceremonial protocols.

Additionally, the village salutation takes clear note of how the genealogies connect to other families on the island, through marriage or extended kinfolk, for one will often find the same family title name—titles such as *Tupua, Toleafoa, Tuala, Papaali'i, Seiuli,* and many more. Often these names or titles are the "prince names" of the various royal families. These families are also known as the village "dignities"—the family members are not dignitaries, but their families have dignity that members carry with them; again, not all family members have dignity, but their families do, and in the salutations, the dignities of their princes and princesses are followed by their respective families', and then the orator dignity.

Thus it is important to understand the island genealogies of the major families if one is to properly address the village. The total of 242 villages and all their respective salutations must be clearly understood and recited from memory when chiefs visit the villages for whatever occasion.

Individual Salutations

Designated positions in the village also come with complete specific salutations, together with an appropriate lexicon to refer to the tools, staffing names, and titles, and the etiquette for ceremonial protocol.

For example, the delegation, by designation, of carpenters to specific families, across the Samoan chain of islands, opened up the knowledge of carpentry to the whole island chain population. Although there were a number of competent carpenters, the skill was still in short supply when it came to meeting the demand of all the islands. So a decree was issued, assigning the gift of carpentry to the following families of Manu'a, Tutuila, Upolu, and Savai'i:[xxx]

1. *Aiga Sa Sao* – the architect title of Manu'a Island
2. *Aiga Sa Lemalama* – the title of the Tutuila Island architect and carpenter
3. *Aiga Sa To* – Tutuila
4. *Aiga Sa Leifi* – Upolu, Atua
5. *Aiga Sa Moe* – Upolu, A'ana
6. *Aiga Sa Logo* – Upolu
7. *Aiga Sa Solofuti* – Savai'i
8. *Aiga Sa Sigi* – Savai'i
9. *Aiga Sa Tagavailega* – Savai'i

So, for example, if you should encounter an architect or carpenter in Tutuila, or from Tutuila, you would address him or her and their family as: "Honorable *Aiga Sa Lemalama*" or "Respectful *Aiga Sa Lemalama*."

The oral history, revealed through specific chief title salutations, makes note that, among a few paramount chiefs, the following have their designated carpenter or architect: TuiManu'a's is *Sa Sao*, Le'iato's is *Tuine'i*, Mauga's is *A'etonu*, Mageafaigā's is *Sea* and TuiAtua's is *Leifi*.

First Established Salutations of Samoa

It's important to note that, after the liberation of Samoa, the King of Toga did not organize a war to fight the battle over again. For as time has shown, Toga and Samoa became allies. Then after the defeat, the father of the Malietoa appointed certain leaders with authority over different regions of Samoa, and thus began the Samoan government.

Unlike Upolu, Savai'i had not been divided into villages at this time. Chiefs *LeTufuga* and *Leaula* became the two foundational paramount chief authorities of all of Savai'i, as was decreed from the authority of the Malietoa Faigā *Uilamatūtū*. They are descendants of the original founding fraternal brothers, *Laifai* and *Fugefe'ai* (or *Funefe'ai* in the post-Christianity polite language) who settled Savai'i.

The brother chiefs *LeTufuga* and *Leaula* became known as *pules* (authorities) of Savai'i around A.D.1360 when they visited the Malietoa during his illness.[xxxi] The conch shells or *pules,* used to balance or anchor the fishing canoe, were gifted to them by their relative, the Malietoafaigā, as evidenced in a decree from the cruel ruler-warrior (*Faigā*) chief, for visiting him during this illness in Upolu. And this is the first time the word *pule* had its other meaning, "authority."

About 545 years later, in 1868, during the war between Malietoa *Laupepa* and his uncle Talavou Malietoa *Vaiinupõ*, Orator *Leaula* promised the districts of Savai'i that, if they allied with Malietoa *Laupepa* and he should be victorious, additional *pule* (authorities) would be decreed to them. And so, when Malietoa *Laupepa* was victorious, Orator *Leaula* promulgated four additional authorities to the following districts of Savai'i: Safotu, Palauli, Satupa'itea and Asau. Hence the new promulgated salutations: *Tulona ia Pule e ono* (meaning six) o *Salafai* (formal for Savai'i). *O Pule Fa'avae ma Pule Tofia* (the founding *pule* and the additional proclaimed *Pule*)...

I mention the story of the first two *pules* because it demonstrates the foundational authority of delegations from a paramount chief with ruling authority, such as this Malietoafaigā *Uilamatūtū* who ruled over all of Samoa at this period. These privileges, decreed in about A.D.1300, still hold true and are still important today, since the customary protocol is that the male-side orator gets the first right of refusal to give a speech. The orator might yield the speech first to the male (brother) side orators. Thus, if you don't know the kindred relationship, you most likely won't know the "pecking order" of orators in competitive negotiations to determine who should take the privilege to orate.

The Overall Island Country Salutation

These complex relationships established a more complete salutation of all of Samoa. Prior to this period (of *LeTufuga* and *Leaula*) the salutation was very simple and straightforward—e.g. *Tulouna Tumua, Aiga ma latou Tama, Tama ma latou Aiga, Faleupolu o tausi va'atele*. (Honorable *Tumua*—Authorities—the Dignity of the Families and their respective Princes and Princesses, and the dignity of their respective families, House of Orator Groups—*Faleupolu*—that serve and protect the Large Vessel of Samoa—*my translation*.) But over time the salutation has changed to memorialize, or witness to, the many milestone events in the history of Samoa.

Today, the short version of the overall "Island Country Salutation" is: Your reverence, honorable royal families and their princes, princesses, and their families, the island divisional authorities, vanguards and rearguard allies, the dignities of all Samoa, Tutuila, and Manu'a and the circle of sitting orator chiefs of all Samoa (*my translation*).[xxxii]

Salutations Example

Today, when you attend a Samoan *fa'alavelave* (a major event), an orator will always stand to recite the salutation of all Samoa. In English translation, the orator would be reciting the major families of Samoa, the families of the four crowns of Samoa. So...

> *Tuloga ia le Pa'ia, o Aiga ma latoa Tama, Tama ma latou Aiga. Aiga o PāPā, ma Aiga o Nofo. Fale Upolu* (talking chief) *o lo'o tausi va'a tele* (protector for all of Samoa) *ia Samoa ma Manu'a ma e'e o le Atunu'u. Tulou, tulou, tulougalava*.

which translates as: "In reverence to the families and their princess and their prince, the prince and their families, and the defined circle of chiefs that carry the authority of the family and the village."

This is one of the various short, all-encompassing Samoa Islands Salutations. There are also completely detailed versions and summary island salutations that include Tutuila, American Samoa, and Manu'a. Greater flexibility is given to orator chiefs as to preference for the Island Nation and American Samoa and Manu'a salutations.

While my translation seems generic, it is nevertheless very specific to the definition of *Aiga* (family), *Nofo* (family of paramountcy), and *Aiga o Pāpā* (families of monarchy), including the honorific orator chiefs and authorities for each respective family. This completes the reference to political structure and, of course, must include the *e'e* (an honorific term for citizens) of Samoa and Manu'a.

Of course, when we have the Samoan *fa'alavelave*, a young person might ask, "What is our relation to that particular person?" And we should begin the breakdown of the genealogy, so that every member can understand. Unfortunately, we are so busy trying to survive, we sometimes neglect to do that. But we need to find the time to communicate with our young people.

The orator, who is giving the speech, has to understand the entire genealogical history. In the dialog seminar for our church youth group, we used the village of Fagasā, Upolu, salutations as our example in public oration. When the orator in the village of Fagasā gets to the part of his speech where he would say, "Ladies and gentlemen," you might hear him continue like this:

"Ladies and gentlemen, the high chiefs, the paramount chiefs, the *Ma'oupū*, the fraternal brothers... I will repeat the history, the ancient history.

"From the day the first *Alo* stepped on this earth, there was no Fagasā—except for one person, and his name was *Mageafaigā*. *Mageafaigā* had the sacred kingdom here. That is why they call this place *Nofoa Sā*, of Fagasā. It's the kingdom of *Mageafaigā*. He had ten different seats, and that became the 'House of Ten' in this island called Tutuila. He presided as the paramount sacred chair; *Nofoa Sā*, of Fagasā, *o le nofoa o le Nofoali'i*, the kingdom of *Mageafaigā*."

So yes, there is a history; there's a dark history of *Mageafaigā*, who was known as a cannibal. He was so powerful that he drew a rope from the mountain of Fagasā village all the way to the harbor of Nu'uuli, and whoever was captured by this rope was brought by a soldier to be stored for his next meal. That is how powerful this man was!

The speech might continue: "This 'House of Ten' was the first foundation of Tutuila, the *Fale gafulu* (tenth house)" *Fa'aliliu mai Sasa'e, fa'aliliu mai Sisifo*, "and the Mageafaigā's son was *Alo*." So, *'Itu'au, ma Nofoa' o le faiā lea le Sa'o o Alo*.

And now, in my culture dialog group, everyone says, "Fata, please, we all know; you don't have to labor yourself with all of this," and they laugh. But for reassurance I'll ask them, "Are you sure about that?" "Yes, yes Fata."

And yes, people are embarrassed, sometimes, when you tell the history. But it's a critical history. And so:

1. First in his salutation, is the paramount chief, the *Sa'o*.
2. Second is the reference to the orator's seat—a seat of multiple legs; *o le nofoa Vaevaeloloa* (the expanse—of his family—is like a great forest).

There are only a few chiefs who have, as part of their salutation, the phrase *O lou nofoa vaevaeloloa*—for example, the Malietoa and Paramount Warrior Chief *Lualemana* of Asu village, in Tutuila. In the case of the Malietoa, the salutation is: *O lou falanofoa* (or *falafolaloa*—seating mat) *ma lou nofoa vaevaeloloa na fa'afofoga iai Samoa* ("he to whom all Samoa listened"). The Malietoa had many fraternal brothers, as well as sisters who married into these titles, and they had their children, but he was selected to be the paramount.

Talking chiefs (or orator chiefs) are as old and ancient a position as the paramount; it's just that their positions are different. So when an orator comes, for example, to the Malietoa during a funeral, he might say in the salutation: "The rain has fallen on Malie, your sacred meeting ground and seat of your government, and on the Vaopipi, the sacred residence of your Honorable Sūsūga Malietoa"—*Ua to le timu i Malie ma le Vaopipi le Afioaga o lo'o Sūsū ai lau Sūsūga Malietoa*.

Funeral Salutation Example

If an orator chief brings gifts and assistance to, for example, a funeral in Chief *Alo's* family in Fagasā village, he will stand in front of the *Malaepule* and *Falepule*, in *Alo's* residence. His speech starts with: *Tulouna ia Malaepule* (sacred meeting ground) *ma Falepule* (*Alo's* residence), meaning, "I humbly address the sacred ground of the *Malaepule* and the residence, *Falepule*, of honorable Chief *Alo*." The orator chief would continue:

> *Pa'ia* (honorific) *o le afioaga o lo'o afifio ai le To'afia o Ali'i, lo'o afio ai lau afioga Alo, o le afioaga o lo'o afifio* (many fraternal brothers) *ai Usoali'i ma le Mātua, o lo'o sūsū le Mātua ia Tuinei o le Ali'ioāiga, o lo'o alala ta'i ai Fetalaiga ia te outou to'afā* (four talking chiefs). *O lagi ma lagi e fia o Samoa: ua gasolo ao, ua ta'ape Pāpā, ua Tō le Timu, ua mafuli le la, ua tafea le tauofe i le Afioga ia Alo, tulou, tulou, tulou-na-lava!*

Which could translate as:

- "Greetings to the three paramount chiefs." This refers to the three chiefs, *Alo, Tupuola,* and *Tuinei*. This greeting is to the honorable senior, who is the firstborn of the mighty Fagasā family, and to Elder High Chief *Tuinei*, Lord of the family.
- "Greetings, honorable fraternal brothers, *Mata'utia, Lili'o, Soliai*."
- "Greetings, Elder *Mamea*: to Your Highness *Tago*, the unstoppable heavenly spear cast on behalf of the two mighty chiefs *Tupuola* and *Tuinei*; to Your Honorable Chief *Tauatama*, to the honorable throne of your mighty village kingdom." This is a metaphor, which speaks to the protection of these two mighty honorable chiefs by a spear that cannot be stopped, deflected, or redirected.
- "Greetings to you, four paramount orator chiefs, heralds and harbingers of Fagasā Village: Orator *Tua*, Orator *Atuatasi*, Speaker *Vaiutusala*, and the unanswered speech of Orator *Sili*."
- "Greetings to the mighty kingdom of the vanguard and protector of your district."

Modern Samoan Titles

Today, the custodians of Gatoa'itele are Fata and Maulolo and the sitting orators Tuisamau. Three subgroups have the same orator group title name: Vaimauga district, Siumu district, and the villages of Afega and Tuana'i, the seat of authority.

Tuisamau is the "title name" of the orator group, headed by Fata and Maulolo, serving the Malietoa monarch. The name, or title, originated with the two warriors, *Tui* and *Mau*, who were brought over from Manu'a by the TuiManu'a to begin organizing a war party to launch an offensive against the Tongans. These preparations took place a few years before the offensive began, and preceded the arrival of *Fata*, *Maulolo*, *Va'afa'i,* and their sister *Luafatasaga*. *Luafatasaga* married the first Malietoa *Saveatuvaelua* (or Malietoa *Savea*). And when *Fata* and *Maulolo* became leaders of the orator group, Tuisamau, giving pronouncements from various Malietoas, they were given the authority Laumua (meaning "capital" or seat of origin of all Tumua) in the Tuamasaga district on behalf of the Malietoa monarch.

An important thing to keep in mind is that, without the warrior group, very little can be done to build a kingdom. As we are periodically reminded by the Tuisamau orators, the village of Afega was settled by the Tuisamau, way before *Fata* and *Maulolo* came along. That's the reason we see the orator group's name recited first in the village, district, and national salutations.

During preparations for the war party, the two warriors, *Laufiso* and *Tapuala*, were placed in the district of Faleatiu, in the villages of Satapuala and Sagafili. The others, *Se'ela* and *Latai* were placed in Leulumoega district. *Se'ela* and *Latai* became the original Tumua authority for the TuiA'ana and the district, until they were defeated by the 'Alipia paramount orator chief and the "Group of Nine" orator chiefs, during the conflict between *Tamālelagi* and TuiA'ana *Sagaate* over the PāPā authority of TuiA'ana.

The other warriors brought over from Manu'a were *Fuga* and *Vasa,* who were placed in the village of Fausaga in the southern part of Tuamasaga district. According to Paramount Chief *Fuimaono Na'oia*, *Fuga* became the first Mau'ava, orator chief and custodian of the ava ceremony of the Honorable PāPā *Vaetamasoaali'i*. Also, the warrior *Leifi* was dropped off at Aleipata, in the Atua district. His fraternal brother *Tautoloitua* had not yet made his appearance in the tales of Aleipata district at this period.

The Vaetamasoaali'i title custodians are the paramount chiefs *Te'o* and *Tuiā* in the southern district of the Malietoa clan territory. And, since *Vae* is a daughter of *Gatoa'itele*, *Te'o* and *Tuiā* have customarily allowed *Fata* and *Maulolo* to bestow the Vaetamasoaali'i PāPā simultaneously with the Gatoa'itele PāPā with their respective protocols. Gatoa'itele and Vaetamasoaali'i are the two female PāPās that, when combined, constitute the monarchy of the Malietoa family clan. Without these two royal PāPās, the Malietoa title would be just another paramount warrior high chief title, i.e. not a royal "King."

My title, Fata, and my fraternal brother's title, Maulolo, both high orator chief titles, are under the authority and custodianship of the PāPā title Gatoa'itele. There are only four of these PāPā titles: PāPā of TuiAtua, PāPā of TuiA'ana, PāPā of Gatoa'itele, and PāPā of Vaetamasoaali'i. When all four PāPās are bestowed on a titleholder, he or she is said to the ruler of all Samoa. We saw this in the story of Tafa'ifa *Salamasina* earlier.

Historical salutations

Some people think that we developed our naming technique after Christianity arrived in A.D.1830. But, in fact, we had established it right at the beginning in Samoa, around 1100 B.C. It began with that simple family who got together and started to assign who was going to go work the plantation and who was going to do the fishing. Out of that beginning, we arrived at these designations: who is going to be the high chief, who is going to be the talking chief, and who is going to be responsible for the ava. We know this because of the genealogies of the royal families—the TuiAtua, the TuiManu'a, TuiA'ana, and much later, the Malietoa clan.

As we shall see, the Malietoa clan didn't come into existence until the year A.D.1235, by which time Samoa had been under the Tongans' yoke since A.D.800. For four hundred years we had been enslaved by the Tongans, and the Malietoa clan came about because of the brothers who orchestrated the army in the battle that defeated the King of Tonga, and hence gave us our freedom. So the Malietoa clan is much later—a thousand years later—compared to the TuiManu'a, TuiAtua, and TuiA'ana clans. And by then we had already established this structure in Samoa.

Every step along the way, Samoans are constantly refining this process. It started out in a very crude way but, as we moved along in the history of our country, the process became ever more refined, more detailed, and more mete to the structure of Samoan culture.

Sūsūga[xxxiii]

Manu'an legend has it that, when Malietoa *Uitualagi* (son of Malietoa Faigā *Uilamatūtū*) journeyed to visit TuiManu'a *Li'a* in Taū, Manu'a, he arrived at the bay in Faleasao village at high tide. When he stepped out of his catamaran, a wave hit him. He was all wet from the sea wave, and TuiManu'a reached out and said to him, "You are all wet,"—*Ua* (you) *sūsū* (wet) *mai* (come). Hence the salutation greeting *Sūsū mai*.

The noun version of this is derived by adding *ga* to the verb *sūsū*. So we have *Sūsūga*, a title. The title, *Sūsūga,* is used commonly but originates from the Malietoa. It is a Malietoa title. It can also be used to refer to a minister, high chief, or talking chief. It's equivalent to "sir" in the English language.

When we hear the title of the last Malietoa, *Afio mai lau afioga, le ao o le malo, i lau* **Sūsūga** *Malietoa*, we should note that the Malietoa is addressed as the *Sūsūga*, and not as *Afioga*. *Afioga* is the title given to the *Ao* (Head of State) *o le Malo*, and you would not say, *Afio mai lau afioga, le ao o le malo, afio mai lau* **afioga** *Malietoa*. That would not be right.

The other two titles that the Malietoa had were: *Lau Afioga Gatoa'itele* (meaning daughter of Malietoa *La'auli*, A.D.1410), and *ma lau Afioga Vaetamasoaali'i* (meaning the mother and daughter royal crowns, respectively, which were decreed by Malietoa *Uitualagi*, the father of *La'auli* around A.D.1380).[xxxiv] These titles refer to the thrones. For there are two female PāPās (Gatoa'itele and Vaetamasoaali'i) that are bestowed onto the Malietoa, and then there are two males with the Tupua family, TuiA'ana, and TuiAtua.

Two villages carry the *Sūsūga* (sir) honorific title for their talking (or orator) chief. One is ours, with Fata and Maulolo and the Tuisamau orator chief titles. The second is Lufilufi, with the six sitting paramount orator chiefs, the Tumua.

The Lufilufi village salutation for the Tumua was decreed by the first Malietoa *Savea* around A.D.1320,[xxxv] and the village of Lufilufi carried a Malietoa title. But the Leulumoega village salutation for the Tumua was decreed by the first Malietoa's father, *Leatiogie,* around A.D.1290.[xxxvi] Hence their salutation for the orator title is *Fetalaiga Leulumoega*.

Paū

When Tagaloa *Funefe'ai* heard a man give instructions contrary from those he had given his grandsons, the Tagaloa asked, "Who is speaking contrary to my command? Is he speaking conspiracy against my government?"

The word for speak, speech, or oration in Samoan is **paū**— among other words, such as *saunoa, fetalai, tulei,* and *fofoga*. So **paū**, *tulei, saunoa, agiagi,* and *Sūsūga* are used to formally address the high chief and also "ordained" ministers and pastors.

Afioga: Usoali'i and Ma'oupū

The **Afioga** class is very particular and includes the fraternal brothers of the paramount chief, **Usoali'i,** and the **Ma'oupū**, *Afioga o Ma'oupū*. The *Ma'oupū* title is given to the descendants of sisters or daughters of paramount chiefs, not just of the *Sa'o* paramount chiefs. And the titles *Afioga* and *Sūsūga* can both be used for the *Ma'oupū*. It depends on how you want to lift the family up.

In the village of Nu'uuli, the high chief Ma'oupūs are descendants of the same paramount chiefs, of the same name as the high chiefs at Fagasā. The difference is in their respective titles: When the high chiefs' names in Nu'uuli are seen, the orator would say **Ma'oupū**, because they are the chiefs, children of the daughters of the paramount chief. In Fagasā, the high chiefs are referred to as *Tago* and *Soliai*, rather than *Ma'oupū*. The lineage is the same, but two different people carry each title in their respective villages. That's why they divided off all the paramount chiefs of their daughters, to make Nu'uuli a residence for them. And that's why they're called Nofoali'i (the kingdom of Itu'au, the vanguard troops in war). They have the same kind of structure, and every chief there has the designated name of their residence and the name of their ava cup.

The various books of salutations of Samoa, Tutuila, and Manu'a, including Aiono Dr. Fanaafi's *LeTagaloa*, have their own preferred salutation titles. In the early part of the 1800s very few titles were given the salutation *Afioga*. This was reserved for the paramount chiefs of monarchy, or for royal family descendants— i.e. princes and princesses. Otherwise, *Sūsūga* was the standard title protocol salutation. So you see that there is a lot of *sūsū mai lau sūsūga*.

The different "salutation books" were commissioned by various churches—first the LMS, then the Methodist. So each of them had their own book, and then other people, like Aiono Dr. Fanaafi, had their own book. And, depending on those people's knowledge, they might use a different salutation if they had to meet with the village. But we should note the use of the *Afioga* title in this particular (Methodist Church) Fa'alupega book,[xxxvii] relative to the village of Fagasā salutations, which listed the Three Chiefs: *Alo*, *Tupuola*, and *Tuinei*. The other high chiefs are listed as *Sūsūga*, and, of course, the orators are accordingly listed by the various speech titles.

Tofā

The titles *Fetalaiga* or **Tofā** may be used to refer to the six paramount talking chiefs of Salafai—the *Pule* (authority) *Ono* (six) *i Salafai*.

Tofā is also a Tulafale title. The *Tofā Fa'atupu* and *Tofā Fa'atamāli'i* (or *fa'atamali'i*) titles mean wisdom, and they are given to the high chief. This does not mean the same wisdom as the *Tofā* title alone.

Fetalaiga, *Lau Tulafale*, *Lau Tuaigoa*, and *Lau Tulatoa* titles are similar, and other such titles include *Tu'ua*, *Tamamātua*, and *Tauto'oto'o*. Tutuila has several *Tauto'oto'o* titles.

Other Titles and Positions

The Aumaga and Aualuma

The *Aumaga*, sons of the chiefs, and the *Aualuma*, daughters of the chiefs, are very important sub-groups that represent the hands and feet of the village Chiefs Council. The leader of the aumaga holds a high chief title name, usually a prince title of the clan's paramount high chief. For example: in our village of Afega, the aumaga title is La'auli (*La'auli* is the name of the son of Malietoa *Uitualagi* who reigned from A.D.1300 to 1370). Many villages that are descended from Paramount Chief Malietoa use the same prince title for their aumaga. Other clans, likewise, use their respective "paramount high chief prince" title for their aumaga—for example: *Tupua*, *Toleafoa*, *Fonotī*, *Afoa*, *Galumalemana*, etc. Again, these are "names" that we will meet as we review the history of the nation in Volume II, *Navigators Founding a Nation*. For example, the leader of the *aumaga* is usually a prince, and *Tupua* and *Salanoa* were sons of royal kings—*Salanoa* is short for *Lealaisalanoa* the grandson of *Va'afusuaga Toleafoa* (*Toleafoa* for short), brother of Tafa'ifa *Fonotī*.

The practice of using the paramount high chief prince title is very much part of the ava ceremonial protocol, whereby the prince, or the son of the paramount high chief, is the cupbearer. Similarly in the Greek classics, Ganymede is the cupbearer to the gods of Greek mythology. And the prince must lead by example if he desires to inherit the paramount title.

The *aumaga* are the ones who will do the work of the family and village. Their responsibilities might extend from preparing the ava ceremony to building the houses of the village. They have their very own structure and protocol, which follows the village Chiefs Council structure and protocol. For example, their designated seating positions in the house—their designated posts—are the same as those assigned to their fathers' title. We will see more about this in the "Seating Arrangements" section on page 191.

You will notice that the name of the *Sa'o Aumaga* (the leader of the Aumaga) is often the paramount high chief's name. It's decreed that the sons of kings chew the ava; they are the *aumaga*. For the Malietoa clan, the Sa'o Aumaga is his son Seiuli, over in Vaiusu: *Faigā le, Sa'o Aumaga, le ava a Malietoa, fa'atupu.*

Titles such as such as *Alalatama* and *Alalamatuatala* refer to those high chiefs seated at the rounded sides of the maota, as we will see when we look at Seating Arrangements. *Alalatama* and *Alala ma Tuatala*, (*ole tala*, meaning you sit in the *tala*) are often given to boys, to a son such as the *aloali'i.*

The *aloali'i* is the oldest son, and the *usoali'i* are the fraternal brothers. The younger children serve the *aumaga* when the chiefs are meeting, and so they learn their responsibility. They are the group who prepare the food and run errands for the *aumaga*. And, as we have already seen on page 74, there is a female organization of the village, The Aualuma, equivalent to the *aumaga.*

Mātua—the Elders

Another honorific title is *Mātua* which stems from the word for an elder. It includes any senior titled person, grandmother, grandfather, or an older mother or father. The word literally means old or ripe, and it covers grandparents and older generations.

Mātua was initially used to refer to the grandmothers that were the foundation of the family. They anchored the family organization. Giving due honor and reverence to this responsibility led to this honorific title and the salutation showing esteem. Then the honorific title and salutation were extended to refer also to older male members of the village. Old age, accompanied with knowledge and wisdom, is esteemed in the culture.

Use of the Mātua title then evolved into a chief title designation—for example, the honorable Mātua of the FaleTuamasaga district, *Fata* and *Maulolo*; the honorable *Alipia*, the Mātua of the House of Nine; the illustrious Mātua of the FaleAtua, venerated *Tafua* and *Fuataga* or orator *Leifi* and *Tautolo*; and the honorable "Ten seated Mātua orators" of Tutuila Island.

Today, the title Mātua is given to paramount elder chiefs—chiefs with ancient genealogies, who are often descended from the founders of great families or dynasties of village and district.

The word "elder" is a Biblical term, translated into the Samoan language as an old person. It is a title in Christian religious ritual, like the title for a senior deacon. But that term is not culturally Samoan, like *Mātua*. That is why the formal title Mātua is revered—like a military title and rank; you salute the rank, rather than the person.

Title Inheritance

Unlike with Europeans, family titles and leadership in Samoan culture are determined by the family at large. Titles are not passed on to the eldest son, nor from his son to the next. When the chief passes on, the titles remain with the family to select the next titleholder.

When it comes to decision-making, the family nucleus is very important. It doesn't matter whether a title comes from the mother's or the father's side. The delegation can also come from the younger generation. In this way, Samoans are very wise when decisions are being made about leadership, because there are lands and customs to be considered too.

When the family at large plans a formal meeting to discuss a potential heir to receive a family chief title, the protocol says you must begin the formal deliberation with the ava ceremony. Otherwise, the chief title would not be recognized and blessed by the family at large—that is, by the entire clan that might live across the island and overseas in New Zealand, America, or elsewhere. Thus, representation from every major branch of the family would be requested, and their participation would be expected in this very critical decision.

One should keep in mind that this decision, once it is concluded, to bestow the chief title on the selected one, constitutes a lifetime appointment. The sacredness of the ceremony evidences the importance of this title appointment process and its successful conclusion to the family.

The Importance of Names

Names and titles are important in Samoan culture. Parents often name their children after themselves because it perpetuates the name.

In our Dialog Seminar discourses, we used Fagasā village as our example, and we looked at the salutations in Chiefs Council settings. In the Chiefs Council, for example, if I hear somebody call, "Hey Matalupe," then, as an orator, I should know that "Matalupe" ("kind eyes of a domestic pigeon"—*my translation*) is High Chief Lilio's ava cup name. So I'll ask, "Are you related to Lilio family?" and Lilio will be that person's grandfather. That's how family members distinguish and identify themselves as members of the family clan, by naming their children with heirloom names, such as the names of the sacred meeting place, chief residency name, the ava cup name, the cupbearer's name, the name of the property boundary and title deed, or other ancient family names.

Ali'i Lelei i Tumua (meaning "Paramount chief's kindness to the Tumua authorities") is the standard ava cup name for the paramount royal chief TuiAtua Mata'utia. The guest orator making a presentation would immediately know the genealogical connection to the paramount family of TuiAtua. Thus, when the name, *Ali'i Lelei Tumua* is said, the response would be, "You must be from the Matautia clan." And the person would reply, "My family is Matautia, in Fagasā. That's how I got the name, *Ali'i Lelei Tumua*."

When you meet someone from Fagasā, you would ask for their name or their family name. They might reply, "My family's name is Tupuola." Then you would automatically think of High Chief Tupuola. If they said, "My father is Sili and I come from…" you would immediately respond, "Oh, the paramount talking chief to Tupuola." This would pinpoint them as a person, a person in a specific family, with a specific title, in a specific village.

So how do we go from one person, to one family, to a village, to multiple villages, to the home district and chiefs? A house does not stand alone, and a family does not live alone. The house is part of the village, which is really part of the district, and it is important to know where you come from; it's important to understand who you are and what your genealogy is.

This becomes clear in village greetings and in salutations for the district. We were looking at Fagasā village together with Nu'uuli and Fageagea; the sub-village, Fagasā, while a third village itself, is really part of Nu'uuli. So we asked, why do we refer to them as a district, together? Why is that important?

The district name and salutation are important because there are times where the whole family gathers together. To avoid having to go through and recite all the salutations for each village at such times, they consolidate the salutation into a shorter "district salutation." So in the case of the Itu'au ma Nofoa district, the salutation might be: "Honorable Ma'oupū and Tamamātua Orator To'oto'o: Greeting, to the honorable three (*To'a-fia o Ali'i*) paramount chiefs, and to your speech-makers, the 'House of Eight' orator chiefs." Here, *fia* means three, so *To'a* (the) *fia* refers to "the three" paramount chiefs in Fagasā village, *Alo*, *Tupuola*, and *Tuinei*. Hence, the venerated three paramount chiefs, or, in Samoan: *Le Pa'ia i le To'a-fia o Ali'i*.

We will see the word *fia* used again as in the house of three (*falefia*), the three (*taufia* or *to'afia*), or the sitting three (*nofoafia*) etc.

At the district level, the salutations honor the titles and honorifics, with salutations for a group of chiefs summarizing all the various chiefs. For example, the honorable Ma'oupū really refers to the four Ma'oupū chiefs in the village of Nu'uuli. It is not necessary to reference each of the four Ma'oupū separately, because they have already been recognized. Likewise the three, or *To'afia*, paramount chiefs of Fagasā village are recognized together, with no need to say, "Your honorable *Alo*, *Tupuola*, and *Tuinei*." And this is where many talking chiefs (or orator chiefs) may run into trouble, because the district salutation doesn't use the names.

So, if you don't know where your family belongs, you have a problem. People might respond: "Hey! Hey! I thought my family was like the big honcho over here; how come I don't hear my name." But the salutation refers to their title on a consolidated basis. "Your honorable *Ma'oupū*; your mighty three high chiefs."

The Oratory Ritual, and the Rod and Scepter

The Importance of Orators

The position of orator chief (or talking chief) and the Samoan and Manu'an oratory ritual form an important part of Samoan and Manu'an culture. The ritual stems from the belief that what separates civilized from primitive societies is oration, or rhetoric, which, as Plato once said, is "the gift of the gods." The system of respect and politeness drives the customs and the formalities of constructing and delivering speeches for every occasion. As orators would say, it's totally uncivilized to be invited to an occasion, and then attend and enjoy the hospitality, and then leave without formally giving thanks to the host family.

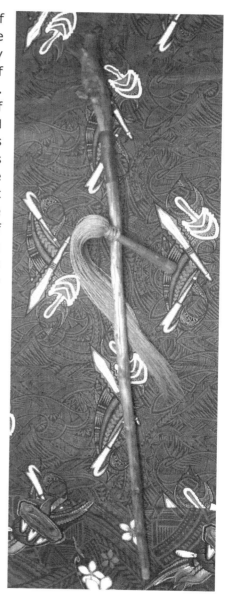

Image 16 Orator's Rod and Scepter, image owned by author

The orators' contest takes place toward the end of the ceremony. Don't forget, the purpose of the speech at this point is to thank the family hosting the event—a wedding, funeral, convocation, etc. So the speech is delivered after the hosts have served the guests.

117

Samoans say that it's a civilized custom, of civilized people, to get invited to a ceremony, then partake in the hospitality and the generosity, and then deliver an eloquent speech of appreciation in gratitude before farewell.

Paramount talking chiefs (orator chiefs) will figure there are a lot of other talking chiefs who would like to speak on behalf of the royals—the kings, the paramount—at an event. They will fight very hard to be sure that they're going to be the one to deliver the important speech. And so there is a whole negotiation ritual (or contest) for them that is quite structured and formal. For example, the order in which the oratory contest is conducted follows the country's hierarchy of senior paramount chief orators, such as orators from Afega and Malie, Lufilufi, and Leulumoega villages, and six from the respective designated district authorities of Savai'i Island. The rationale for the hierarchical structure lies in the Island Nation Salutations order. The authorities cited in the salutations are the ones that should decide who among them should deliver the speech to all of Samoa. So, for example, my village Afega always insists that we are the capital of the Tumua authorities, and so we can present our case that the speech is in our domain and our responsibility.

To put it another way, we should remember that when *Pili* and *Sinaletava'e* made their decrees over each son's responsibility, they gave *Saga* or *Tuamasaga* the rod (or *To'oto'o*) and the scepter (or *Fue*) to guard, and they used the Samoan language to deliver messages to the people of Samoa. Their son *Tua* got the planting or hole digger, the *Oso,* to plant food to feed the Island Nation. *'Ana* was given the spear and war club, the *Tao* and *Uatogi*, to guard and defend the island and people.

There are many different arguments that clever orators can make, to try to win the right to deliver the speech. It's a personal contest, and "may the best person win"—usually the one who is smartest in *Fa'aSamoa* protocols and culture and history. That is a good reason for learning your craft as an orator, so you can cleverly argue your case among your peers, in front of the Samoan people.

Poor performance in a contest could be embarrassing and could cost you your reputation. People would judge you based on your title. The higher the ranking orator chief title, the higher the expectations people have of him or her. For remember, these are the orator chiefs of authority for their country, so they are the last judges to measure your performance.

The speeches themselves are formally organized and orated. Arguing one's case around the desire to deliver the oration is focused on having the most senior status (title, age, and experience), and on one's genealogical relationship to the host family. This shows honor, respect, and gratitude on the part of both the guests and host.

Such a contest would be judgment day for an orator at large. This would be the moment to stand up to participate in the chieftain oral negotiation. This "sacred contest" of orators, *fa'atau Pa'ia o Samoa*, determines who will deliver the speech for an occasion.

As the Bible says in James 3:10, "From the same mouth come blessing and cursing." And the oratory contest is a very important procedure for talking chiefs to argue their rightful responsibility to deliver the very important speech on the day of the meeting.

The Proper Use of the Orator's Rod and Scepter

Improper use of the orator's rod and scepter is a most egregious violation of the oratory chieftain protocols. It's more a case of ignorance and carelessness toward the protocols than of anything else. But it is important to know: how do you hold the rod (or some would say staff) and the scepter (or *fue*)?

The difference between a staff and a rod is that the staff is what a shepherd uses to lean on while walking to the flock. The rod, by contrast, is a symbol of authority in a monarch or king.

My perspective is exclusively Manu'an taught. The Manu'an legend of the origin of the orator's rod or *to'oto'o* (which is also the Manu'an title for orator chief) originates from *Tagaloalagi* instructing his son *Taeotagaloa* to pull up the whole of the coconut tree and use it to lean on, as a rod, to orate. It differentiated him from other people giving messages from the god.

Tagaloalagi also decreed that everything needed for oration must be constructed from the coconut tree. So the stem of the coconut tree is used to carve the rod or *to'oto'o*. The scepter is made from coconut husk; the cup comes from a coconut shell, and the water bottle from coconut shells. The stringers are made of coconut fibers, and sennit is also made from coconut fibers.

Manu'ans believe that the rod is the guardian of the oration or speech, and the scepter is the authority to deliver the oration. The rod must be held with the left hand and the scepter with the right hand. This represents the duality: holding on one hand the scepter of authority to deliver a message and the other hand the rod (like a spear) to protect the speech or the delivery of the message. You cannot hold with one hand both apparatus (or tools) to deliver the message. It is convenient but wrong to hold the rod in the right hand, and many also use same hand to hold the scepter or *fue*. The scepter, or sign of authority, is always held in the right hand. And, since you can't use the same hand to hold the rod simultaneously, this can only mean the rod must be held in the left hand.

There are a few technical orators out there who would challenge you on the *to'oto'o* and *fue* protocols. I have seen a few times where a Manu'an To'oto'o challenges an orator for carelessness and not adhering to the protocols. How can you orate when you don't know your authority? If that's the case, who are you?

Image 17 scepter or fue, image owned by author

We can overlook mistakes of the new Matai or chief and lower-level orators, but the Tumua and Pule and senior orators are expected to set a good example. So here's the Manu'an acid test: In which hand do you hold the *fue*, the authority? What do you do with the other hand? Which shoulder does the *fue* rest on? It cannot be on the shoulder of the hand that is holding the rod. The answers are the guide to the appropriate protocol for holding the *to'oto'o* and the *fue*: left hand for the *to'oto'o*, and right hand for the *fue*—just ask a Manu'an To'oto'o.

As I was in final editing mode of this second book, on August 1, 2021, the New Zealand Prime Minister Jacinda Arden was prostrating herself under a Samoan fine mat or *'ietoga*, offering an apology to Pacific Island citizens of New Zealand for the violent aggression and racist application of their government's immigration policy of the 1970s. The profundity of the occasion is seen in the expression of humility by the Prime Minister, making an apology on behalf of her country, to bring closure to the victims of these "dawn raids" on the immigrant population of New Zealand, primarily on Pacific Islanders. This is a heroic action by a leader of a nation, demonstrating the attribute of great leadership. And so, another observation that I want to point out, as evidence of the protocols of an orator using the *to'oto'o* and *fue* in a formal setting, is of Orator Chief Aupito, Member of Parliament of the New Zealand government, delivering the "thank you" and "distribution of gifts" speech on behalf of the New Zealand government and Prime Minister. It was done exactly as it is prescribed by the protocols. The *to'oto'o* is held on its head by the left hand. The *fue* is held in the right hand. And after three sets of swinging the *fue* onto the left shoulder then the right shoulder, it is rested on the right shoulder to precision.

I have found that senior orators are more precise in the way of using the *to'oto'o* and *fue* in the procedure of speech delivery than are younger chiefs. In an orator contest, the way the *to'oto'o* and *fue* are treated is closely observed, and any slight deviation would be called out for correction.

The Chieftain Oratory Contest

More often than not, the village Chiefs Council will have already designated the orator to orate at a meeting, but it is usually the privilege of the Tu'ua, and he or she would insist, during the sacred oratory contest, on deciding who will orate the day's activities.

The Chieftain Oratory Contest is conducted in a formal orator language throughout the delivery of a speech. The contestant must refer to the orator's salutation, as well as the salutations of the host (family) of the event, and also to the reason the contestant has the right to orate on this occasion. This task includes, often, reciting genealogies and relationships to the family hosting the event. And the contestant must remember, the procedure has a hierarchical structure that, if you don't adhere to it, could eliminate you from the contest, and may even cause personal embarrassment.

The real significance of this oratorical ritual is to show the hosting family the importance of the occasion and show the veneration or status of the family. This form of promotion is very much esteemed. Then the orator who delivers the day's welcoming and thankyou speech is rewarded (in reciprocation) by the host family with money, gifts of fine mats, and an abundance of food baskets.[xxxviii]

In the days of my grandfather's generation (the pre-baby-boomer generation), this contest or negotiation fell under the domain of the those most senior in status, determined by seniority both in age and in the orator's custodianship of the culture. The protocol was pretty low-key and respectful, and adhered to the cultural tenets. But today, it has gotten pretty aggressive and is based on how eloquent and loud the orator is in trying to wrestle the privilege from the mouth of the one decreed.

The Importance of Speech

Importance of Delivery

Wherever you may go in this world, what matters is your message: it's all about expression—how well you articulate in any given situation.

I know the Bible speaks a lot about how to deliver a message. First you organize your thoughts, outline them, solidify them, add language, and deliver the speech out of your mouth into the ears of your audience. This is exactly how the Bible expects you to deliver the messages of God.

It is vital to go through your thought process thoroughly, because once your words are delivered you cannot take them back. All you can do is hope that they successfully land upon the ears of those that are listening.

Your delivery matters: therein lies how you predict and anticipate the landing zone for the message.

Structure of a Samoan Speech

A Samoan formal chief speech can be split into five sections, with two further sections separated out—the *Auga* or *Mataupu*, which give the purpose for the speech. The first sections are:

1. *Tuvaoga* (Introduction)
2. *Vi'iga o LeAtua*. (Praising God for good health and for permitting the fulfillment of this occasion)
3. *Ava* (You must always speak to the ava)
4. *Pa'ia* (Salutation of the special guests and dignitaries present. Reciting the salutations—the dignities—of all of Samoa and Manu'a)
5. *le Taeao* (Salutation of the Morning of the Occasion, as compared to the special Mornings of the dawn of the history of Samoa and Manu'a).

The two remaining parts of the speech are:

6. the *Auga* or *Mataupu* (the purpose or agenda of the day or event) and
7. the conclusion of the day
   a. A prayer to wish the audience health in their departure home
   b. Samoan salutations for the return trip home

Tuvaoga means introduction. Then comes the *Vi'iga o LeAtua* which means "Praise to the Lord." Some people have asked me if Christianity was always included in the speech. But of course, a section praising "god" was always there, because the speech always referenced deities and gods prior to the arrival of Christianity.

The *ava* ceremony would begin the event, and you must always speak to the ava.

Then the next section is the recitation of the salutations, or the dignities, of the guests and the audience; Samoans call this *Pa'ia*. For example, the short versions of the salutations of the village of Fagasā, Tutuila, in American Samoa would be:

- *Afio mai lau Afioga Alo. 'O oe le Sa'o, ma lou Nofoa Vaevaeloloa.*
- *Pa'ia maualuga, aua ua Afio mai le Mātua iā Mamea. Sūsū mai Tago, ma le Afioga ia Salanoa, o le Tao a velo i luga ia Tupuola. Le Pa'ia maualuga ia Fuimaono, sūsū mai Faiumu, Su'esu'emanogi ma Tuvao i tu, maliu mai lou otou Toafa ma le Tofā Vaiutusala, fa'apea le lauti na laulelei iā Nofoa ma Itu'Au.*

Then comes *le Taeao*—the "Mornings" or the "Dawns" of Samoan history—special events and milestones in the history of Samoa. We shall look at some of these in The Oral History, starting on page 137.

And then comes the *Auga* or *Mataupu*, the "purpose" or the whole reason for the occasion. This follows immediately after the Dawn or *Taeao* of the Island Nation history. The purpose is, of course, the main message of the speech, and gives evidence of the senior orator chief's experience in the quality of the message—how it is delivered (or worded), and its relevancy to the occasion.

Modern oratory is woven with threads from the Scriptures, drawing parallels to the culture and the occasion. It includes the summary of your message and overall speech. The technique of stating what you are about to state, then making your point, then summarizing what you already stated, is practiced religiously by experienced orators. For if you just take note of the structure of a Samoan speech, given above, you will see it is an outline that repeats the salient aspects of the culture.

The best advice or mantra is: don't get so carried away with veneration of the salutations that you lose sight of the message, if you have one. Hence, this being the orator's "judgement day."

In my earlier writing, I gave advice to orators to prepare their minds carefully before oration—the Samoan version of this is: *tapega* (prepare) *lelei* (well) *ou* (your) *mafaufauga* (mind or intellect), and that is now a "coined phrase" attributed to Fata Ariu.

Then comes the "farewell," the goodbye. The cultural ritual says it's important to wish good health and farewell to the host family (the head of family or chief, the elders, the ministers and clergy), to dignitaries present, to the ministry and clergy of all denominations in Samoa, and to the reigning paramount chiefs and paramount families of Samoa, reciting their salutations, for orators are the custodians of the culture and service to the families. This farewell can, of course, be summarized and brief.

Structure of an English Speech

A Samoan Orator speech would be organized as follows:

A. Occasion or theme: wedding, funeral, title bestowment etc.
B. Reasons for coming
C. Genealogical connection
D. Agenda
E. Conclusion

By contrast in English, if you were to take a course in public speaking, this is what you would memorize for the organization of an English speech:

A. Introduction
   a. Welcoming remarks
   b. Outline of subject matter
B. Development of the theme
   a. Subject details
C. Summarizing of the subject messages
D. Conclusion

That's the structure of any speech outline in any English-speaking country. As a matter of fact, I saw somebody outline the political speeches of other countries, and they followed that same structure. But is it actually different from the Samoan form?

I wrote an article in Samoa, that was fairly well-read on the Internet, where I took three of President Obama's major speeches: I put them through the outlining process above, showing how he used this format. Then, I took the same speeches, and translated them into the Samoan speech format. And then I realized why Mr. Obama became the President of the United States; it is because of his speech-making and his eloquent delivery to the American voters. He covered the *Ava*, *Pa'ia*, *Tuvaoga*, and *Auga/Mataupu*. He may have used only one word or phrase to cover each section of the speech but, nevertheless, he covered the basics of the Samoan speech format.

With almost all public speakers, you will find that this is how they outline their speeches. But of course, these are educated people who went to some of the most prestigious universities in the United States to learn these skills. For example, Barack Obama and John F. Kennedy are graduates of Harvard, and Bill Clinton a graduate of Yale—the Ivy League—while Samoans had embedded this structure into their culture from the beginning of its development.

The structure of Samoan speeches is indicative of the way Samoans can connect everything together. Learning how to make speeches teaches a civilized way to interact with each other, and is therefore an essential part of their survival, a way of life, and even a religion to the Samoans.

A call to speak

One of the things I would ask students to do is to try this in English; to develop a sort of "elevator pitch." It is valuable to compose this in your own words, so you can begin to understand the structure. And yes, you can find your own words.

You can say, for example, on the passing of a high chief, "On behalf of High Chief *Alo* and the Alo clan, we know the dignity of Samoa and it's designation from heaven to the ground. We know that the Lord has called on Chief *Alo*. We know that *Alo* has his designation into the seventh, into the eighth, into the ninth and 10th heaven, *tulou, tulou, tulou lava*." You could say that, and the people would say, "Wow, did you hear that? This European guy is doing this in Samoan?" It is the eloquence of the Samoan language that really makes the difference here, because of the different lexicon utilized, often with ancient terminology to refer to the setting of the day, the occasion, the Mornings, the sacredness of the family, title, village, district, personal biography, etc.

By the way, you can write your speech down. You don't have to speak Samoan, though I would love for you to speak Samoan, but it's more important that you understand the structure.

So start a speech: "God blessed Samoa with His word. It allows us to seek the Kingdom of Heaven. On behalf of Chief *Alo*'s passing, the gods and the deities that started Samoa are very sacred to this island. I stand before you, on the sacred ground of *Malaepule*, in this sacred residence of the Paramount Chief *Falepule*, knowing that it is time for the paramount chief of Fagasā to prepare for his trip to the 10th heaven." For in Samoa, all families of royalty, every son of royalty, the prince of Samoa and so on, have their designation in the heavens. *Tulou, tulou, tulou le lagi, lau afioga Alo*. And this shows you something. You don't have to labor yourself.

Samoans say they will know a Samoan by the way a person can articulate. They don't say "articulate in Samoan." They wouldn't say that. But they would say they would know you by the way you orate, the way you assemble your intellect, the way you understand your culture, and the way you spit out words of eloquence. Eloquence is what makes a difference. It does not say anything about how educated you are.

I will cover the Sacred Grounds (page 177), the residence, the residence in heaven (the *Lagi*), and the preparations for the high chief getting there (page 220). But here you can relate to the religion part, the Christian part, in your speech. "God has blessed Samoa with His word. The new heavens that allow us to pursue the Kingdom of God... and I do believe *Alo* is on his way."

This aids you to turn the speech right into Christianity. You started out here. If you compare the Samoan ideals and what I did in English, it's very much the same. The eloquence and the sacredness of our culture is the same.

The Welcome Remarks

A ceremony begins with a speech. The welcome remarks will be rendered by the resident orator, and then a response, a reciprocal speech, will be given by the visiting village. Once everyone comes in, they go to their respective seats (see Seating Arrangements, page 191).

There are salutations, required by etiquette, and protocols and overtures, required by politeness, that all must be exchanged. For example, the receiving village chiefs would themselves express greetings of welcome, so one would hear a chorus of welcome greetings from the chiefs. "Welcome, welcome, welcome, please come in take your seat there on front to the right and left of the center front post." Also, short versions of the guest village and chiefs salutations would be repeated during this protocol of greeting: *Sūsū* (the honorific given to the Malietoa, Laumua, and Tumua Tuisamau and Lufilufi and Ministers) *mai, sūsū mai, talamai a'ao* (another term for honor and greetings), *Afio* (a word for high chiefs), *mai, pāpā a'ao mai* (for honored guests and ministers and clergy). *Mamā* (clear) *le lagi* (heaven) in your journey and present. *Malo malaga manuia* (greetings for your safe journey)... The visiting delegations would in return repeat the same greetings, until all are settled into their seats. Then the protocols begin.

This process is the reason why one must memorize the salutation. You need to understand what you are saying, and to whom you are saying it. You do not want to address Chief *Alo* with the salutation of another chief, because then you would have a major problem on your hands. The chiefs would correct you on the spot—it's just how they are with their customs, their formalities.

So in our example, we now welcome two senior orators *Sili* and *Tua*—orator titles of the village of Fagasā, both members of the Tu'ua. They are the ones who will begin the process, by constructing an elaborate speech welcoming all the chiefs into the maota. This is where they would go through the salutations:

Afio mai lau afioga le Sa'o. Afio mai lou afioga le Ma'oupū. Afio mai lau afioga le Usoali'i—these are all different high chiefs.

Ua alalata'i mai fo'i—talking chief in the back, talking chief in the front.

Maliu mai, sosopo mai—these are the salutations and greeting words for the talking chiefs and orator chiefs. Thus, *maliu mai* (the higher-language word for "Come," plus honor), *sosopo mai* (higher language word for "Walk" plus honor), *alalata'i mai* (higher language for an orator conversation, plus honor), *mamalu mai* (as in "Your honor, come in") and a few others, which all mean "Orator, honorable, welcome, come in and take your seat."

So, this is the organization of the welcoming remarks. Then comes a complete opening speech, to follow the salutation.

Salutations and Titles

The protocol is very important, to keep separate the words for orator and talking chiefs, so it's clear they are not to be confused with the salutation words for high chiefs. Then both sets of words, to welcome an orator or a high chief, are again separate and cannot be used to welcome the general population, though a few are in use for dignitaries and clergy.

This is where the Samoan language departs from others except for Balinese and Indonesian; it marks the separation of high chiefs and orator chiefs from the rank and file. It's a very strict protocol that one should not confuse high chiefs and orator chiefs, in either direction. The orator speaks on behalf of the high chiefs. The high chief can orate at will, but taking that out of the orator chief's hand implies something is not right with the family harmony. It also changes the protocol of the ceremony, as in how the corresponding orator should respond to the eloquence oration of a high chief.

As we will soon see, the Seating Arrangements (page 191) dictate in what area each chief sits. The orators take up the front and the back of the maota. The high chiefs take the right and left halfmoon sides of the maota, with respective house-post seating for each group.

The salutations then refer to the respective chiefs under their title salutations. Honorable "fraternal brothers" refers only to those chiefs that carry the "fraternal brother" title salutations as discussed in the seating arrangements section. So, if there is more than one chief with the fraternal brothers salutation, there is no need to mention every chief; the salutation covers all of them.

There is only one Sa'o, Paramount Chief *Alo* in our example. And the maota seating arrangements give us clues about the number of chief categories by their salutations. A chief titleholder might say his title, but one should ask about the salutation, so it can be determined what type of chief—high chief, orator chief, Sa'o, Ma'oupū, etc. These are not classifications of chiefs, but the salutation indicates the chief's relationship to the overall family tree of the village: "Fraternal brothers" immediately designates siblings of the paramount chiefs or of the Sa'o of the village. Likewise, the tile Ma'oupū immediately indicates a son of a sister or daughter of the paramount high chiefs of the village.

The Purpose, Theme, and Summary

Let's go back now, after the welcome remarks, to the introduction, theme, and summary in the speech. The theme of a village council meeting might be to discuss a particular ordinance. They may also want to discuss the summary of the week, or monthly activities. It could even be discussion of a wedding, a funeral, a title bestowment and so forth. We have many *fa'alavelave* in Samoa. So we have to prepare for them. Whatever it is, this becomes the theme of the meeting.

Samoans would say there is a reason for everything. They do not do things, or follow cultural protocol, just for the sake of it. You must have a purpose for a village Chiefs Council meeting. There is an orator's saying: "A day has its morning, and a morning has its events." Every historical milestone event has a date, and therefore the "morning" of that day's event is memorialized in its history. Then history is related to the present and to the purpose. History—The Oral History, page 137—is an important part of the speech.

The Importance of Oral History

Samoans recount, from memories built up over time immemorial, the salutations and "Mornings," or *Taeao*, of events that are foundational to their colorful history. These "Mornings" represent the "New Days," or the dawn, of each milestone that effected change in the course of Samoan history. They include, for example, the dawns of victory in a battle, of last parting words, and of the bestowment of titles or privileges decreed by paramount chiefs or warriors. They also represent the promulgation of assignments and pronouncements of boundaries of districts or deeds of land to clan members. These milestone events were mythologized and became cornerstones to history. And they are committed to memory by the people through their oral history. Orator chiefs memorize these *Taeao* when events took place, as an integral part of their oratory principles and protocol.

As we saw earlier (page 122): *E iai ma'a tulimanu, ma'a fa'avae, ma'a molimau tau'ave* (meaning to bear about, reminding the Orator to bear in mind). For the *Taeao*, the Mornings, are history's cornerstones—*tulimanu* (corner), *ma'a* (stones), *fa'avae* (foundational) stones, and *molimau* (witnesses) of the culture and society—*my translation*. They tell you what took place in the history of this country. They are what mark the history. And interestingly enough, the Israelis, in their culture, also refer to the days of milestone events in their history as mornings.

Of course, some people and chiefs hold on to the belief that the only critical event in the history of Samoa is when we finally accepted Christianity in 1830. Well, the problem is: have you ever heard of a nation, a country, or a people that has no (prior) history? It's a rhetorical question, and the obvious answer is, of course, no. But, as a small digression, here is what happened once to me:

I was in New Zealand, attending a family wedding, and I had to give a formal speech. An orator chief, in his response to my oration, said, "What Morning is more important than the Morning of the arrival of Christianity in Samoa?"

I agreed, "We're not going to deny that's important. We must, however, remember that Samoa has a history close to 3,000 years old. What do we do with that? Aren't we a people, a nation? Yes, we are! We have events that are evidence of the history of Samoa, and we'd better know it."

All the stories of Samoan folklore and legends, before the advent of written records, represent particular milestones and historical events, often "defining moments" in their particular time-period in the history of Samoa and Manu'a. These might be categorized are as follows:

A. Decrees of paramount chiefs and elder orators:
   a. Parting farewells
   b. Greetings at first meeting
   c. War mediation and closure (triumph or defeat)
   d. Gifting or pronouncements
   e. Punishment in defeat
   f. Promulgation of assignments and delegations
B. Family or clannish conflicts and mediation
C. Other defining events

Putting these events in their appropriate time-periods allows us to describe situations in light of the history and evolutionary development taking place in those periods. This helps provide an overall historical timeline and, to some degree, the opportunity, through "regression" (based on proverbs), to predict the future.

Regression is something that Samoans, along with other culture groups, have long practiced, enhancing the ability to understand the past and gain wisdom from this understanding. For example, Samoan history and ancient proverbs have taught us to observe the birds and the stars, study the oceans tides and time of day, and look for patterns between the winds, giving us the proverb: *Ua au mafua manu o le ta'i'o*—meaning the flock of *ta'i'o* birds is enjoying the sardines in the ocean. Studying patterns of the environment and analyzing past situations allows room for predictions and better responses.

The Historical Mornings (*Taeao*) of National Malae and Maota, and of Decrees and Edicts

Listing and retelling all the Mornings in Samoa would be a major effort. I have avoided doing this, because these are legends that would need to be told in the Samoan language and would fill half the book. To do this right, it would have to become the whole focus of the book, much like genealogy diagrams would be, if I were to include them. And the amount of Samoan editing required would be significant because of the need, for my English-speaking audience, of English translation. 45 edicts would be written in Samoan, and we would require accurate and complete wording in Samoan, with no shortcuts. But I am publishing in English and my market is the diaspora, interested readers of history, and maybe academic students. For this, I'm not sure how much added value the Samoan writing would give to their quest for knowledge of Samoan history.

However, I would like to give a flavor for the Mornings and for how they retell our national history. Fuimaono Na'oia Tupua's book is my major reference, together with my own personal knowledge of these Mornings and edicts, for which all chiefs have their own sources.

Among these mornings and edicts are the "National Mornings." As part of the structure and organization of the country's government and its salutations, the "Malae and Maota" (residences of head authority) give these "National Mornings" special recognition. These mornings have gained national recognition and adoption by orator chiefs and historians, and are mandatory in oration, while other mornings, the edicts of history, are included at the discretion of the speaker. But they are all important in the chronology of the history.

Samoan and Manu'an oral history is full of decrees from leaders in the past, memorializing historical events that occurred and made significant contributions to the history of the country. As is the nature of oral history, the more it is repeated, the more eloquent the oratorial presentation is, and the more the population remembers it.

Parting decrees or farewells, given by a paramount chief or ruler at an event in his or her reign, are remembered as dawns of the new day in the history of Samoa and Manu'a. As sunrise precedes the dawn of the new day, so it is the first light of the day. It's the "morning" of the day. And it is said that dawn is actually the darkest period of the night, coming just before the first light bursts through the eastern sky. Thus dawn symbolizes victory from a struggle faced by the population. And thus its use in oratory presents an eloquent method to draw parallels with the meaning and significance of present occasions.

So the "Dawn" or "Morning" of a new day is etched into the memory of the people, in order to honor their history. There are over 50 of these Mornings or Dawns observed by historians and orators—and thus by the people of the Island Nation. An orator would be severely chastised if the Morning part of a speech were missing. The Mornings are as natural a part of oration culture as ethnic food might be in a formal dining experience. Without Mornings, the oration would not be authentic.

Documenting the Oral History

These events memorialized in history are time-stamped (with names and generations) and thus evidence the sociological and psychological developments of the evolving culture. This allows historians to incorporate these events in developing a complete map of the timeline of history.

The development of boundaries, on both the physical level and the sociological (in the people's behavior), is evidenced in these edicts and proclamations in history. Boundaries lead to the development of ordinances and rituals and established norms. And today, one can witness these cultural developments through the telling of these events.

There is more in these edicts and pronouncements than meets the eye. Thus, an orator chief, knowledgeable in these edicts and pronouncements of history, who weaves them into oratorical eloquence, is perceived as a true historian.

The Samoan author Fuimaono Na'oia Tupuola has documented some of these edicts and pronouncements in his Samoan book, *O le Suaga o le Va'atele* (the Findings of the Big Canoe).[xxxix] But it's not easy to find them in the writings, even when we include the missionaries' work.

I feel myself compelled to document these edicts and pronouncements here, because I spent many years looking to collect them, for they really are evidence of events in the historical timeline of Samoa. They help answer questions about when, where, and why certain things are the way they are. And I have found that a chief, armed with knowledge of these events, can be an effective and powerful orator.

Knowledge of history is power. And a prerequisite of eloquence in Samoan oratory is knowledge of these historical events. While the stories are fragmented, in view of the long history of Samoa, they represent pieces of the puzzle, stones in the mosaic tapestry of Samoa's history. The more pieces of the mosaic we have, collected into a cohesive storyline or in a book, the better will be our focus on the beauty of Samoa's history.

I would like to borrow Dr. Failautusi Avegalio's words from his foreword of my first book: *Navigators Quest for a Kingdom in Polynesia*, where he said that if I don't take the time now to document all this in English, it may never be done, and thus it might be buried in the fading memory of our history. So I will take the time.

The Oral History

Mornings in the Period of Tagaloalagi

The Delineation of Ten Heavens

The decree from the god *Tagaloalagi* which delineates the Ten Heavens of Polynesia is mythologized as follows: The first Heaven is the residence of ordinary people. Heavens two through eight are assigned to *Tagaloalagi's* children who are referred to as the "Family of *Tagaloa*" or *SaTagaloa*. The ninth Heaven is the residence of the paramount chiefs of the Tagaloalagi clan and of all Polynesians. And, finally, the Tenth Heaven is where God resides. Prior to the coming of Christianity, this was *Tagaloalagi's* residence.[xl]

The significance of this proclamation lies in its further evidencing Manu'an "Creation" mythology. It's the defining assignment of the Heavens to the children of *Tagaloalagi*.[xli] The pyramid or ladder design of the edict's articulation, regarding the Heavens, is the god's way of positioning the "bridge" for deities to become human. And it's a ladder-step path (or transformation) for humans or chiefs to climb to return to their residence in heaven. This is seen in the establishment of the Funerary Salutations, called appropriately, *O Lagi o Samoa ma Manu'a*, or "Heavens of the deceased Chief of Samoa and Manu'a"—a ritual conundrum that many Samoans don't really understand; they have practiced it but can't really explain it.

This is the brief, final decree by *Tagaloalagi,* after the creation of the Heavens and the humans, as discussed in the Creation Mythology section in my first book, *Navigators Quest for a Kingdom in Polynesia*.

The Edict of Tagaloa *Fa'atupunu'u*

The edict of Tagaloa *Fa'atupunu'u* ("Tagaloa the creator of islands") was proclaimed at Saleaumua, in Atua district, between Tagaloa *Fa'atupunu'u* and his wife *Fue* to their children *Tele* (also known as *Manu'atele*), *Upolu*, and *Tutu* and *Ila* (or Tutuila). This edict declared, "You shall all go forward and find your homestead and grow and multiply, but you shall not enter Manu'a Island for that is the holy and sacred kingdom of the god. If, however, this is violated, you will be severely punished."

The edict granted the children their own authority and respective island residences, but it decreed they must never invade or attack (or attempt to conquer) Manu'a, for that was the sacred land and residence of *Tagaloalagi* and *TuiManu'a*. With this decree, the creation of villages was delegated to these other paramount chiefs.

This proclamation, again, evidences the continuing creation and settlement of the Samoan and Manu'an Archipelago. The assignment of people into each land and property evidences permanent boundaries and "property rights" granted to a person or chief on to a land or "piece of the rocks," to borrow the modern-day idiom.

I should note here that my orator practice and experience are what might separate my narrative, here, vis-a-vis the writings of many researchers and historians. Much of the information and knowhow that I give is learned from the village Chiefs Council and many chiefs I have searched out, in order to interview them and learn from their oral databases.

We should perhaps also note how Dr. Krämer referred to Manu'a as being similar to the sacred island of Delos in Greek mythology.

The Edict of *Tagaloagi* to *Leamoa* and *Lufasiaitu*

This edict was proclaimed by *Tagaloalagi* at Mailata, in Atua, Upolu, to his daughter *Leamoa* (later called *Lagituaiva*) and her husband *Lufasiaitu*. *Tagaloalagi* declared that the vanguard and rearguard of war would guide *Leamoa* and *Lufasiaitu*'s journey to their home in Manu'a, that *Tautai* would captain their vessel, and that the orator *Manufili* would be their family (*aiga*).

Tagaloalagi said, "I am returning to my abode in the Tenth Heaven. I will leave a 'vanguard' to be your frontal lead and a 'rearguard' to protect your rear, a 'warrior leader' to command, and your orator, *Manufili*, 'to serve the command.'"

The orator *Manufili* built the house for *Lufasiaitu* and *Leamoa* in Manu'a. Thus *Manufili* became the first house-builder or architect of Samoa and Manu'a. One of his important inventions was the building of scaffolding for construction.

This particular *Tagaloalagi*, according to Dr. Krämer, lived around the mid A.D.900s, and *Lu* (*Lufasiaitu*) should not be confused with the *Lu* (in A.D.1280) from Uafato who married *Lagifetaupea'i* and begat two girls, *Ma-nu* and *Man-u*. TuiManu'a married *Ma-nu* and gave birth to *Vainu'ulasi*, the progenitor of *Vaetoeifaga*, mother to Queen *Salamasina*. The younger *Ma-nu* is the progenitor of *Gatoa'itele*, grandmother of TuiA'ana *Tamālelagi*, the father of Queen *Salamasina*.

This decree evidences the beginning of matrilineal development, starting with *Tagaloalagi's* daughter, *Leamoa*. Again, we witness the local delegation of the god's genealogy to his daughter, through marriage to a warrior, man-spirit human, evidencing the transition of the archipelago to a human population.

The logical process is seen in not only delineating property rights to a person or persons, but also creating the physical abode or house on it. This house construction would lead to occupying the house, which further leads to the seating assignments in the house. It's important to observe the logic of the development process, to gain insight into the Samoan and Manu'an psyche. Thus the matrilineal culture, leading to a matriarchal cultural organization, begins here, and the genealogical roots descend directly from the god *Tagaloalagi*. So, simply put, Samoa and Manu'a's matriarchal culture and society is decreed by the god *Tagaloalagi*.

The Edict at Alapapa concerning the Selection of the Fine Mat *'ietoga* for the Funeral of *Tagaloalagi*

The word *'ie-toga* comes from *'ie*, a Samoan word for clothing material, and *toga*, the island of the Tonga Archipelago. Often Samoans would refer to the *'ietoga* as simply the *'ie*.

The edict at Alapapa by Paramount Chief *Tauiliili*, concerning the selection of the fine mat, the *'ietoga*, to take to the funeral of *Tagaloalagi*, goes as follows: The girl *Tualafalafa*, a daughter of *Tauiliili*, lived with *Tagaloalagi* and was gifted by the spirit with a sacred fine mat—the heavens opened up with lightning and thunder at the sacredness of this fine mat. And this single fine mat is described as being equivalent to a thousand mats—*Tasi ae afe*—or to the waterproof mat—*matu mai vai*—as, when it was brought up from fermentation in the water-mud pool, it was totally dry, so that it seemed waterproof.

Tauiliili pronounced that all other fine mats should be left, and only *Tualafalafa's Tasi ae afe* state mat be taken to *Tagaloalagi's* funeral. The significance of this decree is as follows:

- The sacredness of the *'ietoga* product or heirloom: This sacredness comes from the legend that the *'ietoga* has a spiritual life about it, to save human lives. Again, the connection to the god *Tagaloalagi* reinforce the sacredness of the *'ietoga*. That is, if we could not define the history of a sacred heirloom product to the god *Tagaloalagi*, we would question the sacredness of it. The intrinsic value of the *'ietoga* is derived from its connection with the god *Tagaloalagi*.
- Also, there is the significance of the *'ietoga* as a medium of currency or exchange. This explains why the *'ietoga* is a sacred currency of exchange in the gifting economy of Samoans but not of Tongans, because the Samoan innovation is blessed by *Tagaloalagi*.
- Finally, this is foundational to the "Gifting Reciprocity" rituals, customs, and formalities of Samoan culture.

Image 18 image owned by author

I covered the innovation of different cloth-weaving techniques across the Southeast Asian archipelago in my first book, *Navigators Quest for a Kingdom in Polynesia*.[xlii] The *'ietoga* (the fine mat) is an innovative Samoan product, and there are several versions of the tales about its original weaving.

The original, large, Samoan *'ietoga* was woven at Matagilemoe in Sauano, in the Atua district, Upolu, by Lady *Feagai*. This is the *'ietoga* that was taken as a gift to *Tagaloalagi's* funeral. And when a Samoan fine mat is presented in formal occasions it is referred to by its formal name: *Lauta'amutafea, Tasiaeafe, Pulouoleola*, etc.[xliii]

The First Samoan Fine Mat, made by *Futa*

There is a Morning commemorating the place, Malaeomanū, at the village of Tula, Tutuila, American Samoa, where the first Samoan fine mat was made by a young lady named *Futa*. The place is called Fagasā, according to the Tulare village version. There are several versions of the story of the original Samoan fine mat, told by several villages, that may precede *Futa's* effort.

There is some confusion between the story of the short version of the *'ietoga*—the size of a wraparound cloth around the waist, as currently worn by Tongan people and called the Vala—and the large, Samoan fine mat. The short *'ietoga* or *tauvala* originated with this young lady named *Futa*, daughter of *Tauaolosi'i* and *Fua'autoto'a* or *Fua'autoa* of Pago Pago, in Tutuila, American Samoa. *Fua'autoa* was the warrior who defeated the Tongans in Tutuila during the Samoa-Toga war.

The young lady, *Futa*, and her mother *Tauaolosi'i*, after weaving the *'ietoga* or *tauvala* (which did not yet have their names), were out night-fishing at the reef during low tide—actually, walking along the reef with a torchlight—when a Tongan vessel, journeying through Tutuila on the way back to the Toga Archipelago, stopped and kidnapped them. At that time, *Futa* was waiting for her mother on shore, seated on her mat, and the names *'ietoga* and *tauvala* had not yet been coined.

The Tongans took the Samoan women with them to Toga, and they were enslaved by the TuiToga. Then they were freed through negotiations by *Fua'autoa*. The Samoan large fine mat (which also ended up in Toga) was integral to the negotiations to release the enslaved Samoan women.

Image 19 https://commons.wikimedia.org/wiki/File:PagoPago_Harbor_NPS.jpg
Tavita Togia, National Park Service, Public domain, via Wikimedia Commons

The TuiToga was aware of and fearful of the Tutuila warrior, and the *'ietoga* used in exchange for their freedom was given both names—*'ietoga* and the Tongan name *tauvala*. The name *'ietoga* represents the fine mat through which the king of Tonga agreed to release and free the Samoans enslaved in Tonga. So the fine mat received its common name *'ietoga* during this occasion.

The Edict of *Magamagaalefatua* to her son as he leaves Fiji Island

Magamagaalefatua was the wife of the sun god, *TagaloaLa,* and the mother of *'Alo'alolelā*. Her son was returning to Samoa and escaping from the cruelty of the TuiFiti. Samoans had taught the Fijians how to fish with a hook, using the whale-tooth and line. Now the TuiFiti pursued *'Alo'alolelā* to confiscate the hook and line for the Fijians. And *Magamagaalefatua* made this proclamation at Alofi o Amoa, on Fiji Island.

Magamagaalefatua counseled *'Alo'alolelā* (who had married the TuiFiti's daughter, *Sinafiti*), to take the fishhook and line to

Samoa and not look back, for dark clouds would fall and cover the sun from illumining his path. "If, however, you should end up in another part of the Fiji Island chain, traverse toward Samoa. And remember your 'fishhook knot must be fastened correctly.'" Then she continued, "The ocean weather is fickle, 'for at times, it yields blessings, and, at times, it yields plagues'"—*Le Pa ne'i fausala. Aua e 'auomanu 'auomanu 'auomala, 'auomala 'auomala 'auomanu. E au a manū* (blessing) *au a manū au a mala.*

The paramount chief title, La'ulu, makes its first appearance in this story, as *La'ulu* is the son of *'Alo'alolelā.*

'Alo'alolelā is a contemporary of *TagaloaUi,* and this period includes the beginning of the *Lu* (*Lufasiaitu*) and *Amoa* (*Leamoa*) genealogy, from which issues the daughter named *Moa* (Rooster) who the TuiManu'a marries, producing a son named *Moa.* This is where the family clan name of TuiManu'a comes from—the "Moa family" or *Aiga o Moa.*

On the island of Olosega, Manu'an people tell their tales that the name SaMoa (*Sa*—sacred family of—*Moa*) refers to the islands of Tutuila, Upolu, and Savai'i, as the colonies of the paramount family of Moa. Thus they are the territories of the sacred family of *Sa Moa* or Samoa.

The Savai'i version of this legend has it that *Magamagaalefatua* is a lady from Sapapali'i village, Savai'i, who married *Tagaloalagi* (rather than *TagaloaLa* as in the Manu'an legend). She bore *'Alo'alolelā.*[xliv] *'Alo'alolelā* married *Fitifiti,* daughter of the king of Fiji or TuiFiti (Manu'an legend says *Sinafiti*) in the Fiji Archipelago. *'Alo'alolelā* heard the maidservants of his wife complaining about *'Alo'alolelā* not having a royal family. So he escaped to his mother at Sapapali'i, Savai'i. He told *Magamagaalefatua* why he'd come back home, because he didn't know his family, let alone whether his status was royal or not.

Magamagaalefatua told *'Alo'alolelā* to go to his father (*Tagaloalagi*) and ask him to tell him his family genealogy. Then *Tagaloalagi* told *'Alo'alolelā* to go to the house of the married couple, *Ao* and *Po,* who were the spirits or demons of *Tagaloalagi.* Their house is called *Fale Tulutuluitao a Ao ma Po*— the house ceiling was made of spears, and entering the house had to be timed correctly, otherwise one would be speared to death.

'Alo'alolelā was gifted with the fishing hook made of a whale tooth that he took with him, back to his wife in the Fiji Archipelago. So this legend leads to teaching the Fijians how to fish with the whale-tooth hook, a great improvement from their spearfishing methods.

The important aspects of this version of the legend are the mention of the house of *Ao* and *Po* and *'Alo'alolelā's* discovery of his genealogy as a descendant of *Tagaloalagi*.[xlv] So the legend of *Magamagaalefatua's* edict begins, as we have seen, with the story of Samoans teaching Fijians about fishing with fishhooks, as opposed to spearfishing. Spearfishing is characteristic of spear-throwing tribes, and is common with Melanesians (Solomon Islands, Vanuatu, New Caledonia, Papua New Guinea). Manu'an mythology dates the legend to the TagaloaLa generation, which would be the mid A.D.900s, using Dr. Krämer's methodology. Reconciling it with the Savai'ian version, and extrapolating through other genealogies, we date it at A.D.1100.

The Morning (*Taeao*) at Sauā, the village of Fitiuta, Manu'a

This is a National Morning given the recognition of the Malae and Maota.

The first ava ceremony at Sauā, a hamlet of the village of Fitiuta, Manu'a, took place between *Taeotagaloa* (grandson of *Tagaloalagi*) and *Pava* the farmer. *Taeotagaloa's* genealogy is as follows: *Tagaloalagi* begat *TagaloaLa* who begat *TagaloaUi*, father of *Taeotagaloa*. This generation comes after *'Alo'alolelā* (above) and after *Pili,* son of the TuiManu'a (not the original *Pili,* who was the demigod son of *Tagaloalagi*, sent down by *Tagaloalagi*). This story can also be found in the legends of *Lefanoga,* son of *TagaloaUi* and brother to *Taeotagaloa, Lele,* and *Leasiosiolagi.*

The first and only two attendees at the ava ceremony were *Taeotagaloa* and *Pava*.[xlvi] This was the event where *Taeotagaloa* lost his patience and disclosed his spiritual power (*mana*) when he became angry at *Pava's* son for constant disruption of the ava ceremony. *Taeotagaloa* grabbed the boy and tore him into two pieces, straight down the middle from head to toe.

Pava was terrified and full of grief. He begged *Taeotagaloa* for mercy, for he now realized *Taeotagaloa* had the *mana* to restore his son's life. And so *Taeotagaloa*, feeling sympathy and empathy for *Pava*, put back together the boy's two halves, and, lo and behold, the boy came back to life. Then *Pava* continued, completing the ava ceremony.[xlvii]

It should be noted that this is the only tale in all Samoa and Manu'a that describes a half-human, half-spirit character both ending a life and restoring someone back to life. This is uniquely unusual in Samoan mythology. The rationale for including this tale in the ava ceremony protocol is unclear, other than that it serves, perhaps, to remind people of the powerful *mana* of *Taeotagaloa*, and of the real human aspect of the demigod—his feelings of empathy and sympathy—and human folly. There are, however, legends that tell stories of taking away the human soul while someone is sleeping, then returning it at a later time, usually within 24 hours, due to empathy and sympathy because of human grief.

This event established the protocols of the ava ceremony and its preparation. The story clearly states the sacredness of the ava relative to the protocols for the convocation of chiefs. And this where it is established that the ava drink must form the protocol for opening a meeting or gathering of paramount chiefs. It's said that without the ava ceremony there would be no convocation.

The ava rituals evidence the separation of civilized man versus uncivilized human, as is maintained in Samoan and Manu'an tenets of belief. Again, if it didn't come from the god *Tagaloalagi*, there would not be a ritual ava drink. The protocols must be proclaimed by the god, as to their sacredness, otherwise the population would not find it necessary to practice them as a norm—the crude metaphor is that blessings and good omens in the water-pool fall from the top of the waterfall—i.e. from heaven where *Tagaloalagi* resides. The water-pool eventually becomes the stream at which all Samoa and Manu'a quenches their thirst and irrigates the land.

Mornings from the First Tuimanu'a Period

The Edict concerning the House of 100 posts

Tagaloalagi's edict at A'opo village, Savai'i, is where *Tagaloalagi* bequeathed the *Faleselau* to the chief, Tagaloa A'opo. The *Faleselau* is the house with one hundred posts and with seashells as decoration for the residence's foundation. Some orators believe the hundred posts really mean posts made up of a hundred humans, making them symbolic of cruelty and primitive authority.

At this time, the village of A'opo desperately "needed" drinking water. *Tagaloalagi* asked *A'opo* what he "wanted" and, having misunderstood, he replied *Paepaelai*, which means seashells. So *Tagaloalagi* said to Tagaloa A'opo, "I thought you would beg me for water due to the severe drought, but you wanted a pile of beautiful seashells for the foundation of your chief meeting house. So I will grant you your wish with a pile of seashells, but for water, you will have to wait for the heavens to hear your prayer." So the moral of this edict is to be precise and always know what you want.

This story evidences the cruelty of the village chief *A'opo* and the use by *Tagaloalagi* of this teaching moment to show how human desires and ambitions are not necessarily logical, nor do they have common sense. What it is becoming clear is the cultural narrative and justification for belief in their god *Tagaloalagi's* wisdom, judgment, consideration, and creative authority.

Applying Dr. Augustin Krämer's dating methodology, this event dates to early A.D.1200.

The Morning (*Taeao*) at Malaetele and Malae o Vavau

This is a National Morning given the recognition of the Malae and Maota. The Morning at *Malaetele* (the vast and great) and *Malae o Vavau* (the ancient land) was decreed during the time of the first TuiManu'a (TuiManu'a *Li'atama*, first Tuimanu'a of the village of Taū) in the village of Taū, Manu'a. It commemorates the division or delineation of the whole of Samoa into a separate district. This Morning gives evidence of the degree of allocation, designation, and delegation of the political division and authority and responsibility of the whole of Manu'a.

Later, TuiManu'a *Lelologatele*, grandson of TuiManu'a *Fa'aeanu'u* (son of *Taeotagaloa*), who lived in Aualuma and married six women, decreed the following:

o To *Soaletele*, daughter of *Leula*, was born *Sotoa*, who was decreed to hold the office of Peace Mediator, residing in Taū, Manu'a.

o To *Sina*, daughter of *TaotoaiseAualuma*, was born *Tuisali'a*, who was decreed the office of TuiManu'a's Valet or Nobleman Servant—the one who divides and distributes the food of the TuiManu'a, and the only one that can eat the TuiManu'a's leftover food.

o To *Anamoatele*, daughter of *Tagaloa* in Fagali'i, a sub-village of Aualuma, Fitiuta, was born *LefolasaAualuma*, who was decreed the office of the title of Tagaloa Chief of Aualuma, Fitiuta, Manu'a.

o To *Sinaigaga'e*, daughter of *Taualuga* in Fitiuta, was born *Lefolasaigaga'e*, who was decreed the office of Peace Mediator for Fitiuta, Manu'a.

o To *Teleilevao*, daughter of *Lega* or *Sega* in Fitiuta, was born *'Ali'amatua*, and to *Moetalaluma*, daughter of *Pua* in Si'ufaga, Taū, was born *'Ali'atama*. Dr Krämer writes that one of the two *'Ali'as* was to become *Lelologatele's* successor to the TuiManu'a title, but because of the families' infighting he did not dare appoint either one. Since the older one, *'Ali'amatua*, claimed the title, the younger one gave in. But then the Taū family got involved and *'Ali'atama* tried to steal the title, in which he succeeded when the other took it off to climb a coconut palm. War broke out resulting in *'Ali'amatua* being killed in Palapala, a hamlet of Taū village, Manu'a.[xlviii] This is the foundation of political division of Manu'a even today.

The Edict of TuiFiti *Suasamile'ava'ava* and the First Ava Plant

This edict was pronounced at the coastal peninsula of Fiji Island by the paramount king of Fiji, TuiFiti *Suasamile'ava'ava* (meaning "ava juice mixed with sea water"). The edict proclaimed that, after his passing, when a plant was seen growing up on his burial mound, his brother and sisters should take it, the ava plant found there, and go find their mother and auntie's homeland at the village of Vailele, Upolu. There they should plant the ava as a gift from him.

This is the source of the Upolu and Savai'i legend of the first ava plant coming from TuiFiti *Suasamile'ava'ava*. The Manu'an version dates this to the *Muiu'uleapai* and *TagaloaUi* generation around A.D.1290.[xlix]

Note, the story of the first ava ceremony precedes this edict, giving evidence for the fragmentation of the island legends and mythology, and the challenge of reconciling genealogy and timelines.

The Morning (*Taeao*) at Samanā, Satupa'itea village, Savai'i

This is another National Morning, given the recognition of the Malae and Maota. The Morning at Samanā, Satupa'itea village, in Savai'i celebrates the occasion when the baby boy *Sālevao*, brother of *Saveasi'uleo* and *Ulufanuasese'e*, stopped crying, thanks to the faithful babysitting service of *Tumupu'e*, daughter of Chief *Valomua*. The obstinate crying boy couldn't stop until *Tumupu'e* made him laugh.

Legend has it that when he finally stopped crying, all the dead people's skulls in Savai'i began to roll about endlessly. Another version indicates that it was a combination of *Tumupu'e's* efforts and the rolling skulls that made the boy laugh and thus stopped his crying.[l]

Sālevao fulfilled his appointment as the paramount chief of the vanguard of war in Savai'i, Upolu, and Tutuila.

The Morning (*Taeao*) of the Farewell at Sea in Alataua, Savai'i

This is another National Morning given the recognition of the Malae and Maota. The Morning of the parting "Farewell at Sea," in Alataua, Savai'i, of the brothers *Saveasi'uleo* and *Ulufanuasese'e*, commemorates the decree under the terms of which one brother, *Saveasi'uleo*, would travel east, toward

Manu'a, to initiate the planning and development of a kingdom, and the other would travel west toward Upolu to marry and so grow the family genealogy.[li] At that time there were very few known inhabitants of Manu'a.

The farewell is a decree to settle their violent differences, caused by *Saveasi'uleo* who turned into an eel and chased his brother to eat him (but to no avail). The brothers thus covenanted that they would live separately, forbidden to meet in person, to avoid conflicts, so they could only meet through their offspring. They decreed:

"We will meet again though our future genealogies," as promulgated by their parent's decree. *Ta toe feiloa'i i i'u o gafa ae le o ulu o gafa* is the proverb that was coined during this milestone historical event.

This legend is well-known, and many versions have been told and written down, originally by several missionaries in their books, including *Samoa: Lest we Forget* by Pule Lameko.[lii] The myth is ancient and is dated around A.D.800-900.

It is a common belief that these two brothers stand at the beginning of many of the foundational genealogies of the major ancient families of Samoa and Manu'a, and are the progenitors the venerable *Tonumaipe'a* family clan. Of the two, one had the form of a creature of the ocean waters (an eel), and lived in the ocean, whilst the other lived on the dry land of Samoa.

The Morning (*Taeao*) at the Residence of the TuiA'ana at Ma'auga and Nu'uausala, in the Village of Leulumoega, A'ana district

This is a three-fold National Morning given the recognition of the Malae and Maota. The Morning at the sacred meeting place and residence of TuiA'ana at the Ma'auga ma (and) Nu'uausala property, in the village of Leulumoega, A'ana district, refers to an ancient meeting place decreed by the early TuiA'ana, before TuiA'ana *Tamālelagi*, for the district and the House of Nine orator chiefs and four major families of the A'ana district. It is a three-fold memorial commemorating:

1. the sacred Malae Ma'auga of the ancient TuiA'ana, at the period of TuiManu'a, and then,
2. the bestowment of the first Tafa'ifa title, Tafa'ifa *Salamasina* TuiA'ana *Tamālelagi*, and also
3. all later, subsequent proclamations of the district, including granting the Tenth House to Tutuila, American Samoa, by decree of Paramount Chief *Mauga*, at the end of the war between Malietoa *Laupepa* and TuiA'ana *Tamasese Titimaea*.

Mornings in the Period of Tuimanu'a *Moaali'itele*

TuiManu'a *Moaali'itele* belongs to the period of the third TuiManu'a, after the founding of the Moa family clan—that is, after *Lu* (also known as *Lufasiaitu*) married *Leamoa* (also known as *Lagituaiva*, daughter of *Tagaloalagi*), begetting a daughter, *Moa*. Some say *Moa* was a son, but this author found evidence it was a daughter, *Moa,* who married the first TuiManu'a and bore a son named *Moa*. This is the *Moa* at the beginning of the Moa family clan. He would be a contemporary of *Taeotagaloa* and *Lefanoga*.

It is said by some Manu'an oral historians that the ancient *Moa* became Tuimanu'a *Moaali'itele* to memorialize the Moa family clan. And so this high chief title, Moaali'itele, exists today in Fitiuta village, Manu'a, and is a significant part of the Tuimanu'a genealogy.

The Edict at Si'uAmoa

TuiManu'a's farewell to his daughter and the village of Amoa, where princess *I'ei'e's* marriage took place, declared: *O le ua e afuafua mai Manu'a*—"I am returning home to Manu'atele; if and when a drizzle or misty rain falls from heaven, that is the messenger bringing my love and greetings to you all, for it is a mist that is sourced from Manu'atele"—*my translation*. The word *ua* means rain or water and is often used to describe a drizzle or very light rainfall, of a type similar to the morning or evening dew that vegetation begs for as life's sustaining "sprinkler system."

The Pronouncement at Asuisui, Savai'i

Around the time of *Moaali'itele's* daughter's wedding in Savai'i, we find the parting words of farewell of TuiToga *Asoaitu* and his sons *Haluilui* and *Hahui*. They both married girls in Asuisui village. After his brief visit, their father now prepared to return to Toga, saying, *Afai e agi* (blows) *mai le matagi* (wind) *mai* (from) *Toga, o le na e momoli* (deliver) *mai* (the) *alofaaga* (love) *i si a'u fanau* (children-sons), meaning "If the wind blows, and you can hear it coming from the ocean shore at Pupu, what you hear are my greetings and my love from Togatapu"— *my translation*.

It is a situation for major grieving, to say farewell when going on a distant, interisland journey. This explains why the Navigators were accustomed to grieving in saying goodbye as their family members departed.

Mornings from the Period of the Twins *Taemā* and *Tilafaigā*

The Parting edict of Chief *Vaea* to his wife *Apaula*

The edict proclaimed at Mauga o Vaea (the mountain of Chief Vaea), in Vaimauga district, Upolu, records the parting words of farewell between Chief *Vaea* and his wife *Apaula*, in the late part of her pregnancy, when she wanted to journey to her family in Fiji Island, so she could give birth to her child in her family there, as was often customary in Polynesian cultures. The chief's words of farewell were, "*Apaula*, my dear wife, go to visit your family in Fiji. If the ocean waves break with white waters, your journey is safe and well; remember me. However, if the ocean waves break with the color of blood, this means I am dead, and I will take your pain with me down to my grave"—*my translation*.

This legend continues with *Apaula* returning to Samoa to visit her husband Chief *Vaea*—whose body had turned into the mountain now known as Mount Vaea in the Vaimauga district— and also to avenge the death of her son *Tuiosavalalo* at the hands of her brothers. Her brother-in-law *Va'atausili* helped her. He had a rather small frame and fragile body and lived in a cave in Savai'i, but he came to life, like a hulk-human with super-strength, and they departed to Fiji Island to thrash and kill the cruel brothers.

There is another *Apauula*, with a slightly different spelling. She was the daughter of *Pili le So'opili* and *Tuamanulele i le mimo*. She married *Ufiufi* and gave birth to *Lealali*. This *Lealali* married *Sinalegogo*, daughter of TuiAtua *Leutelelei'ite*, whose mother was *Lefe'eialali*. Their children were *Salevaogogo* (who was defeated in a club match by *Leatiogie*, father of the first Malietoa *Saveatuvaelua*) and *Sausi*. At this time, the beginning of the population of Samoa and Manu'a, names are often the same, and there are many overlapping tales of their respective family genealogies. As a result, many historians believe there is a close connection between these families with the Lealali name. So Lealali is foundational to populating and organizing Savai'i Island and part of Upolu.

Apauula's husband *Ufiufi* was from Vaimauga, and his is the title family name of the Malietoa ancestors' genealogy, the family of Ufi. The *ufi* is an edible root, or Samoan potato, that grows like an underground vine, providing plenty to feed a whole village. Hence the metaphor that there are plenty of roots to the genealogy of the Malietoa clan. Another family title is named for *Lealali*, the older son of *Leatiogie* of the Malietoa family clan, brother to the first Malietoa *Saveatuvaelua*.

The Morning (*Taeao*) at Solosolo Village

Again, this is a National Morning, given the recognition of the Malae and Maota. The Morning commemorates the journey of the Siamese twins *Taemā* and *Tilafaigā*—some say it was a fishing expedition—when they went ashore at Solosolo village, on a promontory called Namo (or Gamo). It is said that the twins were thirsty for water and hungry for food, but the villagers refused and ignored them, and their dark spirit took over so they both devoured all the villagers.

Again, this illustrates the half-human, half-spirit characteristics of the ancient origin of the population of Samoa and Manu'a.[liii]

The Morning (*Taeao*) at Fatulegae'e, Utumoeaau, and Mālotumau at Faga'itua village, Tutuila

The Morning at Fatulegae'e, Utumoeaau, and Mālotumau at Faga'itua village, Tutuila, is another National Morning given the recognition of the Malae and Maota. It celebrates the sacred place where the twins *Taemā* and *Tilafaigā* sojourned in Tutuila.

Taemā married *Togiola* and gave birth to *Le'iatotogiola*, the paramount orator chief of the district. Then, at a later time, in A.D.1700, Paramount Chief *I'amafana* became Tafa'ifa *I'amafana,* who decreed the Tafa'ifa to Malietoa *Vaiinupõ*. *I'amafana* was defeated by Paramount Chief *Le'iato Tafilele* of Faga'itua and decreed the Tumua authority title to Chief *Le'iato*. And Tutuila became a protectorate of the United States.

The Farewell Decree of the Conjoined Sisters

As the famous conjoined twin sisters, *Taemā* and *Tilafaigā,* parted ways at the coast of Tutuila, facing the ocean between Tutuila and Savai'i (Vasa Loloa), they declared that: if they should meet again in the distant future, they would meet in the "mainsail" and "headsail" of their respective sailing vessels. This signifies that they would not meet each other again in person, but rather in the passing of their traveling vessels. Thus, the sisters vowed to go separately and not meet again, except that they would meet at the tails of their genealogies. This legend and edict are dated around A.D.1200-1230.

The Farewell of the Sisters *Lulai* and *Lulago*

The farewell of the two sisters, *Lulai* and *Lulago,* from Samata, Savai'i, as they departed to Upolu with their husband (*Si'utaulalovasa*), is a farewell made to the father (*Tupa'isafe'e*) of the child that one of the sisters was pregnant with. As their canoe pulled out to sea, the farewell was delivered, using sign language or pantomime, to convey to the father, who was standing on the shore, that the sister was pregnant with his child. The sons, *To'o* and *Ata,* were born from this union between *Si'utaulalovasa* and the two sisters.

Ata continued the genealogy and is the progenitor of the Malietoa clan in Faleata district. His union with *Fa'auliUmi* resulted in two sons: *Si'ufe'ai* and *Tafa'igata*. *Si'ufe'ai* would become grandfather to *Fe'epõ* and progenitor of the Malietoa clan. His brother *Tafa'igata* married *Sauopualai* who bore many sons. When she had just given birth to another son, *Tafa'igata* asked her where the boys' homes were located in the village. She answered, "*Veletaloola* is on the east side, and *Taliausoloi* is on the west side." *Tafa'igata* asked who was on the leeward side. *Sauopualai* said "It is the boy, *Mata* and *'Afa.*" So *Tafa'igata* said, "I decree the name of this last son will be the combined names of *Mata'afa* and this will be the paramount chief title of all my children and my village, and the district." *Tafa'igata* is a descendent of *LeTelesā*.

Ata also married the daughter of TuiToga who bore *Patauave* (A.D.1170). *Patauave* married a woman from Vaitele, who bore the first *Matai'a* and his sister *Tofili*. The Matai'a title belongs to the vanguard of war division of the Malietoa Tuamasaga district. This legend presents the beginning of the major families in Faleata, including the Malietoa, Matai'a, and Mata'afa paramount chiefs, dating back to around A.D.1080-1140.

The Matai'a is the third leg of the tripod ruling authority of the Faleata district (Matai'a, Mata'afa, and Faumuinā). According to sources from the village of Faleata and fragments from Dr. Krämer, the origin of the Faumuinā title in Faleata is as follows:

TuiA'ana *Pilisosolo* (A.D.1170) married *Manavafea'a*, a woman from Faleata who bore *'Ata'atanoa* and his sister *LeTelesā*. Then *'Ata'atanoa* married *Tofili* (*Matai'a's* sister) who bore *Fa'auli* and *Umi* and a boy that was named *Faumuinā* after he was adopted by *'Ata'atanoa's* sister *LeTelesā*. In the story, *LeTelesā* was barren, and so she went to her brother *'Ata'atanoa* and asked him to bring one of his sons so she could adopt the child. *'Ata'atanoa* pointed to his son, who was preparing food in the Samoan cooking hot oven (*umu*), and said to her, "Take him and name him *Fai-umu-mai-ina.*" So the boy was adopted by *LeTelesā* and named *Faumuinā*.

There is another connection with the *Folasa-na-ola-fa'aaitu* paramount warrior from the same family in Faleata (the family of *Manavafea'a*) as follows: The warrior named *To'oa'au* (ancestor of *To'otai* and *To'outa* of Fasito'o) married *LeTelesā*, daughter of the first *Faumuinā*, who bore *Folasanaolafa'aaitu*.

Folasanaolafa'aaitu married *Punefulealofioa'ana*, daughter of *Apenamoemanatunatu*-II, the son of the original *Ape* who fought and won the war with his brother *Tutuila* of Fasito'o, on behalf of the Malietoa, against *Mageafaigā* of N'uuli; she bore him two sons; *Apenamoemanatunatu*-III and *Folasāitu*-II.

Mornings from the Period Leading up to the War between Toga and Samoa

The Morning (*Taeao*) at the Sacred Meeting Place Moamoa, Falefā village, Upolu

This is another National Morning given the recognition of the Malae and Maota. The Morning at the sacred meeting place at Moamoa, Falefā village, Upolu, celebrates the occasion when *Leatiogie*, son of *Fe'epō* and progenitor of the Malietoa dynasty, won the overall club match against the last formidable opponent, *Salevaogogo* son of Paramount Chief *Leutelelei'ite* of Falefā village, in Atua district.[liv]

The Edict known as the Tu'itu'i

Fe'epō, the blind grandfather of the first Malietoa *Saveatuvaelua,* gave a blessing to his son *Leatiogie,* in thanks for his faithful caring for him while, at the same time, participating in Upolu Island's annual stick-fighting games at the Moamoa meeting ground at Falefā village, in the Atua district. At these games, *Leatiogie* defeated the well-known *Salevaogogo*, son of the Paramount Chief *Leutelelei'ite* who later became TuiAtua *Leutelelei'ite*.

Fe'epō was touched by the faithful love of his son, who had cared for him by preparing three separate meals (breakfast, lunch, and dinner) for each of the two days he was going to run off to enter the contest. *Leatiogie* hung each day's meals in a coconut basket on a house-post close to his father's bed for ease of retrieval.

The blind *Fe'epō* said, "Son, go to the games contest; may the god be with your strength and skills. May the blood (or blood, sweat, and tears) of your body, from the contest, run through your path. May your vision be clear and bright. May your body be dark and camouflaged. And may your genealogy be like the abundant fruit of the first *ufi* plant"—*my translation*: *Ia tafe toto* (flowing blood) *ou ala* (your path), *malamalama* (clear) *lau va'ai* (view), *pouliuli* (dark) *lou tino* (your body) *ma ia tanumia* (buried or planted) *lua'iufi* (the first planted *ufi* plant—a potato-like root).

This famous pronouncement is quoted ubiquitously by speakers to departing sport teams on farewell occasions at tournaments. It emphasizes that love for parents, faithful caring, and responsibility gives you the blessing of the parents—the key to blessing and success.

We should also note here the story of TuiManu'a's shining red residence house. In around A.D.1225, this shining red house, or *Faleula*, was given as a gift to TuiManu'a's wife, *Sina* who was from the Ufi clan. The house was called the *Faleula*, and *Sina* was to take it to her family in Faleata, Upolu, together with her brother, *Malalatele* or *Malālatea* (the great-grandfather of *Fata*, *Maulolo,* and their sister *Luafatasaga* who married *Fe'epõ*'s grandson, the first Malietoa *Saveatuvaelua*). *Sina* had another brother, *Leatiogie* (the father of *Fe'epõ*'s grandson, the first Malietoa *Saveatuvaelua*), and because of this the Tuimanu'a's *Faleula*, that shiny red house, was given to be the Malietoa's residence in the village named after the *Faleula* in the Tuamasaga district of the Malietoa clan.[lv]

Mornings in the Period of the Malietoa Dynasty

The Edict of the Defeated Togan King

This edict was proclaimed at the Bay of Tulātalā, Mulifanua, Upolu. The defeated Togan king, TuiToga *Talaifei'i*, while escaping on his war vessel to return to Toga, stood up on the deck and announced in a loud voice, saying to the warriors standing at the beach shore, "*Malie tau* (well fought), *malie toa* (well done and heroic), you warriors. I will not come in dark clouds of cruelty and war, but I will come in the white clouds of peace and friendship and fair weather." This commemorates the founding of the Malietoa title and dynasty and records the founding of the first Malietoa *Saveatuvaelua* in the generation around A.D.1225-1240.

The Edict of Samoa and the Royal Aualuma

The proclamation at Le Vaisā in Tufu Gataivai village, Savai'i, commemorates the edict by Paramount Chief La'ulu *Nofovaleane* (a name which means "La'ulu sitting idle") to his three daughters, *Fa'atupuigati*, *Tuaetali,* and *Maupenei*, whose prodigious genealogy would produce the sons who would shape the structure of the Island Nation's foundational families and monarchies—his daughter *Tuaetali*'s union with Tonumaipe'a *Saumaipe'a* produced *Tapumanaia* who married Tafa'ifa *Salamasina*; *Fa'atupuigati's* union with Lilomaiava *Seveailaomanu* bore *Pesefeamanaia*, ancestor of the prestigious Lilomaiava dynasty; and *Maupenei* married TuiToga and bore *Le Aumoana* who was decreed to be the prince and ancestor of the modern SaMuliaga clan. The proclamation came about this way:

As punishment for mocking the enlarged head size of *Maupenei's* son *Le Aumoana*, La'ulu *Nofovaleane* decreed to *Maupenei's* sisters (*Fa'atupuigati* and *Tuaetali*) that *Le Aumoana* would inherit the title Aualuma (head of the formal unmarried young virgin girls of the village) of his family clan; the mighty clan SaMuliaga would be appointed to him. As for the other daughters' sons: *Tapumanaia*, son of *Fa'atupuigati* was to be given to the Lufilufi and Leulumoega districts to serve as the head of their Aualuma (Lufilufi is the home of the Tumua orator authority of Atua district, and Leulumoega of the Tumua orator authority of A'ana district), and *Pesefeamanaia,* son of *Tuaetali,* was to be head of the Aualuma of the Three-Legged-Stool—*Vae o le Nofoafia*—family clan, Liliomaiava (in Safotu, Palauli and Satuimalufilufi villages).

These three Aualuma heads are considered the Royal Aualuma of Samoa. And the boys are also called the *O Tama o le fa'atolotologatama na i papa, the* "Princes that were raised by having them crawl every morning on the flat smooth sea rocks at the beach at Lealatele"—*my translation*.

The significance of this decree is that it represents the first establishment of the aualuma into the royal office of the monarchic structure of Samoa. Prior to this assignment, aualuma were exclusively at the village level. With this decree, the title was now held at the national level, much like the *Sa'o Aumaga* title, named after sons of monarchs and their princes.

The Edict concerning the Rainforest Parrot

This edict was issued at Talagavae, between *Taeotagaloa* and the warrior *Taeoiatua* of Atua. *Taeotagaloa* was the son of *TagaloaUi*; he brought the beautiful Pacific rainforest parrot called *sega* to Samoa. The warrior *Taeoiatua* of Atua was the son of *Tanu* and *Fili* of Uafato, and he is credited with introducing saltwater in cooking food, by soaking the food in sea water when this had been made taboo by Malietoa Faigā *Uilamatūtū* at Tuana'i, Upolu.

The warrior *Taeoiatua* requested of *Taeotagaloa* that, at his funeral, he should be buried together with the beautiful tropical parrot, the *sega* (*sega* or *sega'ula* where *sega* is the bird and *ula* describes the beautiful red feathers—*ula* was also used to describe Tuimanu'a's house, the *Faleula*, gifted to *Sina,* daughter of *Fe'epõ* of Faleata, Upolu).

The *sega* was a bird, much sought- after by all the paramount chiefs. *Fo'isia*, the man from Onegoa, Tutuila, had trained and domesticated the *sega,* and then gifted it to the TuiManu'a. The *sega* had been tamed to perch on a stick and then on the back of the hand.

According to the stories, Malietoa Faigā *Uilamatūtū* requested that he might obtain the *sega* from TuiManu'a, and it was brought over by *Taeotagaloa*, who, in turn, bargained with the Malietoafaigā to free the slaves in exchange for the *sega* bird. This marked the end of the Malietoa's cruelty and his enslaving of his subjects.

In the Manu'an version of this legend, *Lefanago* is sometimes substituted for *Taeotagaloa*. The legend is about the taming of Malietoa Faigā *Uilamatūtū's* omnivorous cannibalism and cruelty by *Taeotagaloa* (or *Lefanago*) from Manu'a. According to this legend, Malietoa Faigā *Uilamatūtū* gave up, at least temporarily, his cruelty, when presented with the *sega* bird.

This is the generation in which both brothers (Malietoa *Gagasavea*, the older, and Malietoa Faigā *Uilamatūtū*) each married the daughters of the TuiToga, the sisters *Pate* and

Alainuanua respectively. *Taeotagaloa* lived around late A.D.1290 and Malietoa Faigā *Uilamatūtū* lived around A.D.1350.

There is another well-known legend in Malie, Tuamasaga, which tells the story that led to Malietoafaigā *Uilamatūtū* giving up his cannibalism permanently, with the help of his adopted son *Poluleuligaga*, as will be told next in The Morning (*Taeao*) at Malie and Vaito'elau. *Poluleuligaga* was the biological son of Malietoafaigā's brother-in-law, TuiToga *'Ulufanuatele* (or TuiToga *Talaaifei'i*).[lvi]

The Morning (*Taeao*) at Malie and Vaito'elau

This is another National Morning given the recognition of the Malae and Maota. The Morning at Malie and Vaito'elau, in the villages of Malie and Afega in Tuamasaga district, marks the proclamation of the District of Tuamasaga as a sacred meeting place and residence of the Malietoa dynasty. It also commemorates the morning of the new day when Malietoa Faigā *Uilamatūtū* (nephew of the orators *Fata* and *Maulolo*) finally gave up his cruelty and the practice of cannibalism, as orchestrated by his adopted son *Poluleuligaga* (the biological son of his wife's brother, TuiToga *'Ulufanuatele*). This Morning signifies the giving up of cruelty and primitive behavior and turning toward more civilized human customs.

Malietoa Faigā *Uilamatūtū* was also known by his salutation: *Sūsū mai le Tapaau Fa'asisina Lau Sūsūga Malietoa ma lou falafolaloa* (large seating mat) *ma lou Nofoa vaevaeloloa na fa'afofoga iai Samoa* (all Samoa listened to), meaning "The Malietoafaigā whose command all Samoa listens to"—*my translation*. He married a princess of Tonga, and the princess' brother—the King of Toga, Tuitoga *'Ulufanuatele*—had a son, *Poluleuligaga,* whom she and the Malietoafaigā adopted. According to the legend, at this time Malietoafaigā ruled over Upolu, Savai'i, and Tutuila, where he created a schedule for when each village would sacrifice one human being. His army of men would relay the schedule to each village.

A man called *Palaugi* had two boys scheduled for sacrifice. The staging area for the event was Salemoa. And one early morning, *Poluleuligaga* was walking along in Samoa. During his walk he heard a crying voice. Concerned, *Poluleuligaga* asked who was there and, as he searched for the crying voice, he found the two boys. The boys explained they were next to be sacrificed for their villages.

Poluleuligaga told the boys he would return tomorrow with a plan. As the next day arrived, he found the boys still crying. He told them to climb up the coconut tree and cut down the leaves. The two boys brought the longest leaves and laid *Poluleuligaga* down on the leaves. They wove the leaves into a basket, just as Samoans would do to prepare fish. Then they carried *Poluleuligaga* to the boat and paddled to the Malietoa.

Poluleuligaga instructed the boys to lay the basket, face down, in front of the Malietoa. The boys did just as *Poluleuligaga* directed, and the Malietoa was excited to see such a large basket. As he flipped the basket upright, he asked "How many Malietoas are there? There is only one."

When Poluleuligaga insisted that he stop cannibalism practices, Malietoa replied, "What? Do you know if there are two gods Samoans worship?" meaning "There are no two gods. Only me, Malietoafaigā." But *Poluleuligaga* replied, "If you keep this up, you will eventually run out of people to serve your kingdom." And, so Malietoafaigā said, "You requested this, that I stop, and I will do so." Hence, *Poluleuligaga* received his second name, *LuaAtua* or *Luātua*, at the village of Saleimoa, Upon (not Savai'i), and this is the origination of the Lua (two) Atua (god) family in Savai'i.

This Morning also commemorates the designation of the Tumua and the two Pule (Safotulafai and Saleaula) national authorities (and hence the beginning of the national salutations), the *Tumua ma Pule* authorities. The original authorities were in Safotulafai and Saleaula districts, later promulgated to Safotu, Palauli, Satupa'itea, and Asau districts in 1868-80 for Savai'i Island. We again witness the rollup of the country's governmental structure and organization through promulgating these offices as national authorities.

The Morning (*Taeao*) at Lalogāfu'afu'a and Mulinu'ū in the village of Lufilufi, Atua district

Another National Morning, given the recognition of the Malae and Maota, is the dawn of a new day at Lalogāfu'afu'a and

Mulinu'ū in the village of Lufilufi, in the Atua district, commemorating when this was promulgated by the ancient TuiAtua family clan to be the sacred meeting place and residence of the TuiAtua and the House of Six orator chiefs and six councilor chiefs of the Atua district. It also commemorates the allocation (or designation) of Tumua authority to the Atua district.

The Edict of Tagaloa *Funefe'ai* abdicating war with TuiAtua

The edict at the sacred property at Utufiu in Savai'i, between Tagaloa *Funefe'ai* and his daughter *Utufa'asisili* is when Tagaloa *Funefe'ai* instructed his daughter that he would abdicate his war campaign against her husband TuiAtua *Fepulea'i*. TuiAtua was cruel to *Utufa'asisili,* but, it should be noted, accumulating authority and thus power was the mantra of the period. Tagaloa *Funefe'ai's* marriage to *'Ulalemamae* produced two daughters who each married into the Atua district genealogy. One daughter married *Taua*, who became TuiAtua *LeTaua*, and bore *Leifi* and *Tautoloitua*. And the other daughter produced the Atua district warrior *Manusamoa*. Additionally, Lady *'Ulalemamae* also married *Leutelelei'ite* at about the same time as Tagaloa *Funefea'i* married *Utufa'asisili's* mother *Tauanu'nufaigā*.

Funefea'i abdicated the war by making TuiAtua *Fepulea'i* promise to bestow the TuiAtua title onto *Utufa'asisili's* child, who turned out to be a strong boy and was named after the Samoan word which means abdication—*Tologataua* or *Tolonataua* (*tolo* means postpone, but in fact he actually abandoned, *taua,* the war effort). So, with the war effort abandoned, when *Utufa'asisili* gave birth from her current pregnancy, all of the honorifics and assets of the TuiAtua were bestowed on the child.

The parting decree at Falepunaoa

The parting decree at Falepunaoa, Falealili, Atua district was a farewell decree between Warrior Chief *Manusamoa* and his sister *Tautiapagofie* as he departed for war. *Manusamoa* said to his sister, "Blessings be with our farewell. Blessings be when we part, and blessing when we meet again."

Some Samoan historians orate that *Manusamoa* was making a journey to fight in the war on behalf of Malietoa *Tuilaepa* against the formidable warriors of the Manono Island district. It is said that *Manusamoa* hauled up a very large, strong tree and split it down the middle into two halves to be his war clubs. A well-known high chief orator is named after this, *Tofilau* (*Tofi*, meaning to split down the middle, and *lau* meaning tree half).

The Decree pronounced in the Cave at Seuao

During the war between Tuamasaga and Atua district, between Malietoa *'Ae'o'ainu'ū*, leader of Tuamasaga, and TuiAtua *Muagututi'a*, leader of the Atua district, Malietoa *'Ae'o'ainu'ū's* warriors were driven to find cover in a cave named Seuao at Safata village in the southern part of Tuamasaga district. When the Tuamasaga war party was trapped in the cave, the Atua tried to burn and smoke them out. Malietoa *'Ae'o'ainu'ū* began to negotiate safe passage out of the cave.

As the Malietoa war party was tightly huddled, deep in the cave, they heard some of the war party of Atua speaking in the Tongan language. So one of Malietoa *'Ae'o'ainu'ū's* warriors, an old man from the village of Vailele, Upolu, whose ancestors were Tongan, suggested that he could go out and speak to the Tongan-speaking folks, and maybe he could negotiate their way out. Malietoa *'Ae'o'ainu'ū* decided to allow the old man to do this.

So it happened that Senior Orator *Iuli* of Falefā village, who was related to Malietoa *'Ae'o'ainu'ū's* genealogy in their district, began a long-winded oration to the Atua war party, calming them down and seeking some resolution for the trapped Malietoa *'Ae'o'ainu'ū* war party. As historians tell the tale, the oration lasted two days and two nights! Hence Orator Chief *Iuli's* salutation of "he who orated two days and two nights."

At this time Malietoa *'Ae'o'ainu'ū* reached an agreement whereby he decreed that his authority over the whole of Tutuila was ceded to the TuiAtua in trade for their safe passage out of the cave. Thus, Tutuila Island became Atua's political district until partition by the United States in 1899.

The time-period of Malietoa *'Ae'o'ainu'ū* is A.D.1680-1720 and this event occurred at the tail end of his reign. But the reign of the Malietoa over Tutuila goes back to when Malietoa *Uitualagi* defeated Paramount Warrior *Mageafaigā* (*Magea* the cruel) in the early A.D.1300s. Later, in the mid-1500s, *Tapusalaia*, the princess and sister of Paramount Chief *Asomua*, great-grandchild of *Fuaoleto'elau* (who was brother to *La'auli*) of the Malietoa family clan, was given Tutuila Island to rule over. It was called the Island of Tapusalaia and is still under the Malietoa dynasty.

Mornings from the Period of the Tafa'ifa

The Edict at the Forest, proclaimed between TuiSamoa *Nonumaifele* and *Li'amanaia*

This edict was proclaimed in the period of Malietoa *Uitualagi*, son of Malietoa Faigā *Uilamatūtū*, at Tuavao (which means forest). The edict was between TuiSamoa *Nonumaifele* of Falealili, Atua district, Upolu, and *Li'amanaia*, son of Senior Orator *Fineitalaga*, progenitor of the Sagapolutele family clan in SaLuafata, Atua district, Upolu.

An outing hunting fruit pigeons turned into a contest where each wooed the other's sister respectively. TuiSamoa *Nonumaifele* was victorious, for he succeeded in gaining *Li'amanaia's* sister *Letutupu's* hand in marriage. But *Li'amanaia* was unsuccessful in capturing the TuiSamoa's sister's heart.

The proverb, "we shall meet in victory and not in defeat," references their contest, and the significance of this edict is that the marriage of TuiSamoa *Nonumaifele* to *Letutupu* gave birth to the famous sisters *Gauifaleai* and *Totogata*. These two maidens both married Malietoa *La'auli,* giving birth to the two girls *Gatoa'itele* and *Gasoloaiaolelagi*. Both daughters married the Tongan prince *LeSanalāla*, who fathered *Vaetamasoaali'i*, *Atougaugaatuitoga* (the mother of *Valasi*), and *Lalovimāmā* (father of *Mata'utia Fa'atulou* and husband of *Valasi*). Hence the "Celestial Constellation" that Dr. Krämer refers to, that produces the first consolidated ruler Tafa'ifa of Samoa, *Salamasina*.

The Edict at the Motu Tu'ufua

The Motu Tu'ufua is the abandoned island in the Tuvalu Archipelago. Here were heard the parting words of farewell between Lady *Leutogitupa'itea* and her son *Fa'asega*. Lady

Leutogi instructed *Fa'asega* to take the Tonumaipe'a and Tauiliili titles, and the princess title, Tilomai, to her brother *Lafaitaulupo'o* in Ulusuatia, Savai'i.

We have already seen the legend where *Leutogitupa'itea* married TuiToga *Manaia* (the same TuiToga *Manaia* who later married *Nafanua* (or *Suaifanua*). *Leutogitupa'itea* was barren, but the other wife of TuiToga *Manaia* had a child. *Leutogitupa'itea* asked to babysit and, out of jealousy, poked the baby's eyes with a toothpick of coconut leaves. The child died, and the TuiToga banished her to an abandoned island, to be tied to the *fetau* tree and be burned with the tree.

Fortunately, *Leutogitupa'itea's* brother in Savai'i, Samoa had a premonition (or was warned) of her punishment. He sent the flock of white Pacific fruit bats to save her. The bats flew over the fire and urinated, putting the fire out. Her cook-oven on the beach was buried with sand and fine seashells (*iliili*), for there were no leaves to cover the Samoan-style *umu* oven—hence the name and title, *Tauiliili*.

Paramount Chief TuiUēa of Uēa, of Wallis Island just west of Savai'i, found *Leutogitupa'itea* on the abandoned island and took her for a wife, and she gave birth to the boy *Fa'asega*. *Leutogitupa'itea's* brief genealogy is: *Muliagalafai* (also known as *LeMuliaga*, descendant of the prodigious *Laifai* who, together with his brother *Funefe'ai,* organized Savai'i Island) united with *Poulifataiatagaloa*, daughter of *TuiAsau* of Vaisala, Asau, Savai'i, with the issue of a boy *Lafaitaulupo'o* and a girl *Leutogitupa'itea*. *Lafaitaulupo'o* became the first Tonumaipe'a whose great-grandson *Tapumanaia*-I married Salamasina, giving birth to *Tapumanaia*-II.

The Edit of *Saveasi'uleo*, made to *Nafanua*

This well-known and important historical edict at Pulotu, Alataua, Savai'i was issued by *Saveasi'uleo* to his daughter, the "Warrior Queen" *Nafanua*. The famous Samoan female warrior would lead the battle to defend *Saveasi'uleo's* cousin *Tonumaipe'a's* kingdom, in the district of Alataua, Savai'i, and avenge the cruelty of Paramount Chief *Liliomaiava* over *Tauiliili Tonumaipe'a* and his people.

164

Saveasi'uleo instructed *Nafanua* that the battlelines must not cross the boundary of Paramount Chief *Tauiliili Tonumaipe'a's* residence. The command was to neither advance the war nor battle beyond the residence of the "Elder and Firstborn" (*Ali'i o Aiga*) Paramount Chief *Tonumaipe'a* for it was sacred: *Afai e pa'ia le pā i Fualaga, sua le tuli auā le Ali'i o Aiga*—"If the war arrives at the boundary (*pā*, meaning rock or erected fence) of the sacred residence (i.e. at Fualaga village, Alataua, Savai'i) of the head of the family and the firstborn (*Ali'i o Aiga*) of the monarch, stop and turn back (*sua le tuli* is a Samoan phrase meaning stop or turn back)"—*my translation*.

This story is dated to around A.D.1230 but is included here because of the earlier date for *Saveasi'uleo*. It signifies the sacred boundary in brother-sister relationships and the sacredness of a paramount chief's residence.

The Proclamations of the PāPā royal titles

There is a prodigious and historical set of proclamations given at Analega, Alataua, Savai'i. For there were conflicts and wars within each PāPā royal title—the TuiAtua, TuiA'ana, Gatoa'itele and Vaetamasoaali'i royal titles—to determine the ownership and holder of each title. In each of these conflicts, involving kin related to *Nafanua*, those with such kin relationships sought assistance from Warrior Queen *Nafanua*, seeking fighting warriors to strengthen their military forces.

First TuiA'ana *Tamālelagi* (grandson of *Gatoa'itele* and father of *Salamasina*) sent a message to *Nafanua* asking for assistance, and *Nafanua* responded through her ambassador, *Tupa'i* as follows: "*Tupa'i*, go and take the warriors to help fight in the conflict between *Tamālelagi* and *Sagaate*. If *Tamālelagi* is victorious, bring the royal PāPā of the TuiA'ana to me."

Now, TuiAtua *Mata'utia* (grandson of *Gatoa'itele*) sent a message to *Nafanua*, asking for war party assistance. *Nafanua* responded with assistance through her ambassador *Tupa'i* with slightly different instructions, that the title Tupa'i should be installed in the TuiAtua government, to assist in establishing the new government. TuiAtua *Mata'utia* was victorious and the royal PāPā of TuiAtua was taken to *Nafanua*.

Gatoa'itele and the brothers *Fata* and *Maulolo,* together with the Chiefs Council Tuisamau, likewise went to war with Malietoa *Sagagaimuli*. The orators' council group 'Auimatagi of Malie village (the Malietoa residence) fought with *Tupa'i's* fighting warriors. ('Auimatagi is the orator chiefs' council of Malietoa. And Tuisamau and Fata and Maulolo is the orator chiefs' council in Afega and Tuana'i.) *Tupa'i's* warriors were victorious, defeating the Malietoa and the 'Auimatagi orators' council. *Tupa'i* was likewise installed at the Tuisamau to help with the new government. The name Gatoa'itele was taken to *Nafanua* to be made into a PāPā royal title, for up to this point neither *Gatoa'itele* nor Malietoa had a royal PāPā.

Shortly after the Malietoa and *Gatoa'itele* conflict, a war broke out between the Alataua at Safata village and the Satunumafono of the *Vaetamasoaali'i* family clan. *Nafanua* responded to a request from *Vaetamasoaali'i* (daughter of *Gatoa'itele* and mother to *Tamālelagi*), sending ambassador *Tupa'i* and providing the assistance of fighting warriors. This resulted in victory for *Vaetamasoaali'i*. The name *Vaetamasoaali'i* (not yet a PāPā) was taken to *Nafanua* and likewise the Tupa'i title was installed, to assist Paramount Chief *Te'o* and *Tuiā* to build the new government at the Togamau and Nu'usuatia meeting ground, and at the *Vaetamasoaali'i* residence.

Tupa'i, younger brother of *Valasi*, was now the ambassador title of *Nafanua*. *Nafanua* proclaimed or designated the title Tupa'i for her ambassadors after the war, to be installed in the various victorious government organizations, to assist in the establishment of those governments. The Tuisamau of Afega has a Tupa'i; likewise the Satunumafono at Nu'usuatia and Lotofagā villages for *Vaetamasoaali'i's* government, and at Lufilufi on behalf of the TuiAtua. The exception is Leulumoega, on behalf of TuiA'ana, because of the boundary between *Nafanua* and *Valasi* and TuiAana *Tamālelagi*. But the Tupa'i did not relocate to these physical residences.

In a period of about 30 years, *Nafanua* had gained total custody of all four titles (TuiAtua, TuiA'ana, Gatoa'itele and Vaetamasoaali'i). The two PāPās, Gatoa'itele and Vaetamasoaali'i, were prophetically decreed by Malietoa *Uitualagi* (the son of Malietoa Faigā *Uilamatūtū*, son of the first Malietoa

166

Saveatuvaelua according to the Malietoa monarch genealogy) to be bestowed on the Malietoa. This was done with the agreement of *Fata* and *Maulolo* for the Gatoa'itele PāPā, and of *Te'o* and *Tuiā* for the Vaetamasoaali'i PāPā, for they were custodians of the respective PāPās, to ensure the Malietoa title rank equaled that of the royal TuiAtua and TuiA'ana titles. *Nafanua's* decision, and her act of bestowing these titles on *Salamasina Tamālelagi*, commissioned the Gatoa'itele and Vaetamasoaali'i titles and respective PāPās.

Tafa'ifa *Salamasina's* Deathbed Pronouncement

This pronouncement was made at Mulifusi and Tanumaleu, Lotofaga, Atua district. On her deathbed Tafa'ifa *Salamasina Tamālelagi* decreed that her family should not erect a burial mount for her (the rock pyramid monument, customary for paramount chiefs), because she did not want her brother's family from Leulumoega village in A'ana, to come and take her body (or bones) to be buried in Leulumoega, the capital of the A'ana government. "But bury me under the Samoan cook oven, the *umu*, using banana leaves for covering, and material residue to disguise my resting place of burial"—*my translation*. *Afai* (If) *ou* (I) *te oti* (a common term for death or died), *'aua ne'i faia so'u tuugamau* (the burial pyramid for royalty, thus, don't erect a burial mount) *ne'i maua mai a'u e le fanau a lo'u tuagane* (*Tuala* was her brother: *tuagane* means sister's brother) *eli a'u ave i Leulumoega, ae ia tanu a'u i le valusaga o le umu*. "Otherwise, my brother's children will come in time to take my body to be buried in Leulumoega, the capital of the government of A'ana."

History notes that her oldest brother, the firstborn of TuiA'ana *Tamālelagi* was *Tuala*, progenitor of the prodigious SaTuala family. *Tuala* was given the responsibility of serving his sister Tafa'ifa *Salamasina*. He, in turn, delegated the responsibility to his three older sons, *Malufaitoaga* (at Amoa village), *Tauālelei* (at Amoa village) and *Tauimalie* (at Tufu, Savai'i and Lefaga in Upolu).

Some historians, close to TuiA'ana affairs, say that Tafa'ifa *Salamasina* was miffed by the unfaithfulness of *Tuala's* children in service. Their poor service caused her to go to stay with her "mother," *Valasi*, the progenitor of the venerated SaLevalasi family in Lotofaga, Atua. Hence, the profound meaning of the Tafa'ifa's decree with her family in Lotofaga stems from disappointment in how she was served by the *Tuala* children. This action by the Tafa'ifa deviates from royal burial rituals customary in Faleolo, the location of the TuiA'ana royal burial ground.

The cultural thread here, of tireless service to authority, particularly to the paramount Tafa'ifa, is integral to affirming the organizational structure. Rewards await the faithful servant, as evidenced in the numerous pronouncements dedicated by paramount chiefs raising their servers to personal and family status.

The Decree promulgated at Tu'ofe

The Decree promulgated at Tu'ofe is a milestone pronouncement by TuiA'ana TuiAtua *Taufau*, granddaughter of Tafa'ifa *Salamasina*, who proclaimed that her son *Tupuivao* would be disinherited from the (TuiAtua TuiA'ana) throne, because of his obstinacy and disobedience to Queen *Taufau*. After he declined numerous messages and requests from his mother, the queen, asking him to come so she could decree the TuiAtua and TuiA'ana throne to him, *Taufau* sadly called on her sister *Sina* to bring her son *Faumuinā*, so she could proclaim the edict on him. And so *Tupuivao*, the cruel, disobedient son, was disinherited of his mother's royal heirlooms.

This edict also marks the beginning of the *Faumuinā* dynasty, with his three children (two sons, *Va'afusuaga* and *Fonotī*, and their sister *Samalaulu*) that caused the first and only civil war in Samoa. *Va'afusuaga* was later called *Va'afusuaga-Toleafoa* when his son, *Toleafoa,* fought on behalf of his father in the war against his uncle *Fonotī*. *Fonotī* was victorious and claimed the Tafa'ifa title, making him the second Tafa'ifa:

Tumua (authority) *ua tafea* (my vessel being blown away by the wind) *la'u utu* (heirlooms in the fishing bamboo receptacle) *ae aumai le tama a lo'u uso* (bring the son of my sister, the boy *Faumuinā*) *tou te fa'afegai* (will face your authority) *e e'e i ai PāPā* (and for you to bestow the TuiAtua and TuiA'ana PāPā— *my translation*).

The Proclamation at Salani and Alofisula

The proclamation at Salani and Alofisula (the principal residence of Paramount Chief *Fuimaono*), Falealili, Atua district, was made by Chief *Fuimaono* and his wife *Oilau*, giving their only son, Tupua *Fuiavalili*, at Tafa'ifa *Muagututi'a's* request, so he could be adopted as heir apparent to the crown titles. The significance of this is the fulfillment of Tafa'ifa *Salamasina's* parting farewell decree, to remember her only male heir, her son *Tapumanaia*-II, who was stolen from her at birth by the senior orator chiefs *Talolema'agao* (*Talo*) and *Ofoia* of Falealili.

This pronouncement tells further how Chief *Fuimaono* said to his wife *Oilau* that she should go to her brother, the prodigious Warrior Chief *Te'o* to bring one of his sons for them to adopt, as heir apparent to the Fuimaono title. The boy *Leliulagi* was adopted and became heir apparent to all the titles and heirlooms of the Fuimaono family. He was given a first name *Na'oia*, meaning the only one, or Fuimaono Na'oia.

The Decree in the period of *Tiumalumalilomaiava Tumailagi*

In the period of *Tiumalumalilomaiava Tumailagi*, *Lilomaiava Tumailagi* sojourned in Tutuila or on the Island of Tapuisalaia (the princess of Paramount Chief *Asomua* of the Malietoa family clan), visiting his brother's father-in-law's family, that of Paramount Chief *Tuitele* (a descendant of TuiManu'a), ruler of the Alataua district of Tutuila Island. The parting words of farewell, decreed by Chief *Tuitele,* as *Lilomaiava Tumailagi* was about to get on his vessel, were the following: "*Lilomaiava*, go with your paramount salutation, 'Lilomaiava the Royal Honorific' family. May clear white clouds guide you; let no bad or formidable ocean waves be obstructive to your path, but sail with calm ocean currents to take you home to Savai'i"—*my translation*.

Lilomaiava, sau i na alu ma lou Fa'asisina or Tapa'ufa'asisina lea. Ia e folau i lagimamā, ia 'aua nei laga se peau vale. A ia laga peau matamataloloa.

Lilomaiava Tumailagi's brother *Lilomaiava Nailevaiiliili,* had married *Tuitele's* daughter *Sinagautaala*, giving birth to two boys, *Momo* and *I'aulaualo*, in Palauli, Savai'i. The title chief names of

169

these two sons, as well as the senior orator chief name Lavea of the district of Palauli, Savai'i, are also gifted to Leone and found in Leone village of Tuitele.

The Edict at Sepolata'emo, Atua district

This edict proclaimed the transition of the Tafa'ifa to *Tupua*, the adopted son of Tafa'ifa *Muagututi'a*. *Tupua* was a descendant of Tafa'ifa *Salamasina's* son *Tapumanaia*-II. Hence the transition of the throne to the male descendants of the first Tafa'ifa *Salamasina*, as it was recorded in Tafa'ifa *Salamasina's* last wishes and requests where she declared that people should remember her son *Tapumanaia's* descendants, the male heirs of the title. And so Tafa'ifa *Muagututi'a* felt it was time to accomplish this promise, which had been made prophetically, with the adoption of *Tupuafuiavailili*, offspring of his wife's sister's grandson, the son of *Fuimaono*.

Tafa'ifa *Muagututi'a* proclaimed: *Tumua e, o le tama lea o Tupua o le a outou feagai, Fepulea'i o le a tautua. O Aiono o le a e fa'a'ele'elea Aua le tama lea. O le toeina lea o Taimalieutu, o le a te'a i Lupese'e e fai ma fofoga o le Vai e fofoga ia te ia upu o SaTuala auā upu o si o'u atali'i*—"Orator chiefs' authority the Tumua, the boy there, *Tupua,* will take my place, and you will serve him. My (biological) son *Fepulea'i* will serve the family and the title Tafa'ifa. High Chief *Aiono*, you will labor on the distribution of the fine mats on behalf of my son, Tafa'ifa *Tupua*. The old man there, Chief *Taimalieutu*, will go to Lupese'e (the sacred residence and meeting ground of *Muagututi'a* in Nofoali'i) to be the orator voice to the SaTuala mighty family, giving the oration on behalf of my son"—*my translation*.

Another important decree by a Tafa'ifa, concerning the transition of government authority, details the genealogical connections of *Muagututi'a* and *Tupua* to *Salamasina*. *Muagututi'a* is the descendant of Queen *Fofoaivao'ese* from a different father, and the elder child of Tafa'ifa *Salamasina*. And *Tupuafuiavailili* is the descendant of *Tapumanaia*-I, son of Lafai *Tonumaipe'a*. For five generations—from *Fofoaivao'ese, Taufau, Faumuinā, Fonotī* to *Muagututi'a*—the title had been carried by the female line (through *Fofoaivao'ese*). If, however, we include the generation of Tafa'ifa *Salamasina,* we have over 300 years during which the

TuiAtua and TuiA'ana PāPās had been carried by the female lines of the major families of Samoa. This serves as a reminder that the title, Tafa'ifa, means the PāPās of *Gatoa'itele* and *Vaetamasoaali'i* are also included.

The Mornings Commemorating the Arrival of Christianity

The Morning (*Taeao*) at Mataniufeagaimaleata in Sapapali'i village, Savai'i

This is another National Morning given the recognition of the Malae and Maota. The Morning at Mataniufeagaimaleata in Sapapali'i village, Savai'i, celebrates where Malietoa *Vaiinupõ* received and accepted the missionaries and Reverend John Williams of the London Missionary Society of London, England, with the Protestant Message of God and Salvation for the people of Samoa in 1830.

The Morning (*Taeao*) at Faleū and Utuagiagi at Manono Island

Another National Morning given the recognition of the Malae and Maota is the Morning at Faleū and Utuagiagi at Manono Island, which celebrates where Paramount Chief *Le'iatauaLesā Putetele* received and accepted the missionaries of the Methodist denomination, led by Reverend Peter Turner in 1835. New historical data shows that the Methodist denomination actually arrived in Samoa about three years before Reverend John Williams' arrival in 1830, brought by Tongan missionaries.

The Morning (*Taeao*) at Malaeola and the Gafuaga Sacred Meeting Place at Lealatele, Savai'i

The Morning (*Taeao*) at Malaeola and the Gafuaga sacred meeting place at Lealatele, Savai'i is another National Morning given the recognition of the Malae and Maota. This Morning celebrates where Paramount Chief *Tuala Talipope* and Chief *Salā* received and accepted the mission of the Roman Catholic church in 1845. The arrivals of other religious denominations are commemorated at the church organization level.

Tafa'ifa Malietoa *Vaiinupõ's* Final Proclamation to Abolish the Tafa'ifa title

This edict was to all of Samoa, pronounced to Fata and Maulolo and the 'Auimatagi at Malietoa *Vaiinupõ's* principal residence, the seat of government of his Tuamasaga district at Vaopipi, Malie, Upolu in 1842.

Tafa'ifa Malietoa *Vaiinupõ* said, "Proclaim to Samoa that, when I depart from this world, I will take the title Tafa'ifa with me down to my grave. The titles TuiAtua, TuiA'ana, Gatoa'itele, and Vaetamasoaali'i, and their respective PāPās, will be returned to their respective families and custodians. The Tafa'ifa (or King, a term learned from the Bible) of Samoa is the God and Father in Heaven. Samoa will be anchored in its foundation and cornerstone in God. The ministers of the gospel and churches will be given my salutation title, Sūsūga."

Officially there are only three authorities whose salutation title is "Sūsūga." The first and original is the Malietoa and his immediate family clan (children, villages, and district). That is, every title originating from his genealogy carries the same salutation, Sūsūga. The other two are:

- Fata and Maulolo and the Tuisamau council (Fata and Maulolo are the heads of the Tuisamau council) and
- the Tumua authority of Lufilufi village—any orators from Lufilufi will carry the Sūsūga salutation.

Interfacing with the (king) Tafa'ifa is sacred only to the Tafa'i, not the whole council. These two authorities received their respective salutation from the first Malietoa *Saveatuvaelua*, hence their having the same salutation as for the Malietoa.

The authorities of Leulumoega (seat of government of the A'ana district) and the six Pule authorities in Savai'i are given the salutations of Tofā (Orator) or Fetalaiga (which means to orate). These salutations were also proclaimed by the Malietoa or, in the case of Leulumoega, decreed by *Leatiogie*, father of first Malietoa *Saveatuvaelua*.

Tafa'ifa Malietoa *Vaiinupõ* also proclaimed that the missionary work would be supported hand-in-hand with and chaperoned by the Samoan chiefs' authority of Tumua, Pule, To'oto'o (the Manu'an Orators group) and Ponao'o (of American Samoa). It's generally an acid test for a chief, when addressing any of these authorities, because they were all decreed by paramount chiefs, mostly from Malietoa.

The significance of Malietoa *Vaiinupõ's* gifting his title to the ministry is that it facilitated engagement and interactions with the village chiefs, satisfying the requirement of Samoan customs for a chief titleholder or a guest with a significant title salutation, such as a European with a title, office, and appropriate salutations. The title is similar to the formal title, "Sir," in Great Britain. It's impolite and disrespectful for anyone without this title to be seated or to speak in the gathering of chiefs. Thus, in order to deliver the message of Christianity to the villages, the missionaries had to speak through a chief to the Chiefs Council group in the village. In fact they couldn't enter the house of Chiefs Council, let alone speak themselves with the chiefs.

For this reason, Malietoa *Vaiinupõ* used his children to help chaperone the initial delivery of the mission to his extended family, for example sending his nephew *Tuimaleali'ifano Sualauvi* to be the chaperone to the missionaries in Falelati village. Likewise, his son *Talavou* (a member of team that translated the Bible into the Samoan language) chaperoned the mission to the Manono Island district. His son *Moli* helped with the mission in the Tuamasaga district.

This procedure and proclamation were also carried out with the Methodist denomination with the Le'iatauaLesā in the Manono Island district, with the paramount chief giving his salutation of Afioga (meaning "venerated honor"). In the same way, the Catholic priests were given Afioga by *Tuala* and *Salā*, chiefs of Lealatele village in Savai'i.

The relationship between Malietoa *Vaiinupõ* and the missionaries became strained due the missionaries' unhappiness at the Malietoa's exercising too much authority over the management activities of the mission at their Sapapali'i headquarters. And so, the Tafa'ifa's feelings being hurt because he was being undermined and marginalized by the missionaries, he decided to relocate to his official, principal residence and seat of government to Malie, Upolu, at the tail end of his life.

This marked an emphasis on the separation of church and Samoan cultural authority, which has deep attitudinal consequences in the separation of the chief's cultural practices from the religious practices and management authority of the church. While there is mutual respect between church clerks and the chiefs' members of congress, there is still the desire with a few clerics to keep the chiefs at arm's length. Still, the reality is that Samoa's constitution evidences the fulfillment of Malietoa *Vaiinupõ's* last proclamation.

As a footnote: when Tafa'ifa Malietoa *Vaiinupõ* returned his official and principal residence and seat of government to the Malie and Afega villages, his son *Moli* and family also accompanied him, going to live in Malie where his humble burial ground (or *Tia*—the Samoan humble and crude version of a rock pyramid mausoleum) stands. *Moli* was attending the Malua LMS Seminary College at the time. It is here that Tafa'ifa Malietoa *Vaiinupõ* made his parting request to Fata and Maulolo and the 'Auimatagi to look after his son *Moli,* asking that *Moli* should follow him as the next Malietoa. The Tafa'ifa Malietoa's wish was fulfilled, and Malietoa *Moli* followed his father, the first and only son of Malietoa *Vaiinupõ* to graduate from Malua Seminary College.

Malietoa *Moli* likewise made his parting words of farewell to Fata and Maulolo and the 'Auimatagi, to remember his son *Laupepa* who was Afega village's first church minister at the time of Malietoa *Moli's* passing. Subsequently, *Laupepa* followed his father *Moli* as the Malietoa *Laupepa* who spearheaded the Island Country, with a few opposing paramount chiefs, through foreign colonizers to the founding of a nation.

The Morning (*Taeao*) at Gagamoe at Pagopago village, Tutuila, American Samoa

This is another National Morning, given the recognition of the Malae and Maota. The Morning at Gagamoe at Pagopago village, Tutuila, American Samoa, commemorates Tutuila becoming a protectorate of the United States of America in 1899.

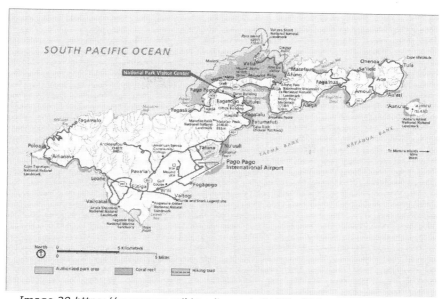

Image 20 https://commons.wikimedia.org/wiki/File:NPS_american-samoa-map.jpg U.S. National Park Service, restoration/cleanup by Matt Holly, Public domain, via Wikimedia Commons

Houses and Sacred Grounds

Sacred Grounds

Every village has a sacred ground. It's a part of the whole village—not a particular house, but a literal piece of property that is designated to be the meeting place for that village. When the village meets, they will come together at a place called *Malaepule* or *Malaeti'a*.

The meeting place is sacred because of the mythology behind it. The high chief doesn't just select a place and make it a sacred ground. There are always ancient stories that tell how the sacred ground was discovered and named. Often Samoans will use other ancient ground names to name additional meeting places for various villages, and the same names will be found elsewhere. But there is always folklore behind how the people arrived at that particular meeting place, and how this whole area was given a name.

In Samoa we say that there is no land that does not have a name. Can you believe that? If you're on the mountain, there's a name for it; a name for every place in Samoa. That's why Samoans say that in the whole island, from the land to the people and to the culture, everything has been "decreed." It has already been divided, defined, delineated, and destined.

This being the case, then, you might think learning Samoan culture should be very simple, for it's already been determined. But therein lies the challenge. How do you get the information from the family?

In any village, the house, even the posts of the house, the land, the meeting ground, and the high chief have all been given a name. In our Culture Dialog class, we explained this as we considered the case of High Chief *Alo*; the name of his house is *Fale Pule*.

In a lot of villages there are two different meeting grounds. One will be for the war party, and the other will be for the peace meeting; *malae a le manino*, and *malae a le aava*. *Aava* is where the word ava (or kava—the European English word for the ava plant) comes from. But there is also a different ava ceremony, as well as a different meeting ground, for war. And the seating

177

arrangement, which we will soon look at, is also different when it's time to deliberate for war. The high chief doesn't sit where he would normally sit, because now everyone is looking at the warriors; the *tulatoa*.

In the case, for example, of the district of Falealili, Atua, in a war convocation at the House of War (*Fale o Itu'au ma Alataua*) at Falepunaoa Malae, the two paramount warrior chiefs, *Te'o* and *Patea,* would occupy each end post facing each other in the maota seating arrangements. All other chiefs would be seated elsewhere in the maota. Paramount Chief *Manusamoa's* children and war warriors would take up their post positions in the maota—that is, *Le'avasa* and *Ma'aelopa*, *Lutu* and *Solosolo*, and *Tuiloma* and *Taitu'uga,* and the others who would constitute *Manusamoa's* war organization. The *Te'o* and *Patea* ava cups would be the only ones that would be called out by their cup names. For all the other chiefs' ava, the ava would be called out by their names, not by their respective ava cup titles—for example: *Lau Ava lea Lutu! Lau Ava lea Tuiloma! Lau Ava lea Tuatagaloa!*

The meeting to deliberate over war must occur, to prevent the loss of many lives. And before such deliberation, it would be important to have the ava ceremony.[lvii]

The Story of *Tagafa* and *Fatumanavaoupolu*

On many occasions, after war had been fought in Samoa, the decision to appoint a king would have to be made. And the bestowment of the throne would have to take place at the right location, or the people would go to war again.

Aumua *Tagafa* and his half-brother *Fatumanava o Upolu* (*Fatumanavaoupolu*) were sons of TuiAtua *Tologataua*, the son of TuiAtua *Fepulea'i* and *Utufa'asili* (daughter of Tagaloa *Funefe'ai*). They fought, contesting the title of TuiAtua. Aumua *Tagafa* defeated *Fatumanavaoupolu* with the assistance of the war machine of the orator mātua (elders), *Leifi* and *Tautoloitua*. Thus, Aumua *Tagafa* was appointed to the TuiAtua title. However...

Subsequently, Orator *Leifi* heard that the TuiAtua bestowment was held at the wrong sacred Malae, at Lufilufi, the Tumua authority. So they came back from Aleipata district and fought another battle, and this time Aumua *Tagafa* was defeated, and *Fatumanavaoupolu* was elected to the TuiAtua title.

Aumua *Tagafa* continued contesting the title, and he went back to Orators *Leifi* and *Tautoloitua* to present his case for the TuiAtua title and try to convince them. He was successful in his campaign and, again, *Leifi* and *Tautoloitua* helped Aumua *Tagafa* regain the TuiAtua title.

Thus *Fatumanavaoupolu* inherited the paramount Tagaloa title in Saluafata village and was also decreed the Sa'o Aumaga of the ava ceremony of the FaleAtua (the House of Atua) district.[lviii]

There is a genealogical relationship between the two sets of brothers in this story—the half-brothers Aumua *Tagafa* and *Fatumanavaoupolu*, and the orators *Leifi* and *Tautoloitua*—and blood is thicker than water. As mentioned, Aumua *Tagafa* and *Fatumanavaoupolu* were great-grandsons of Tagaloa *Funefe'ai* through their grandmother, *Utufa'asili* (from Tagaloa *Funefe'ai's* marriage to *Tauanu'nufagā*, daughter of *Tuliaupupu* of Letogo, Upolu.)[lix] Their mother, of the same name, was the daughter of *Va'afa'i*, of Tuna'i, in Tuamasaga, Upolu.

At the same time, Orator Chiefs *Leifi* and *Tautoloitua's* grandfather was also Tagaloa *Funefe'ai*, for Lady *Ulalemamae*, a descendant of *Tolufale*, married Tagaloa *Funefe'ai* (or, in another version of the stories, Tagaloa *Letula*) and bore two daughters, *Sinaauvale* and *Taupifagalau*. Lady *Sinaauvale* married TuiAtua *LeTaua* (or *Taua*) and gave birth to *Alei* and *Pata*, later called *Leifi* and *Tautoloitua*. Lady *Taupifagalau* married *Punaoa* (of Sapunaoa, a descendant of *Liliolelagi*) and bore the warrior *Manusamoa* and his sister *Tautiapagofie*.

The village of Sapunaoa is the seat of Samoa's "House of the Vanguard and Rearguard of War" (*Fale o Itu'au ma Alataua*), anchored by *Manusamoa* and his warriors. The House of War was brought over by the warriors *Leifi* and *Tautoloitua* (*Alei* and *Pata*), having been gifted and decreed to them by the TuiManu'a, and they thought it only appropriate that their cousin, Warrior *Manusamoa,* and the warriors *Le'avasa* and *Ma'aelopa* should be the custodians of it.[lx]

In the same decree from the TuiManu'a, *Leifi* and *Tautoloitua* also received a "post" of the Faleula (the residence) of

Tuimanu'a, and a "Tumua" authority was designated to them. Manu'an legend has it that High Chief Orator *Leiato* and the Safotulafai authority also received respective "post" designations of the TuiManu'a residence at this ceremonial occasion.

On their way home to the Atua district, *Leifi* and *Tautoloitua* stopped at Leone village in Tutuila; they received such wonderful hospitality from the orator Mātua chiefs, *Olo* and *LeOso*, that they reciprocated by gifting the Tumua title they had received from TuiManu'a to *Olo* and *LeOso*. Thus the salutation of *Olo* and *LeOso* of Leone is *Tamafa'aTumua*, or just *Tamamātua le Tumua, Olo ma LeOso*.

These same two orator chiefs, seekers of fortune and fame, went to Malietoa *Savea* and requested a Tumua authority from the Malietoa, arguing that they, TuiAtua *Tualemoso's* warrior sons *Tapuloa* and *Taputoa*, and TuiAtua *Tuanu'utele's* sons *Lagouta* and *Lagotai,* had all fought right alongside the Tuamasaga warriors during the Tongan War.[lxi] According to Tuamasaga legend, the decree noted that Malietoa *Saveatuvaelua* decreed to them his Tumua, the last Tumua, decreed from and by his father *Leatiogie*, and changed his authority to Laumua (capital or seat of origin of the Tumua). This was later acquired by *Fata* and *Maulolo* and the Tuisamau at their victory in the war over the PāPā of Gatoa'itele.

Leifi and *Tautoloitua* took the Tumua and decreed it to *Lufilufi* to guard the TuiAtua PāPā. In return, *Lufilufi* gifted to the two orators the "head" of a very large fish-catch they were carving out among the villagers at the time. The occasion of carving-out the fish evidenced decreeing the distribution of authority across the Atua district government, and the symbolism of the gifted fish-head is the privilege of head authority over Atua district and the proclamation of the TuiAtua title.

Thus we see how the Tagaloa *Funefe'ai's* genealogical connections with the TuiAtua clan continued to proliferate with the enterprise and ambition of these illustrious senior orator chiefs.

Fale and *Maota*

<u>House Design</u>

Samoan customs, protocols, and rituals center on the *Maota* (house of the high chief) or *Laoa* (house of the orator chief). And the structure of Samoan society is mirrored in the structure of the Samoan *fale* or house.

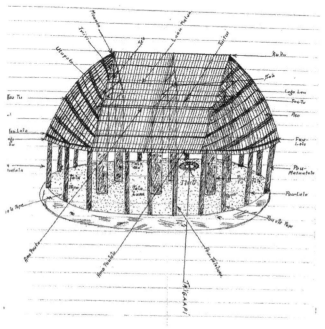

Image 21
https://commons.wikimedia.org/wiki/File:Samoan_fale_tele_architecture_diagra m_2.jpg Teo Tuvale [3], CC BY-SA 3.0
<https://creativecommons.org/licenses/by-sa/3.0>, via Wikimedia Commons

Samoan house design is simple—some would say primitive—and practical, open, and welcoming, as well as mobile and artistically pleasing to the eye. Architecturally, the circular design of the *fale* reflects the circular process of huddling in conversation and decision-making. This is quite unlike the Western square design that leads to huddling in corners, an idea completely opposed to Samoan meeting in the middle of the *maota*—the high chief's house—or the *laoa*—the orator chief's house.

The rooftop of the house evidences the heavenly direction of the gods, or God, as the supreme authority that sees and hears all the affairs being conducted and decreed within, while also providing shade and shelter from the sun and rain.

The openness of the *fale* is welcoming and lacks restrictions to entry or exit. Similarly, the open-arms hospitality and generosity of the Navigators are contagious to all who have experienced them.

The house-posts serve as pillars to equally carry and shoulder the burden of support of the ceiling and upper roofing of the *fale*. This is a collective approach, representing open and equal voice for discussions, deliberations, and decision-making within the family or village chiefs. Note, only the chiefs sit in the circle (see Seating Arrangements, page 191), because they are the ones representing the family's interests; collectivism is the mantra in the definition, delegation, and conduct of responsibility by the family members.

The ceiling structure is often described as being analogous to the various support groups of the family and or village. It is made of straight and easily-fastened wooden branches from a particular tree, similar to bamboo. Some villages use bamboo if it is plentiful.

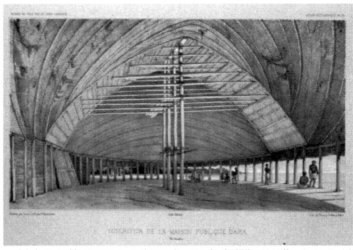

Image 22 https://commons.wikimedia.org/wiki/File:Urville-Apia-public.jpg
Interieur de la maison publique d'Apia [interior of the public house of Apia]. Ile Opoulou. In: "Voyage au pole sud et dans l'Oceanie ....." by the French ships ASTROLABE and ZELEE under the command of Dumont D'Urville, 1842

The *fale's* foundation is built on large boulders and groups of large-sized rocks, followed with smaller rocks on top, then pebbles, and filled with sand to get rid of any open pockets, with, finally, seashells as the topmost layer. The significance of the different layers is that they represent different aspects of the culture's layers, such as the natural separation of things, the dogmas of custom and formality, the family-centric dedication of responsibility and authority, the governance of all aspects of culture by the system of chiefdom, and the practice of oration as a way of perpetuating oral communication to sustain the culture and history of the people.

Samoan and Manu'an Houses

Samoans and Manu'ans have separate houses for different purposes, each called either by its purpose, or by the material—timber or tree—that is used for its construction. Interestingly, homes were built around the responsibilities of each member, so, for example, cooks lived near the kitchen or *umu* (oven). *Fale* is the common word for house, vis-a-vis *maota* for high chief's and *laoa* for the orator chief's residences.

Some examples of houses are:

- *faletunoa* a polite term for the cooking house in the presence of the high chief (from *fale*, meaning house, and *tunoa,* for cooking)
- *faleo'o* a casual resting house (from *fale* and *o'o* for laying around or resting)
- *faleafolau* longhouses, used to accommodate the size of the double-hulled canoe (the *fale* for the *afolau* vessel) and used for family meetings due to their large capacity
- *faletofā* the high chief's sleeping house (from the "high chief word" for sleep—not to be confused with maota, which is the meeting residence. For example, you cannot say to someone who is not a high chief, not even to an orator chief, to come in to your *faletofā*. For the formal name of the sleeping residence of Tuimanu'a, and subsequently of other monarch titles, would be given the same name for their sleeping *faletofā*)

- *fale'ulu* meaning a house, *fale*, made of the *'ulu*, breadfruit tree, which is very popular for building houses because of its strength and flexibility; also it withstands termites, humidity, and monsoon weather. It is the best house-building material
- *faleolemea*—a house made of the *'olemea* tree
- *falemao*—a house made of the *mao* tree
- *falesae*—a house made of trees whose skins have removed, therefore a very beautiful house
- *falemaa*—a spirit-demon house, made of *maa* stones for the spirit, as in the legend of *So'oialo* and the boy raised by a demon spirit in a house built into the rock (*falepouma'a*). In this story, the boy receives his name *Momoemaaitu*, meaning "sleeping with the demons"
- *falelauasi* is literally a crude mausoleum, complete with a full mini version of a house, of profound significance for its sacredness to a departed chief. It is made from the leaves of the *asi* tree, and includes the *tia*, a rock pyramid, for the paramount chief version of a mausoleum. Some have been noted to be the size of a large *maota*. The building of these rock pyramid mausoleums often commanded participation of the whole district and complete clan, in hauling the rocks from across the island.

So, the residence for the high chief (*Ali'i*) is the *maota,* and the *faletofā* is the sleeping house. *Laoa* is the orator's house. And *fale* is the house for ordinary people.

From Shelter to House to Identity

When did a shelter become such a well-designed house? The answer turns out to lie in the story of the human "hunter-gatherer's" migration and metamorphosis, in the exhausting and yet indefatigable chase after food supplies across the earth's landscapes, and, in the case of a seafaring people, across the oceans and rivers.

Historians and anthropologists all agree that hunter-gatherers first lived in caves around 20,000 B.C.[lxii] Then a half-shelter, built from tree branches, leaves, ferns, and tree bark, with an open side, became common when crossing open desert landscapes.

Then the invention of spinning and weaving and the use of animal fur and skins, around 6000 B.C., led directly to the creation of tents.

The Christian Bible, of course, is an example—from all history books available to the layman—that describes in detail the form and concept of abodes used during the period of Abraham and the Israelites in the land of Canaan. The Hebrews dwelt in tents way before their sojourn in Egypt (Hebrews 11:9), while the Canaanites and the Assyrians were the builders of cities, according to Scripture. Tents were used, not only as places of recreation in the evening, but also sometimes as sleeping places at night (1 Samuel 9:25; 1 Samuel 9:26; Daniel 4:29; Job 27:18; Proverbs 21:9), and even as places of devotion (Jeremiah 19:13). The Scriptures also indicate that, throughout their exodus from Egypt across the Sinai desert, the Israelites were living in tents. And the Children of Israel's migratory journey— using tents as opposed to permanent buildings, then settling in Judah and Jerusalem when they started to build towns and cities—was easily understood by Samoans, as the Samoan house can be disassembled, like a tent, into four sections, the two ends and the two sides being carried separately to each new location.

2 Samuel 11:2 shows the Israelites' move from temporary abodes to more concrete, permanent structures. It illustrates the evolution of society toward building towns, cities, and metropolises. As I mentioned in *Navigators Quest for a Kingdom in Polynesia*, this evolution was driven by the dawn of agriculture that required a stationary population as opposed to one constantly moving, chasing the hunt, and pitching tents.

This change was then followed by the building of centralized places for worship. I once saw a TV program that showed the ancient Celts' primitive abodes and their original architecture which mirrored the structure of tents, except that it was built on stones and rocks. The design incorporated spiritual worship, reminding me of Samoan house design, leading me to believe these concepts are not born in isolation but relate to the whole issue of cultural diffusion—of boat design, navigational tools, knowledge, weaponry, etc.

This same process of settling into a central village and district happened here, where the district *malae* is the place where major district convocations are held. So Samoans easily understood Biblical accounts of the journey of the Israelites and their progress—how, from the time of Abraham to the time when Joseph was sold to Egypt, they were a nomadic people. The Bible is very clear on it, and Samoans identified with the migratory nature of the appointed People of God.

As human migration continued snaking through the Asian continent to Southeast Asia and the Malay and Indonesian Archipelagos, shelters developed and changed accordingly, based both on the environment and on the influence of other cultures and societies encountered in their sojourn. *National Geographic Concise History of The World: An Illustrated Timeline* by Neil Kagan offers a timeline for when many societies began to erect bigger houses and buildings—such as the mighty city of Jericho around 8,000 B.C. and Catal Huyuk around 4,000 B.C.[lxiii]

National Geographic's online articles tell how the buildings and architectural designs of cities like Mohenjo Daro and Harappa in Pakistan, dated to around 2,500 B.C., evidence skills in urban planning with reverence for the control of water and respect for the environment—the area had a history of flooding due to drainage from the Indus River during the monsoon seasons.[lxiv]

Thus, by the time the seafaring people arrived in the Asian archipelago, their idea of shelter had long been honed to mean a house, with the concept of home as a place of identity. Their next 10,000 to 13,000 years in the Asian archipelago is the period when the Polynesians, as members of the Austronesian language family, began to move out into the Malay and Indonesian archipelagos and occupied those islands, some time after the arrival of Malayans on the Southeast Asian mainland.

Austronesian Houses: Perspectives on Domestic Designs for Living

A well-represented study by the Department of Anthropology of the Australian National University, Canberra, Australia, in association with the Comparative Austronesian Project, Research School of Pacific Studies,[lxv] included Jennifer Alexander's review of the Lahanan longhouse on Borneo, noting how the design relates to:

- Social status
- Social activities
- Ritual practice
- Domestic space as it relates to patrilineal and matrilineal residence designs

Another author, Clifford Sather, provided an additional perspective on the Iban longhouse from Saribas Iban along the Paku River in the lower second Division of Sarawak. He provided a detailed view of how the arrangement of house-posts within a defined structure provides a physical representation of order and origin.

Research author Cecilia Ng's paper on the other hand—part of her PhD dissertation—is concerned with principles of domestic spatial organization among the Minangkabau of Sumatra's longhouse. And researchers at Nagari Kotonan Gadang, working in the district of Lima Puluh Kota in West Sumatra, examined the usage of space within the longhouse. They concluded that houses are associated more with women, who act as a "source" of continuity in society, in contrast to men, who act more as "agents" of continuity. While men's lives derive from a series of outward movements, women's lives derive from movement within the house. Thus generations of women provide continuity to the family lineage within the house. And the form of the house illustrates the definitions of male and female identity.

The parallels are compelling between the architectural structure, design considerations, and intrinsic purpose—as seen in this limited sample of Malay Austronesian houses—and the *maota* and *laoa* of Samoa and Manu'a. And so, throughout this work, I will labor to show that the development of a people's culture is so integrated, so cohesively bound into one single human system, that it can only be fully comprehended when viewed in its totality. The development of the Navigators' culture must be understood in conjunction with its language, history, ancient origin, oral mythology, migration paths and destinations, genetics, and their whole way of life.

So we find that the Navigators' house designs differ slightly, depending on the type of house being built. The house's design incorporates all aspect of the people's culture. And everything is driven by the culture, from architectural design, building materials, functional purpose, and even to the appointment of seating arrangements.

The Wooing of the Princess

House-building is such an integral part of culture that it becomes part of the protocol for a chief or a warrior to ask a lady's hand in marriage; he has to actually build for himself, and then move into, a house on her parents' property, so as to effectively court her on a daily basis. He would take his *aumaga* (servants) with him, to cater to himself and the lady's family. This also meant doing the food planting, harvesting, preparation, and serving of food to the family. In essence, he would have practically relocated to his new house, in order to woo the lady.

The lady would be someone with princess standing in the family and village. She would, of course, be the daughter of an important chief, and part of the major family genealogy of Samoa and Manu'a. Such daughters—of high-ranking chiefs or warriors or orator chiefs—are referred to as princesses because, culturally speaking, they are the princesses of their family. Thus their proper salutation is Princess.

It was not unusual to have two or more chiefs courting a princess at the same time. The chief's first task was to construct a good speech or oration and deliver it to the parents; then, if they liked you, they would present it to the princess. The chief wooing the princess would be prepared to stay as long as it took to get an answer from her. The longer it took for her to make up her mind, the better the chance she would agree.

A princess could be attractive to many paramount chiefs and warriors for many reasons: title, family name, land ownership, and, of course, beauty. Often, because of this, the suitor might offer "the world" to the princess' parents and family. Legends often allude to the limited number of women present in the early part of Samoan and Manu'an history. So, when all the paramount chiefs heard of a princess being available, anywhere in the archipelago, they would immediately sojourn with her family to woo her. This ritual shows evidence of the male abandoning the family and choosing to live where his future wife's family resides. Though, obviously, the unsuccessful proposer would return home empty-handed.

As one might deduce, this multi-male courtship arrangement meant it was quite natural that a princess would be married multiple times, but not simultaneously. That is why connections are made via the genealogy of the same princess in various different family genealogies. It should be noted that this practice, and this marriage protocol, is a residual custom from the matrilineal and matrilocal culture of Polynesia. The practice was made severely *tapu* by the missionaries, starting in 1830.

When looking at the genealogies of the princess names later, one would immediately note the authority vested in women and, of course, the remnants of the matrilineal and matrilocal society structure: *LeTelesā*, *Valasi*, *Iliganoa*, *Sina*, *Talaleomalie*, *Ulalemamae*, *Lelāpueisalele*, *Falenaoti*, *Fuatino*, *Tapuisalaia*, *Maupenei*, *Poto Taumulimalei'a*, *Oilau* and others. We have already met several of these names in this book.

Samoan and Manu'an history is full of folklore and anecdotes about paramount chiefs' marriage proposals. The higher the princess' lineage, the greater would be the number of suitors from across the islands, including even the King of Toga, TuiFiji, TuiManu'a, and other paramount ranking chiefs.

LeTelesā, daughter of High Chief *Faumuinā* of Faleata in A.D.1470-1530, had several successful suitors including Tagaloa *Fa'aofonu'u*, *La'ululolopo*, *Taulapapa* (nephew of Malietoa *Taulapapa*), and So'oialo *Momoemaaitu*. But again, this was one of the last few practices and rituals of the old matrilineal and matrilocal culture of Samoans and Manu'ans. Now, the remnants of the matriarchal culture of the Navigators of the East Pacific Ocean have evolved into the current bi-lineal culture.

And so we see, the more you drink water from the ancient well of the Navigators, the more you are thirsty for more; the earth cannot quench its thirst with intermittent rain.

Seating Arrangements

The structure of the Samoan house is mirrored in the structure of seating arrangements and formalities. Generally, village council meeting or convocations are held at the village mayor's residence, which is usually an orator chief's *laoa*. The high chiefs and orators, with their different levels of responsibility, are the authorities decreed and appointed by the paramount high chief and the village Chiefs Council. Each has been assigned a seat in the *maota* or *laoa*.

The traditional *Fale Samoa* (the Samoan house) has designated seats near each house-post which are allocated to the paramount chief and his children, the talking chief (i.e. the orator chief), the *Sa'o Tama'ita'i* (or the *Oilau* who is also known as *Sa'o Galua*—remember, we have already seen some of these names, but here they are titles), and others with authority. Among the high officials, the *aumaga* (the men servants who will soon be chiefs themselves) and the orators also sit in the *Fale Samoa*.

Every title has its specific seat in the *Fale Samoa*. The paramount chief's seat may not be taken by anyone else, whether the paramount chief is there or is not. To sit in that seat, you must obtain the title of paramount chief.

The talking chief is the same as the orator chief. It is a literal translation of the Samoan title *Tulafale* (he who stands outside the *fale* and orates) or *Fetalaiga* (speech).

Quite often a person might be ridiculed for not understanding this very complex seating arrangement and its purpose, which defines a family's activities or role in the village. For each family member's role is defined and distinct.

Positions and Titles

The (oval) house is divided into to four sections—the right rounded corner, the left rounded corner, the front side, and the back side, with steps at the front. The high chiefs' seats are assigned to both rounded corners of the house, going from the right to the left of the house. Orator chiefs are assigned to seats at the front and back of the house.

The simplest way to understand the hierarchy of the village organizational structure is to locate the seating positions of the village chiefs. This is important, in order to know who's who in the seating arrangements, particularly if you are not sure of the hierarchy. These seating arrangements are very particular; you don't just sit anywhere. As a guest, you would ask the village talking chief, or ask the people who understand the structure of the village, which post is allocated for guests.

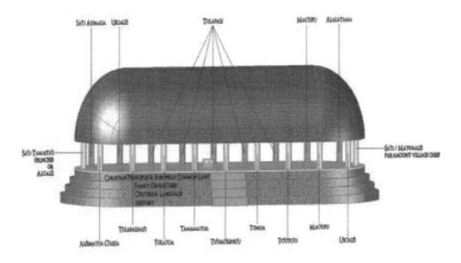

Image 23 drawn to scale for the author by a Samoan architect

Look Right

First, one should look to the far-right corners and identify the *Sa'o*, the head paramount chief of the village. There may be more high chiefs, and we would also use the "paramountcy" salutation for them, but they are not to be confused with the head of the village—they have their own designated seating positions.

Once you have located the paramount high chief of the village, then you can go from left to right, remembering that the positions are assigned to high chiefs, with different title designations that should have been studied before the visitors arrived.

For example, there is the *Alalatama* title for sons of the paramount village chief—in some cases the paramount village chief might relinquish authority to them. In the diagram, the *Alalatama* sit on the *Sa'o's* right, and so further toward the back of the house. In my village of Afega, Tuamasaga, this title refers to Paramount Chief *Savea* and *Ututa'aloga*. If the *Matuaali'i Manu'aifua* is not present, the *Alalatama* would take the house-post of the *Sa'o* and the opposite post, where the *Sa'o Tama'ita'i* sits, because they share the head title paramountcy. (We don't have a *Sa'o*, in the strictest sense of the word, but we have a paramount "head chief" *Manu'aifua* followed by his prince sons, *Savea* and *Ututa'aloga*; their sister is *Tu'uamaleulua'iali'i* who married TuiA'ana TuiAtua *Faumuinā* and bore "Queen" TuiA'ana *Samalaulu*. Also we don't have a reigning *Sa'o Tama'ita'i*.)

Returning to the diagram, there is the *Ma'oupū* title, the high chief designation for sons of a sister or daughter of the paramount village chief. Their seats are next to the *Alalatama* in the diagram.

The *Usoali'i* title designates other fraternal brothers of the paramount chiefs of the village—of the paramount village chief or of paramount chiefs who reigned in the past. In the diagram, these are seated on the *Sa'o's* left, toward the front of the house.

Keeping in mind the ancient history of these villages, we can appreciate the division of village structure and authority that has evolved over a long time. Thus, some titles date back to different heads of the family's leadership and their respective designations over the evolving history of the village.

Look Left

If we look to the opposite round corner of the house (on the left of the image), we can locate the post directly opposite to that of the *Sa'o* or village chief. This post is allocated to the *Sa'o Tama'ita'i*, or to the fraternal or biological brother chiefs of the village *Sa'o*. In some cases, these fraternal brothers share authority with the *Sa'o*, to manage the village affairs.

The *Taupou* (or, using her title *Sa'o Tama'ita'i*) has responsibility to serve the ava. The *Taupou* of the Malietoa title is *To'oa*, and in Sapapali'i she is known as the *Sa'o Galua*—a title which means the second head of the family. When the *Sa'o Galua*

193

title is bestowed on her, she removes herself from the ava task, and the family will, therefore, designate a new *Taupou* to take on the responsibility of the ava.

The prince titleholder, the *Aloaliʻi* of the village, or son of the *Saʻo* of the village, also sits here. The importance of this post designation is that whoever occupies this post during a meeting will drink the last (*moto*) or concluding ava cup of the ceremony. The protocol for the meeting closure, or *e moto i ai le ʻAva*, calls for a son of a "king" or his descendant.

Once the occupants of this house-post have been located, going from right to left one will find other fraternal brothers, *Usoaliʻi*, and the *Saʻo Aumaga* (labelled toward the back of the house in the diagram). The *Saʻo* (or head) of the *Aumaga* is a title equivalent to the *Saʻo Tamaʻitaʻi*. The *Aumaga* are the young warriors who serve the Chief's Council. And the title designation for the *Saʻo Aumaga* names a son of the paramount village chief or of the original founder (or head) of the village, district, clan, or dynasty. You can expect to see the title name of a son of a monarch—like Fonotī, Muagututiʻa, Galumalemana, Tupua, and (for the Malietoa) Laʻauli. For example, in my village Afega, in Tuamasaga, Upolu, our *Saʻo Aumaga* title is Laʻauli, for the son of Malietoa *Uitualagi* and father of *Gatoaʻitele*.

Other high chief titles are found like *Maʻoupū*, *Matuaaliʻi*, the elder high chiefs, *Alalamatuatala*, other prince titles like *Alalatama*, *ʻAuimatua Ofana*, or *Aliʻimatua Ofana*, high chief elder of the sacred malae and residence of the village dynasty.

At the Front

At the front of the house are posts that would be assigned to the various classes of orator chiefs and their respective title designations, such as the orator categories *Tumua*, *Laumua* (capital or seat of origin of the *Tumua*), and *Pule* authority. And yes, a very powerful post, in any village, is at the front. This is not to say the "eyewitness" sitting there has the greatest power though. There can also be very powerful people sitting at the back.

Posts here are assigned to the senior (*Tuʻua*) and elder (*Mātua*) titles of the village council. Again, their designations are *Tuʻua*, the head orator chief leading the village council, and

Mātua, the elder titles of the village or clan. The *Tu'ua* is appointed by the village Orator Chiefs Council. The *Mātua* is a title decreed from the family or clan's paramount chief.

For example, my salutation is *Sūsūga* (orator) *Laumua Fata ma Maulolo*. One of the six Pule in Savai'i would be addressed as *Fetalaiga* (orator) *Pule Safotulafai LeTufuga ma Leaula*. Likewise, there are *Sūsūga* (orators) *Tumua Lufilufi Fa'amatuainu* and twelve other orator chiefs. Other senior orator designations include *Tamamātua*, which is equivalent to *Tumua* and *Pule* in Tutuila, and *To'oto'o*, an exclusively Manu'an orator title in same class as *Tumua* and *Pule*. Posts for these titles are at the front in the illustration.

Then there are a few orator chiefs who are also high chiefs and are called *Tulafale-ali'i* (talking high chief). These include, for example, *Fata* and *Maulolo*; *Alipia* of Leulumoega village; *Le'iato* of Faga'itua, Tutuila, *Olo* and *Oso* of Leone, Tutuila; *Savea* and *Le'aeno* of Faganeanea, Matu'u, Tutuila; and a few others. Also the *Tulatoa* title is a special designation for ancient orator warrior (*Toa*) chiefs: for instance, Malietoa Paramount Warrior Chief (*malie*, meaning well-done or satisfies, *toa*, meaning warrior or hero). These are founders of villages, districts, and dynasties.

Additionally, posts at the front of the house would be allocated to the orator chiefs of the visiting village delegation. This is arranged from the middle, where the leading orator sits. To the right and left of him are the rest of the delegates. High chiefs of the visiting delegation are directed to seats at the rounded corner of the house opposite from the *Sa'o* of village, following a similar standard seating arrangement to the above. The occupants of this rounded corner would make room for the seating of the visitors' paramount chief. So, for example, if the visiting delegation included a paramount *Sa'o* of their village, he or she would sit opposite the receiving village's paramount *Sa'o*. In the diagram, he or she would sit at the post marked *Sa'o Tama'ita'i*.

At the Back

Finally, the fourth section of the house is the back, occupied by the talking or orchestrator chiefs (*Tulafale*) and the *aumaga* warriors with the wooden ava bowl. Again, seating starts at the center going to right and to left based on service, seniority, and protocol in the village meeting.

The administrators of the Chiefs Council affairs and protocols are seated here, as we might see in the proverbial fish skeleton metaphor—"The fish has many bones, and sometime too many to count, but each bone performs a critical function to the life and survival of the fish." Remember, the major parts of the fish—such as the head, gills, backbone, rib bones and tail fin or caudal fin— must all work in unison to allow the fish to swim. So these are the orators orchestrating the meeting and protocols of the ceremony. They will orchestrate the gathering, including the food and the ava. This is their duty. When they look to the side, they are facing eye-to-eye with the chiefs. The chiefs will let them know what the next item on the agenda will be. They are the orator chiefs.

The back of the house is where the ava is prepared before being carried to the front. The *aumaga*, which consists of young men, prepares and serves the food for the high chief and the rest of the authorities. As the high chief and other officials are meeting, the *aumaga* are served by the children. This is done to reinforce the tradition through generations.

The *aumaga* are the sons of chiefs, and the *aualuma*, wives of the young men involved in *aumaga*, are the daughters of chiefs. We have seen that the leader of the *aumaga*, the *Sa'o Aumaga*, is the son of the paramount chief and sits on the rounded left side of the house, toward the back.

When the *aumagas* have their own meetings, in their own house, their designated posts are the same as those of their fathers.

Entering the House

The importance of viewing the house from the front is to know which is the front and back. The front is where the ceremonial activities will be conducted. And the paramount chief sits at the head post, to the right from the front. It is important not to confuse the right and left sides of the house or forget where the paramount village chief sits.

When entering the house, from the front, one must immediately look to the right and greet the paramount village chief by saying *tulou, tulou, tulouna lava* meaning, for example, "excuse, excuse and pardon us profusely for disrupting the sacred residence of *Malaepule* (the meeting ground of Fagasā village) and *Falelupe* (High Chief *Alo's* residence)." You would say this as you bow and approach your seating position.

Everything in Samoan culture is defined—from seating arrangements in the house to the words to speak in the chief's house. The paramount chief is designated to sit at the head post. (In most villages there's only one head.) And every section of the house has its designated purpose. All the high chiefs, including the *Sa'o*, sit at the front. And the ava is prepared at the back.

When you go to Samoa, you will see this within any meeting structure; no matter the location, you will see this same structure. Even within a church setting, you will see this exact structure, with the additional inclusion of the minister. The rest of the chiefs will work out the seating arrangement, within the church setting, by locating the seating position of the paramount chief and head reverend. Then they seat themselves accordingly.

At night you will find this in the family worship tradition. In the evening, when the sun sets, the village bell will ring to begin worship. Then the aumaga will stop any traffic going in and out of the village.

A Personal Anecdote

So, every chief title has a designated seating-post. You must know the designation of your family's seating arrangement. It's quite embarrassing when you are questioned on this particular arrangement and you have no response.

There was an occurrence in my sister village, when I was not in attendance. When the story was told to me, I was in total shock and disbelief. This story relates to my village Afega, in Tuamasaga, Upolu, in around 2004. Our village Chiefs Council called a meeting with our sister village Tuna'i—our next-door neighbor. Historically, since ancient times, the two villages were really only one village, until the mid-1970s when, for reasons of practical management due to their size and growth, they agreed to split into two independent villages.

The occasion of this anecdote was a scheduled joint meeting with Tuana'i village. Afega was the visiting village. And when the

Afega Chiefs Council arrived, they immediately took up their seats at the respective seating posts allocated to the Tuna'i village Chiefs Council, and of course the *Sa'o* post of *Saena*. What happened illustrates the technical seating protocol that shows evidence of respect, good etiquette, cultural compliance, and good leadership.

While *Sa'o Saena's* seating post was available, the opposite post from him was occupied by the wrong title chief. In this case, it was occupied by a Ma'oupū title, which is not in compliance to our combined village protocols. The only title that can face the *Sa'o Saena* is Paramount Chief *Manu'aifua*, and if Chief *Manu'aifua* is not present the post is left open.

This is why, when Paramount *Sa'o Saena* came and saw, from the outside before entering the maota, that a Ma'oupū title-holder was seated at the opposite post, he told him, in a didactical way, to "Get off the seat. Who instructed you on the protocol and etiquette of the village?" And he started to scold the leadership, including *Fata* and *Maulolo* and the rest of the Chiefs Council. For the culture is very precise and unforgiving, and mistakes must be corrected immediately. So that was a learning experience.

Subsequent to this meeting, when our village delegation returned to the village, they immediately held a meeting to discuss the infraction. The council not only reprimanded the leadership, but also assessed punitive fines to the Tu'ua (*Fata* and *Maulolo* and *Taliaoa*). More important than the fines was the embarrassment of being lectured and schooled by a paramount chief. It's often said, by Samoan chiefs, that if anyone needs to know the truth of Samoan culture, history, and language, they should go ask a Tumua or Laumua and Pule authority, like the Afega.

The unfortunate thing here is that the Ma'oupū chief who sat at the wrong post left the meeting before Chief *Saena* finished his lecture, and he never again attended any more village meetings. Two weeks later, he emigrated to New Zealand to live with his children and never returned to Samoa, and he died there.

The Story of High Chief *Saena* and Afega Village

The hierarchical structure of my village of Afega, before the split, began in history: After Malietoa *La'auli* decreed his daughter *Gatoa'itele* to be the paramount chief of *Fata* and *Maulolo* and the Tuisamau, around A.D.1410-1420, nothing changed until the passing of Paramount Chief *Gatoa'itele* around the mid-1500s. After *Gatoa'itele*, *Fata* and *Maulolo* needed a paramount chief, for they now didn't have one of their own. So they went to Paramount Chief *Saena*, next door in Tuana'i village, and asked him to give them one of his sons to be their paramount chief.

We should remember, orators without a paramount chief have no kingdom. Remember the tales of the orator chiefs *Ape* and *Tutuila*, when they had to ask for LeTagaloa *Fa'aofonu'u's* son *Selaginatõ* to be their paramount chief (see the story of *Vaetamasoaali'i*, page 67).

High Chief *Saena* told *Fata* and *Maulolo* to take the firstborn, and make his first name a chief title, *Manu'aifua*. So he became their first paramount chief since *Gatoa'itele*. But why did *Fata* and *Maulolo* go to *Saena* to ask for a chief? They went because *Saena* was a descendant of the *Gatoa'itele* lineage through his mother *Sinalemanaui*, sister of Malietoa *Taulapapa* (the one who went to *Nafanua* to ask for a PāPā but was too late). The mother of *Sinalemanaui* and Malietoa *Taulapapa* was the daughter of TuiA'ana *Tamālelagi*, an older sister to *Salamasina*. Then *Saenafaigā* was designated by his uncle, Malietoa *Taulapapa,* to go to Tuna'i village to be the prince, to interface with *Fata* and *Maulolo*, and to represent the Gatoa'itele genealogy in the government of the Tuisamau (which covers Afega, Tuana'i, Vaimauga, and Siumu).

So, Paramount Chief *Manu'aifua* is a son of Paramount Chief *Saena*, and *Saena* represents the Gatoa'itele lineage in Afega. Therefore, Paramount Chief *Saena* maintains an elder paramount chief status in the hierarchical structure of the villages of Afega and Tuana'i, with his appointment decreed by Malietoa *Taulapapa*. For example, in a joint session, where all the high chiefs are presiding, the first ava cup goes to *Saena*, and the last cup, to close the ava ceremony, goes to Paramount Chief

Manu'aifua, seated across the room, opposite from Chief *Saena*. In the earlier explanation of seating arrangements, this would be the seat designated for the *Sa'o Tama'ita'i* or the *Aloali'i* when there is no (elder) *Mātua Manu'aifua* present, the exception being if one or both of the paramount *Alalatama* are present. Also, in a joint session, Paramount Chief *Saena* is the only chief who can deliver a response to an oration of *Fata* and *Maulolo*.

Fagasā Village: Culture Dialog Role-Play

The Importance of Identity

The Culture Dialog class were curious to learn from experience, by seeing and feeling the sacred circle process. But first, I told them, in any venture, you must know who you are. To define yourself as a person, you must acknowledge yourself, your family, and your extended family, that which has now been transformed into the village and into a district. Then you can go anywhere in the world and know who you are, by knowing this information.

The question is: do you know who you are? Can you answer that when someone asks you? The hope for participants in the Culture Dialog was that the students would retain enough information from the class to research and document exactly who they were and where they came from—information that could then be passed to the next generation. The class would function much like the elders who, during the evening hours, would call upon the family so they could pass on the family genealogy to the next generation.[lxvi]

For example, when there are court hearings to protest a chief title, the judge will give you the opportunity to explain your side of the story, and you will begin to recite your genealogy. The judge may ask the name of your grandfather and great grandfather, or may even, on purpose, ask questions that cause you confusion, to make sure that you're not being deceitful. In some cases, they may ask you for the Taupou name for your chief title—if you stutter in confusion, that could jeopardize your chances of winning your protest.

The judge may also ask the seating designations of your chief titles and, if there is no reply, it could cause major devastation. These small particulars may seem insignificant, but they are of extreme importance when it comes to a court decision.

It's easy to claim a family, but you must remember that the family is well-defined. Remember that it starts with you, your family, and then your village. And it ultimately leads into the *maota* or the *laoa* that governs the village affairs and defines the family and village activities.

You must understand where your titleholder sits in the circle of chiefs. And you must remember, in the final analysis, these people are all your family.[lxvii] So first you should picture, in your mind, your title and your family, and then, if you know your history, you will know where everyone sits. And so, when you look at the house and seating structure, common to all Samoa and Manu'a, you will see that we can reduce the whole country into this metaphor of a house.

Preparing to Role-Play

So now we were ready to imagine a village council meeting together. We planned to play out the seating arrangements and protocols in our Culture Dialog process, and I asked a friend to help out in the class. My friend, Paramount Tumua Orator Chief Fa'amatuainu Vasaoāiga Jones Iakopo Tu'ufuli from Lufilufi, the seat of government of Atua, Upolu, now lived in Southern California. His late father was a titleholder of Paramount Orator Mātua Chief Savea, one of the two orator Mātua chiefs (Savea and Leaeno) of Matu'u and Faganeanea villages, in Itu'au district, that are the "Senior Speakers" (*Tamamātua* or orators) on behalf of all the Ma'oupū in Tutuila. Thus, I solicited his assistance.

Fa'amatuainu Jones Iakopo Tu'ufuli acted the role of orator chief in our sessions where we practiced village ceremonial protocols, such as the convocation of a village council meeting, the serving of the ava ceremony, and the welcome of a delegation from another village to discuss district property rights and boundaries.

One Family, *Feoi*

Remembering the seating arrangements described earlier, we considered, as a group, the importance of seats and titles. For example:

- *Sa'o,* the high chief: You would never want to disrespect anyone by referring to them with the wrong title. You would not refer to the talking chief with the high chief's title. And to the high chief, who is the *Sa'o,* you could not just say "High Chief." You would have to refer to him, for example, as "the high chief *Saʻo* from the village of Alo."

- *Aloaliʻi,* the prince: In the same way, you must refer to the prince with his title—for example, Aloaliʻi Tupua. The title *Aliʻi o aiga* means the eldest child, so whenever you hear *Aliʻi o aiga*, you know that this the oldest in the family. (If the king does not have a son, the title does not exist. But when he has a son, the son has this title—it's the royal genealogy and it does not change.)
- *Usoaliʻi,* the fraternal brothers: For example, *Sūsū mai Tautama ma Tupua*.

At one time, the whole group seated in the maota was actually one family. We were all brothers and sisters at one point. So I told them a Samoan word, *feoi*. *Feoi* means the genealogical members of the family. So, we are all genealogical family members. We are all *feoi* of the *Alo, Tupua, Tuinei, Salanoa, Tago, Soliai, Fuimaono, Tautama,* and others of Fagasā village district. *Feoi ole aiga* means that we are all brothers and sisters. Even the person who sits in the back has equal rights to a title, for the family could will their designation to the younger brother before the eldest, and the eldest would have to render his respect because this was the will of the family.

Fagasā Village

Many of the participants of the Culture Dialog, which led to this book, were descendants from the village and district of Fagasā. So I chose the village of Fagasā as an example where we could discuss salutations, village Chiefs Council seating arrangements, and general etiquette and protocols. The idea was to make the discussion more relevant to the group members, for they understood their own family and ancestral background. It's much easier for a participant to understand when they hear about their own family titles, village, and ancestry—their own background—rather than hearing about another village unrelated to them.

I could have used my own village, Afega, to illustrate the Chiefs Council seating designation and protocols, but no one would have related to it except me. Instead, because Fagasā is a real village, and the dialog participants could relate to it, it made the example real for the dialog.

Apology for Any Error in Our Interpretation of Fagasā Village Salutations

But first, before telling readers about Fagasā village, I must apologize for any errors in our interpretations of Fagasā village salutations:

To Fagasā o Itu'au ma Nofoa.

Le Pa'ia maualuga o Malaepule ma Malaeti'a o le afioaga o lo'o Afifio ai le To'afia o Ali'i. O lo'o Sūsū ai le Mātua ma Usoali'i. O lo'o alala ai lo ou tou To'afa o Tulafale ma le Lauti na Laulelei ma upu ia te oe Itu'au ma le Nofoali'i. Ia, laga ia le mulipapaga ae ou sua le tuli i muliaō ae tu'u le tuli o mulianõ, auā le foaga o lo'o lalovaoa mai i'i ma õ. Ia, o Samoa o le fue lavelave, o le i'a iviivia, ae tau ia na ou lafo fa'aaufala le falalafo aua Samoa o le atunu'nu na tofi mai le lagi. Tulou, tulou, tuloulava. Ou te fa'amaualalo atu i lo ou tou Nu'u Pa'ia on ua matou fagota i le sao i ou Pa'ia tulutulu i tao lea ua ma'ea ona ta'i ona aō. Ua matou sagolegole ai e pei o le igoa o le nu'u i i le Alataua, Savai'i. Ona o le sailiga o se malamalama ma se fiailoa o mataupu Fa'aSamoa i o na talafa'asolopito ma lana agaifanu auā outou alo ma fanau mo nei ma ataeao. O le toatele o la matou vasega o outou alo ma fanau mai lo outou afioaga ma le Itu'au. O le ala lea na ma tou a'oa'o ai le tulaga o fa'alupega o Fagasā e pei na lomia i le "Tusi Fa'alupega o Samoa Atoa" e le Methodist Church of Samoa,1985. A fai ua sopovale le manuvao i foātia sala se gagana ia fa'amaglo mai le faiaoga ae lafo i le va'a o Tumua e foalo ia Samoa. Ia alo maia alo lupe le tapuaiga Fagasā. Ia, mamā le lagi i le To'afia o Ali'i, a'ua ne'i paū ni aotauila i le Mātua ma Usoali'i. A'ua ne'i motu fa'atuaafa lo ou tou Fue ae mauá le lauga a lo ou tou toafā o Fetalaiga. Ae manū fa'aifo mai lagi le soifua manuia i le falelua o Fagasā, o le Nofoali'i o Itu'au.

Short Translation:

The honorific sacred residence, Malaepule and Malaeti'a, of the Three Paramount Chiefs of Fagasā village, the crown seat of Itu'au district, where the Elder Mātua and fraternal brothers

(*Usoali'i*) reside and the Four Paramount Orator Chiefs orate, and the guardians of the village of Fagasā: I would only awaken the sacred spirit of the ancient ancestors that are guiding us from their graves below. For the young current and future generations are present and anxiously awaiting knowledge and wisdom from the well of the past. The Islands of the Archipelago have been settled and structured by our ancestors, and therefore no one has omniscient knowledge to change Samoan culture and language by any iota, ever. Thus, I can only humbly ask for your indulgence, as we proceed to understand the Salutations of Fagasā village and their meanings relative to the village Chiefs Council structure.

We selected Fagasā Salutations because the majority of our dialog seminar members' families are from Fagasā and Itua district. Thus, I profusely ask for your forgiveness if we erred in your sacred Salutations and in the dignity of The Three Paramount Chiefs, Elder Mātua, and fraternal brothers, and the four Orator Chiefs, and the honor of Fagasā village. Such errors were never intentionally committed. But cast it on board the vessel of the Tumua for they are the mediators, to mend the differences of the people of Samoa.

Farewell and blessing:

May the heavens be bright and clear on the wellbeing of the Three Paramount Chiefs of Fagasā. Let not dark clouds be falling on the Elder Mātua and Paramount Fraternal Brothers. May the Four Orators' Fue (scepter of speech) be steady and wise and may you find in your oratory wisdom to guide and protect the dignity of Fagasā.

Introduction to the Village and Titles

And now I should tell readers something about the village: There are four main sub-villages within the whole of Fagasā, Tutuila. Itu'au is the title of the district. Nofoali'i (Fagasā) is the seat of government of the district—the headquarters or the crown—and the technical name is *Itu'au* and *Nofoa* (or *Nofoali'i*, seat of government): Itu'au ma Nofoali'i. The "kingdom" of Itu'au is the home of the vanguard troops in war.

The villages of the district of Itu'au are: Matu'u, Faganeanea, Nu'uuli, and Fagasā. And the "helmets" of Fagasā village are: Fagasā Faga Tele and Fagasā Faga Le'a. And the sacred meeting grounds of the villages are *Malepule* and *Maletia*. The village princes have the titles, Tupua and Lealaisalanoa.

The table below lists the paramount chiefs of the overall village of Fagasā. There are many chiefs in the village, but this gives an orator the net of who are the key players in the whole village. An orator should always know the pecking order, because an error in this would be a family embarrassment, and a defeat for the orator. So look in the table; you can see here, right away, the chief title, the princess *Sa'o Tama'ita'i* title, and the residence, and you should have already ascertained the *Malae*, the meeting ground.

Chief Title	Princess	Residence Name
Alo	Sina	Falelupe
Salanoa	Pafuti	Moso'oi
Tupuola	Fenunuivao	Apati
(Mātua Tuinei)		(Oloapitoamoa)

The names of the royal fine mats of the village of Fagasā are:

- *Aneanea* (Queen *Salamasina*)
- *Pulu ma le leuleu* (Royal family SaLeValasi)
- *Lauta'amutafea* (King Malietoa)

The names of the village ambassador (or harbinger messenger—*Maina* is translated "harbinger" because it is often the war messenger) are:

- *Le Malo* (Village appointed messenger)
- *Maina* (He who lights the path for the messenger)

And the names of the chieftain ava cups are:

Chief	Ava Cup Name
Alo	*Faifaimalie-upu-o-Samoa*
Tupuola	*Pisaina-ua-i-va'a fa'amoana ma se tausala, aumaia alalafaga ma Lufilufi*
Tuinei	*Nu'u tamali'ia*
Mamea	*Taua ua maui'u*

Lili'o	*Matalupe*
Soliai	*Atua na sau i fanua*
Tago	*Seu i Avatele*
Salanoa	*Aofaga o manu, aumaia le ipu a Salanoa*
Tupua	*Lalagofa'atasi*
Matuaivaotu	*Aiga fealofani*
Fuimaono	*Tuaoitau, aumaia le ipu a Fuimaono*
Faiumu	*Moe i le pua*

Those high chiefs and orators with no ava cup name would be called out with "Your *ipu*," for a high chief, or "Your *ava*," for an orator chief, as in "Your ava lea Fata ma Maulolo," or for Tuimanu'a, "Bring the *ipu* of Tuimanu'a"—there is a very special protocol for the searching and delivery of the *ipu* by the *aumaga* of TuiManu'a

The Story of the Malietoa Royal Mat Name

The state mats in the village are heirlooms of the various monarch families and, while they have their history, that history is the domain of the respective monarch family. With no documentation to reference, any explanation of the mat name would be hearsay and incorrect. For mat names are specific heirlooms, and I prefer to leave it for the family themselves to tell their own origin and name derivation. I do, however, have authority to tell the origin of the Malietoa monarch state mat, *Lauta'amutafea*—from *Lauta'amu* meaning the leaf of a large taro indigenous to Manu'a Island, and *Tafea* meaning floating by.

Legend has it that Malietoa *Uitualagi* and TuiManu'a *Li'a* were having an ava ceremony on their vessel in Manu'a harbor; the Malietoa saw the ava chewing-spits being delivered to the ava preparer on the *ta'amu* plant leaf, floating by, and was impressed with the size of the leaf with the ava chewing on it, so he said, "Great! That is the name of my state mat—*Lauta'amutafea*."

The Story of Chief *Alo's* Ava Cup Name

Every chief has a title for their ava cup. This is a prime example of how everything in Samoa is defined in detail. The name of Chief *Alo's* cup comes from this story:

It begins with Malietoa *Laupepa* (grandson of Tafa'ifa Malietoa *Vaiinupõ*) sending a messenger to *Mauga*. The Malietoa was searching for warriors to help fight a war for him. *Mauga* had limited numbers of men to fight, because they too were struggling. The messenger prepared to return to the Malietoa with this information, but *Mauga* made one more attempt to find more warriors, by sending the messenger to Fagasā. He sent the messenger to Itu'au Nofoali'i. The messenger delivered the request of the king and, lo and behold, *Alo* said, "We'll find the warriors to meet the Malietoa's request."

The Malietoa defeated *Tamasese*, and one of the gifts that *Alo* received from this battle was his second *ipu* (cup), *Faifaimalie-upu-o-Samoa*. So *Faifaimalieupuosamoa* refers to this battle between the Malietoa and *Tamasese*. The name of *Alo's* cup comes from this local legend and the history of Malietoa Laupepa's reign.

The Story of *Tupuola's* Ava Cup Name

Tupuola's ava cup name is *Pisaina-ua-i-va'a fa'amoana ma se tausala, aumaia alalafaga ma Lufilufi!* which means "Pandemonium at sea, while sailing at sea with the princess; call out the Ava presentation with Lufilufi, the Tumua"—*my interpretation and translation*. There are several chiefs that carry the same name for their ava cup because of their genealogical connection to each other. The *Sa'o Tama'ita'i* has a name for their ava cup as well.[lxviii]

The Story of the Sina Title

I spent almost a year with Paramount Chief Alo Dr. Paul Stevens and Senior Orator Chief Sala (Vaiutusala), both of Fagasā village, in a political campaign for Governor of American Samoa with Paramount Chief Lealaifuaneva Peter Reid of Pago Pago village (for governor), and Paramount Chief Afoa Moega Lutu of Utulei village (for lieutenant governor). High Chief Alo Dr. Paul Stevens was the chairman of the campaign committee, and Orator Chief Sala was the orchestrator and orator chief of the campaign committee. We spent many evenings conversing about *Fa'aSamoa* and Fagasā village history and practices.

I took advantage of my investigative interviewing tactics that I'd honed as an EDP-auditor in Bank of America Corporation's auditing division. And I had the privilege of meeting and engaging with several paramount and orator chiefs of the Fagasā Itu'au district during the campaign experience. These included Paramount Chief Lutu T. Fuimaono of Fagatogo village (President of the Senate house of government), Orator Chief Taisaliali'i Si'ua'i Sam Matagi of Fagatogo, Tamamātua, Orator Chief Tuilefano, Paramount Mao'upū Chief Soliai Tuipine Fuimaono of Nu'uuli village, and many others.

I remember the looks from both Alo and Sala when I told them the legend of where Alo's princess Sa'o Tama'ita'i name, Sina, originated from. They were incredibly surprised. It comes from the story of the dolphins (*munua*) on the village shore in Fagasā:[lxix]

Li'ava'a's traveling party, returning from Manu'a on their way back to Savai'i, pulled in at the Fagasā bay lagoon and decided to sojourn at Fagasā village, to replenish their drinking-water containers. *Li'ava'a* was the son of Tagaloa *Va'afuti* (or *Va'afa'i* (around A.D.1320) of Sili, Tufu Gautavai, Savai'i—the older brother of *Fata*, *Maulolo,* and their sister *Luafatasaga*, who were all descendants of *Sinalagilagi*, daughter of *Tagaloalagi*. This was during the reign of the Mageafaigā, and it's not known if *Alo* had yet been born.

After a few days of resting, *Li'ava'a* commanded that they should get the vessel ready for departure. And so the vessel pushed out to sea, and they said farewell to the village of Fagasā. The vessel reached the end of the bay, and *Li'ava'a* called out the crew to prepare the ava. And he called out to his daughter *Sina* to come and prepare to serve the ava. But *Sina* did not answer her father's calls.

Li'ava'a instructed the crew to look for *Sina* and tell her to come and prepare to serve the ava. But the crew could not locate *Sina*. It appeared they left without her or had forgotten her at the village!

Li'ava'a was angry, and he commanded the crew members responsible for looking after *Sina* and the provisions to take some *nonu* fruit (morinda citrifolia, an excellent medicinal fruit) and swim back to look for *Sina*. And if they couldn't find her, they would turn into fish. For *Li'ava'a* was well-known for his cruelty and cannibalism, as described in the legend of Tu'uleama'aga, A'opo, Savai'i.

When *Sina* had come to the vessel's dock, the journey had already begun, and she immediately swam after the vessel. But it was too far gone, and her water bottles broke by the harbor reefs—there is fresh water at the edges of the harbor reefs, even today. The crew members that swam back never made it to shore, and they all turned into dolphins—there is a seasonal coming of the dolphins to Fagasā bay lagoon, and Fagasā village tightly manages the fishing of the dolphins and their distribution throughout the village residents, so very limited gifts are allocated to outside villagers.

Sina is often seen standing on the edges of the harbor reef, waving her finely woven fan, as though she is calling out to her father's vessel. And according to Dr. Krämer, her name, the name of *Li'ava'a's* daughter, is *Sinatauata*. This is the "Sina" of the Sa'o Tama'ita'i of Paramount Chief *Alo*.

I tell this story because sometimes one must find commonality with different village chiefs, in order for them to open up to share their village tales and history. Thus I offer my familiarity with Fagasā village's organizational structure and history.

The Story of the Tupuola Title

Dr. Krämer mentioned in his footnotes that the paramount chief Tupuola title was a gift to the village from Paramount Chief *Mata'afa*. The implication, in Dr. Krämer's note, appears to be that such paramount chief titles are easily handed out as gifts, without consideration of genealogical connection, but this is not so easily done; the profundity of title bestowment and proclamation of such a paramount royal chief, of the TuiAtua genealogy, requires a deep-rooted connection through genealogical relationship.

The Tupuola title is not owned by a specific village. Tupuola are "Country of Samoa" titles, such as many of the titles in Fagasā village are. They are national heirlooms, like Fata and Maulolo, Leiato, Alipia, Mauga, Tuitele, and others. Holders of these titles are called chiefs of the country and culture, often defined by their role in the history of Samoa and Manu'a.

As I mentioned earlier, this district is Nofoali'i o Itu'au, which includes the Nu'uuli, Fagasā, Faganeanea, and Matu'u villages. It consists of paramount Ma'oupū chiefs—i.e. descendants of the royal paramount chiefs of Samoa and Manu'a through marriage connections in these villages.

For example, the first *Tupuola* was the son of the illustrious Paramount Chief *Asomua*, the descendant of Malietoa *Fuaoleto'elau* (brother of Malietoa *La'auli*) and *A'atasilogogoa* (daughter of TuiAtua *Fotuitama'i*). *Asomua's* wife, *Falenaoti Fūfe'ai*, was the daughter of *Tauiliili* of Amaile, Atua (A.D.1530). At this period, Tutuila was under the control of the Malietoa dynasty, and Paramount Chief *Tauiliili* (father of *Asomua's* wife) was the bedrock of the TuiAtua lineage, of TuiAtua TuiA'ana *Taufau* through her son *Tupuivao*, who was disinherited from the throne. *Taufau* was Tafa'ifa *Salamasina's* granddaughter and progenitor of *Taua'a*, *Tago*, *Tupuola*, *Leilua*, *Tuimavave*, and finally Mata'afa *Fa'asuamaleui* who was banished to Tutuila after being defeated by his cousin TuiA'ana *Nofoasāefā*.

Mata'afa *Fa'asuamaleui's* mother, *Salaina'aloa*, was the daughter of *Luafalemana*, son of Tafa'ifa *Tupua* and brother of the princes *Afoafouvale* and Tafa'ifa *Galumalemana*. And we already know that *Tupua* was adopted by Tafa'ifa *Muagututi'a*, son of Tafa'ifa *Fonotī*.[lxx]This was the reason for Mata'afa's claim to the Tupua title, for he was a descendant of both the male and female lines of Tafa'ifa *Salamasina's* genealogy.

Paramount Chief *Asomua* (a descendant of the Malietoa and TuiAtua lines) was also married to *Vaemanu*, daughter of Mageafaigā of Nu'uuli village, in Tutuila, giving birth to a girl *Fa'aitenu'u* (in A.D.1532). Dr. Krämer noted that her descendants have died out. But this is the connecting point between *Tupuola* and *Fa'aitenu'u*, for they were siblings, and the relationship between *Asomua* and Mageafaigā was that of son-in-law to father-in-law. It can also be said that *Tupuola* was a descendant of Mageafaigā and, for all practical purposes, all the chiefs of Fagasā village are descendants of Mageafaigā.

As noted above, there is also a genealogical relationship between *Tupuola* and Mata'afa *Fa'asuamaleui*, father of

Fanamanu and grandfather of *Va'ailua*. *Va'ailua* was the father of TuiAtua TuiA'ana Mata'afa *Iosefo*, who was elected king just before the partitioning and German annexation of Western Samoa around A.D.1890.

Thus *Tupuola's* royal genealogy makes his title a national chief title. That is why Mata'afa bestowed it in Fagasā, because it belongs to his genealogy—TuiAtua, Tupua, Mata'afa *Fa'asuamaleui* and TuiA'ana TuiAtua *Taufau* through her son *Tupuivao* through *Togafau* marrying to *Suluo'o,* daughter of *Tago* in Amalie, Atua district. As the *aiga* (family) relationships show in the above genealogy, Paramount Chief *Alo* or, collectively with other descendants of Mageafaigā and Tupua and TuiAtua Mata'afa, could choose to bestow the Tupuola title on anyone of their *aiga* in Fagasā village. Likewise, TuiAtua Mata'afa could also bestow the Tupuola title to anyone with the genealogy of the *Tauiliili* ancestor. Remembering service to the family, for example during war, can still be seen as an example of gift-giving reciprocity at play.

Since Tutuila had been a major supplier of warrior troops to the campaigns of various Mata'afa chiefs in their attempts to secure the TuiAtua and Tupua titles, this is probably what Dr. Krämer was referring to, when he said the title was a "gift" from Mata'afa. But he was absolutely wrong when he said there was no family relationship.

Even so, Samoans are very careful about title bestowment relative to genealogical ownership, because "there are more roots in a family than those of a tree," as the Samoan proverb says. Thus a clear understanding of the village chief's genealogy is essential to effective engagement in village settings.

As shown in the list of chiefs in the village of Fagasā, they are all descendants of Mageafaigā, *Asomua*, and TuiAtua *Tupuafuiavailili*. And Paramount Chief *Lealaisalanoa* is a descendant of Toleafoa *Va'afusuaga,* who was defeated by his brother Tafa'ifa *Fonotī* in the civil war for the Tafa'ifa title.

This is an example of why a chief must be familiar with major family genealogies and history. It should be pointed out that, in a village setting, the family members know their genealogy; they just want to learn if the chief delivering the oration knows it.

Fagasā Village Titles

One member of the dialog group made a sharp observation and asked about the differences in some of the chief titles in Fagasā village that are also listed in the village of Nu'uuli, with a salutation of Paramount "Ma'oupū"—for example, Paramount Chief *Soliai* and *Tago* (as listed earlier in the ava cup titles list).

According to Paramount Chiefs Alo Dr. Paul Stevens and Soliai Tuipine Fuimaono, the titles in both villages are of one and the same family and are one and the same title. The difference comes from the "founding" paramount chiefs' agreement and their decree that Nu'uuli village should be the residence of all paramount *Ma'oupū* titleholders of their paramount families. It's not clear in which time-period these edicts took place but, as mentioned earlier, the practice of marriages between the paramount royal chiefs from Manu'a, Savai'i, and Upolu Islands and the ladies, or princesses, of Tutuila Island marks the innovation of the title and is evidence of the inclusionary approach (*ma upu i alo o tama'ita'i*, hence "Ma'oupū" or *ma-upu*) to their genealogical offspring in their specific family genealogy.

Around the period of A.D.1530, we have the legend of Princess *Tapusalaia*, sister of Chief *Asomua*, who had a misunderstanding with her brother *Asomua* and so relocated her residence to Tutuila Island. Tutuila was under the Malietoa dynasty at the time, and so Tutuila Island was known as the Island of Tapusalaia (*tapu*, meaning forbidden, and *salaia*, meaning punishment), for the island was where ostracized victims were sent for punishment.

Asomua and *Tapusalaia* were descendants of Malietoa *Fuaoleto'elau* and TuiAtua *Fotuitama'i*. *Tapusalaia's* illustrious genealogy spans time and extends with connections to the various paramount families of Samoa, Manu'a, and Toga and Fiji.[lxxi] These connections include SaMuliaga, Fiame of TuiA'ana, Samatau, and TuiToga, in addition to the Malietoa and TuiAtua and SaTupua families. *Tapusalaia* was a progenitor of the Ama-ia-Fiame family clan. *Ama ia Fiame* was the son of *Ama-ia-Alo-levave* (*Alo* the quick and expedient, of Safata village) and Lady *Fausia*. We should note the practice of combining names, as in

Ama ia Fiame, to distinguish people from other family members of the same clan.

Lady *Fausia, Ama ia Fiame's* mother, was the daughter of Paramount Warrior Chief *'Ale* (of Safata village) and *Taleta* (the daughter of TuiToga *Tupoufei'a* and one of the pride princesses of the illustrious Paramount Chief *Toefaeono* of Siumu village, in Tuamasaga district). And *Ama ia Fiame* is an ancestor of *Ama o Tauaituatasolo,* whose son was *Ama Lele,* who married *Soliai,* daughter of Mageafaigā of Nu'uuli and Fagasā village, giving birth to *Ama-ia-Pesetā,* which is the name of a son of TuiA'ana *Tamālelagi. Ama-ia-Pesetā* sired six children, of which there were two girls, *Poto* and *Fuga. Poto Taumulimalei'a* married Prince *Afoafouvale,* the older son of Tafa'ifa *Tupua Fuiavalili. Fuga* married *Nonumasesē,* giving birth to a girl, *Usipua,* who is an ancestor of the first TuiA'ana Tamasesē *Moegalogo.*[lxxii]

I would be remiss if I didn't also mention Malietoa *'Ae'o'ainu'ū* (A.D.1680), who unfortunately gave Tutuila Island to TuiAtua and the House of Atua government in his defeat at the cave of Seuao (see page 162, The Decree pronounced in the Cave at Seuao, around A.D.1720). The grandmother of Malietoa *'Ae'o'ainu'ū* was a daughter of *'Ae,* the son of Mageafaigā of Nu'uuli village, Tutuila. This *'Ae* Mageafaigā frequently came to the bays—to Fagafaga in Atua district and to Ti'avea, Uafato, Fagaloa, etc.—to indulge in the sport of pigeon-catching, and this is where his daughter met and married Chief *Ta'amai* of Salufata and gave birth to *Tofoipupū,* who became the wife of Malietoa *Toatuilaepa* (A.D.1650). Malietoa *Toatuilaepa* was the father of *'Ae'o'ainu'ū* and his sister *To'oā.* Malietoa *'Ae'o'ainu'ū's* sister *To'oā* was later named Sa'o Tama'ita'i of Malietoa, and her salutation is *Sa'o Nalua* or *Sa'o Galua* (the second *Sa'o*). On such an occasion, Malietoa *Toatuilaepa* received his cup or *ipu* name: *A'umai Seufagafaga,* for the aumaga would call out to the servant, *Taumasina A'umai Seufagafaga*—Taumasina bring the Seufagafaga.

Malietoa *Toatuilaepa* received his servants from *'Ae* to build the Malietoa's pigeon-catching huts during these pigeon-catching sports between *'Ae* and the Malietoa. And Malietoa *Toatuilaepa* took these servants, with their names that were coined during the pigeon-catching sport—*Toelupe, 'Afa, Tuloa, Saunia'au, Si'a,*

Tulusunui, Tuiatafu—their apparatus, and their practices. They were are all made orator chiefs by Malietoa *Toatuilaepa* at his residence in Malie village, in Tuamasaga, Upolu. So the paramount families of all of Samoa and Manu'a are well represented in the village of Fagasā. And the paramountcy of the honorable Ma'oupū *Soliai* should be clear at this point.

A Personal Connection

As a footnote to the history of the village of Fagasā, I should add that the early Samoan ordained ministers of this district were from Olosega Island, Manu'a. In fact, the early ministers, assigned to Fagasā around 1860-1890, were my grandfather's cousins from Olosega Island, Manu'a. These are Reverend Nu'utai Sauasili F.S. Malemo, Iosefa (1868) and Reverend *Iatamo Tu'uaga* F.S. Malemo, Iosefa (1875). Reverend *Iatamo Tu'uaga* married *Sala* of the Ologa family of Fagasā. He is buried in Fagasā village.

Meeting Protocols

We role-played several different situations in our Culture Dialog class—a village gathering, visitors' welcome, wedding, funeral, and so on—and completely different sets of protocols apply for a wedding, a funeral, a village convocation meeting, and a title investiture meeting.

The point is, because the protocols are different, each event requires a lot of thorough planning and preparation: the gifts are different, the fine mats are labeled differently, and different guests are anticipated. Also, each occasion calls for different types of speeches. A different language lexicon is used, and "thou shall not" mix them up.

The Village Gathering

The village gathering is usually the monthly Chiefs Council meeting. A messenger tells the village chiefs that you have, say, a meeting on Monday morning; he tells you who the designated host chief will be, etc.

The seating arrangement of the chiefs, by their respective titles, shows the "pecking order" or hierarchy of the village social structure. The differences among the high chiefs are clear by title and seating arrangement, as we have seen. Fraternal brothers of the high chief, the prince, the orator chiefs, senior orator chiefs, and the sitting orator chief each have responsibilities in directing the agenda and program from the back of the house. The high chief is seated at the right-hand corner. And at the front of the house will be orators, family members and elders.

The orator chief, or talking chief, is like the "sergeant of arms." But the sergeant of arms actually sits in the back. In front are the people who orchestrate the activities of the village. Then the paramount chief basically blesses something or does not bless it. The others will circle around and debate and finally make recommendations to the paramount chief. If the paramount chief says it's a wise decision, he blesses it, and we're done.

That's the decision-making process, the responsibility of the chiefs. But remember there are orators, or paramount spokespersons, for the family high chief, for the village high chief, for the district high chief, for the region or the county, and ultimately for the islands. There is a pecking order that goes all the way up, and they all know where they stand in that pecking order. They all know how they must give and take, and how they should carry out their responsibilities.

The Wedding

The planning of a family wedding is a culturally involved event. Samoan culture reminds the family and people that each person has, in his or her core being, two families—the mother's family and the father's family. But then the mother, likewise, has two families—her mother's and father's families. And the same with the families of the father's parents. Thus to plan and prepare a wedding celebration, the bride must remember that, just from her immediate family, she has to incorporate the considerations of six whole families, those of her parents and of their respective families. And of course, likewise with the groom's preparations. So, at this immediate point, the would-be young family is dealing with twelve separate families, not including any extended families. The planning and organization can be a challenge and, for some, a nightmare.

The bridesmaids are usually negotiated with the mother and other close family relatives. The bride's wedding dresses (a minimum of four—the grandma's, aunt's, new mother-in-law's, and one of her own choosing) are also subject to negotiation.

Once the logistics are ironed out into a cohesive plan, the orator chief "orchestrator" will plan out the cultural protocols accordingly, based on the master plan.

A major function here is the process and management of exchanging gifts. Procedures for oratory presentations are incorporated into the protocol, to ensure every family is recognized. The objective is to show their pride and love for the bride and groom, and the family's cohesiveness. Also, the young married couple shows off their respective extended family genealogy and status (title, wealth, size, cohesiveness, and evidence of a peaceful and loving clan).

The most involved process is the presentation of the *'ietoga* or the fine mats. The names of the different mats and, of course, the state mat names and designations must be properly labeled and presented, usually to paramount chiefs of the groom and bride and the family's church pastors or ministers.[lxxiii]

So now we imagined a wedding in our Culture Dialog, and we role-played a visitors' welcome to our guests from the Tupuola family.

I gave my students their assignment: We imagined my friend, Paramount Tumua Orator Chief *Fa'amatuainu* Vasaoāiga Jones Iakopo Tu'ufuli, was going to be the talking chief for a family which was coming to present gifts. We had to remember, we were connected with him through the female side of the family. Our family gifts would be put together with his family's, to assist in the wedding.

Fa'amatuainu's family was now coming from Upolu. He knew that "my" daughter was the person getting married. He understood that, because we were cousins, he would gather his family in Western Samoa. They would travel by plane to us. And obviously, we would know he was coming, hence the reason why we would be sitting in the maota.

So: the role-playing occasion was a wedding, and we had contacted the "family." Again, he and the family lived in Western Samoa; we had not seen them in a long time; and they were coming to assist us in this occasion. We were all one family. So we would note the arrival of Tupuola, Tuinei, and Tupua, the Usoali'i, the Tu'ua and Tamamātua. In this case, we called the Tamamātua *Vaovasa*, as *Vaovasa* is a very old paramountcy title.

We obviously had to think of all this in English, as some of my students didn't understand *Fa'aSamoa* (Samoan customs and etiquette). So we asked, what do you do when you have guest? You welcome them in, right. "Welcome, your Honorable Chief..." using the forms of salutation given earlier in this book.

Once the greetings were done and everyone had gotten reacquainted, then we had to designate the seating. I walked the group through it as *Fa'amatuainu* played his part. Each person had their designated sitting post.

What I wanted to do was to have *Fa'amatuainu* enter the house or maota. As he entered, he would first excuse himself to come in, as we have seen earlier. Our family would now shift to the left, to make space available for the visiting family to sit, as

219

described earlier. The chief Tupuola would sit on the left of the house, where my family had been. The Usoali'i would sit to his right and left. The orator chief, *Fa'amatuainu,* would sit at the back. Everyone would have their designated place.

The Funeral

The planning and preparation of funeral services in the *Fa'aSamoa* is also ritualistic and quite involved. The customs and protocols are detailed and specific to the family, title, and village, and the material preparations are significantly complex, due to the protocols of the title and family.

For example, on the occasion of a funeral, if an honorable chief has died of severe illnesses, and he or she is a member of the Malietoa clan, you should address the situation like this: "Honorable Chief, *ua to le timu* (torrential rain has befallen on) *ia* then the chief's name, *i le malomaloā* (severe) *o le fa'atafa gasegase* (illness of a chief)."[lxxiv]

Funeral Salutations

A whole set of protocols must be referred to on the occasion of the passing of a paramount chief. It is a time in which the preparation for the chief's trip into his place in the heavens is honored. We have special words for such a critical process. We might say, for example:

- for this village, the sun has turned over his face
- the sun has turned over to his dark red, sun-setting face
- the moon's face has turned blood red
- there are dark clouds of rain on the mountain
- the dark clouds are hovering over the village sky
- the rain has fallen in the village heaven
- a storm has taken the orator staff and the authority scepter
- the paddle of the mighty fishing canoe has floated away.

All these salutations honor the sacred path for the dying chief.

The history of Samoa is regal, for it is comprised of royal families, warrior heroes, elder orators, and paramount chiefs.

Warrior heroes are those who have distinguished themselves in service during national conflicts for the family, village, district, and country. When they pass on, we would come up with a phrase to indicate that this warrior or king has passed on.

For example, *Salamasina's* mother, *SaLeValasi*, was of a royal crown, so you could expect that the salutation would refer to the crown. Hence, "The royal crown has been put aside—been laid to rest." *Ua gasolo ao.* "The clouds in the heavens have moved on into the mountains. There is darkness. The dark clouds are hovering in the mountain for this village, because the royal crown has been laid to rest. The sun has turned red. The moon has stopped rising."

Care for the deceased person's body, particularly that of a chief, whether male or female, is designated to particular members of the family. For example, the ladies who are sisters or female genealogical descendants are assigned to care for the deceased body and stay with the body, day and night, until burial.

Parting Farewells

The parting farewells to heaven are very particular to each paramount chief. The belief is that we are all descendants of the deity *Tagaloalagi,* and his family clan is assigned to nine heavens with, of course, *Tagaloalagi* residing in the tenth. Therefore, when the paramount family heads pass on, they're returning, back to their respective, heavenly, family residence, hence the "farewell when departing to heaven."

There are several heavenly farewells for paramount chiefs noted in this section, including the monarch's heavenly farewell for the Tafa'ifa: [lxxv]

- SaTupua:
  - *Ua ta'ape PāPā ua gasolo ao* (The PāPā titles are scattered, for they are returned to their respective honorific royal families and their custodians. The dark clouds have befallen on SaTupua—*my translation*)
- TuiAtua:
  - *Gasetoto le masina, Ua mafuli le la ia TuiAtua* (The moon has turned its color red, symbolic of blood and

the moon setting, and the sun has turned over onto its back or to darkness, opposite from light, on the TuiAtua—*my translation*)

- TuiA'ana:
  - *Ua gaugau auta, ua tātā fa'aali'i le TuiA'ana* (The drumstick handles are broken, for the drumbeat is the sound of a paramount chief's passing, the TuiA'ana—*my translation*; the drum is a harbinger to the village people. It communicates convocation meetings and deaths in the village)
- Gatoa'itele:
  - *Ua ta'ape PāPā, ua gasolo ao, ua tõ le timu ia Gatoa'itele* (The torrential rain has fallen—*my translation*)
- Vaetamasoaali'i:
  - *Ua tõ le timu, ua Po le nu'u ia Vaetamasoaali'i* (The torrential rain has fallen, and the village is fallen to nightfall—*my translation*)
- Malietoa:
  - *Ua tõ le timu i le Malietoa* (The torrential rain has befallen the Malietoa—*my translation*)

Translating these cultural heirloom rituals and funeral protocols is difficult, due to the need to capture the essence or profundity of the sacred dignity of the paramount families. Between the farewell parting to heaven and the distribution of the family chiefs' *'ietoga* or fine mats, everything always tests the seniority and proficiency of the presiding orator.

The Title Investiture

When a chief passes on, the title remains with the family to select the next titleholder. In our Culture Dialog, we looked at the selection of a new titleholder after the death of a paramount chief. We said, "The paramount chief, *Lutu*, has lived to be 90 years old, and it is now time to assign the new responsibility to the next chief." Of course, *Lutu* did not necessarily have to be the "chief" titleholder; it could have been another titleholder, as there are the *Ta'isali* title and the *Ta'amuvaigafa* title that also connect with the paramount chief title of *Lutu*.

In this example, even though he was not physically there, the *Lutu* title name would have to be bestowed unto a new person. And this newly selected person would not only inherit the chief title name, but would also inherit the designated "seating post."

For example, if someone says, "In Fagatogo, my grandfather is *Lutu*," one might ask, "Did he take the title *Lutu* and, if so, what year did he take it?" The reply might be, "Oh sometime in the 1930s." Then we would know this *Lutu's* seating position would be the paramount chief position.

The next questions might be, "What about the other chiefs? Where does *Tiumalu* sit?" "Where does *Mailo* sit and *Afoa*, the *Alo Ali'i* sit?" For Samoan people can identify an individual, just by hearing the name, and with that they can automatically trace you to your family and the chief name. That's why the elders place such emphasis on their children knowing who they are. It's important.

Selecting the Chief

The cultural protocols for selecting a new family chief or chiefs are perhaps the most involved customs and formalities in the Navigators' culture. This is the acid test for knowing your genealogy in general, and your position in the family tree in particular.

Fundamentally, it begins with the original person who started the title and family, the progenitor of the original family name (which became a chief title) and clan. From that starting point, the genealogy comes down to two categories by generation:

1. First Generation:
    1. Male heirs (from the male house or *Faletama*): son 1, son 2, son 3, etc.
    2. Female heirs (from the female house or *Faleteine*): daughters 1, 2, 3, etc.
2. Second Generation:
    1. Male heirs, grandsons and granddaughters 1, 2, 3, 4...
    2. Female heirs, granddaughters and grandsons 1, 2, 3, 4... [lxxvi]

223

These two lines of the title genealogy continue down to the current generation, however many generations that takes. Thus knowing your genealogy is crucial to your participation, so you will always know who you are and where you stand or sit with respect to the genealogical tree, which can be challenging to the researching mind.

Deliberation is the effort required, not negotiation. Custom dictates that the male heirs progress toward the title inheritance, and the female heirs carry the genealogy and property rights and must agree to the title-holder selection.

The family deliberations can take several sessions and the timeline can be lengthy. The whole process could take several months or years. This is where the service records of individual candidates can make a difference. Remember the Samoan cultural mantra: *O le ala i le Pule* (authority) *o le tautua* (service)—"Your path to holding the title is in being a faithful servant"—*my translation*.

There are many families that have chosen female heirs for the titleholder role for obvious reasons, to promote and elevate the family's wealth and status, hence evidencing the sound decision-making process to select a competent, caring, educated culture and genealogy expert, a gifted orator, and a strong leadership candidate to lead the family. It's no different from selecting a corporate leader for a company, such as the CEO or any of the other C-suite positions.

The Ritual

The ava comes first, before anyone can proceed with the meeting to select the new titleholder. The ava is a religious ritual, in that its purpose is to pray for wisdom and a peaceful deliberation to find a candidate who can lead the family and become a custodian of family heirlooms, titles, and landholdings.

There are times that can be intense during the deliberation and discussion, because there may be several candidates proposed from different branches of the family, requiring the promotion of each by their respective nominating body. At such a point in the discussion, a chief may interrupt the meeting, just by clapping his hands, signaling to the ava preparer and cupbearer, the young prince *Aumaga*, stating: *Paki*—clap—*le Ava*! meaning "Serve the ava cup drink."

In Greek mythology, as told in that famous literary work the Iliad, by the ancient historian Homer, Hermes was a cupbearer. Also Hebe was originally a female cupbearer for the god, Zeus (this later changed to Ganymede, a male cupbearer). Nehemiah was a cupbearer for the Lord, the Hebrew God, as shown in *Nehemiah 1:11* which states, "I was cupbearer to the king." And so the role of the prince, son of the paramount chief, as a cupbearer is consistent with classical mythology and the Hebrew Old Testament. The role of cupbearer is assigned to a prince or princess, because of the father's trust in him or her to sacrifice his or herself for his protection.

The interruption, provided by the ava ceremony recess, serves the purpose of letting people deliberate and search for ancient wisdom to guide their positions with due patience and the exercise of good judgement. So really, the ava is a call for patience, wisdom, peace, long-term intellect, and short-term expediency in deliberation. The ava ceremony is a way to manage the process, the tone, and the whole deliberation aspect of such a meeting. Colloquially speaking: "It's time to calm the waters."

In my village, before I received a chief title, I had to figure all this out because they would just randomly select... "Fata Ariu, the ava ceremony, please." It didn't matter where I was sitting, I would remove myself and I would be the one calling them up. And just as an aside, in the old days, we didn't have clothes other than the pe'a and tea leaves. So when these guys go through this ceremony, you'll see that they're practically naked. You've probably have seen pictures of it. For this is a sacred ceremony.

It's at the conclusion of this iterative process that a titleholder, or titleholders, is or are selected. Then the family moves to the ceremonial protocols for title investiture.

The proclamation

The first process in the protocols for title investiture is the proclamation to all members of the family. It's equivalent to

225

issuing a press release to the family, village, district, and the island country.

A date is set for bestowment of the title at the village ceremony held by the Chiefs Council. It should be noted that this is the same village Chiefs Council that sanctioned the title bestowment. The investiture takes place in an orator chief's ceremony. At this ceremony the new titleholder is directed to his or her new seating designation going forward.

Bestowing the Title

Now imagine the scene: Through much deliberation and negotiation, a chief has been selected. The family is in unison with this decision. The title will be bestowed by the village Chiefs Council to honor this person, who has now moved from their personal house to the village Chiefs Council house. And again, we have the seating arrangement:

> *Le Pitovao or Lau fetalaiga Le Pitovao or Lau tofā le Pitovao. Alala mai lau Tofā Tuainoa. O se na fa'atua i upu o la i tou nu'u.*

The LePitovao and Tuainoa titles are the elder orators (in seniority) of the Chiefs Council—*LePito* (the corner) *vao* (forest), means "your corner of the forest" so, metaphorically, someone sitting in the back side of the maota council house; *Tuainoa-tua* (back) *inoa* (names designated) are corner seats designated especially for these titleholders, for the seniority system is very much a part of the chieftain system. The culture very much reveres "old age" chiefdom, not male or female. It's the fountain of wisdom.

The former titleholder might be sitting in the back of the house, because he's retired. For example, he might have relinquished his "front" position and the responsibility of the Tu'ua due to old age. So now he has retired to Tuainoa. But the Tuainoa might still be Tu'ua. He may still use the Tu'ua title while he sits in the back, but another Tu'ua—one who may be younger—will sit in the front. The former titleholder will now be referred to *Tofā Tu'ua* or *Tuainoa o la ou tou Nu'u.*

A chief title has its own salutations, no matter what the age of the chief. There is a lexicon of words that are used to honor elders and senior orators. So, Tuainoa and LePitovao are titles that will not be used for young titleholders.

The salutations used in a speech, such as *Fetalaiga, Tofā, Sūsūga, Fofoga,* etc., are based on the speaker's preference. However, certain words are particular to a certain set of orators. For example, *Sūsūga* is used to refer to the Lufilufi group of orators, the Tuisamau group of orators and Fata and Maulolo, and the LMS ministers and clergy. *Tofā* is often used to address senior orator chiefs, Alipia, and the likes of the Tamamātua Group of Nine senior orators in the Tutuila Island structure. The application of this protocol is a test of an orator's knowledge of orator chief etiquette.

Titles are important. But *afioga, afio o ali'i*—so are the places where everyone sits. (*Afioga* means honorable, and *afio o ali'i* means "come in your honor, High Chief," hence, "Welcome, your honor, High Chief *Alo.*")

I'm indebted to Sūsūga Tumua Lufilufi, Orator Chief Fa'amatuainu Vasaoāiga Jones Iakopo Tu'ufuli, for the role-playing and subsequent discussions of this involved cultural title investiture ceremony and other cultural protocols.

Arrival

The village Chiefs Council arrive at the family residence that has been prepared for the ceremony. The Council occupy the front of the house, and the *Aumaga* take their position at the back with the ava bowl and the dried ava plant sticks.

The titleholder is directed to sit at the rounded side of the house, opposite from the seat of the paramount chief, *Sa'o,* of the village.

Oratory

Immediately after the welcoming greetings, the head orator, the Tu'ua, of the village council presides over the ceremony. The Tu'ua's oratorial eloquence is directed toward complimenting the family for reaching a decision to select a leader who will lead the family and help the village council.

A critical part of this speech is the reciting of the genealogy of the title being bestowed. Often, the Tu'ua will be begged not to

227

continue, because of the sacredness of the title history. The Tu'ua would immediately honor the family's request and move on to the next section of the bestowment speech.[lxxvii]

Bestowment Process

For the actual process of bestowment, one of the orator chiefs will stand up with the bottle of oil, made up of dry, ripe, shredded coconut meat, fermented in the sun for six weeks or more to produce its oils. This is the oil that will be sprinkled on the head and upper body. It is rubbed over this new titleholder's chest, arms, and shoulders, as evidence of ritual consummation.

Then the Tu'ua finishes his or her oration by giving advice to the new titleholder.

Ava Ceremony

Immediately after the Tu'ua's speech, the *pati*, or clapping, to the ava ceremony begins. The first ava cup is given to the new chief, followed by the Tu'ua, and then the paramount chief of the village, and then the protocol of the ava continues.

Upon completion of the ava ceremony, the paramount chief blesses the title investiture proceedings and the new chief. Other senior orator chiefs also give speeches of advice. And the final process is the gift-exchange protocol and the closing speeches.

Gifting of Fine Mats

The gifting of "fine mats" or "State mats" (commonly referring to mats of the respective monarchs like Tupua, Malietoa, TuiAtua, TuiA'ana, Gatoa'itele, Vaetamasoaali'i, SaLevalasi, LeTagaloa, SaTuiManu'a, and other paramount titles), must be anticipated by all families involved. These are heirloom mats and are treasured by all. They represent the highest value in mediums of exchange, and one of these mats can be worth a thousand other mats.

There are different fine mats that are labeled and earmarked for different parts of the protocol. For example—an example of fine mat distribution of the (monarch) Malietoa, on title bestowment and on funeral protocols—at the passing of a

Malietoa titleholder, the protocol for gifting his honor's fine mats is as follows:

- 1st *Tetoga* to Sūsūga Fata
- 2nd *Tetoga* is to Sūsūga Maulolo
- 3rd *Tetoga* is to Sūsūga Usoali'i Taliaoa
- 4th to Auimatagi
- 5th to LeTofā Li'o
- 6th to the Malietoa's Toetaufanua:
    - Vaimauga district
    - Faleula village
    - Tufulele village
- 7th to Faleata district
- 8th to Safata district
- 9th to the Tumua and Pule Authorities

The Ava Ritual

Legends of the Ava Ceremony

How the Ava Plant Came to Samoa

Samoan legend tells of *Tinopoula* (or *Sinapoula*) and *Sinafaalua*, daughters of Chief *Faluaseu* (also known as *Faleaseu*). TuiFiti married them, giving birth to *Suasamiavaava* (or *Suasamile'ava'ava*) and *Sao-lateteleupegaofiti* (this Sao name originated from Manu'a with the brothers, all named *Sao*, including Tuimanu'a *Sao'io'iomanu*),[lxxviii] and a daughter *Muliovailele*.[lxxix]

The family lived in the village of Vailele, in the district of Tuamasaga on the Island of Upolu. The father, *Faluaseu*, went hunting for fruit pigeons in the mountain forest behind the village, which bordered the village of Siumu. When the father was late returning, the mother sent the two daughters to search for him. In their quest, the daughters crossed through to the villages of Siumu and the district of Safata, and continued westward on the Island of Upolu, but their search was in vain.

The daughters decided to return home, following the coastal route around the district of A'ana. Upon reaching the village of Mulifanua, they stood on the beach and motioned to a catamaran that was heading out to sea. They waved for it to stop so they could catch a ride to their village.

The boat returned and picked up the girls. The sailors introduced the girls to the captain, who was the TuiFiti (the Fijian king). Shortly after the girls joined the ship, the TuiFiti suffered an illness, and the sailors and servants were filled with fear that he might lose his life to this sickness. The sisters remembered the old Samoan remedy of taking a ripe green coconut—not one of the dark brown ones—and opening a tiny hole in the top, so seawater could be added inside, then shaking it thoroughly for about half an hour until it is well mixed, in a similar manner to modern-day cocktails.

The sisters strongly insisted that the king should drink this concoction to relieve his illness. The king reluctantly accepted the drink, and before long he began to feel strong, and his health returned to normal. Filled with elation and desire for the Samoan sisters, he then took both girls to be his wives. *Sinapoula* gave birth to a son, *Suasamiavaava*—which means juice-of-sea water and ava roots—and *Sinafaalua* bore two children, a boy named *Saolateteleupegaofiti*, and his sister, *Muliovailele*.

The TuiFiti found great pleasure in his children borne by the Samoan sisters. His joy was short-lived, however, in that, not long afterwards, his son *Suasamiavaava* took ill and died. On his deathbed the son asked his mother and aunt to promise him that, if he passed, a plant that grew up and out of his grave would be uprooted and taken to Samoa and planted there in memory of him and of their sojourn in Fiji (see The Edict of TuiFiti *Suasamile'ava'ava* and the First Ava Plant, page 147)

The plant that sprang forth from the grave of *Suasamiavaava* took on the shape of a man's fingers and became an attraction to the people of Fiji. This plant (Piper methysticum, from the Latin for "pepper" and the Greek for "intoxicating") was named the ava.

Muliovailele and her brother *Saolateteleupegaofiti* wished to visit their mother's homeland in Samoa, so they took with them the ava plant. During the course of this journey they visited various villages in the Samoan chain of islands, where they gifted the ava plant to be planted. Then they landed at the beachfront of their mother and aunt's village, Vailele, Upolu.

The Manu'an Legend of the Ava Plant

A different legend of the ava plant is told by Manu'ans, involving the god *Tagaloalagi* and his ava ceremony in his residence in the tenth heaven; this is clearly a different kind of story, like the Manu'an story of creation: *Tagaloalagi's* grandson, *TagaloaUi*, sneaked up and stole the ava, despite its being *tapu* (forbidden) because of its sacred nature. Then *TagaloaUi* brought the ava down onto earth for the first TuiManu'a.

This Manu'an story shows a creative way of imagining the "origin" of the ava, for the Manu'an is ever aware there has to be an "origin" and beginning for everything, just as in the mythology of creation. So, to their credit, in the absence of a legend that tells where the ava originated (other than that it's from another island such as Fiji) Manu'ans understood and accepted that everything originated in heaven and was administered by the will of *Tagaloalagi*.

The First Ava Ceremony

The well-known legend of the first Ava ceremony begins with *TagaloaUi* and a man named *Pava,* as we saw in The Morning (*Taeao*) at Sauā, the village of Fitiuta, Manu'a on page 144. The "half-human half-spirit" *TagaloaUi* was having an ava ceremony with *Pava*, a plantation owner. And *Pava's* son, a three-or-four-year-old, was playing and running around, making a lot of noise and disrupting their ceremony. He was being... rather annoying and, after couple of orders to keep the boy quiet and well-behaved were shrugged off, *TagaloaUi* became angry and grabbed the boy; he literally "split the boy in half" and laid him down in front of himself and *Pava*. Then *TagaloaUi* said, "This is our 'meal' for the ava ritual ceremony." This is the first time a "meal" was to accompany the ava ceremony. But, of course, *TagaloaUi* had observed the whole ceremony up in heaven earlier, when he sneaked up to steal the ava for TuiManu'a down on earth.

Pava was shocked and petrified, not to mention full of sorrow and heartbroken, and he begged for boy's life to be returned, because *TagaloaUi* was a deity. *TagaloaUi* thought that this was a learning moment, so he restored the two halves of the boy, and the boy came back to life. Afterward, *Pava* went out to fetch taro, palusami (baked taro leaves and coconut milk juice), bananas, and different types of fish for their meal.

Because of *Pava's* lackadaisical way of conducting the ava ceremony, *TagaloaUi* banished him to a village now called Falealili, Upolu.

Some people believe that this ava ceremony was done in the village of Pavaia'i, on Tutuila Island, hence the somewhat eponymous village name. The legend does not say they consumed the boy's body, of course, and the reference to cannibalism simply illustrates the need for a meal to accompany the ava ceremony. Also, the story demonstrates *TagaloaUi's* spiritual power to restore life.

History of the Ava Ceremony

The Value of Ava

As with anything that is given attention and attracts enough interest to be studied, the ava is something where gaining understanding and being armed with all-around knowledge will provide many benefits. And researchers have uncovered a lot about the history and the nature of the ava plant, as it relates to Pacific Island culture—such as the Hawaiian, Tongan, Samoan, Maori, and many Micronesian cultures. According to many researchers, both modern and from the 1800s, the ancient origins of ava-drinking (or kava to use the European English name) trace back at least 3,000 years or more, and are associated with both social and ceremonial functions.

Ava is more than a traditional remedy for ailments. Highly valued for its medicinal uses, it can be a sedative, muscle relaxant, diuretic, and a remedy for nervousness and insomnia.[lxxx] It is a botanical marvel that has been used in parts of the Pacific, at traditional social gatherings and in cultural and religious ceremonies, to achieve a "higher level of consciousness." The roots of the plant can be used to produce a drink with sedative, anesthetic, euphoriant, and entheogenic properties.[lxxxi] Extract from ava has also been mentioned for treating anxiety.[lxxxii]

The ava plant is a shrub that thrives in loose, well-drained soils where plenty of air reaches the roots. It grows naturally where rainfall is plentiful. Ideal growing conditions are moist soil with high humidity. The plant cannot reproduce sexually, and female flowers are especially rare; they do not produce fruit even when hand-pollinated. Cultivation of ava is achieved entirely by propagation from the stem. And plants are traditionally harvested at around four years of age, as older plants have higher concentrations of the "active ingredient," kavalactones.[lxxxiii]

The Chewer

George Forster, a naturalist on Captain Cook's voyage back in 1777, wrote a description of the process by which the islanders prepared the ava (or kava—Tongans and Fijians, as well as

Europeans, refer to it as kava, but for Samoans it is always ava). He described it as being made in what he considered the most disgusting manner that could be imagined![lxxxiv]

Ava, he explained, comes from juice taken from the roots of a particular species of pepper-tree. Small pieces of root are chewed by a group of people, who spit the "macerated mass" into a wooden bowl, where coconut water or coconut milk is added. Coconut fiber is used to strain the resulting mixture, squeezing everything till the juices are well mixed with the coconut milk. Then the whole liquid is poured into another bowl. In his opinion, this "nauseous stuff" would be swallowed as fast as possible; and some ancient experts valued their ability to drain many bowls in one go.[lxxxv]

It is amazing how accurate Forster's description is, and how much the procedure has not changed since it was observed by him in the 1770s, over 240 years ago. Mr. Foster did not understand the significance of the procedures or protocols, for he was not armed with detailed knowledge of the relevant culture, customs, and formalities. For example, he did not know that traditionally the chewers of the paramount (or royal) chiefs' ava are the virgin princesses and the sons—the princes—of the paramount chiefs. The main reason for this is the "trust" factor. In ancient times trickery was often deployed as a way of defeating or eliminating one's enemy; the paramount chiefs set up this practice to protect against this risk. In the same way they would utilize "tasters" to taste the food before the paramount chief would eat at a meal presented to the chief.

I recall the legend of Paramount Chief *Asomua* (in A.D.1500), a descendant of the Malietoa *Fuaoleto'elau* royal house. He became outraged when he did not see his stepsister spit her ava chewings into the ava bowl for his ava. His open display of anger caused the sister to run away, filled with sadness, because she had actually chewed the ava at the back of the maota (house), where the young warriors were seated, and Chief *Asomua* could not see her. This, of course, caused a big misunderstanding with the chief. *Tapusalaia* was so hurt and embarrassed that she decided to run away to Tutuila and live there, never to return to Upolu.

The Cupbearer

The appointment of trusted tasters and chewers, of course, is not unique to Polynesian culture. It was practiced throughout ancient cultures across the globe. The idea of identifying a cup name, cupbearer, and protocol, is present in Greek, Egyptian, and Mesopotamian mythologies, and many others noted in the literature of the Classical Antiquity period.

A cupbearer was an officer of high rank in royal courts, whose duty it was to serve the drinks at the royal table. On account of the constant fear of plots and intrigue, such a person must be regarded as thoroughly trustworthy in order to hold the position. Cupbearers had to guard against poison in the king's cup, and they were sometimes required to swallow some of the wine before serving it. The cupbearer's confidential relationship with the king often gave them a position of great influence. The position of cupbearer was greatly valued, and it was only given to a select few throughout history.[lxxxvi] For example, the Egyptian hieroglyph for a cupbearer was used as late as 196 B.C. in the Rosetta Stone, to represent the cupbearer of King Kanephoros—Areia, daughter of Diogenes. Sargon of Akkad was also a cupbearer, in the 23rd century B.C.[lxxxvii] Nehemiah became a cupbearer to King Artaxerxes, the sixth King of the Persian Empire, as told in the Old Testament of the Bible, *Nehemiah 2:1*. And cupbearers are also mentioned in *Genesis 40:1, 1 Kings 10:5,* and *2 Chronicles 9:4*, where they are noted as examples of royal splendor.[lxxxviii]

In Greek mythology the daughter of Zeus and Hera is Hebe, the goddess of youth, who was the original cupbearer to the Greek gods of Mount Olympus, serving them nectar and ambrosia. She was later replaced by Ganymede, after Hebe married the war hero Heracles. The Roman gods are also closely related to Greek mythology, with their Goddess of Youth, Juventa, being the Roman counterpart to Hebe.

And the King of Bohemia held rank as arch-cupbearer of the Holy Roman Empire. At other times, the Count of Limburg and, after A.D.1714, the Count of Althan, served as cupbearers to the emperor.[lxxxix]

Samoans, Ava, and Christianity

There was a program on the Samoan radio news broadcasting station, whereby listeners could call in and share their opinions on a subject being discussed. A group of professors and academicians had traveled to Samoa for a conference with the University of the South Pacific in Samoa. The conference opening ceremony was held with the University Board of Academics on a Sunday. And, of course, it began with the ava ceremony.

The ensuing debate on the radio program centered around whether the ava ceremony should have been conducted on a Sunday, the Sabbath day. A lot of senior orators and Samoan historians weighed in on the debate. Some held to the opinion that Sunday was God's Day, and that the ava appeared to be an offering to a deity—that the ava was a heathen way of worshipping idols. Others said: Wait a minute, let's not forget that, when Malietoa accepted Christianity, his words were, *Pati le Ava a le feagaiga fou*, meaning "Clap and welcome the new ava of the new God of all gods, and let this be the integral principal foundation of Samoan society." So it becomes the new ava ceremony, an offering to the Christian God almighty. And the "new ava ceremony" promulgated the new relationship between Samoa and the one true God.

An elder Chief called in to the radio program, from the village of Sale'imoa, with his opinions on the matter. He went on to say, "Have you all forgotten that, way before we knew the heavenly God and Jesus as our Savior, Samoans worshiped a god named *Tagaloalagi* and other spiritual deities. That was the belief, and it is a part of our cultural foundation."

The ava ceremony between the Chiefs Council was extended to meeting with the clergy, as ministers became recognized as the *feagaiga,* or go-betweens, between God and the Samoan people. *Feagaiga* means an interface, go-between, ambassador, or the boundary between people. Thus, Samoans use it to refer to the boundary between sister and brother, or between the seating of Chiefs (hence the title *Ma'oupū* or *ma upu i le feagaiga*, meaning to extend courtesy to the children of sisters and daughters). If God were perceived in a feminine perspective, the ministers would probably be the *Ma'oupū*.

The story goes that, when Malietoa *Vaiinupõ* understood the translation of the word "servant of God," he thought the word was too impoverished for a servant of God. So he used the word *feagaiga* or ambassador instead, and he bestowed the *Sūsūga* title so the ministers could interface with the village Chiefs Council. And so the ava ceremony between the Chiefs Council was extended to meeting with them.

Why Samoans accepted Christianity

Samoans accepted Christianity easily, because it mirrored our ideals of life. Unlike other countries in Melanesia—such as Papua New Guinea and the Solomon Islands that worshipped idols and thus struggled to accept the new, heavenly, spiritual God—we didn't have a hard time receiving the "message of peace and love." There's no question that Samoans had idols of course. But their understanding was that their gods and deities were spirits. When they finally understood the Scriptures of the new message, they recognized that Scripture too speaks of the Spirit.

The people of the Solomon Islands had difficulty accepting this concept, because they fought the idea of worshipping the Spirit versus an idol. It's much like the people of Israel in ancient times. They worshiped idols, like Baal and other deities. It didn't take Moses long to go up the mountain to receive the Ten Commandments but, to paraphrase Old Testament Scripture, when he returned, the people of Israel were already building the golden calf to worship. They continued to return to their idols—to foreign gods—because they didn't accept the concept of God's spiritual relationships. It wasn't until the Hebrews were galvanized by the idea of the Spirit that it began to resonate with the Israelites.

But Samoan culture is anchored in the idea that we are earthly people. Samoans believe they come from the earth, and, therefore, they believe that this is a temporary stage of life. They have always understood that there is a spirit that interacted with them on a daily basis.

Classical European Christianity centered on belief about the heavenly world. The teachings were all about the soul's preparation for admission to the next world. Of course, some in the ministry took advantage of that, using the scare tactics of "heaven or hell" preaching. But that was an alien concept to the Samoans. The idea of weighing all your hopes for the future on the heavenly new world is anchored in hope and fate.

Samoans believed that they were able to communicate with their ancestors, so it was not difficult for them to conceive of what the future looked like in real terms. Even when people have passed on, they can still speak through their spirits. A Samoan grandmother might say, "Listen; listen to the whispers of your ancestors that speak to you, for they guide you to the truth." And truth, in this language, is the same word as "right" or "correct"— that is *sa'o* or *moni* or *fa'amaoni*. "They will tell you where they come from and where they are going. Just listen."

The Samoan proverb advises: Don't drink water from another person's well. Drink the water from your own family well, because it is the well of your ancestors, and that is the source of the truth. In this way, the ava ceremony summons the spirits, to assist the village Chiefs Council in their meeting. They call upon the spirits for wisdom during testing and trials.

And so it was always about the spirit for the Samoans, and this made it easy for the people to transition into accepting Christianity's Holy Spirit and His message.

Structure of the Ava Ceremony

Family Meetings and Presentations

So now we come to the structure of the ava ceremony. After the welcome remarks by the resident orators and high chiefs, the welcome response by guest orators and high chiefs and ministers, and the opening speech by the lead orator, then comes the presentation of the *sua* (gifts) to the family or to the *Sa'o* (the high chief), followed by the presentation of further gifts, fine mats, foods, money etc. and other discussion. Then comes the closing portion of the orator speech, followed by the farewell portion of the orator speech.

Welcome remarks are made as chiefs arrive the meeting, assuming their designated seating positions.

Next there is a speech for the gathering of the ava, followed by blessing the ava and presenting it to the aumaga for

239

preparation. The aumaga begins preparing the ava at the back of the maota, behind the *tanoa* ava basin. They have procedures they follow as they mix the ava with water. While the orators begin negotiation, the *aumaga* whisper communications among themselves, to ensure the sacredness of the ava preparations.

The senior orators negotiate upon who among them will deliver the welcoming speech—the village protocol. Then the welcome speech is delivered, and a response is made by a senior orator based on village structure.

A speech is made for the ava, and the sacred ava is presented to the high chiefs, guests, orators etc., in an order dictated by village protocols. Then, after the ava, the meeting agenda is addressed. And next, a recess is called for lunch. An ava presentation restarts the meeting when the agenda continues. Then comes a closing speech by the senior orator with a response by the corresponding senior orator. And then the farewell. [xc]

The Welcome Speech

At the start of the meeting, the senior orators might debate as to who's going to say the first speech, which is called the welcoming speech. Usually this is held in the morning, and we should remember now: it has seven different sections. The orator may have repeated this speech a thousand times, but he will not miss one of the seven or he will get scolded. Everyone is listening.

Fa'atau means "negotiating," and this is the term used for deliberating—for deliberating who will make the welcome speech. Deliberating is an honorable thing; it's the moment where you say, "This is your turn;" where, the more you give, the more is given back to you. They might say, "The circle wants to hear; you have been gone a long time in America. The circle wants to hear you." When this is not the way we do things today, then we have lost the meaning of this very critical process. Today we have arguments—negotiation rather than deliberation.

So the senior orators first negotiate among themselves, to designate who will deliver the welcoming speech. Once this is determined, the orator will go through the whole speech process, starting with the introduction. So, time for a reminder: how do you phrase the introduction?

1. Firstly, the orator must acknowledge the sacred ground, because these sacred grounds are sanctioned by the gods.
2. Secondly, this is followed by acknowledging the paramount chief's residences.

Sometimes there might be two sacred meeting grounds. One is *Malaepule* and the other is *Malaeti'a*. The introduction has to cover and recognize the sacred ground because it's what you're standing on.

This is very much like in the Bible: for example, when Moses was standing on sacred ground and was asked to take off his shoes as he witnessed a burning bush—you know the story: "This is sacred ground." And so you must reference the sacred ground, because you must show honor and respect for it. So, remembering our Culture Dialog example of the High Chief *Alo*... we recognize that this is one of the ancient sacred grounds in this island of Tutuila. This is where the kingdom of Mageafaigā began, the ancient sacred ground that we know as the "House of Ten."

This "House of Ten" was the first foundation of Tutuila, the *Falegafulu—fale* meaning house, and *gafulu*, meaning ten. And so the salutation would begin:

- *Fa'aliliu mai Sasa'e, fa'aliliu mai Sisifo*—from the East and from the West of Tutuila Island, I must honor it.
- *Itua ma Nofoa o le faiā lea o le Afioga Alo*—Mageafaigā's son and the first *Alo*.
- *Afio lau Afioga Alo ma lou Nofoa vaevaeloloa i le Nofoali'i o Itu'au ma Nofoa, tolu!*—a seat or chair (*nofoa*) with multiple legs (*vaevaeloloa*) is only decreed to those who have a kingdom-like structure in the village or district ruling authority, such as *Alo* and *Lualemana* of Asu village, Tutuila, hence its being Chief *Alo's* part of the salutation.
- To address the village, you would start with the word *To'a* then *Fia* (the number three) for the *Ali'i* or three paramount chiefs—*Alo*, *Tuinei*, and *Tupuola*. So you would say *Afio le to'a Fia o Ali'i, lau Afioga Alo ma lou Nofoa vaevaeloloa.*

In this way you would honor the residence of the venerable Paramount High Chief *Alo* and his mighty seat as the foundation family of the village of Fagasā.

You all understand this, right? I'm not speaking (or writing) in Samoan. But this is very important! If you don't explain this properly, then you just blew it, like a feather in the wind. So why would you use other words? I would ask the Culture Dialog participants to look up these words in the dictionary: venerable, reverential, pious, numinous. They are important. We should look them up!

I know a lot of people don't like to use such words. The missionaries didn't want to know all those words, because they started to sound like they were addressing the pope, or like these guys were beginning to sound like gods. And yes, there was a time when *Alo* was considered a "deity." It's just that now we have made him more human. He *is* a human, but if you understand the genealogical beginning of *Alo* (which we will look at in Volume II), you'll know why he became paramount. *Alo* was a pretty tough guy in his day.

And that's what it means: Respect is how you should refer to these people. If you are speaking of Paramount High Chief *Alo*, you would appropriately give him the title *Lau Afioga*. Otherwise it would be perfectly okay to say *Sūsūga*, *Lau Sūsūga*. Be sure that you can recognize this.

The Ava Speech

So, the welcome speech is completed and delivered successfully. Now there is a protocol whereby the high chief, the *Sa'o*, responds to the orator. He thanks him for a great speech and for the wonderful meeting. Senior orators would also comment on how appropriate the delivery was. And, after all that is done, then comes the presentation of the ava. The speech for the ava is ready.

There is another full-length speech now, about the ava ceremony. In my village and in Manu'a, they do not allow a memorized poem. They do not allow you to *kauloko*, saying that is for the young and immature. The older people speak from their heads. So, let's say if we're getting ready to go to Nu'uuli. Every one of us that's taking the trip to Nu'uuli must know who and what we are going over there for.

Image 24 ava cup or tanoa, image owned by author

Suppose we're going to visit *Soliai*. Then *Atua ua sau i fanua* (The deity that came on shore) is his ava cup in Fagasā village. And *Fatu* (heart) *Palalaua* (depend or rely on us) is *Soliai's* cup in Nu'uuli village when they go to war... It means "the heart of relying on us, Nu'uuli/Fagasā, the 'Vanguard of War,'" or "the Heart of the Vanguard of war." And how do I know this? I research it. There is no book that will show you *Palalaua*. I also know that his ordinary cup is *Logo i tino matagi lelei*, which means "You can feel in your body, the wind of good fortune coming."

The ava speech refers to the sacred nature of the event and the gathering of ava from visiting chiefs and the village or family chiefs. In our example, we had a mat that we circulated around for the chiefs to place their ava upon. Once all the ava (roots and sun-dried stems or sticks) were collected, they were placed in front of the talking chiefs, who made a speech about the sacredness of the ava.

That's what you would call "the gathering of the ava speech," or "the blessing of the ava." Then the *aumaga*, the young warriors, begin the preparation of the ava. The princess would come in, take a seat in the back, the part called *tanoa*, and begin the process of the mixing the ava with water.

Sua—Presentation of Gifts

Everyone in the Culture Dialog would have been familiar with the *sua* presentation; they would have witnessed it at a family function, or in a church setting.

The *sua* includes the presentations of gifts, fine mats, money, and food, etc. In our example, when presenting the *'ietoga*, we had a *sua* presentation. In my speech, I wouldn't refer to this as the *tao ma le uatogi* (spear and war club), because I was the one that would *ta'i* the *sua* to a guest—i.e. present the *sua* (food for the chief's meal, such as pig, taro, chickens etc.). It is up to the receiver to refer to the *tao ma le uatogi*. During his speech of appreciation, he would say, "Fata, you have reached back to the ancient tradition of this village. You have opened the finest of all riches in Fagasā, the *tao* and the *uatogi*. It is the fine mat that states how mighty *Alo* is, *ole Sa'o, o lona nofoa vaevaeloloa*."

Note, he wouldn't simply say "a fine mat"—*tao ma le uatogi*. For it would be very impolite not to recognize the beautiful royal mats, because they don't open these mats up every day; they save them. The fine mat of Valasi, and the *aiga* (family) of SaLevalasi are also fine mats that you wouldn't open every day. Even if my *'ietoga* wasn't all that good, he would promote it by giving it the highest praise:

> *Fata, ua e a'apa i le toga Pa'ia a le malo o Samoa. Ua tatala* (open) *le 'tao ma le uatogi,' aua e fa'asigo iai le Sa'o, le afioga ia Alo ma lona nofoa vaevaeloloa. O lo'o fa'asigo ai le ali'i o aiga, le Tamamātua, ma le Usoali'i, le tofā o lo'o tausi I upu a Fagasā, fa'amalo; fa'afetai—*

"Fata, you have opened up the 'ietoga of the paramount chiefs and royal monarchy of the paramount chiefs and the Sa'o Alo, and his multi-seat extended family, the Mātua or Elder Tuinei, Senior Orator Speakers Tamamātua, fraternal brothers, and the four orator speakers on behalf of Fagasā village." *Tao* is a spear, and *uatogi* is a war club; the words are used here as a metaphor for the heirlooms that protect the island population; this is the same as the *'ietoga* being used as a medium of exchange—a tradition that can save lives.

I should tell you, the Samoan fine mat is valued for its fine weave. In ancient times, the fine mat would have been the sail used on the mast of the double-hull canoe. It is still made in the same way by the women of the village in the *fale lalaga* (the weaving house). The beautiful mats are family heirlooms, and are exchanged as gifts at weddings and funerals, chief title ceremonies, and other special occasions, including house blessings and church openings.

Usually each chief, when they come in, will bring their own piece of ava, "dry ava" sticks (roots and sun-dried stems). If you see them carrying this, you know they are going to some kind of special occasion, to a Chiefs Council meeting.

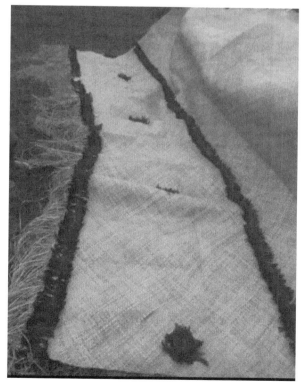

So, they take the mat and collect the ava sticks, first from the high chiefs and the talking chiefs. Then they pull the mat over to the paramount chief and he puts his roots on top.

Image 25 Fine Mat image owned by Author

One person makes the speech to collect the ava. Another one makes the speech to sanctify it. Then it is taken to the back where the aumaga prepare it (in old days they used to chew the ava, not in the back, but outside in the sun. They brought the ava bowl outside and followed the procedure—water to cleanse the mouth, then chew, then take out the spit.) The Taupou mixes the ava with the water.

Distribution of the Ava

When you hear clapping from the back, this means the ava is ready for distribution. The presentation of the ava begins.

Various ava names would be called out in a loud voice: *Aumai* (bring) *Faifaimalie upu o Samoa!* Who's that? You forgot? *Lau ava nei Sili!* Who's this guy? See these guys. *Iseiluamaivasa! Fa'atafeamatausala! Aumai alalafaga ma Lufilufi!* Who's that guy? *Salanoa*. And you'll hear people say, "Man, I want to sound like him," for orators speak from the diaphragm.

The Taupou sends the ava bowl from the back with all its customary decorations. The decorations all have meanings. They are not accidents; not even the feathers. You can trace which bird that feather came from, and what color, and who did the coloring and the dying. It's all very particular.

Once the ava is concluded it would be announced, *Ua moko le ava, Aumaia le ava Aloali'i!* The last ava always goes to the prince; in this case it would be *Salanoa*.

Conclusion

After the ava ceremony, they take a break and have lunch. Just before the break they have one more go at the ava. In other words, they've been at it for hours discussing various subjects. Now they recess for lunch and then resume the meeting, calling it to order with the ava ritual, and continuing the meeting until the end.

There may be several rounds where the ava is served, until the subject under discussion is done or postponed to another day. Then they will have a closing ava serving, to close the meeting. This is where the last and final ava cup is served to the prince or Sa'o Tama'ita'i, or the paramount chief seated opposite the Sa'o. This ava ceremony will conclude the meeting.

Organization and Laws

So now we come to the section on Samoan and Manu'an organizational structures. In Volume II we will see how the arrival of the Western world influenced our rules. But in this volume we will concentrate on the cultural aspects of the organization and laws.

Rules and Organizational Structure

History of Government

The *Tagaloalagi* Period

The demigod *Tagaloalagi* is the creator of the islands, of the first Samoans and Manu'ans, and of every living thing.

Manu'an and Samoan organizational structures begin with the organization of the expanding family structure through intermarriage. In the beginning, *Tagaloalagi* was the progenitor of the expanding foundational families in Samoa (Savai'i, Upolu, and Tutuila) and in Manu'a, as told in the legend of *Lu* and his sacred flock of chickens (see *Navigators Quest for a Kingdom in Polynesia*). At this time warriors emerged whose heroic efforts were rewarded with chieftain titles. They in turn accumulated authority and corresponding land or property in particular geographical areas which would later be known as districts.

The distribution of designations, appointments, responsibility, and authority, through decrees or proclamations by these early rulers, became foundational to early development of the national organizational structure and culture of Samoa and Manu'a. This also began the importance of keeping account of family identity and genealogy. The chronology of historical events shows evidence of how these progenitors' genealogies have shaped the subsequent organization of the major families of the islands, Samoa and Manu'a.

In this period, the core single-family structure existed as it had since the arrival of the earliest migrants. It is *Tagaloalagi* who decreed sacred places called *Malae* with specific names for

247

the Chiefs Council meeting—names such as *Malae Toto'a* (for peaceful meetings), *Malae o Vevesi* (for meetings to deliberate war), *Malae o Vavau* (for meetings to view the ancient, distant past)—in Taū, Manu'a, Alamisi in Samatauta, and Samatatai in Savai'i—and a resting *malae* when *Tagaloalagi* sojourned in Savai'i as told in the Manu'an "Poem of Creation."

Residences of chiefs were also given special names, locations, and designations in the sacred village property, as a point of family land identification. And these practices continued with subsequent paramount chiefs or rulers at the village and district level.

The *Tagaloalagi* time-period is ancient, and the corresponding mythology and legends clearly indicate the development of early organizational structures stemming from original pioneer families, dating from this period.

The TuiManu'a Period

The rule of the paramount monarch Tuimanu'a over all Samoa and Manu'a is evidenced with early decrees and proclamations of authority to different chiefs in various villages where he visited, or from where he secured marriages—these were given special names and designations. The promulgation of these proclamations became foundational to the early development of the organizational structure and culture of Samoa and Manu'a.

The recognition of warrior leaders of various districts across Samoa and Manu'a is evidenced in the ruling authority of geographical areas—for example, the recognition of the Atua and A'ana districts and Savai'i as a separate group, with its own warrior rulers, such as the brothers *Laifai* and *Funefe'ai* and their respective descendants who helped unify it as an extended family organization.

The Tuamasaga district emerged as a distinct entity after the Toga war and the founding of the Malietoa dynasty, around A.D.1225. Right around that time, both Samoa and Manu'a had a loose organizational structure at the family and district level. But they were evolving rapidly into a recognizable district authority that would become the permanent structure, evidenced in its salutations even today.

The practice of intermarriage was honed as a process of externally growing the family, and hence the acquisition of land and territories together with, of course, authority and power. This "human force" propelled an evolutionary "survival of the fittest" organizational anatomy.

The Role of Orator Chiefs

The delegation and designation of the orator chief as the messenger or harbinger of a tyrant ruler represents a paradigm innovation in the development of the culture and society. This function and title, orator, accumulated considerable authority in the daily operational management of the family, village, and district over time, to the point where some orators could often have significantly more authority at different levels of the hierarchy of the extended family. Examples include: *Tafua* and *Fuataga* of the Aleipata, Atua district; *Alipia* and the nine orators in the A'ana district; the six paramount orators and their six counselors in the Lufilufi, Atua district; and *Fata* and *Maulolo* in the Tuamasaga district, together with a few others. Many of these orator chiefs are genealogically connected to the paramount family they served.

The Acquisition of Royal Crowns

The period of warring to acquire PāPās, or royal crowns, was critical to the division and authority of the Island Nation with respect to politics and tribalism. The concept of empire-building was very much practiced at the local district level; wars to consolidate the PāPās were guided by Warrior Queen *Nafanua*, and the royal crowns were headed by prodigious women such as *Gatoa'itele*, *Vaetamasoaali'i*, *Leutogitupa'itea*, *Salamasina*, *Valasi*, *Atougaugaatuitoga* and others.

Samoan historians are in agreement that the bestowment of the first two honorific royal crowns (PāPās), TuiAtua and TuiA'ana, onto Tafa'ifa *Salamasina Tamālelagi* took place around A.D.1560. The other two PāPās, Gatoa'itele and Vaetamasoaali'i, were installed at later, separate ceremonies that took place at their respective *malaes* at Vaitoelau, for the Gatoa'itele crown, and at Togamau, for Vaetamasoaali'i. The protocol is that each

249

title must be bestowed in its respective, sacred *malae,* or meeting ground and residency. The "Fine Mats Gifting Ritual," a mandatory procedure, must be held at the sacred *malae,* otherwise it's not valid.

Dr. Krämer noted that Tafa'ifa *Salamasina* brought the fine mat *Fa'aoti i Salani,* a name which means "completed weaving in Salani." This mat was woven by *Sivalavala,* second wife of Tonumaipe'a *Saumaipe'a,* and begun in Saginoga, where the precious ancient mat *Lagava'a* was completed. *Lagava'a* is the ancient mat that was woven onboard vessel by the married couple, *Fane'a* and *Fane'a,* who landed in Saginoga, in the district of Salailua, Savai'i, and its name means "weaving on a vessel."

Tafa'ifa *Salamasina* brought the mat *Fa'aoti i Salani* to Tuisamau and gifted it to *Fata* in exchange for the Gatoa'itele PāPā. This evidence shows that the Gatoa'itele and Vaetamasoaali'i titles were not bestowed in Leulumoega by *Alipia* and the House of Nine.

A mishap in details like this is a usually a cause for war. Thus, the legendary *Alipia's* salutations were directed to the Tumua (*Leulumoega* and *Lufilufi*) and Pule (*Safotulafai* and *Saleaula*) of Savai'i. A technical title of Fata and Maulolo and Tuisamau is Laumua, seat of all Tumua.

The bestowment of the first two honorific royal crowns onto *Salamasina Tamālelagi,* in around A.D.1560, marked the first time a paramount orator chief, *Alipia* of Leulumoega, A'ana district, gave the formal salutation to all in attendance at the ceremony. The event took place in Leulumoega village in the A'ana district. At this time, Orator Chief *Alipia* addressed the audience of all Samoa with the Salutations as follows:

➢ Honorable *Tumua* and *Pule...*
- *Tumua* (meaning to stand first in deliberation) refers to the orator councilors of Lufilufi village, on behalf of the Atua district, and to *Fata* and *Maulolo* and the Tuisamau councilors of the Tuamasaga district, and to *Alipia* and the nine orator councilors of the A'ana district.
- *Pule* (meaning ruler or authority to rule) refers to the two ruling orator group authorities in Savai'i, consisting of orator councilors in the Safotulafai district

and the Saleaula district. This was subsequently extended to six orator group authorities at the end of the war between Malietoa *Laupepa* and his uncle *Talavou* (often referred to by the European consuls as Malietoa *Talavou*) in A.D.1868. Authority in the Safotu, Palauli, Satupa'itea, and Asau districts was promulgated from the two original authorities: Safotulafai and Saleaula in Savai'i, where TuiAtua *Mata'afa* was defeated.

> ...the venerable foundational families of Samoa and Manu'a and their princes and families... This would include:
> - The Honorific Families of Nofo (Seat of foundational)
> - Honorific Families of Monarchs, or *Aiga o Fale*, and
> - Honorific Aiga o PāPā.

Many of the families have additional Salutations in honor of their family. For example: Aiga Sa Tuala is the *Aiga Fa'alagilagi* (Heavenly foreshadowing protection of his feagaiga Tafa'ifa *Salamasina*). For Tuala is the first born of TuiA'ana *Tamālelagi* and thus also referred to as *Ali'ioāiga*. But he was decreed to take care of Tafa'ifa *Salamasina*, his feagaiga. The war families of the TuiA'ana district are the *AigaTau* (fight) of A'ana. Hence Aiga TauA'ana. *AigaTaulagi* (Heavenly Salutation) is the honorific salutation to the royal family of TuiA'ana TuiAtua *Faumuinā*. And the three royal families (*Aiga i Fale*) are:

1. Sa Tupuā
2. Sa Malietoa
3. Sa TuiManu'a[xci]

> ...Honorable, the war fleet of Warrior Queen *Nafanua* (*Auva'a*)

Government Constitution

So now, the current government constitution's framework is based on the established political organizational structure, as defined by the divisions evidenced in the country salutations. The cultural and political division of Samoa, not including Manu'a, led to the selection of representatives from the districts, who then became the voice of the people directed to a collective body of government administration. The representatives, in essence, took on the role and authority of the *Tumua* and *Pule* as the voice or messenger of the district, or of the paramount chiefs' ruling authority in the district, or of the major divisions of the Island Nation.

Manu'a is a separate kingdom, not under the structure of Samoa, but the TuiManu'a lineage is still foundational to the genealogies of the Samoan families.

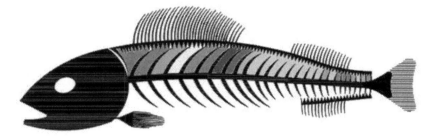

Image 26 Image owned by Author

Using the metaphor of a fish skeleton again:

1. The head represents the paramount royal crown ruling the families.
2. The so-called "backbone" really consists of separate rib bones that are tied together by tissues and cartilage. It appears as if there is a single, solid, continuous bone. Beside it, the rib bones represent separate families and clans which are "genetically engineered" together into a cohesive body.
3. The skeleton is flat to symbolize a flat surface structure with a linear flow of authority, as opposed to a pyramidal hierarchical structure.
4. Responsibilities are equal in importance, and thus the fish cannot move any part of the anatomy if others are not working.
5. The bone marrow that flows from head to tail feeds the whole body's anatomy.
6. The meat and skin represent the language that ties together the body and brings it to life.
7. Finally, it's almost impossible to count the number of bones in a fish, much like the threads of Samoan genealogy and kinship.

For example, the vanguards and rearguards are in charge of fighting wars. If they don't agree to go to war, the "fish" does not go to war. Likewise, if the orators in charge of the ava ceremony choose not to participate, there won't be an ava ceremony. Then, since according to protocol we cannot start a meeting without an ava ceremony, we won't have a meeting either.

This illustrates how the culture is based on interdependence. The culture is a collective whole formed by its parts. The parts, by themselves, cannot move as any kind of whole.

By looking at the "fish skeleton" metaphor, one can see that there are more separate chief titles, delineating functional responsibility, represented in the anatomy of the fish, than in a typical corporate business or government organization. The (modern) science of division of labor, accompanied by the creative assignments of titles, many of them chief titles, has long been used to delineate functions and processes in the protocols and customs of the culture.

It should be noted that the Navigators had long practiced the chiefdom system of organizational structure, prior to their immigration journey to the archipelago. Then, as we can see, when the islands' population increased, they honed the system to facilitate economic and cultural development.

Administration of Justice

The organization for administering and delivering justice to the people is the chiefdom system or chiefdom organizational structure. At the family, village, and clan levels, the chief has responsibility to deliberate and deliver decisions on justice, based on the hierarchical structure of rank. At the village and district levels, the Chiefs Council deliberate and deliver justice decisions, although this also follows a hierarchical structure of chiefs, based on rank and seniority in the Chiefs Council.

The authority of the village Chiefs Council is foundational to overall law and order and to the administration of justice throughout the Island Nation. It is foundational to the current government of Samoa and, to some extent, the same with American Samoa, which includes Manu'a, with changes implemented by the United States of America to comply with the Constitution.

These Chiefs Council sessions are closed to the public. The accusers represent themselves, and witnesses can be invited and cross-examined by the members of the council. It's said, by many experts, that the village authority in Samoa is a critical aspect of the Island Nation's effective system of law enforcement. Again, it provides another example of the role of strong cultural adherence in keeping the peace and maintaining the safety of the population.

Administration of Districts

Looking at the history of these islands and their respective district and village administrations, we see it goes back to the ancient founding families that first settled the various geographical areas. Thus, the Island of Upolu, the two small Islands of Manono and Apolima, and Savai'i are combined into one government administration. Within this administration, there are three major district administrations. The districts are Atua, A'ana, and Tuamasaga, with the district of Aiga i le Tai being included in the A'ana political district because of geography and family ties, and Manono and Apolima being included with Upolu under Atua.

Although it's included in the A'ana political district, Aiga i le Tai is included in the overall Samoan vanguards and rearguards of war, which includes several districts of Savai'i—Safotulafai, SaLeMuliaga, the Alataua district of Palauli and Satupa'itea, and the Faleata and Safata districts of Tuamasaga. They all supply troops to fight a war, depending on which side they pledge their support to. For example, during the Civil War between the brothers, *Fonotī* and *Va'afusuaga*, Aiga i le Tai provided the fleet of navy vessels and Faleata the ground troops for *Fonotī*, while the majority of A'ana and half of Atua and Safata and Tuisamau were on *Va'afusuaga Toleafoa's* side. Savai'i split right down the middle for both royal princes.

Aiga i le Tai has its own salutation and honorifics. In terms of their genealogy, the people of Aiga i le Tai are descendants from the same stock as the Malietoa on one side, and from the *Fata* and *Maulolo* genealogy on the other side. The relationship between *Fata* and *Maulolo* and the Aiga i le Tai district is through *Le'iatauaLesā,* the paramount chief of the district, who is the son of *Lelāpueisalele*, sister of *Oleaifale'ava*. *Oleaifale'ava* is the blind ancestor of *Fata*, *Maulolo*, *Va'afa'i*, and *Luafatasaga*, hence the salutation *Feagaiga,* which means "Sister or Brother of the Sacred Covenant." All cultural "boundaries" and *tapu* (taboos) are adhered to in the Feagaiga covenant. For example, Aiga i le Tai, in war, would not cross the physical boundaries of Afega and the seat of Tuisamau district, and vice-versa.

Savai'i, in its ancient structure, is divided into six administrative authorities. They are Safotulafai, Saleaula, Safotu, Palauli, Satupa'itea and Asau.

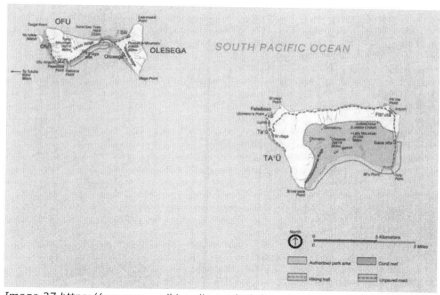

Image 27 https://commons.wikimedia.org/wiki/File:MapOfManua_NPS.png NPS, converted into .png by Telim tor, Public domain, via Wikimedia Commons

The Island of Tutuila was under Malietoa rule before the late 1600s. Then it came under the Upolu administration, as a part of Atua. Today it is a possession of the United States of America, under the Deed of Cession Agreement, signed in April 1900. This agreement did not include the Kingdom of Manu'a but, after further negotiation, the Deed of Cession of Manu'a was finally signed by the TuiManu'a Elisara, Tufele, Misa, Tui Olosega and Asoau of Faleasao village in early 1905.

The Tutuila Administration consists of ten districts. These are Sua, Vaifanua, Saole, Fagaloa, Itu'au, Nofoa, Fofo, Itulagi, Leasina, and Satoa.

The Kingdom of Manu'a has Taū, Faleasao, Fitiuta, Ofu Island, Olosega Island and Sili hamlet.

Subdivisions and Villages

In 1898, Dr. Augustin Krämer, in the conduct of his project, visited every village in the islands of Samoa and Manu'a. He noted that the average size of a village population was around 30 to 40 people, though some larger villages could number in excess of a couple of hundred people. Today's populations average around 200 to 500 for a small village (a hamlet of a big village). Some village subdivisions can number around 500 to 800 people now, while populations of larger district headquarter villages can number in excess of 1,500 to 2,000. For example, the population of my village is hovering around 3,500 registered voters in the last two elections (2015 and 2010).

Counting the villages and hamlets, Dr. Krämer found that Savai'i had a total of 36 villages, including hamlets, each with separate administrations. Today, Savai'i has 78 villages. In Upolu Island, the A'ana district had a total of 16 major villages and hamlets in 1898, including Apolima and Manono Islands. Today it has 24. Tuamasaga district had 39 villages and hamlets in 1898, and now has the same number of major villages. And Atua district had 40 villages including a few hamlets; today it has 48.

The Island of Tutuila, including Aunu'u, had 27 villages and a few hamlets in 1898; today its count stands at 48 villages. Manu'a Island, which includes Ofu, Olosega, and Sili Islands, had a total of 6 major villages in 1898 and today has the same number.

So, while the population has grown on a per-village basis, the number of villages has, for the most part, stayed the same or similar: the total number of villages for Samoa and Manu'a is 242.

For every village, there is a salutation, designating certain authorities to various seats in the maota. These village salutations are also the same today as when Dr. Krämer documented them in his 1902 publication. Although some titles may differ in the salutations of 1898, compared to current salutations, this simply reflects some old family titles that have been revived.

Honor

In any highly civilized society, you would expect that over time there would be war treaties and rewards that must be bestowed on the victor of a war. The practice with Samoans is very simple. If someone is a defeated warrior, the procedure is to kneel down in front of the warriors that won the war. The hands are positioned, hanging straight down and folded toward the back of the waist, with the head extended out. It's very much like the behavior we see in Greek mythology, like that of the Babylonians, and that of the Egyptians—the same posture all throughout the ages.

You might wonder how Samoans, being in the middle of nowhere, came up with this idea? Why didn't they just sit on a rock and say, "Go at it, brother?" Why go through this ritual? But no, it turns out that Samoans practice the same exact posture as so many other cultures. For this is a sign of a highly civilized society. First, they go to war. When it's completed, they establish the victor over the defeated. The warriors that have been defeated must "assume the position." They kneel down, with their head extended. Of course, if you choose not to do this voluntarily, the victorious warriors may decide that your head should remain with them, to be used as a football, and not returned to your village at all. Then you will not be honored as a mighty warrior.

A good warrior accepts defeat. For an honorable defeat displays the character of a true warrior, because saving the family dignity reinforces the fortitude of the ancient ancestors; it ensures the sustainability of future generations of the family. Thus they celebrate heroes and their gallant efforts, celebrating not just memories of the "agony of defeat," but the honor of the family for posterity.

Have you ever heard the Manu Samoa Rugby Theme song? It says, *ae e malolo* (when you're defeated) *e malolo fa'atamali'i*.

This means: if you are defeated, do you want to receive defeat like an animal, or like a high chief. The *malolo* of the *fa'atamali'i* is to receive defeat with dignity like a high chief, so that you may live to fight another day. But, if not, it is your duty as a warrior to get down and do what is necessary for you to prove that you will receive defeat with honor, as a representative of your ancestors before you, and for your children after you.

Laws and Property

In an ancient oral-based society, cultural customs and etiquette and their formalities are the foundation of governance and management of the community. The first established sets of laws, ordinances, *tapu* (taboos), and regulations governing family, village, clan, district, and the Island Nation are based on anecdotal lessons from past experience, coupled with a need to hone the cohesiveness of cultural norms, rituals, and ceremonial protocols, and to establish practices maintaining individual boundaries between people and groups. Early development of this process began during the TuiManu'a reign and the emerging TuiAtua and TuiA'ana regimes.

The approach is basic, and the methodology leads to a tightly woven culture with organizational threads that become the glue, tying governing processes to the community and society. These administrative processes all continue to reaffirm the chiefdom system of organizational structure; and the role of the orator as a spokesperson for the family, village, clan, and district is further elevated in the hierarchical structure of the culture and its governance.

When missionaries and business entrepreneurs arrived in the early 1800s, the obvious differences between Samoan and Manu'an practice and European common laws and torts, as well as between them and ordinances governing European business trades and practices, led to a perception of Samoan and Manu'an norms as being primitive, based in the practices of primitive culture. For example: almost all European writers chronicling the early years of the colonial period commented on a Samoan behavior that they considered the handiwork of thievery. It became a major source of European complaint, because they did not understand the culture.

Theft and Acquisition

The taking of someone else's property, without asking or gaining permission, is forbidden in law in almost any culture or society. And the early European assumption of Samoan "thievery" was really a misunderstanding of Samoan tradition.

Before the island government implemented European-style laws and torts, the "old" Samoan culture relied on asking, giving, and reciprocity. The same custom, or medium of exchange, was studied with the Trobriand Island tribe in the Solomon Archipelago, Melanesia in 1922, by Dr. B. Malinowski, and was made famous.[xcii] This field research became fundamental in looking at early development of functionalism in indigenous culture organizational structures.

Samoans would ask permission, but if there was no one available to give permission, they would and did just help themselves, with the expectation of gift-giving reciprocity later. This is particularly true with agricultural products such as fruits, coconut, taro, bananas etc. But the trading currency was still, effectively, "please," "thank you," and gift exchange, where gift exchange is the focus in the gift-giving oratory protocol of ceremonial occasions. Often, the more eloquent the oratorical presentation, the more the gifts that flow back to the orator's family, so that sometimes, if the orator gets carried away in his oration, it may begin to sound like begging. For eloquence is an art and a science, but common sense is a balancing wisdom.

The rationale, of oratory and of gift-giving, leads back simply to genealogical connections. The whole Island Nation can be reduced to a few families, some say about 15 major families. On another level, there are only three royal crown families: SaTuiManu'a, SaTupua, and SaMalietoa. This provides motivation to memorize the families' genealogies, so one can easily and quickly recite the family's genealogical connections during ceremonial oration. Leadership is defined by your oratorical proficiency. You can't lead if you can't master the gift of God. It's the science and art of developing a narrative—the storytelling gift that is the heart of God's gift to the Navigators of the Pacific Ocean.

The new set of common laws and torts, based on European laws and Christianity's Biblical commandments, was a major challenge to the Samoans, requiring behavior modifications in this aspect of their cultural transformation.

Economics of Gifting and Exchange

Bronislaw Malinowski first studied the real live practice of bartering and exchange of goods and services as an economic model in 1917, with the Trobriand natives in the Papua New Guinea Archipelago. He coined the word "reciprocity" to describe it. But he did not know that the Navigators of the Archipelago had been using this "gift-giving" practice as an integral part of their economic system and culture for over 3,000 years.

Fundamental to gift exchanges is the understanding of "give and take," or "I give to you; you give to me." The rationale is that you give because of honor and respect, and then, in a market setting, it becomes a question of need versus supply. The recipient, likewise, gives to reciprocate out of honor and respect.

Much like any practice, this is eventually subject to abuse, whereby one might manipulate the goods or gifts, and manipulate the exchange value process.

Samoans believe excessive gifts, relative to the weight of the occasion, imply manipulation, meaning there is perhaps another motivation behind the gifts. In fact, a Samoan proverb mentions the "excessive gifts of a beggar," meaning that to get more, you give more, and appeal to the recipient's pride, honor, and status. In return, this leads to reciprocity plus more, commensurate to the status of the family you are elevated to.

Next comes the concept of a medium of exchange, which implies an assignment of value—nominal, intrinsic, or a combination of both. Value assessment is based on supply and demand for the goods or services being exchanged. The nominal price or value is determined by usage or appropriate application of the goods or services. For example, the more you need flints and black obsidian for weapons, cutlery, and tools, the higher the assigned value would likely be. Likewise, more available supply might the lower the value assigned. Ocher is rare, so its limited supply could mean a high value assessment. Food crops, fish, pigs, and other food products are all subject to the medium of exchange. Competition occurs when supply and demand are out of balance, or what the economist calls not in "equilibrium."

Then there are the psychological aspects of value assessment—that is, the recognition of intrinsic value, which considers the value the owner puts on the product or commodity, based on their own emotional aspect toward it. This applies, always, in cases involving heirlooms of historical value. It usually means, no matter how much value is offered, the seller would not accept. The concept of there being a price that would eventually clear the market does not usually work in these cases, because of the psychology of intrinsic value assessment.

The experience of the traders allows the whole process to function smoothly and efficiently. Thus, during the ceremonial gift-giving exchange, the orator who is conducting the oration does it all and will be efficient at it. Merchant-traders are then an offshoot career for the gift-giving orator.

So, value pegging is an attempt to standardize value assessment, to simplify the exchange process. The Samoan "fine mat" or tapestry, for example, is a standard cultural heirloom that can have a standardized value assessment. It has been used to standardize value exchanges, through managing the quantity and quality of the mats throughout the population. The balancing of supply and demand is intuitive. Production of fine mats can be controlled, and the mats can be stored. The division of labor has been put in place and can be reshuffled, to optimize productivity.

The real issue is: can this system of exchange sustain the livelihood of a community? The answer is the system of exchange works, in the context of the overall cultural norms and practices. It is integral to the cultural protocols for an occasion. Thus, self-governing of the process is integrated into the Samoan protocol procedure. Measurement of successful exchanges is part of the value assessment equation. Costs are integral to the production assessment and its dependence on labor. And land is abundant, therefore its value is often ignored.

Today, there is a study of the gift-giving economic model at the university level and, of course, bartering has been included in micro-economics models. Studies of public goods and services often reference the "gift-giving" or "exchange" theoretical model. Some public goods and services (e.g. government via taxes) follow an economic model which parallels the philanthropic economic model (gift-giving) and mirrors the economic value proposition of reciprocity in the gift-giving system.

To appeal to the emotions for philanthropic value proposition parallels the gift-giving exchange proposition.

Property Rights

The Samoan concept of property rights and administration is well defined in the culture. Samoans have rules with respect to property ownership as it relates to family, clan, village, and district. They have laws and administrative processes with respect to the sacred grounds (meeting ground) and the heirlooms which are integral in a person's identity.

In business and other organizations, and in other countries and cultures, there are completely different ways of defining property rights, as dictated, for example, by a country's constitution. This leads to a philosophical difference between Samoans and other countries, such as the United States of America where the U.S. Constitution guarantees rights, even inalienable rights, to ownership of property.

A major difference between Western society's idea of property and the Eastern (Chinese, Russian, Anatolian etc.) idea lies in the way property rights can be used as collateral for borrowing money. Samoan property rights are viewed as a factor in building wealth for the family, as opposed to just in meeting the needs of welfare. Western society views the individual as an independent member of the community, thus having sole ownership of his or her property—a selfish and lonely way of looking at life.

This idea of Western individualism or singularity also shows up in religions in the sense that, to Western thinking, religion has one God. Samoans believed in *Tagaloalagi* as supreme god, and all other figures were local demons, orchestrated by local shamans, but they were not equal to *Tagaloalagi*. For example, *Taeotagaloa, TagaloaLa, TagaloaUi, Pili-i, ii, iii* etc. are not gods; they are half-human, half-spirit and are children of *Tagaloalagi*. This substantiates the singularity of *Tagaloalagi* as god of the Samoans and all of Polynesians.

The influence of this Western idea of individualism leads to the most critical aspect of Samoan cultural foundation being under attack by the new generation. Individual freedom—property rights, the right to free speech in the family circle or village Chiefs Council, the right of public protest against the government's authority—all this is pitted against collective freedom, and thus the authority of the family, village, region, clan, and government is challenged.

The idea of individualism is now challenging the core of Samoan family-centric authority and property ownership. The lines, distinguishing the natural family member's freedom from that of family authority, are blurring and to some extent even eroding altogether. The boundary-based culture is challenged in virtually every seam of the culture's woven mat. And the growing pains of growth in isolation now challenge the strength of the knots of the metaphorical fishing net.

However, continuing the Samoan metaphor, there is daylight still to open and hang the net, in order to repair and re-tie the knots for the next fishing expedition. This will require leadership at all levels of society—starting with the family chieftain level, then the village Chiefs Council—to exercise that chieftain wisdom to repair the net.

Natural Order and Duality

Boundaries

Samoans and Manu'ans knew from the beginning that there was a natural order to the division of things. They observed the division, and they called it the "boundary" or "border." But the Samoan word for this is more profound; *O le tu-a-oi*. It's the division of everything in life.

This very simple, primitive, but intuitive logic (of a natural order to division) is foundational in the development and subsequent understanding of the Navigators' culture and way of life.

- It's the natural division between human beings and the "gods," and the Christian God—which is why Samoans believed there were times when we are half-human, half-spirit

- it's the natural division between male and female
- it's the natural division between "opposites"—as the famous Greek mathematician and philosopher Pythagoras of Samos, Ionia (570 B.C.-95 B.C.) observed, the world depends on the interaction of opposites[xciii]
- it's the natural boundary or separation between a family and an individual member, a family and the village, or a village and district, region, and country.

Also, there are boundaries to the district ordinance and village *tapus* or taboos, and borders between all different levels of municipal authority and that of the central government.

Natural Duality

So it begins with the family, as a unit which evolves into an organization. Then, following on, come responsibilities that must be clearly defined and assigned or delegated to each member of the family. The naming of each task and responsibility gives it a sub-unit identification. And the assignment of authority corresponds to the level of responsibility needed to facilitate the role of decision-making, within both the family and village organizational structures.

The natural order of things was the foundation of how Samoans decided to construct their customs, formalities, traditions, and rights. We have shown how the process of delegating responsibilities, titles, and authority is integral to Samoan culture. And so, we've got the division between men and women, the division of their responsibilities, the division between members of the family as they relate to each other, and the sacred division between the sister and brother. This last one is called, in Samoan, *O le feagaiga Sa*—it's a sacred *tapu* or boundary that separates male and female siblings. There are very specific etiquettes and procedures as to the governance of the male and female—the sister and brother. For example, when the sister is in the maota, the brothers cannot enter the maota unless there is a meeting. Otherwise, he sits and speaks to her from outside.

The sacred boundary between a person and their body, *O le tuaoi a le tagata ma lona tino* (a man's boundary with his body— *my translation*) is another concept that Samoans readily incorporated into their cultural tenets. Before Christianity, Samoans knew this and honored the body as sacred. The human body has boundaries with everything else—for example between your heart and your physical body; your spirit and your heart and desire; the duality of two arms, hands, eyes, etc. Samoans knew there were natural separations within the body—male, female, mind, soul, inhaling, exhaling etc. Through that spirit and understanding, Samoans moved toward understanding the process and development of thought, *O le Tofā manino*, or human philosophy. In doing so, they reproduced, in isolation, the same ideas found in well-known Western philosophy.

Ancient Philosophy

Teaching just before the Trojan War of 1290 B.C., the Greek philosopher, Thales of Miletus (624 B.C.–546 B.C.), advocated "explicit preference for the life of reason and rational thought."[xciv] He is considered by classical philosophers to be the first Western philosopher.

Another Greek, Plato, is famous for his theory of the "tripartite" soul (or psyche)—reason, spirit, and appetite or desire—stating that reason is responsible for rational thought and so is the center of control of the soul.[xcv]

Also, there is the idea of duality, dating to the Greek philosophers. However, a new version of duality became more enlightening in the 17th century with Rene Descartes' timely re-articulation of the idea that human beings consist of two quite unlike substances which could not exist in unity. The body was subject to mechanical laws; however the mind was not, according to Descartes. He further stated that the mind was unextended— an immaterial but thinking substance—whereas the body was extended—a material but unthinking substance. So it turns out, a person lives in two spheres of histories, one comprised of what happens in and to the body, the other of what happens in and to the mind. Thus, the events in the first history are events in the physical world, while those in the second history are events in the mental world. The difference becomes profound in chronicling

265

the physical events in a culture's long history and understanding the psychology of the origin of those events.[xcvi]

Thus the Greeks had discovered there was, somehow, an "unnatural" order whereby things, by definition—by the ways they are constructed—are separate.

According to the Greek historian Hesiod, in his *Theogony* (c. 700 B.C.), the genealogy of the Greek primordial gods began with one: first came Chaos, then second the Earth, hence the first "duality" of this version of creation.[xcvii]

Hesiod continues, with series of "dualities":

- Tartarus and Eros
- Darkness and Night
- Light and Day
- Heaven and Ocean

Inherent in the forming of this "genealogy" of creation is the existence of Male and Female.[xcviii]

Pythagoras was one of the most famous and controversial (self-proclaimed) ancient Greek philosophers. He lived from around 570 to 490 B.C. Besides being famous for mathematics, he was really famous as an expert on theories of how the soul was immortal and went through a series of reincarnations.[xcix] He recognized the soul as being separate from the brain, and the coexistence of science and religion (another duality).

The Bible begins with Adam and Eve and the perfect, natural division of man and woman as a duality that began with one, single Adam. And in fact, all throughout history, mythology across multiple ancient cultures continues to reaffirm the theme of the natural order of the separation of things.

The French philosopher, René Descartes (A.D.1596-1650) is closely associated with the philosophy of dualism. To paraphrase his main (familiar) statement: thought exists and cannot be separated from "me." And an ultimate example of "separate but equal" duality is found in the U.S. Constitution—separate but inextricable.

Samoan Philosophy

There are no monuments, nor is there any concrete evidence that the Navigators had knowledge of the classics. But what we do see in the Samoans is evidence of a people's existence and their culture for over 3,000 years (since 1150 B.C.), living in isolation in the largest ocean in the world, compelled by their inquisitive minds to seek rational and logical answers to this conundrum.

Samoans always believed that, in this body, there is a natural division between the feminine and the masculine. There is a natural division of the human body, the soul and the mind, the left eye as opposed to the right eye, the left hand and right hand and so on. Samoans knew this and thus developed the belief that there should also exist half-human, half-spirit beings, similar to the "demigods" of other cultures. Hence the advent of mythology.

The Social Contract

As in building any organization, whether it be a business, government, family, village, or clan, there are certain fundamentals of organizational structure that must be conformed to. The purpose and objective of the organization and the necessary functional components of operation must be clear. Cultural rules and dogmas must be developed to ensure the operational machine works with all parts in unison. Communication must be effective in delivering messages to the organization and, of course, in ensuring compliance to the culture's rules.

Orators communicate and, finally, leaders must have the trust and the credibility to lead the organization.

Individualism and Collectivism

The more we differentiate the parts of a family, the more we give each part individual identity followed by recognition, eventually followed by responsibilities and corresponding authority. This is a serious challenge facing the current millennial, X, and Z generations in Samoa and Manu'a, especially those that have been educated or reside outside the islands. As we have seen, the outside culture of individualism goes against the foundation of Samoan and Manu'an culture. But understanding the development of the culture and its foundation might lead to a better way of enhancing and evolving it further.

Understanding how profound the importance of the family authority and structure is, in Samoan culture, provides the catalyst to understanding the Navigators' psyche. It helps us understand the motivation and the courage leading them to undertake such an intrepid voyage.

The family is the authority in Samoan culture. The individuals are defined as members of the family and derive from this their respective freedom. The individual is a person with his own freedom, but that freedom is defined within the overall family structure. Similarly, property rights are defined within the family structure as communal family property (collectivism).

This may not appear to motivate or promote individual creativity other than through collective action. But the family's collective efforts, given the size of the family, can command power and authority at local and regional levels, so it was natural that attempts would be made to consolidate power, through marriages of family chiefs, princes, and princess, to combine resources.

Building a Social Contract

Logic and Reasoning

The great Greek philosopher Aristotle (384 B.C.-322 B.C) was a prolific writer about reasoning. He wanted to define a universal process of reasoning that would allow man to learn every conceivable thing about the whole of reality. He proposed reason as the source of the first principles of knowledge, in that it deals with the abstract and ideal aspects. But he suggested it might only be a potential source of ideas, for it leads to them only by a process of development whereby reason gradually clothes sense in thought, to unify and interpret that which is presented to the senses.[c]

So everything goes back to the development of logic, or reasoning—this common sense of the Samoans, which was later divided into *O le Tofā tamali'i* (high chiefs) and *ma le fa'autaga ma le moe a le tulafale* (orator chiefs)—the "old wisdom of the high chief" and the "common sense and expediency of the orator chief"—*my translation*. It begins with the concept of thinking through who they are as a people, where they came from, and therefore their whole existence.

The reasoning process of human development over thousands of years led, in different times and places, to discovering the natural separation of "things" and "boundaries." It gives the Samoans their own version of a social contract—a concept defined as the recognition, within a society of people, that each person's moral and political obligations will depend on the agreement of the people within the society.[ci]

The U.S. Constitution

In the United States of America, the social contract is embodied in that treasured document, the U.S. Constitution, which defines the concept of freedom and guarantees freedom to its citizens as their inalienable right, a human right. The construction of this document was very much influenced by many world philosophers including John Locke, widely regarded as one of the most influential of Enlightenment thinkers of the period. It is a marvelous document, the U.S. Constitution, and it has a life of its own. It lives and breathes life into the governance and justice systems of society in the United States.

The Samoan Approach

Samoans, on the other hand, had to discover their own methodology to define their freedom and rights—recognizing that freedom is a gift, given from the god.

By their very existence, Samoans knew there is freedom. And so the natural order of things and boundaries (*Tuaoi*) became the foundation of freedom in their cultural development. The Samoan cultural perspective demonstrates freedom achieved through responsibility—freedom based on responsibility and adherence to boundaries.

The Samoan family structure and organization leads naturally to the delegation of responsibility. And this defines freedom. Thus personal freedom is tied to the family and to the family structure. Individual liberty has boundaries, implying responsibilities not only to other humans but also to the family, village, chiefs, church, and government. But this system of human rights is now being challenged by the current generation, influenced by knowledge from the outside world which pushes against the delineation and definition of "boundaries" and priorities. What are the rights and priorities of an individual, and where do they stand relative to family or village authority, relative to the government', and, finally, relative to God?

Tuaoi (*tuā'oi*) and *Tapu*

Boundaries

With the United States' concept of ownership and property rights, you are not only free, but once you consume something it becomes yours. The Samoans would say no. And they don't need a document to spell it out; they know it already. Samoans' innate belief tells them this. All they have to do is understand the boundaries—the Samoan's *Tuaoi*.

Samoans know the *Tuaoi* between a sister and a brother; a wife and a husband; the church and the village; the family and the village. There is a *Tu-ā-'oi*, meaning boundary, to virtually everything. The idea of *Tuaoi* is to get people to think in terms of boundaries. But how do we get them to understand about these boundaries?

The *Tuaoi* is the guiding dogma of Samoan culture. It's natural; it's unwritten. In Samoan history there is no document that spells out the *Tuaoi* other than the Bible, which supports the belief but only came with the arrival of Christianity. The oral history of the dogma of *Tuaoi* (of boundaries) defines the Samoan legal system.

But we struggle with this idea here in the USA. Of course, these things are written in the Constitution, and all the law books spell them out in detail so that, maybe, one doesn't have to think too much about it. But if one understands the *Tuaoi*, why would one even need someone else to define it?

Know your borders

This very unique concept, this *Tuaoi*, is how we define our freedom. If a Samoan would ask, "How do you know you're free?" the answer is simple: understand your *Tuaoi*. Know the *Tuaoi*, the border.

Know the border between a man and a woman, a husband and a wife, a sister and a brother, the minister and the chief, the aumaga and a chief, the paramount talking chief and the other Tulafale, the paramount high chief of the whole village and other high chiefs; know who are the sisters (the children of their sisters or the daughters) and the Ma'oupū. That's the Samoan *Tuaoi*. That's how Samoans know they're free!

And so Samoans would say: just memorize the *Tuaoi*(s) and we won't have any problems. If you don't understand this concept then, guess what? Guess what happens to those that step over the *Tuaoi*? You get reprimanded, counseled, fined, or outright ostracized from the village.

In typical tribal culture, violation of these boundaries usually leads to war. You've violated the *Tuaoi,* and "I'm not a happy camper." We go to war to sort things out. Wow! If we only respected the borders or boundaries, we wouldn't have this problem.

Male/Female boundaries

Here is an example: I was watching Fred Sakari's weekly program on CNN one Sunday morning, where he was discussing a documentary he had made, sponsored by CNN, on the problems caused by the lack of civil rights for women in Indian society today. While I found it shocking to hear of the horrible treatment of women by their male counterparts in India, I was particularly puzzled by not understanding the source of this behavioral practice.

The size of the middle class is increasing in India. And it appears that women, in the middle class, are now courageously speaking out about their lack of civil rights. They're bringing an awareness of this issue into Indian society. But what I did not hear Fred Sakari say is how the Indian culture receives and treats women. How are boundaries so obviously absent from the culture? I don't know.

Well, dear reader, we might spend a great deal of time talking about how Samoan culture thinks about women. Including that study, we've learned the different titles that are given to

271

Samoan women. I've given you at least 12 different names, from to *Sa'o Tama'ita'i* to *Taupou*. All these names are not names that point women to the back of the house or the bus. No, these are our princesses.

These "natural boundaries," governing right respect between, say, men and women, are not the same as the sort of "unnatural boundaries" society sometimes places between people of different social class (Indian untouchables for example), or people of differently colored skin, or differently colored hair.

Respect

One of the key characteristics of Samoan culture that Samoan people have exemplified is the human etiquette of respect. Respect can be a noun or a verb which expresses esteem, high regard, or high opinion, admiration, reverence, and honor. It is a fragile concept that hopes to solicit reciprocity. It is fragile because it is delicate and easily fractured or shattered if even slightly mishandled.

The Samoan people have learned, by looking back on past experiences, the simple lesson that to give and receive respect can avoid conflicts, such as wars, major disputes, and disagreements. Building an etiquette, based on leading with respect, into the cultural dogma can result in lowering the defense mechanism of the engaging party. If the leading message is one of respectful behavior, followed by the eloquence of an orator's words reaffirming this respectful protocol, reciprocity will always become the expected response. So it should not surprise anybody that all the customs and formalities of etiquette in Samoan and Manu'an culture are derived from and driven by this fragile word "respect," be it verb or noun, depending on grammatical usage.

This, of course, is not unique to the Navigators' culture. All human cultures have learned and embraced the concept of respect. But for the Navigators, the difficult and, at times, warring path of their migration—through mainland Asia and the Malay Archipelago, and on into the Pacific Ocean among unfriendly tribal cultures in Melanesia—would have caused the people to sharply hone this form of defense mechanism.

Fa'aaloalo

And now, after looking at the *tuaoi*, the boundaries that lead to the responsibility, the delineation, and the titles in Samoan culture, we must not forget the glue in the culture, which comes from understanding the *fa'aaloalo*:

The *fa'aaloalo* is best seen as an upside-down pyramid. But why would we "respect" an upside-down pyramid? It is true that it is a very fragile concept, though simple and profound. It's fragile because once you lose that *fa'aaloalo*, then you must declare war.

Everything we do is *fa'aaloalo*. We keep peace by *fa'aaloalo*. We give gifts because it's *fa'aaloalo*. Why? Because it glues Samoan culture together.

In conversation, people have said to me, "Fata, you know: from the government of America we have this wonderful document called the Constitution of the United States. In Samoa, you must have also such a magical, beautiful document." And I've told them, no we don't. They ask why? And I answer, well, you see, Samoans have always believed that freedom is its own inalienable right. We did not need a philosopher to tell us that we are free.

This freedom, we believe, is the way God created us. Then He gave us independent freedom of thinking and decision-making, to choose our own individual path. The *Fa'aSamoa* would say *e pule oe i ou mafaufau*, which means you have authority (*pule*) of your own (*oe, ou*) thinking (*mafaufau*).

How it works

My Culture, My View

Studying a culture of any specific ethnicity requires an understanding of various academic disciplines, such as anthropology, ethnology, archaeology, linguistics, sociology, mythology, history, genetics, and many other specialized fields of study. A student may choose to study a culture from the outside looking in, or may participate with the community and society being studied.

Since I am a member of the Samoan and Manu'an culture and society, I recognize the risk of bias in my observations—in my view—of the events and facts of the culture and the culture's history. But, having been in business for over 40 years and, in fact, being educated and trained in business, I have a natural inclination to view things from a business point of view—that is, not necessarily from a viewpoint of profit and loss, but perhaps looking particularly at efficiency and effective leadership used in guiding an organization to fulfillment of its objectives. Thus studying the Samoan culture has been, for me, a study in organizational structure and behavior, management practices, and leadership.

Samoan Culture

Samoan culture has been evolving for over 3,000 years, including the period before entering the Eastern Pacific Ocean. And business organizations, or the "business of making a living" as economists would call it, must have begun at a similarly ancient time, as an integral part of human development. So all the value-drivers of what makes cultures thrive—for example, family-centric, with established dogmas, systems of compliance, assignment of responsibilities, and corresponding authority structures, leadership, communication systems, and so on—are, not surprisingly, very much applicable to business organization.

The "collective consciousness" is defined by Emile Durkheim in *Division of Labour in Society* in 1893 as the set of shared beliefs, ideas, and moral attitudes which operates as a unifying force within society.[cii] This concept very much parallels the contribution of Professor Peter Drucker to the philosophical and practical foundations of modern business corporations, in his *Management: Tasks, Responsibilities, Practices* in 1973.[ciii] But these academic ideas and theories are sourced in ancient social practices.

Peter Drucker explained that the assignment of responsibility is a sophisticated way of managing an organization. It's the basis of the revolution of streamlining tasks, where tasks are broken down to their lowest level. Understanding the micro-tasks and their relationship to other tasks is essential to determining whether they are dependent or independent. As the Hawthorne

Studies by Elton Mayo in 1927 revealed, this is an essential part of measuring the timeline for the performance of the task, giving light to the efficiency of the overall process.[civ] It leads to the era which birthed Alfred P. Sloan's and Henry Ford's assembly-line manufacturing processes in the early 1900s.

The challenge in human resources, of mapping responsibilities to the skillsets of the personnel—skills in areas such as fishing, farming, cultural ceremonies, leadership roles, or the skill of a gifted orator—is an evolving learning process. There are numerous examples where a family's selection of a chief with limited competence ended in failure, due to lack of leadership, and caused deterioration of the family's status with the village and district governments.

The transformation from hunter-gatherer society to organized agriculture is evidence of a paradigm shift in social structure. Man would no longer need to roam the earth, searching for food, but could look upon it with an understanding of the concept of tilling the earth so food would grow. This entailed a deliberate effort that had to be planned and executed. Once this concept was mastered, the process moved on to the next natural step of evolution, namely the delegation of responsibilities to particular members of the family or clan, to streamline the process of agriculture for efficiency, so as to anticipate scalability of food production.

The important thing here is to lay out the evidence of how the Navigators, as a society, came to develop the same understanding that was achieved by their "high culture" society counterparts during ancient times. We cannot ignore the reality of this. We are exposed to it today. Listen to the whispers in the morning; these are our ancestors telling us the events in our ancient histories which confirm how unique and organized Samoan society was from the beginning of time.

Adapting and Retaining Culture

Much like the children of Israel, we spent a long time roaming around in our own desert. We were busy building the foundation of the Samoan structure.

I've used the picture of the Samoan *fale* as an analogy, to show how Samoans went about building a structure that begins with the family. It's probably the only culture that can claim that such a family-centric culture. But there are generations of Samoans that have come to this country (the U.S.) at a very young age, and some were even born here. These individuals have adapted to the way of life here as part of their second home. And we have crossed over cultures.

American culture places emphasis on the individual—"I am-ism"—but Samoan culture emphasizes "We-ism." Individual liberty is the essence of the United States of America's system of government—our newly adopted country. It is what makes the U.S. attractive to many people around the globe. Of course, the abundance of natural resources, enveloped into a system that promotes personal freedom to pursue opportunity, and a government that guarantees these inalienable rights is the magic of God's blessing to the U.S.A. But in Samoa, the "we" is given to the family, contrasting with the "I am" of your own liberty and freedom to do anything you want, of your defining your own opportunity, while leaving family second to that—and in some cases, imagining family doesn't even exist. In Samoan culture, everything is defined through the family. "Me," my person, is defined into the family and the family's "location."

The village location is very important because it's the home of the family and the extended family. Margaret Mead realized, in her studies, that this is a critical part in raising a family—particularly a challenge for adolescents in the village. She referenced a famous African's statement that "It takes a village to raise a child," and Hillary Clinton quoted her in one of her speeches. Think about it: it's a very logical process. And in this multi-cultural environment, we begin to struggle with that. How do we live out these two diametrically opposed concepts? "We-ism" versus "I am-ism." How do we do that? How do we survive and take advantages of all the opportunities here?

Let's further define the difference: For example, in American culture we need the Constitution to define liberties. This document, the Constitution, was written to define everything. So, what about in Samoan culture? Is there a constitution written for Samoans? Yes, there is. There are copies of the Samoan Constitution with very basic laws. It doesn't define a lot of stuff. And we might ask, why is that? Well, the Samoans developed this structure in the beginning, with a structural belief that there is a natural order of things. Samoan culture states that when you are born into this wonderful island environment it (the island environment) is your inalienable right. You are defined by the land where your umbilical cord is buried. That's your inalienable right.

In the United States we found out, in history and political science, there was a lot of influence by heavy thinkers, John Locke being one of them. Locke said everything on earth is free—conceptually everything, man, animals, everything, is free. The difference between man and animal is that, when man consumes any part of the earth, it becomes his. Hence the concept of ownership and property rights.[cv]

In fact, the cultural development of many cultures, in the West and East, was highly influenced by social scientists and political philosophers who promoted new ideas about how to optimize the organization of social community. For example:

- The Chinese ancient philosopher Confucius (551-479 B.C.) advocated a way of life with emphasis on the importance of family and social harmony. This results in a religion which regards "the secular as sacred."[cvi]
- John Locke, in his *Second Treatise of Government*, in 1689, said everything on earth is free; conceptually everything— mankind, animals, everything—is free. The difference between man and animal is that when man consumes any part of the earth, it becomes his.[cvii]
- And, as we have seen, in United States history we find many of its forefathers were heavily influenced by prodigious thinkers such as John Locke, among others. Hence, the birth of the concept of ownership and property rights in the United States Constitution.

Business Models

Reward Through Service—*Tautua*

In business, you study management to understand how promotions and appointments are used as a system of reward, with a built-in dogma that perpetuates the system of control over cultural enforcement and adherence to culture. Division into departments with separate functions is a part of business.

Samoans have our own way of promoting or appointing to the rank or class of chieftain. The Samoan way to promotion is *Tautua,* meaning service: *O le ala i le pule, o le Tautua*, which means the path to authority (*pule*) is service (*tautua*).

What does it mean to be a good servant? The good servant is the one who is honest to their craft. You must be honest to your responsibility and service. Samoans say, *a e pule i mea ititi, e ave oe e pulea mea tetele*, meaning if you are honest in your duties and responsibilities, your reward is authority over major and significant things in your defined responsibility.

Throughout the history and cultural development of the Samoan and Manu'an people, more activities began to arise that required new responsibilities and assignments to members of the family. In some cases, an individual might receive a promotion for doing some great thing, such as conquering the enemy in battle. As a result, if your performance in a very critical war was so exceptional that it caused victory in battle, you would earn praise from the family and they would bestow the title of chief warrior, gaining additional responsibilities for you.

Communication and Information Flow

Information systems and frameworks in business, showing how information is disseminated to the organization, work in the same way as that with which Samoans chronicle flow. Samoans have an information flow structure, whereby the ambassador carries information to specific destinations, villages, and chiefs. The "chronicle" of the message must include the correctly titled person, and it must be delivered to the exact village location and the exact chief. Otherwise, the message may be declined, given an unexpected response, or totally ignored.

The protocol and etiquette for messages have been decreed by ancient customs, by the founding Chieftain Council of the district, and throughout all of Samoa. This is very critical, of course, in times of war among family members, villages, or districts. The process of soliciting support for war troops must be done via these protocols.

Again, the people have a highly-defined process and protocol for communicating messages to families, villages, paramount chiefs, and district authorities—one that is similar to that of a modern company or organization. This process has to be passed on to the chiefs, from one generation to another, to ensure that the know-how for executing these procedures will be available when warranted.

All these things—protocol, etiquette, rules for communication, and behavior—require a solid foundation in history, culture, and language, and a genealogical understanding of what underlies these practices. You have to have a history. You need the study of archaeology to understand the ancient history. You have to understand what your folklore says, and how the rules developed, and where you came from, because that's all part of this culture.

Accountability

You cannot have "loosey-goosey" rules, in business or in a culture, for then nobody would be accountable for anything. They'll correct you—if you're speaking, they'll correct you right in the middle of your speech. But Samoan culture is self-auditing, in the sense that every member of the society audits each other as to correct usage of the language, customs and formality, etiquette, and ritual protocols. There are corrective answers and corrective decisions, meaning, for example, if I go into my meeting at the village council and they say, "Fata, your children were out there violating the ordinance," then they tell me whatever the fine is, I will have to pay. That's just the way it is.

For example, at night there is the family worship tradition. In the evening, when the sun sets, the village bell will ring to begin worship. And the aumaga will stop any traffic going into and out of the village. The aumaga acts as law enforcement in the village. No one crosses the line, to get into or out of the village, during the protocols or ordinances of the worship service. You would have to be aware you were now trespassing. And the consequences can be severe. If you choose to violate the ordinance you are taking a risk with your life. For aumaga are not trained law enforcement officers; they are citizens and members of the village, whose job is to protect and enforce property rights, and boundary rules, and culture protocols. They will stop you from crossing into the village. If you are in a vehicle and you don't stop, you will be stoned, and you and your automobile may not survive the altercation.

The leaders of the aumaga have to be in total control; otherwise a violation could turn into a terrible disaster. Several circumstances have occurred where the violator was intoxicated and the automobile ran over a young man and killed him—unfortunately, the aumaga lost control and burned him in his car. The government legal system will intervene but the village Chiefs Council will invoke the customary cultural protocols, such as *Fa'aSamoa* apology or *ifoga*, with the village paramount chiefs prostrating themselves under a fine mat or *'ietoga* for a period of time.

If you are a member of the village and you survive the aumaga, the Chiefs Council will assess the degree of your violation and render a punishment or punitive fines. If you caused damage or hurt any person, you will absolutely receive a severe punishment which could include being ostracized from the village—not only you but the whole family—for a definite period of time or, in extreme cases, a permanent banishment from the village. And you would still have to face the government's murder charges for killing somebody with your automobile.

Rules-Based Decisions

At their simplest, rules-based decisions are decisions based on standardized procedures and practices that have been established, based on very specific rules. They can be protocols or formulas or well-defined, step-by-step processes. These have been adopted as rules or customs in performing the respective functions and processes. In business, these rules are automated through computing systems and therefore are executed automatically.

The idea is foundational to artificial intelligence (AI). That is, the more "smarts" you can standardize in the form of computer language, the smarter the computer system will be in performing the expected commands or functions. To put it another way, the more data you give or feed into the computer system, to learn the patterns of doing a task in a standardized way, the smarter the system will be in performing those protocols or tasks. Thus we have rules-based decisions and data-based intelligence, or smart decisions. The obvious conclusion is clear—no data means no smart decision, nor any decision probably.

Likewise, we find that Samoan cultural protocols are "automatically" executed. The standardized, step-by-step protocols for ceremonies and rituals are executed, almost automatically, by the people. They move in cadence, from the ava ceremony to the gifting of fine mats or 'ietoga and various ritual protocols.

So, rules-based decisions mean: don't deviate, don't get inventive, just follow the rules. In business you don't have to think about this, because the rules of the firm tell you what to do. But in the village and district, we follow custom and formality. When an orator chief stands up and delivers his speech, if he commits an error in facts, salutations, protocol, sequence (the order of the sections of the speech), or simply mispronounces a title, it is considered a "defeated" speech. So, it is all about rules and data—about preparation, studying, and rehearsal.

If you watch the detailed analysis of the Osama Bin Laden mission, for example—how he was captured and how he was killed—you might think about the decision theory that was necessary here. For there is a certain amount of information you need in order for you to make effective decisions. When you have too much information, you're paralyzed. When you don't have enough information, you're constricted. Decision theory, rules, and accountability are very important.

The Samoan Village/District Chart

So... we've covered the rules for function and policy decisions in "this" village. We have partnered in the village. And now we ask: are there particular rules, that are very specific to your village, that are slightly different from rules in the rest of Samoa. But only you and your village would know. You would have to learn them.

281

Decision theory provides control and accountability. And we've discussed how everything is controlled by the definition of responsibility. The better you define the responsibility, the better off you will be. If you put the right people in position to exercise responsibility, you will have better accountability.

Village and District Organization	Business Organization	Study Discipline
District Government	Board of Governors	Organizational Theory
Village Chiefs Council	Local Board of Directors	Economics
Decreed Responsibility Title	Board Bi-Laws	Management Theory
Functional Responsibility	Organization Chart and Responsibilities	Economics & Organization Management
Rules/ customs/ religion/ common sense	Operational Standard Operating Procedures Manuals	Anthropology
Rules Based Decisions	Title Definitions and Responsibilities	Decision Theory
Policy Decision	Culture Customs and Formalities, & Decrees	Decision Theory
Controls and Accountability	SAME	Management Theory
Corrective Decisions	SAME	Management Theory
Promotion and Appointments	SAME	Management Theory
Information System and Framework	SAME	Management Technology
Protocols and Etiquette	SAME	Behavior Science
Historian	SAME	Archeology
Property Rights Administration	SAME	Law and Justice
Sacred Grounds and Heirlooms	NONE	Archeology and Anthropology, Political Science, Theology, Ethnology (origin of race), Ethology (ethos, moral beliefs), Etymology (word origin), Philology (Language origin), Philosophy

Cultural Skills

In this section, we will look at the various cultural skills which are or were a part of Samoan and Manu'an culture. They are part of everyday life, and describe a way of life, how it developed through history, and where it stands today.

Sailing and Navigation

Navigational Skills

To talk about the Navigators' seafaring skills and acumen is to highlight the one skill that the Polynesians and Oceanians had to have mastered to enable them to conquer the vast Pacific Ocean and colonize their current homeland. It is important here that I return to my preferred point of view, an aerial view approach, to review the origin and development of this vital skill that made possible the Polynesian migration across the East Pacific Islands.

A Seafaring People

In my earlier book—*Navigators Quest for a Kingdom in Polynesia*—I put much effort into tracing the migration path from the multiple layers of human migration and the colorful mosaic of their tracks left behind. The resulting path takes us across North Africa to the Levant, around and through the Indian continent, traversing many major rivers (the Indus, Ganges, Yangtze, Yellow, Irrawaddy, etc.), as far as Southeast Asia and the Malay and Indonesian Archipelagos. It is the consensus of social and physical scientists that the "seafaring people" were the dominant migrants in and throughout the Asian Archipelago.

"Sea People" are found in the Greek Classics, causing major disruption up and down the Mediterranean Sea and the Aegean Sea. Both Herodotus and Hesiod point to the Phoenicians as the Sea People, but the Phoenicians came into existence around 1200-800 B.C., after the fall of Troy. In contrast, the seafaring people populating the Asian archipelago had been in Southeast

Asia and the Malay and Indonesian archipelagos tens of thousands of years before Homer wrote about the fall of Troy.

The navigational skills of this seafaring people were very much honed from the beginning of their migration, following the coastal contours of the Indian continent until they reached the Malay and Indonesian archipelagos. Additionally, those travelers that followed the major rivers—across India and the Eurasian steppes, and across China's major rives until their arrival at the Asian archipelago—had occupied and populated the rivers' major ports and peripheral areas and become proficient in the mariner's way of life.

So, through island-hopping across some 18,000 islands in this body of water, this seafaring people now began looking at the vast East Pacific Ocean, with more and more curiosity, and more desire to explore.

The urge to explore

The configuration of islands in these archipelagos—the Malay, Indonesian, Bismarck, Philippine archipelagos, etc.—made them particularly conducive to travel by island-hopping. As a result, the people could occupy and colonize, or pause and re-strategize on a continuing migratory journey. Understanding this process, which took hundreds and thousands of years, helps us see the reality that this skill is, metaphorically, ingrained into this people's DNA.

The extended stay in North Maluku and Halmahera and the Bismarck Archipelago, on their journey to the East Pacific, allowed them to pause and reorient themselves in a new ocean environment. They developed the ability, or the logical thinking skills, to go back and reexamine events—now called a regression learning capacity—and this too is fundamental to the psyche of the Polynesians. They depended deeply on it as they continued their intrepid journey. And at each of the stopping areas they found archipelagos—Bismarck, Vanuatu, Solomon Islands, and Fiji—made up of many islands with a configuration that was, again, very similar to the previous archipelagos. These kinds of seascapes and configurations became well-known to the Polynesians.

The spirit and courage to push forward to the next unknown ocean was greatly enhanced by the experiences of the past. The proximity and configuration of the Fiji archipelago led to the last stop of the Polynesians, before the Togan migration which discovered the Togan chain of islands. Shortly thereafter, the Navigators migrated to the Manu'an and Samoan chain of islands.

There is an established oral consensus among Polynesians that their sojourn in the Fijian Archipelago (described as Rotuma in Manu'an oral history) lasted between 1,000 and 1,500 years before they moved on. The lingering question is: Why so long? The answer might be that their familiarity was with an archipelago oceanscape; they were not accustomed to the idea of rather isolated distant islands. The learning curve here would have been a little bit more substantial than before.

Speaking of a learning curve, and of learning, we should note that Samoan oral traditions—as discovered by early missionaries and men of science through interviewing older generations— confirm some of the "oral consensus" of the legends and folklore that are still today being promulgated by the culture.

What the Master Sailor must Know

To get an appreciation of the learning process involved in navigational knowledge, we need to understand which aspects of the environment are critical to navigating the ocean. The Samoan orator would say the following:

- The winds and their patterns and directions are known to the Samoans; they have been observed over the centuries.
- The birds and their flying paths and patterns have been learned.
- The different fish and their traveling paths and seasons have been learned.
- The ocean currents and swells are known to the Samoans— their strength and directions.
- The configurations of groups of islands in an archipelago are known to the master sailor (*Tautai matapalapala*).
- The outlines of the various island land masses have been memorized.

- The stars for fishing, and the stars for a long journey, are known to the master sailor (*Tautai 'Alia* and *Tautai o Vasaloloa*).

The Winds

The winds are very critical to the navigator, for they determine the planning and timing of the sea voyage, whether it be for fishing or for a long-distance journey. But Samoans and Manu'ans have no standard geographical names for North, South, East, and West. The current terminologies are Samoan translations of English words for directions, such as *saute* for south, *matu* for north, *sasa'e* for east where the sun raises, and *sisifo* for west where the sun sets.

Geographical directions, instead, are somewhat ambiguous, like "here," "there," "over there," etc. However, the directions themselves are clear; they are each named after an island, village, or district, etc. For example:[cviii]

- While *Saute* is just the Samoan translation of the English word South, the name given to South is *Toga,* because the wind that blew in from that direction came from the location of the Island of Toga.
- The south to southwest wind, or *Tuaoloa*, is characterized by the fact that it brings rain.
- The southeast trade wind is called *To'elau*, the name of an island northeast of the Samoan chain of islands.
- *Mataupolu* is the northeast or easterly wind. The missionary Stair interpreted this as East, while Pratt translated it as the easterly wind.
- The *Matu* wind is dry and calm before the storm. This is usually associated with very strong winds such as a storm, tempest, hurricane, typhoon, or super storm. Both Pratt and Stair labeled it the northern gale.
- The *matalepola* is a wind that begins from the northwest then moves to any direction as wind patterns dictate.
- The *La'i,* according to Pratt, is the westerly wind.
- The *Fiasaga* is a gentle northwesterly breeze. Both Pratt and Stair agreed it also means a splendid wind.
- *La'ilua* is the west or southwesterly wind.

- The *Fa'atiu* is the north wind, according to both Stair and Pratt.
- *Pi'ipapa* is the cold wind from the South Pole during the monsoon season; the name comes from how it causes people to press against cliffs due to the cold.

The Stars

The heavenly bodies and the patterns they traverse are the domain of the seasoned master chief navigator, *Tautai matapalapala*. For the stars will have been observed and committed to memory by the master navigator—it is said the god *Tagaloalagi* gifted this critical skill to the builder of his vessel. So:

- The *Sumu* (a cluster of stars) is Samoan for the Southern Cross, with the two Centauri (alpha and beta Centauri) or *Luatagata* (the twins—two people).
- The Great Bear, if at all visible, is called the *Anava* (warrior's club), as described by Dr. Krämer.
- Orion is *Amoga* or *LeAmoga* in Samoan (which means carrying something heavy on your shoulder), and *Taumatau* (the right side of canoe) and *Tauama* (the left side float).
- In the southern Milky Way, the three stars in the Delphinus constellation are, in Samoan, *Ti'otala*, *Tulalupe,* and *Faipa* or *Toloa* (again, as recorded by Dr. Krämer)—the head of Scorpio is *Faipa* or *Toloa* in Samoan.
- Among the fixed stars, Sirius is *Fetusolonu'u* in Samoan.
- Among the planets: Venus is *Tapuitea* or *Fetuao* in Samoan; Jupiter is *Tupua Legase* in Samoan; Mars is *Matamemea*.
- The Milky Way is *Aniva* or *Aolele* or *Aotea* in Samoan (the Maori's Aotearoa).

TuiAfono's Navigators

Fiji to Samoa

The way the ancient Navigators calibrated the skies, applying the patterns of the various stars, was to first observe the point where the star is rising, perpendicular to the horizon, and set the vessel's direction along a perpendicular to the star's position. The Navigator then awaits the next rising star until its direction can also be defined. The knowledge of the rising stars is, of course, very important.

The Navigators were proficient in reading the positions of stars rising at the edge (horizon) of the sky. Their reference points were derived from a knowledge of the directions to the neighboring islands. The three most popular or most traveled islands were Toga, Niue, and Fiji. And the direction to Toga is south from Samoa, hence the wind from Toga that blows from the south. The Samoans also knew that Niue is in the same direction toward Toga. Fiji, on the other hand, is located in the direction where Orion, *LeAmoga*, rises, which we now know is in the Western sky. And the Milky Way, *Aolele* or *Aotea,* is in a southwestern direction from the *Amoga*, a direction toward the long white cloud of Maori.

The Manu'an legend of *Gaiuli* and *Gaisina,* who travelled to Fiji to take *Taeotagaloa* to visit his sister *Muiu'uleapai*, is recounted in Dr. Krämer's first volume of *the Samoa Island*.[cix] *Muiu'uleapai* had sent a message to her brothers (*Taeotagaloa* and *Lefanoga*) saying she needed help, for her husband, the TuiFiti, blamed her for the famine that devastated Fiji Island, and had banished her to an inland promontory. *Taeotagaloa* took the wild yam plant (potato) and he planted it in the fertile land, toward the mountains, where it grew rapidly. And then *Taeotagaloa* instructed his sister *Muiu'uleapai* to tell her husband to move the whole village to the land toward the mountains to harvest the yam roots. The TuiFiti moved the whole village and cured the food shortage, thanks to *Taeotagaloa*.

It was here that *Taeotagaloa* caught and domesticated the colorful Pacific parrot bird and brought it with him to Manu'a. Malietoa Faigā *Uilamatūtū* heard of this parrot bird (the *sega*) and later asked for it, when he finally met one of the brothers, *Taeotagaloa* or *Lefanoga*.

Other Manu'an historians say it was *Saoluaga* who went with *Taeotagaloa* to Fiji. For the two chiefs, *Taeotagaloa* or *Lefanoga,* were brothers and were the navigators of Paramount Chief TuiAfono. Thus, other members of the traveling parties were *Saoluaga*, *Lepolofa'asoasoa* and TuiAfono.[cx]

The time-period of these characters and events is around the 15th to 18th generation (between A.D.1100 and 1250), as calculated by Dr. Krämer—estimates pegged to Malietoafaigā's (Malietoa Faigā *Uilamatūtū's)* generation, which also corroborate the story of *Saoluaga's* visit to Malietoafaigā in Malie village, Upolu. This is also the legendary journey where *Taeotagaloa* gave the navigator brothers the breadfruit branch and coconut branch with coconuts attached to take with them to Samoa—the first story evidencing crops being brought over from Fiji.

In the legend, Krämer recounts how the navigators looked to the part of the sky where the constellation *Amoga* (Orion's belt) stands, to use it for a compass on the journey, by steering directly toward *Amoga* (Orion). Of course, we now know that Orion rises in the Western sky, exactly at the geographical location of Fiji Island as viewed from Samoa. There are other stars that rise at the horizon that further guide and confirm the direction of the journey. And directions could be given to the helmsman by one man, who would lie on his back, lengthwise, in the hold (*liu*) of the boat, trying to keep the three stars directly above with one in the center, another to the right, *taumatau*, and the third to the left, *tauama*.[cxi]

Tutuila to Manu'a

Another account of the two navigator brothers, *Gaiuli* and *Gaisina*, documented by Dr. Krämer, comes from Paramount Chief *Le'iato* (whose brother was Paramount Chief *Savea* of my village, Afega, Upolu at the time). *Togiola* was the paramount chief of Faga'itua, Tutuila. This voyage departed from the shore, in the village of Tula where Paramount Chief TuiAfono reigned in the district of Afono:

The navigators *Gaiuli* and *Gaisina* wanted to sail to Manu'a but didn't know the route. So *Gaiuli* said they should keep the stern of their ship exactly in line with Mata-Tula (the foothills of Tula village). Then they sailed steadily, keeping the ship's stern exactly in line with the foothills of Tula until night fell sea.[cxii] Then they watched for the appearance of the Evening Star, *Tapuitea,* above the sea in the westward part of the sky, while the stern of their ship was still kept in line with Mata-Tula.[cxiii] The journey continued until, at about 10 o'clock at night, the chiefs observed that the star was now in its right place, i.e. its setting position. Another star, named *Faipa* and *Tulalupe,* rose in the part of the sky in the east; and then the *Toloa* (the three stars in the Delphinus constellation or Southern Milky Way), and the *Sumu* (the Southern Cross) with the *Luatagata* (alpha and beta Centauri), rose—these stars are very close to each other.

The chief's vessel went steadily on, and the *Ta'elo* rose—this is the name for the moon in the wet or monsoon season[cxiv]—and they directed the bow of the ship exactly toward it. Then they also noticed the *Ti'otala*—one of the other three stars in the Delphinus constellation—and again they directed the bow of their ship toward it.

When morning approached, the chiefs looked out again to see if other stars, the *Amoga* (Orion's girdle) and the *Li'i* (the Pleiades), had appeared yet. They directed the bow exactly toward the *Amoga*. Next, the morning star came up, which appears in the half-light of dawn. And so the chiefs saw to it that their ship entered the reef channel. "When it grew light, the bow of their ship faced that place exactly."[cxv]

Practical Navigation

Lessons passed on

While we can read the account of travelling from west to east, which a journey from Tutuila to Manu'a approximates, I'd like to note that this technique is confirmed in my own grandfather's instructions about knowing and understanding the timing of the rising stars. Depending on whether it is dawn or the evening part of the day, and on whether a star is rising or setting, it will appear at a different point on the horizon, indicating a different direction. And the appearance of the stars on the horizon is used to indicate direction.

My reference for this and for the oral stories is my grandfather *Niu Tavita*. His grandfather was Rev. Baker, the English missionary to Toga. His sons brought the mission to the Elise Islands, hence the name *Tavita*, from the Biblical King David. My grandfather was born and grew up on Elise Island and was employed by the missionary steamship Va'alotu in the late 1800s until his retirement in 1926. He was selected because of his proficient sailing skills and knowledge of the Fijian, Samoan, and Micronesian archipelago seascapes. I spent a lot of my childhood life with my grandparents on our humble plantation, and I recall how much I enjoyed interviewing both of them about anything and everything to satisfy my insatiable curiosity. So, this is how I heard all these things.

The Learning Process

In sailing and navigation, there was always a need to simplify the learning process, so it could be adapted easily and quickly. Thus fingers and arms are used, for example, as a measuring stick (or yardstick)—the distance between the thumb and small finger, in the movement of a star, is sometimes "how long to follow the star until the next star appears." The measurement is similar to defining a yard as the distance (about three feet) from your longest fingertip to your Adam's Apple.

If one considers that Samoa lies approximately on latitude 13 degrees south, and if one assumes that Orion rises at the same latitude, it is very simple to see the orientation provided by the star. But moving, using sails, and cruising against the trade wind, or being driven off course in bad weather, complicates things. The Navigators looked for setting stars which set at the same latitude, at the time when Orion rises—for example, Arcturus and Boötes.

Experienced navigators might simply wait for better weather. This was customary with any kind of ocean travel. For time was not of the essence for the Samoans. They were not in a race to conquer something, or to meet a schedule, and thus they had patience—and were aware that it is clearly a virtue. We now appreciate that they needed to develop this level of patience in order to travel long distances in the Pacific Ocean. In particular, the pattern of the trade winds was to move from east to west, while the northwest and northeast winds blew south toward the Pacific Ocean. We now understand how the Polynesians waited until the westward winds blew easterly, so they could go east.

Where the navigator starts

The apprenticeship program to becoming a master navigator starts with being a very good fisherman. The idiom is: if you cannot feed the family with fish, you cannot be depended on to master the vessel on a trip. So mastering fishing skills came first, then a graduation to learning long-distance navigational skills.

The fishing mantra is: "the master fisherman knows where to fish the species he wants." This requires developing a knowledge of the ocean tides and currents, as well as winds and their directions. It is important to observe and learn the migration patterns of the fish, and the changes in fish behavior during different weather patterns. It is equally important to learn and understand the migration patterns of birds as they feed.

Of course, cyclical weather patterns are observed also and are associated with all other environmental factors. This separates the learning skills of the young inexperienced fisherman from those of the older wise master.

Sails, Weaving, and Fine Mats

In ancient times, the fine mats woven by the women would have been used as the sail on the mast of the double-hull canoe. These fine mats are still made in the same way by the women of the village in the *fale lalaga* (weaving house). The beautiful mats are family heirlooms, and are exchanged as gifts at weddings and funerals, chief title ceremonies, and other special occasions including house blessings and church openings.

The Samoan fine mat is valued for its fine weave, and fine mats are used by Samoans and Togans as a medium of exchange during the exchange of gifts. The current going rate for a really fine thin weave is around $1800-2500 USD. Fine mats become heirlooms of the family.

The mats are named and have history. The mat called *Lagava'a* was woven onboard vessel by a married couple named *Fane'a* and *Fane'a—Laga* is short for *lalaga*, which means weaving, and *va'a* means a vessel or canoe, hence the name. The legend of this mat is part of the story of *Saveasi'uleo* returning from Pulotu, in Fiji Island; *Fane'a* and *Fane'a* were members of his crew. The mat's history includes several names, such as *Pi'imale'ele'ele*, *Moeilefuefue*, and *Tasiaeafe*, and the name is a function of who is creating the story of the mat.

One of the Mornings of Samoan and Manu'an history tells how *Tauiliili* of Atua, whose sister married Tagaloalagi, selected a fine mat *'ietoga* to take to the funeral of *Tagaloalagi* (see The Edict at Alapapa concerning the Selection of the Fine Mat *'ietoga* for the Funeral of *Tagaloalagi* on page 139). *Tauiliili's* daughter, *Tualafalafa*, was gifted by the spirit with this sacred fine mat—the heavens opened up with lightning and thunder at its sacredness. So this mat is described as being equivalent to a thousand mats, given the name *Tasi ae afe*—and it is also the waterproof mat— *matu mai vai*—because, when it was brought up from fermentation in the water-mud pool, it was totally dry.

There is another story about the fine mat of *Futa*. This mat was brought back to Samoa from Toga when it was gifted by the TuiToga to *Tauiliili* of Atua for helping to find TuiToga's brother *Lautivunia*, hence *'ie toga* because it came from Toga.[cxvi]

293

Image 28 images owned by author

Fine mats at funerals

The gifting of "fine mats" or "state mats" (commonly referring to mats of the respective monarchs like Tupua, Malietoa, TuiAtua, TuiA'ana, Gatoa'itele, Vaetamasoaali'i, SaLevalasi, LeTagaloa, SaTuiManu'a and other Paramount titles), at funerals is an important cultural protocol. These are heirloom mats and are treasured by all. They represent the highest value of medium of exchange, and one of these mats can be worth a thousand other mats.

I remember the funeral of TuiAtua Tupua Tamasese *Lealofi-IV*, when his village of Salani, in the Falealili, Atua district, came to do his funeral service in Vaimoso village, in the Faleata district of Tuamasaga. Almost all the village (three or four hundred people) came, and they brought one *'ie*, or one fine mat.

The names the two state mats were: for Tupua, *Laufafa o Fenunuivao* (meaning the garment of Princess *Fenunuivao*), and for Tamasese *Lealofi's* family, the *Aiga o Mavaega*, *O le Falase'ese'e o le TuiA'ana* (The sliding seating mat of TuiA'ana).

Local witnesses indicated that the *'ietoga* that was presented was the *Laufafa o Fenunuivao*. Its history is said to be that, when his father died from a gunshot during the peaceful protest march of the Samoan Mau in 1929, this fine mat was given to cover his wounded body, and it filled with blood. Subsequently, the mat was gifted to the family of Paramount Orator Chief *Tofuaeaeofoia* (*Ofoia*) of Salani village, in Falealili, Atua district.

Another example of the *'ietoga*, state mat, is the mat Tafa'ifa *Salamasina* brought to Orator Chiefs *Fata* and *Maulolo* and *Tuisamau* in exchange for the title and PāPā of Gatoa'itele. This mat is called *Fa'aoti i Salani* (weaving began on the mat in Saginoga, in Alataua, Savai'i, and was completed in Salani village, in Falealili, Atua, where her son *Tapumanaia-II* resided). Orator Fata kept the mat, and it is long since fallen to pieces.[cxvii]

House-Building

The Story of the First House

When the Navigators settled in their new island home, they began to build homes on their islands. In Manu'an mythology, the origin of the house is that it comes from heaven, gifted from the god *Tagaloalagi* as a home for his son TuiManu'a. Somehow the gift, the *Fale Ula* or Golden House, was placed originally on top of the mountain between Taū and Fitiuta in Manu'a. Nobody could reach up into the sky to get it down, until the boatmen urged *Pili*, son of TuiManu'a, to go up and bring the house down. *Pili*, according to the original genealogy, is the son of *Tagaloalagi*, but he's also known as the son of TuiManu'a, son of *Tagaloalagi*.

Manu'an folklore tells how *Pili* woke up from his rest and used the mast of the vessel as a ladder which he climbed up to bring down the Golden house, the *Fale Ula*, for TuiManu'a, who was Paramount High Chief of all Samoa and Manu'a.[cxviii] The myth serves to indicate the original source of the first house, as being a gift from the god to the Manu'ans, as a sacred residence of TuiManu'a and, later, of the chiefs. Hence the name of the TuiManu'a's residence title: *Faleula*.

It is said that the original Golden House (*Faleula*) had posts made from human beings to hold and support the house. This house was populated with the spirits, to assist in governing the affairs of TuiManu'a. So other half-human and half-spirit paramount chiefs or warriors showed off their power and authority by emulating TuiManu'a's house, using posts made from humans. For example, TuiAtua *Lu* had his "house of hundred posts" (*Faleselau*), Tagaloa A'opo also had his house of one hundred posts. And, of course, *Tagaloalagi* also had a house with one hundred posts of human beings, at Le Faga, Fitiuta, Manu'a.

Further legend has it that Tagaloalagi gave his decree to the first carpenter, *Manufili*, at the same time that scaffolding (*fatamanu*) was first created. So the legend of how the god *Tagaloalagi* gifted and decreed the art of architectural design for the Samoan *maota* (chief's house), *laoa* (orator chief's house) and *afolau* (long house) to Samoa, Tutuila, and Savai'i is combined with Manu'an practicality in the construction of the house as an integral gathering place and shelter, a construction that evolved into building a formal meeting place and residence of paramount leaders of the family and community.

In a rational sense, after struggling through the construction process, it would have become evident that an apparatus would be needed to build and lift the ceiling—the arched purlin—to the top of the house. To rationalize the origin of scaffolding (*fatamanu*), this too had to come from the god *Tagaloalagi*. But in practical terms, the scaffolding used was copied from the process that warring troops used to build their observation decks up in the trees, as well as from the camouflaged shelters used for the sport of catching pigeons in nets. These were two of the models that led to Manu'ans honing their skills in construction of scaffolding.

In an elementary sense, the general design of the house was primitive but functional. But as it evolved the design became a genuine architectural creation. We can see further evidence of evolution in house-building, following the multiple regression model, from basic necessity to the use of more complex architectural design apparatus, when we look at carpentry. For the skill for carpentry is also a gift from the god.

Samoan House-Building

Researchers have found that the way Samoans constructed the *fale* is ideal, because it exemplifies the formalization of the family circle.[cxix] The foundation of the house has evolved into a platform built with rocks and filled with sand, with the top layer being completed with seashells (see The Edict concerning the House of 100 posts on page 146).

The Samoan metaphor, since accepting Christianity, views the foundation and functional value-system of the house as being derived from God, as a Christian-based foundation in the Word of God. It follows that the architectural design of the house should, metaphorically, show the structure of the culture, the history, and the way of life. The house is where the family begins with birth, with a healthy adolescence, then responsible adulthood, raising a family, and being a good teacher of the family history and culture. The repetition of cultural customs and traditions, through oral reinforcement, grows over time and develops into a routine process that governs the family, clan, and village. And this foundation is mirrored in the foundation of the *fale*.

The organizational structure, created to govern the original family, is mirrored in the design of the house, and is very much the same structure that governs the village organization. For example, in Nu'uuli and Fageagea and the sub-village, Fagasā, we may have three different villages, but all have the same architectural organization and structure. It is the same cultural foundation, family organization, protocol, and procedures that in turn drive the economic system for the family, village, district, and country.

Design of the House

The design and construction of houses are basically very simple, but they have evolved over the centuries. Dr. Krämer, in the second volume of his *The Samoa Island*, describes how two man-sized poles, each with forked tops form the ridge props. These are rammed into the ground, then the ridge beam is placed on top of them. A second, similar structure, only one foot high, is erected about six feet away. This is joined together to the ridge by a row of rafters which are each strengthened with several "purlins."[cxx]

The oval house for a chief's dwelling evolved from the basic circular form of house with the addition of the span roof. The rounded part is split and joined to both sides of this span, enclosing the gable area to the eaves, so that in this way the shape of the rectangular house becomes rounded. The *fatu* (lashing) of the *lagofau* (edge bar), is nicely visible. The big arched purlins are lashed first, and only then the small, lower arched purlins are lashed onto the posts. Dr. Krämer describes the ground plan is being comparable to a round, extendable table after a small section has been added (for a large house) or several sections (for a long house).[cxxi]

The additional architectural design, needed for building a very large house, centers on a number of ridge pillars (*poutu*) and brace-beams (*so'a*) that are needed for the round house. For such a house, often referred to in Samoa as the orator chief's house, the size is determined by the number of *utupoto,* or ridges—four or five.

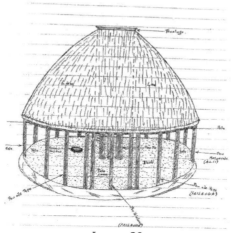

Image 29
https://commons.wikimedia.org/wiki/File:Samoan_fale_tele_architecture_diagra
m_3.jpg Teo Tuvale [3], CC BY-SA 3.0
<https://creativecommons.org/licenses/by-sa/3.0>, via Wikimedia Commons

A House without Nails

One unique aspect of the Samoan house comes from its ancient history, as no iron or steel nails were used to build it, because Samoans did not "discover" nails until the Europeans arrived. The whole house was built by lashing pieces together, using the plaited coconut sennit (*'afa*), which is similar to twine or string.

- The *fatu le ulu 'aso,* or lashing of the heads of the rafters, the pin spar, is different from the type of lashing used for the ribbon.
- The *fatu le lagolau* is applied to the ledge, half bright, small arched purlins and rafter.
- The *selemanu,* or birds' nest design of lashing, is used for the arched purlins and the continuous buttoned seam of rafters.
- The *'sumu,* or cross lashing, is used particularly for scarfing two beams which butt up against each other, such as braces (*so'a*) and big roof purlins (*amo*), ridge beams, and supporting posts, etc.

Dr. Krämer emphasizes that the choice of lashing methods is not arbitrary, but that the same form of lashing is always used for certain joints, thus giving the house a particular charm, due to the patterns rather than to the variety of colors.[cxxii]

The Roof

The roof covering materials used for the Samoan house are coconut tree leaves or leaves from the large palm Dubius Pandanus plant, popular for making "thread" and fruits for chief leis. These were later substituted or subsidized with sugarcane leaves, once sugarcane became available in the islands.

The leaves are strung up on light sticks, called *lafoa*, a finger thick and 3 to 5 feet in length. The roof thatch, called *lau*, is sewn to the roof spars, by means of a wooden needle, each piece as close as possible above each other, and firmly lashed so that they are proof against rain. The details of the roofing task are, again, the domain of the carpenter and his construction crew.

Agriculture

Indigenous Agriculture

With the arrival of the first group, or the family core, on the islands, the Navigators began to interact with their new environment. Indigenous agriculture is a result of the cultural development that began at that point in time. The ecology of the immediate landing site was explored by experienced travelers, to ensure the necessary food supply would be available to sustain the family, clan, and village. Then the already-developed family organization wove together the division of labor and the delegation of responsibilities, which helped accelerate agricultural development.

The original focus, on arrival, was very simple: How to feed and sustain the family, hopefully forever, in the new homeland. Exploration of the new land was an immediate task and of foremost concern, for the purpose of building a sustainable family that could exist for a long period of time. Failing to find and nurture a sustainable ecology would mean having to continue to move in search of a fertile land.

Not all geographical areas of the islands are as fertile as others. For example, Savai'i is the largest of the Samoa chain, but large parts of the island have a significant covering of volcanic rock. Tutuila is mostly mountainous, similar to the Manu'an chain of islands ('Ofu, 'Olosega, and Tau). The small size of its population—of family, clan, and village—ensures that the land still provides plenty to support them all. In fact, the assumption is that the population of the Manu'an islands consists of one extended family—if you are descendant of the Tuimanu'a family then you are descendant of *Tagaloalagi*.

Intrusion onto the land by new migrants would surely mean war, fought to fend off such unwanted visitors. Thus the development of indigenous agriculture is also the beginning of land ownership, property rights, and an economic system for the Samoans and Manu'ans. It is also the root of the Samoan justice administration, which mediates disagreements over property ownership and punishes petty theft of a family's plantation or food crops.

The family's land defines the person's identity. This is the essence of the Samoan proverb: A person is their designation, family, title, sacred residence, sacred meeting ground, village, and clan, all the way to the core of the earth—*'O le tagata ma lo na fa'asinomaga*.

The Story of the Breadfruit Tree

We have looked earlier at stories of the ava plant (see How the Ava Plant Came to Samoa on page 231). There are myths and stories associated with other plants as well. For example:

According to Hawaiian legend, a man named *Ulu* had a sickly baby boy, whose life was endangered due to the scarcity of food. *Ulu* went to the god, *Mo'o* (this is the same as *Pili* in Samoa). He prayed at the temple at Pu'ueo for help for food and, when he returned, told his wife he had heard the voice of the god and that, when the volcano goddess, *Pele* lit the night sky above Mount Kilauea, then the "cloth will cover my head." At his death, *Ulu's* wife had to bury his head near a spring of running water, and his heart and entrails near the door of the house, hiding other parts of his body similarly. Then she was to listen throughout the night, perhaps hearing the sound of heavy fruits falling to the ground, which would tell her *Ulu's* prayer had been granted and their son would be saved. *Ulu* immediately died, and his wife sang a lament and obeyed all his instructions. In the morning, her house was surrounded by a thicket of vegetation and breadfruit.[cxxiii]

In another story, TuiAfono *Taeotagaloa* gives the navigator brothers, *Gaiuli* and *Gaisina*, the breadfruit branch and a coconut branch with coconuts attached to take with them to from Fiji to Samoa. This is the first story evidencing these crops being brought over from Fiji.

Later, missionaries discovered a cave containing a buried mound. When they excavated it, they found well-preserved, slow-baked, breadfruit bread. When tested, they noted the bread must have been buried for over 25 years. This is the way Samoans preserved food—taro, bananas and ripe bananas, and breadfruit by slow baking under the earth.

The Story of Salt

The salting of food, for flavor and preservation, is essential. This story tells how salt was first used in Samoa.

In the village of Uafato, *Taeoiatua* and his sister *Talalaufala* were born from parents *Tanu* and *Fili*. Their parents were summoned by the Malietoa come farm the Malietoa's plantation at Tuana'i village, in the Tuamasaga district. And so *Taeoiatua* and his sister *Talalaufala* went searching for their parents, and they found them at Tuana'i village, where the Malietoa resided. The first Malietoa *Saveatuvaelua* lived here, for his first wife *Amaamaula* was from the village of Tuana'i.

Taeoiatua discovered that the people did not salt their food... with the exception of the Malietoa. And *Taeoiatua* wanted salted food for his parents and family. So, in spite of the tapu by Malietoa, forbidding going to the sea, *Taeoiatua* went to the sea to fetch saltwater, which he used to dry the food and thus salted the food. Because of his powerful warrior strength, the Malietoa then decided to allow all the people of Samoa to use salt for their food.

The Malietoa's sacred meeting ground in Afega and Tuana'i is named after *Tanu* and *Fili*, hence *Tanumafili*. The custodian of this Malae is *Fata* and *Maulolo* and the Tuisamau Orator clan. Later, Malietoa *Laupepa* was the first pastor or minister of Afega village, thus this was his residence, and he named his first son Malietoa *Tanumafili*-I, followed by his grandson Malietoa *Tanumafili*-II.

Land and Crops

The rich, fertile, life-sustaining soil of the island is the second greatest environmental gift from God to the Navigators, superseded only by the Pacific Ocean itself. The volcanic-based soil in these islands is so rich in nutrients that there is a familiar idiom: throw any green plant outdoors and it will turn overnight into a plantation or a forest.

The volcanic ancestry of these islands has, over millions of years, produced rich topsoil that is abundant with fertile nutrients to support a population of people. From early primary school geography class onward, it is often repeated that only one place on earth has a higher concentration of nutrients in its soil than Samoa; that place is Java Island.

Bringing Plants to the Island

To understand the level of preparation that must have been invested by the Polynesians in organizing and planning their migrations, we must not forget their investment in ensuring that sufficient provisions were loaded to support and sustain the group or family during such a long journey—provisions that then led to the crops they grew in their new homeland.

Looking at the mythology and culture of various Austronesian societies, we note that the following crops are "native" to the Malay, Indonesian, and Bismarck archipelagos:

- breadfruits
- many types of taro
- manioka (cassava)
- banana
- coconut
- paper mulberry
- many fruits, such as mangoes, papayas, and others
- ti leaf
- noni (cheese fruit – a plant in the coffee family)
- umala or kumara (sweet potatoes, which were brought over from South-Central America at a later time)[cxxiv]
- ufi (dioscorea wild yam root)
- lega (turmeric)
- ofe (bamboo)
- vi (spondias ambarella is very good for medicinal purposes, particularly when the tree bark is ground up in a drink)[cxxv]
- and many medicinal and edible plants

Some of these crops were transported during various waves of migration.[cxxvi] Special care would have been applied to securing and protecting the precious plants on the vessels, during open ocean voyaging. According to folklore, the root suckers were wrapped in well-rotted coconut husk fibers, and then the whole plant wrapped in dried ti leaves and banana leaves, before being secured in baskets woven from coconut leaves.[cxxvii]

The Use of Slash-and-Burn Cultivation

Crops were cultivated with simple, ancient agricultural techniques. For example, the Samoans and Manu'ans knew that some species of taro and some other roots are grown in areas with water marshes; however there are several taro species that grow very well in good fertile soil. Also they had always known the slash-and-burn method of clearing thick forests and had practiced this throughout their history. In the absence of steel tools like the axe or saw (which were not available 2,500 year ago), the ancient slash-and-burn technique was the only method available to use in clearing the thick forest land.

I grew up and spent my early teens on a plantation with my grandparents, where I witnessed and participated in using this method to clear very thick tropical rainforest. Usually, after the fire has been out for two or three weeks, the fire residue is cleared, and the planting of crops commences.

Fire

Fire and cooking are important to agriculture. According to legend, fire was wrestled away from *Mafui'e* and the demonic god, *Fe'e* (the octopus) by *Ti'eti'ei-talaga* (also known as *Ti'iti'i*— the Maori *Tikitiki* is now the name of a piece of land near Taū, Manu'a). *Ti'eti'eitalaga's* legend parallels the Greek story of Theseus.

The Legend of Fire

The octopus, *Fe'e*, was known as a demonic god and he lived in the underworld, in Salefe'e, together with the guardian of fire, *Mafui'e* (which means earthquake). It's not mentioned where fire originated from, anywhere in the legend. But the name *Mafui'e* (meaning earthquake) implies a deep crack in the earth's surface, which seems to imply a volcanic or lightning origin for fire.

Ti'eti'eitalaga was the son of the Uluelepapa and a man called *Talaga* from the village of Fagali'i, Upolu. The Uluelepapa was the sister of *Mafui'e* in Fue'aloa and of *Tauaifu'efu'e* near Taū, Manu'a. But she was childless. One day, on her way to get salt water, the Uluelepapa saw a maiden (a *Taupou*) named *Ve'a*, taking a bath at the place named Saletua. The Uluelepapa took the young maiden, *Ve'a*, to *Talaga* so they could produce a child. *Ve'a* did produce a boy, and later he was given a name *Ti'eti'eitalaga* (for he was always carried or sitting—*ti'eti'e*—on his father's shoulders).

The Uluelepapa was extremely fond of *Ti'eti'eitalaga* and cared for him very well. She cracked rocks to catch water from the rain, both for drinking and to bathe the boy. While all other people did not have cooked food, her family ate meals cooked and prepared by *Talaga* in the underworld, in Salefe'e, where her brother *Mafui'e* and the *Fe'e* lived.

When *Ti'eti'eitalaga* inquired about why other people didn't have cooked food, Uluelepapa told her son that there was a magic spirit, down in the underworld, that was used by *Mafui'e* and by *Ti'eti'eitalaga's* father *Talaga* to cook the meals. And so *Ti'eti'eitalaga* decided he would go down to Salefe'e to bring the spirit up to cook everyone's food.

When *Ti'eti'eitalaga* got to Salefe'e, he discovered that he had to fight *Mafui'e* through various wrestling matches. Upon defeating *Mafui'e*, he was given fire. *Mafui'e* instructed him then to use dry wood to keep the firebrand lit.

In another version of this legend, according to author Ali'i Felela Fred Henry,[cxxviii] *Ti'eti'eitalaga's* original name is *Maui*, the child who was born as a blood clot, implying a miscarriage, and was left at sea by the mother, *Maeatutala*. But the high tide's waves washed the clot to shore, and the father found it and raised the child to life. Thus his complete name is *Maui Ti'eti'eitalaga*, the fire fetcher. The name *Maui* is known across all Polynesia, including Hawaii and Maori. This title appears in this writer's family genealogy in Taū and Olosega Islands.

The myth is set in the period where *TagaloaLa* and *TagaloaUi* are contemporaries, for *Tagaloalagi* begat *TagaloaLa* who bore *TagaloaUi*, father of *Taeotagaloa*. *Fe'e* (the octopus) is a war deity, the war god of A'ana and Vaimauga districts. Vaimauga district is where Fagali'i village is located, the birthplace of *Talaga*, father of *Ti'eti'eitalaga* who obtained fire.

Livestock and Fishing

Livestock would also have been brought to the islands on double-hulled canoes: for example, pigs, chickens, fowl, fruit pigeons, dogs, rats, and some insects.

The Story of the Pig

We know the pig has been a subject of ancient Greek mythology, with the rites of pig sacrifices in the myth of Persephone, who was conceived of Zeus and Demeter, the Cretan goddess of agriculture and fruitful soil. Thousands of pigs were sacrificed to negotiate the retrieving of Demeter's daughter, Persephone from Hades, as recounted by Joseph Campbell's *The Masks of God: Primitive Mythology*.[cxxix]

Tales about pigs spread across the Near-East and Eurasia to Southeast Asia. So we know that pigs must have been transported from the Western Pacific. But how did they get here?

Early Samoans and Manu'ans were traveling back and forth to the Samoa/Manu'a Archipelago. So the oral legend has it that when *Taeao* and *Lefanoga* were in the Fiji Archipelago, rescuing their sister *Muiu'uleapai* from the cruel king of Fiji (the TuiFiti), this is when they concocted the idea of stealing piglets to take to Manu'a.

The two Manu'an warriors were given cooked pigs for meals for their journey. But instead of eating the pork straight away, they kept it whole. Then in the evening, they took two piglets, a male and a female; each was hidden inside the stomach of the much bigger cooked pigs, which was then rewoven shut. Once they were far away from the Fiji Archipelago, they opened up the cooked pigs and then carefully cared for their piglets. That is how pigs were transported and domesticated in Manu'a and Samoa.

Samoans and Manu'ans agree, in their oral history, that these pigs were brought over in around A.D.1100.

Stories of Fishing

We cannot finish this section on foods without including fishing. A proverbial expression says, "let the fishing methods of Fiji remain a secret." For the weaving of a fishing net is a Samoan innovation, according to oral history. And it is said in the legend that the Fijians only used spears to catch fish. The Fijians were very secretive about their innovation in fishing methods— spearing the fish—but the Samoans copied it in secret and improved on it; they came out with whales' teeth hooks for large fish excursions.

We saw the story of the whales' tooth hook memorialized in The Edict of *Magamagaalefatua* to her son as he leaves Fiji Island on page 142. *Magamagaalefatua* was the wife of the sun god, *TagaloaLa,* or else was a lady from Sapapali'i village, Savai'i, who married *Tagaloalagi*. She bore *'Alo'alolelā*,[cxxx] who married *Fitifiti*, daughter of the king of Fiji or TuiFiti. When *'Alo'alolelā* heard the maidservants of his wife complaining that he did not have a royal family, his mother told him to go to his father (*Tagaloalagi*) and ask him to tell him his family genealogy. *Tagaloalagi* sent *'Alo'alolelā* to go to the house of the married couple, *Ao* and *Po*, who were the spirits or demons of *Tagaloalagi*. And *'Alo'alolelā* was gifted with the fishing hook made of a whale tooth that he took with him, back to his wife in the Fiji Archipelago. Later *'Alo'alolelā* took the fishhook and line back to his family in Samoa, and his mother uttered the Edict recorded in the Mornings.

Tattooing

The Story of the Tattoo

The Samoan legend of the origin of *Tatau* or tattooing is the story of the conjoined twin girls *Taemā* and *Tilafaigā*, descendants of *Ulufanuasese'e* and *Sinalalofutu-i-Fagaiofu*, of Falelatai, Upolu.

The twins' journeys took them to Solosolo village in Upolu, and on to Manu'a and Tutuila, where *Taemā* married Chief *Togiola* and bore *Le'iatotogiolatu'itu'iotoga*, after which they continued travelling on to Fiji Island. After some period of time, the twins desired to return to Samoa. In their farewell parting with the TuiFiti—the Fijian king—they were given a gift, a little box containing the tools and apparatus for tattooing the body. This was originally for tattooing women and not men. As the twins journeyed to Samoa, they sang their song as follows: "Tattoo the women and not the men."

The twins arrived at the seaside village of Falealupo in Savai'i, and one of them looked down to the bottom of the ocean and saw there a trident shell—the Samoan word—*faisua*—really means a very large oyster. She dived down after it and brought it up into the boat. In the process she forgot the song, and so she asked her twin sister how the song went. Then the sister said, "It goes like this: 'Tattoo the men and not the women.'"

It is not clear whether the meaning of this incident is that the sister really got confused and changed the verse from women to men, or whether there is some symbolism attached to the oyster, relative to the women, that motivated the change in the practice.

The twins arrived in Safotu, Savai'i, where Paramount Orator Chief *Lavea* resided. The twins called out to Chief *Lavea*: "Hey there! We have a skill we brought with us on our journey from Fiji." But Chief *Lavea* did not pay any mind to the women, and so their journey continued on to the village of Salelavalu, Savai'i, to the residence of High Chief *Mafua*. But he too wanted nothing to do with women's gift box.

The twins went on to the village of Safata, Upolu, where Chief *Su'a* lived, and they were kindly received by the chief's daughters. When they arrived, Chief *Su'a* was out at work in the plantation. So the chief's daughters had the twins welcomed to the house, served with fresh water to drink, and invited to rest for a moment, while they ran off to get their father. When Chief *Su'a* arrived home, he immediately greeted the ladies with kind, honorific remarks, and the twins were very impressed with the generosity of the Su'a family. They then told *Su'a* about their gift box from Fiji and how the purpose of it is to tattoo the body. The twins, desiring to express their thanks for the Su'a family's kindness and generosity, gifted the skill box to Chief *Su'a*. The gift included the architectural design of the *tatau* (tattoo) and construction implements as his heirlooms, and his ava cup name which must be called out during the protocol as to when he should receive (be served first) his ava drink in the ceremony of tattooing or of a house (maota) dedication. This came with the following decree:

"This is the container and in it are all the tattoo hammers. These hammers are our tools; we will gift it to you, Chief *Su'a*, and your family. When the ava ceremony is served, during the ritual you shall have the first cup to drink before every chief's term. Your ava cup is called *Logotaeao* (to welcome in the morning), and your sacred meeting grounds shall be named Tulau'ega, Lalotalie and Fagalele and Fa'amafi in Safata" (four sacred meeting grounds).

After this the village ladies presented the twins with gifts of barkcloth and curcuma yellow, and the twins were elated.

The Use of Tattoos

As with the ancient tattoos noted in other ancient cultures, tattoos usually covered the whole body. Samoans and Manu'ans have always held onto the belief that Tatau is the "clothing of civilized men." Several explorers—including Jacob Roggeveen in 1722, and members of the expedition of Lois-Antoine de Bougainville in 1768—noted that, from a distance, the native males appeared to be clothed in a wrap-around material, until they came closer; then they realized that the native men were not wearing material clothing, but rather the explorers were observing their tattooed bodies only.

Ancient Egyptian women also appeared to use tattoos as a form of cosmetic decoration—and also, perhaps, for medicinal purposes like acupuncture treatments. In the same way, the Samoan legend clearly indicates that the original instructions for tattooing was to tattoo the women and not the men. But, as we have seen, the instruction was changed, and tattooing was now for men also. Today, young men are eager to have a *tatau* put on them, so they can serve the Chiefs Council and be proud young warriors.

Women can still have a tattoo, but a woman's tattoo is called the *malu*, and it is done on the thighs above and just below the knees, when the young woman shows signs of entering adolescence and experiencing puberty. The procedure is this: when a man decides to get a *tatau*, then a female member of his family, such as a sister or a female cousin, can be a dual tattoo partner; they then accompany each other during this painful ceremonial ritual practice. This is one of only two occasions whereby the boundary taboo, between a male and his sister, is lifted. That is, the sister would be the only one to assist the tattoo architect, to help with the brother's tattooing while he is naked. The other exemption from this taboo is when a brother passes away and the sisters are to prepare him with his burial attire.

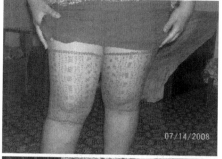

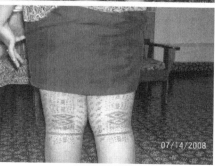

Image 30 images owned by author

The Women's Tattoo

A woman cannot decide one day that she wants to have a *malu*. First a young girl must be of age, 15 or 16 years old, to have a tattoo put on. And there are proper protocols that entail how she must go about getting one. A young girl must have a male partner in order for her to get a *malu*. The first thing a chief architect will ask you is if you have a *Soa*. Now the *Soa* must be a male and female combination, such as a brother and sister, a niece and uncle, etc. This is the traditional way in which a female receives a *malu* and a male receives the *pe'a*. It is the ultimate definition of the male-female *tuaoi*.

Navigators and Tattoos

Much of the literature on Samoan tattoos deals with their historical and cultural importance to the Navigators. However, nothing has been done to examine the Samoan standard warrior and chieftain tattoo, or *tatau*, considered as a series of messages from the immemorial past. One might question: Does art need to have a message?

"Art without a message is like a perfume without a smell," says one reply in DEBATE.org. But 67% of people replied that art does not have to have a message and can simply be enjoyed for its aesthetic beauty. Similarly, three quarters of all viewers of the Samoan tattoo might fall into this group, believing that tattooing is an art and can be enjoyed simply for its aesthetic beauty. The other one quarter of viewers would always be deciphering possible messages from the tattoo, like messages in a bottle so to speak.

So, what if the tattoo is more than an art? What if, in fact, it could be considered as the early "raw initial stages of pictorial script," as the German historian Heinrich Wuttke (1818-1876) suggested?[cxxxi] What if the common practice of modern society—the assumption that if we cannot decipher something, then it must be purely art to be enjoyed for its beauty—is wrong?

Starting with the birth of writing with the Sumerians in southern Mesopotamia around 3500-3000 B.C., followed by attempts to decipher the Egyptian hieroglyphs on the Rosetta Stone in 1822 by Jean-Francois Champollion, then on to the

Mayan hieroglyphs of 300 B.C. in Mesoamerica, we are still awaiting the results of efforts to decipher the Rongorongo—a writing system of pictographs—of Easter Island, of Polynesia.

But if we now go back and follow Dr. Krämer's thought process, in his investigation of the tattoo in *The Samoan Islands, Volume II*, where he isolated a microscopic view of the design patterns of the Samoan *Tatau*, we will note clearly, with him, that these are symbols describing environmental items such as tools, and patterns representing birds and house designs in worm-like and millipede-like style. For example:

- *Togitogi* represents a dot or pecking, as in the woodpecker pecking or drilling through the tree.
- *Aso* is the rafter or cross beam of the house, for Samoa does not have word for "line."
- *Fa'avaetuli* is like footsteps, the leg of a golden plover or tuli bird. As we will see in the Manu'an Creation poem, *Tuli a le Tagaloalagi* is the ambassador of Tagaloalagi. *Fa'avaetuli* represents the repetition of the golden plover's footprints.
- The fishing net design is often used as a metaphor for the close-knit structure of the family unit and how it must be cared for diligently.
- Viewing the male tattoo from the back side, one would see an illustration of the Samoan concept of two halves making one whole in the design. The usage of the *ivitu* (backbone) to divide the halves is clever and elegant.

It is a well-known fact, in linguistics, that writing is formed of symbols for the sound patterns, or of pictorial shapes or glyphs representing an object or concept. "It is physical manifestation of a spoken language," says Joshua J. Mark, Professor of Philosophy at Marist College, New York.[cxxxii] So it is a natural development for human communication to evolve into writing, much as it did in the Sumer (the southern region of Mesopotamia or modern southern Iraq) some 5,500 years ago.

The development of writing was driven by distant trade and the need for documentation of transactions. The frequent travels of Polynesians, and the need to document ocean routes, as well as recording culture and daily activities, might lead to a similar need, fulfilled by the tattoos. In particular, the symbols of objects—representing tools and processes used in house design and building practices—and of deliberations—such as *tatou velo'aso i ai,* deliberation in council (*velo'aso* means consider), like deciding on the best rafter or cross beams and passing them up to the house builder to lay and tie them—are etched in the memories   of cultural customs and protocols, with metaphors relating to these concepts:

- A vessel's sail design is evidenced in the profile, or side view, of the male *tatau,*
- as well as the laying of the Samoan house *'aso* (rafters) as viewed from the back side of the *tatau*.
- The names given to the different sections of the *tatau* design are clearly metaphorical, representing the *fale* (house) design
- and the sections: *'aso fa'alava, 'aso fa'aifo, 'aso e tasi, 'aso laititi, tafagi, pulatua, fa'aulutao,* etc., sections which are designed in such a way as to facilitate rapid relocation if desired, so the house can be disassembled and relocated if necessary.

Language, Words, and Expressions

The Old and the New

Current usage of the Samoan language differs in its intuitive understanding of the implied diacritic spellings of Samoan words (the use of accents and marks). In this volume, I am aware that I may seem to suggest perpetuating the incorrect use of language, but changes in the actual practice of the language are now the norm. We can insist on the original usage but if, in actual practice, the prevailing language usage is accepted as the norm, then the correct diacritic language becomes the exception.

This is evidenced in more modern translations of the Bible vis-a-vis the "old" or early translations, which followed strictly the diacritic spellings of the words. In fact, many in the younger generations stay away from reading the "old" translation, because they struggle with understanding it. For example: is it *ia, iā, ua, uā, oe, oē*, etc.?

So yes, *ia* is used to call attention, like "ya," in the middle of a speech, or "well, then." But iā is used before pronouns to say *to* him or tell *to* him. Also, a predicative particle with the imperative is pronounced iā, as in *Ia e alofa mai*, meaning "Well, then, you love us," or, "Remember to love us." Indeed, there are seven different uses and meaning of ia and iā, and I will try to explain some of them in this section. But within this document, you may find them used with both the old and new diacritic.

A Continuing Study

As discussed in my earlier book, *Navigators Quest for a Kingdom in Polynesia*, language begins with symbols. And Samoan tattoos, as we have just seen, contain in themselves a language of Samoan culture and history.

After signs come words, and the most important gift from the gods is language or rhetoric, according to the Greek philosopher Plato. Language also turns out also to be the "greatest weapon" ever gifted to man. It is used to secure food, protect and defend the family and homeland, conquer new land and people, proselytize with a gospel or cultural belief (Hellenic, Christianity, and other religions), build empires, and identify or brand a race.

315

Language gives identity to a group of people or race. It shapes how we form our ideas and how we convey them to other members of our community. Analytic dissection of your language can even lead to understanding why you think the way you think today. And the relationship between language and culture provides a mirror to show who you are and what you are, as a person, family, culture, community, and citizen of the world.

My intention, in this next section of this book, is that it should be a continuation of the *Navigators Quest for a Kingdom in Polynesia* Linguistics section. Readers of this section should probably start with the Linguistics Section, pages 175-208 in *Navigators Quest for a Kingdom in Polynesia*, which gives the details of the origin of the Polynesian Samoan language and its development from the Asian continent through Southeast Asia and into the East Pacific Ocean. For the structure of Samoan speech grows out from the structure of Samoan language, which grows out of history and is a vital part of culture.

Symbols and Grammar

Dr. Dan Everett, author of *Dark Matter of the Mind* and *How Language Began*, explained that language, in its fundamental definition, is composed of "symbols and grammar." He divides such "signs" into three categories:

- Index: in the same way as "smoke" is an index for fire-related messages.
- Icon: where the symbol is associated with a specific meaning, such as a piece of art or a deity.
- Symbol: for example, where a shovel indicates digging the earth.[cxxxiii]

According to Everett, grammar is initially the arrangement of very simple sounds with words in a linear fashion. At a time before the verb and noun were differentiated, the simplest sentence might be something like "go I." Then a second level of grammar came into being through the development of inflections of linear grammar, so a sentence has more words, and their order implies their specific meaning.

316

Samoan Word Order

There are seven basic sentence patterns in the Samoan language, all starting with a verb or verb auxiliary.[cxxxiv] Examples of these are given in my earlier book, *Navigators Quest for a Kingdom in Polynesia.*

A strict Verb-Object-Subject or Verb-Subject-Object word order holds in the older version of the Samoan language, which is spoken by the chiefs and sometimes referred to as the "polite language." And Samoan cultural belief holds that the relationship of the sentence content to its subject or object should be described by the verb or verb auxiliary or by adjectives, since each describes an action, emotion, mood, tense, or occasion for the noun.

Samoan word order, therefore, is fundamentally different from word order in other societies or western cultures, in that the Samoan sentence starts with a verb (or verb auxiliary), rather than following the western subject-verb-object (SVO) word order.

Language and Orators

Word order is particularly important to a Samoan orator for, in Samoan culture, the verb describes the occasion (the type of meeting for example), and the occasion dictates the contents of the speech and the structure of the message. Because of the oral-based cultural customs and traditions, content must be constructed to include the relationships of the object or subject to the message—for example: *Tulona le mamalu o le Aiga Malietoa...*, meaning "Respectfully," or "the venerated Malietoa family..."—the verbal phrase, describing different occasions such as weddings, funerals, everyday meetings, or dialog, should alert the speaker as to the appropriate lexicon and protocol in the content and method of delivery.

There are different sets of vocabulary words earmarked for each special occasion. The introduction is the salutation of the sacred residence and meeting ground, followed by the veneration salutations of the various families involved in the occasion. Thus, the occasion or the object of the day might be the wedding, but to the orator it is first the glory and honor of the families; their salutations are critical in the introduction of the speech. Each family and their respective chiefs have very specific salutations as we have seen, together with idiomatic words and expressions that describe the mood of the occasion.

For the orator, the occasion is viewed in terms of how effectively the protocol is delivered. The gathering of the families, together with respecting their relationships or genealogies, is paramount. Every special, ceremonial occasion in the culture requires a recitation of the genealogical connections of the families involved. So a real test of an orator chief is how much they know of the family genealogies. Some can recite up to 55 generations, say, in the case of the TuiAtua family, and 42 generations of the Malietoa title.

While the ava ceremony is the immediate "object" or prerequisite to the gathering of chiefs, to the orator clan the most important things are the protocol and procedures for the conduct of the ceremony.

Formal Language

These occasions are where one can observe the difference between the common language and the formal, polite, or chieftain language. The old chieftain's idiom holds that the "Samoan culture was built on words" (or rhetoric)— *'O Samoa na fau i upu*, where the verb object *'O Samoa* is built, *fau*, with rhetoric or oration, *upu*. So, anything can be resolved through words or oratory. Smart and eloquent can be a panacea to discord in human conflict.

Another phrase says, "Samoans live and survive through their oratory, their dignities and honorific titles, and through respect to one another." An elaborate system of gift-giving and reciprocity (you give gifts, and the recipient in return gives you gifts) keeps the peace within village and clan.

Ultimately, in Samoan thinking, it is of utmost importance to understand the inextricable nature of relationships between things, people, and the physical world. The subject or object of a sentence will become obvious from the verb describing it.

In the case of a wedding or a funeral, for example, the isolated disposition of Manu'ans and Samoans in these very small islands has naturally resulted in intermarriages and close kin relationships. Thus knowledge of kinship, together with knowledge of the type and nature of the occasion, is what matters, making it even less important to lead a sentence in the European way, with the subject or object—they are obvious. The verb comes first.

Verbs

Since the word order places verbs first, we shall look at the structure of the Samoan language, starting with verbs. We should note that, in Samoan, the verb itself does not change for the past or future tense. Instead, the tense is shown by verbal particles, which are called indicators, such as the past tense indicators **sa** or **na**. Also, the verbs "to be" and "to have" do not have direct equivalents in the Samoan language. However, there are other ways (equivalent structures) to express these.

Verb tenses

The five main tense indicators are as follows:

1. **E** or **Te** expresses the present tense, or the vague, implied future.
    a. **E** is used when the subject follows the verb, as in **E** *alu Siaki i San Francisco* (Jack goes to San Francisco)
    b. **Te** immediately follows a pronoun. It tells what the pronoun is about to do: *'Ou* (I am) **te**, *E* (you) **te**, *latou* (they) **te**, *matou* (we) **te**, etc. Hence: *'Ou* **te** *alu i le falemai*. (I go to the hospital)
2. The participle **'O lo'o** expresses continuous action in the present.
    a. **'O lo'o** *Moe Ioane*. (Ioane is asleep or is sleeping)
3. **'Ua** is used in three different ways.
    a. To express the perfect tense. This is its most common use, as in **'Ua** *alu Pele*. (Pele has gone)
    b. With impersonal verbs, to express the present tense, as in **'Ua** *po*. (It is dark)
    c. Also it is used with an adjective, to express a past state which continues into the present. **'Ua** *leaga le fuamoa*. (The egg is bad)
4. **Sa** or **Na** expresses the past tense when the action has finished, as in

    a. ***Na*** *moe Pita.* (Pita slept)

    b. ***Sa*** *e alu i le a'oga ananfi?* (Did you go to school yesterday?

5. ***'O le 'a*** expresses the immediate or the definite future, as in

    a. ***'O le 'a*** *tamo'e le tama.* (The boy will run)

Verb Participles

Verb particles, such as ***ia*** are used to denote the imperative (i.e. commands).

    a. ***Ia*** *alu loa.* (Go immediately)

    b. *Se'i faia e a'u.* (Just let me do it)

Sometimes the ***ia*** is used after the verb, as in:

    c. ***'Ina*** *sau* ***ia****!* (Come here!) where the emphatic form of the imperative is ***'ina***

Subjunctives

'ina 'ua and ***ona 'ua*** are subjunctive participles that come before the verb and mean "because" or "that." Although these conjunctives are only possible as indicating the past subjunctive, yet the principal clause of the sentence, upon which such a conditional clause depends, may be either present or past, as in:

    a. *E lelei* ***ona 'ua*** *'ou alu.* (It is good *that* I went)

    b. *'Ua le o* ***ona 'ua*** *matagi.* (We did not go *because* it was windy)

The subjunctive can also express purpose. Sometimes called the "Final Subjunctive," this is indicated by a conjunction ***'ina*** with the particle of the subjunctive ***ia*** as in the following, indicative of a strong desire and hope:

    d. *Soso mai ia, lo'u atali'i e,* ***'ina ia*** *'ou tagotago ia te oe.* (Draw near, my son, that I may feel—touch—thee)

    e. *Tatalo,* ***'ina ia*** *manuia.* (Pray that it be blessed)

Negative causality is expressed by ***'ina ne'i*** as in:

    f. *Sola ia 'oe,* ***'ina ne'i*** *malaia 'oe i le sala a le nu'u.* (Flee thou, lest thou shouldest perish in the punishment of the place)

And the subjunctive of remonstrance—for giving an earnest reason for opposition—is **se'i** as in:

g. *'Ua le **se'i** ta'ito'atasi ma lauga ile leo 'ua ia masani ai?* (Why should not each person preach in the voice that he is accustomed to use?)
h. *'Ua le **se'i** mau se alavaa?* (Why do you not steer a straight course?)

Finally, the subjunctive used to express a wish is indicated by the particle **'ia** as in:

i. ***'Ia** manuia.* (May you be blessed)
j. ***'Ia** manuia Samoa.* (May you prosper and flourish!)
k. ***'Ia** tupu i se fusi* (May you grow in a swamp—a Manu'an proverb referring to the prolific growth of taro plants when planted in a swampy landscape. Hence a good blessing for fruitful reward)

Conjunctives

The conjunctives **'ina ia**, **'ina 'ua** and **ona 'ua** are exemplified in the following quotation:

Ona 'ua *leai 'ea ni tuugamu i Aikupito, na 'e aumaia ai i matou 'ina 'ia matou oti i le vao? Se a le mea na 'e fai ai lenei mea ia te i matou ina ua 'e aumaia i matou nai Aikupito?* (Exodus 14:11) meaning: "Was it because there were no graves in Egypt that you have taken us away to die in the wilderness? What have you done to us, bringing us out of Egypt?" (NRSV)

According to Pratt, **Ona** is preferred for the commencement of a sentence, or for the more strongly emphasized statement of a condition or fact upon which something else depends.ᶜˣˣˣᵛ

'Ina is derived from *'i na*, combined to give the word *'ina*. There is another word *inā* which is a verb particle meaning "to urge." **'Ina** follows a verb in the definite past with **na** or **sa** (expressing the past tense) and seems to preserve historical sequence better than **ona**, used instead of **ona 'ua**.

Samoans frequently express the same idea in composition more forcibly, and more in accordance with the genius of the language, by using the indicative followed by **O le mea lea... ai** (therefore). So the following example illustrates how *O le mea lea* may be used instead of *Ona 'ua*:

Na 'ou vala'au, a e lei mafai outou; na ou faaloaloa lo'u lima, a e leai sē na faalogo mai... **o le mea lea** *ou te ata* **ai** *a'u i lo outou malaia; 'ou te tauemu pe a o'o mai lo outou fefe* (Proverbs 1:24-26) meaning: "Because I have called and you refused, have stretched out my hand and no one heeded, and because you have ignored all my counsel and would have none of my reproof, I also will laugh at your calamity; I will mock when panic strikes you." (NRSV) The Samoan text emphasizes "I," referencing God's speaking (command) and the people not listening, **therefore** (*o le mea ea*) "I" will laugh, and "I" will mock. In the Samoan language it's important to address the superior ranking chief or clergy at the beginning of the sentence. Here, the meaning is that you admit to disobedience, therefore there is an expectation of something punitive to come. By starting the sentence with "Honorable, you called but the people didn't listen," a direct command is implied and His mocking and laughing at their misery is expected. This is just another example of the Samoan translation of the Bible, retrofitting it into the word order and grammar of the language.

Nouns

Relative Pronouns

The extremely important word **ai** performs the function of a "relative" (not necessarily relative pronoun)—a word referring grammatically to a pertinent, relevant antecedent. It always implies the existence of an antecedent—a word that precedes or goes before; perhaps the conditional element in a proposition—but it is not always a pronoun, nor is it always possible to define its use in the sentence or, when associated with a verbal particle, to interpret it.

As a "relative pronoun" **ai** must be translated in accordance with the antecedent in the sentence in which it is used. In this way the word **ai** may be said to mean *which*, or *by which* as in:

   a. *Ona taomia lea, oti* **ai**. (Then he was crushed, *by which* he died)

b. *O le malaga lea na ia momoli **ai** le alofa o nu'u 'ese i le Ekalesia o i Ierusalema e fesoasoani **ai** i lo latou mativa.* (That was the journey *in which* he conveyed the gift of other lands to the church which was in Jerusalem *with which* to help their poverty)[cxxxvi]

Ai may be used to take the place of the personal pronoun, singular or plural, as in these sentences, where the antecedent would be found in the previous sentence:

c. *Le aupito ane i **ai**.* (He was next to *him*)
d. *'Oe mai **ai** le tasi Tui.* (Another Tui answered *her*)
e. *Se'i lua, silitonua mai **ai**.* (Do you two ask of *them*)

The relative pronouns of the nominative case are, **'O le** (singular) and **'Oe** (plural), being translated as *who*, as in:

f. **'Oe** *'aupito ane **ai**.* (*Those* with *whom* you come)

Indefinite Pronouns

The indefinite pronouns are:

a. **Nisi** *(ni isi),* **isi** (Some, others)
b. **Ni** (Some, as in any)
c. **Nai** (Some, as in few)

These can be seen in the following examples:

d. *Se ta**si**, le ta**si*** (One, another, the other)
e. *a se **isi**** (Another, certain one)
f. *Le **isi**** (The other)
g. *'Au mai **ni** niu* (Bring me some coconuts)
h. *'Au mai se **tasi*** (Bring me another)
i. *'O le **tasi** tagata sa mau i Moapi* (A certain man who dwelt in Moab)

Demonstrative Pronouns

Singular demonstrative pronouns are:

a. **leneni** (this)
b. **sinei** (this—diminutive)
c. **lea**, **'o lena**, **'olela** (that)
d. **sina** (that—diminutive)

Plural demonstrative pronouns are:

    e. **la, nei** (these)
    f. **na** (those)
    g. **la** (those near at hand)

Diminutive pronouns are:

    h. **Sea, sisi** (That—diminutive)
    i. **Siasi** (That—diminutive)
    j. **Sinasi** (That, more distant—diminutive)

Distributive Pronouns

The distribute pronouns **ta'itasi** (meaning each) and **ta'itasi uma** (meaning every) might come before a personal pronoun, as in:

    a. *Ia **ta'itasi** ma sau.* (Let each one come separately).
    b. *Sa maua* (We went, we did this).
    c. *Sa 'oulua* (You two or you all did it together)
    d. ***Ta'itasi** ma alu i lona aiga* (Let each go to his family)
    e. *Sau ia so oulua taeao* (One of you come tomorrow)

Possessive Singular and Plural Pronouns

It is probable that the possessive pronouns are formed from the personal pronouns by prefixing the article, *le*, or *se*, and then eliding (suppressing a sound or syllable to join together) to give:

    a. **la'u** (my)
    b. **sa'u** (indefinite, my)

Singular possessive pronouns are then:

    c. **Lo'u, la'u, lota, lata** (mine)
    d. **Lou, tau, lo, la'oe** (thine)
    e. **Lona, lana** (his, hers)

From

    f. **O'u, a'u, ota, ata** (my)
    g. **O'u, au** (thy)
    h. **Ona, ana** (his, her)

And plural possessive pronouns are:

    a. **Lo maua, la taua** (ours)
    b. **Lo matou, la matou** (ours, exclusive)
    c. **Lo tatou, la tatou** (ours, inclusive)

d. **Lo oulua**, **la oulua** (yours plural)
e. **Lo outou**, **la outou** (yours, exclusive plural)
f. **Lo laua**, **la laua** (theirs)
g. **Lo latou**, **la latou** (theirs, exclusive)

From

h. **maua**, **a maua** (our)
i. **matou**, **a matou** (our, exclusive)
j. **taua**, **a taua** (our, inclusive)
k. **oulua**, **a oulua** (your—plural)
l. **outou**, **a outou** (your plural exclusive)
m. **laua**, **a laua** (their)
n. **latou**, **a latou** (their exclusive)

Examples include:

a. *Ua fai la* **laua** *galuega*. (They two are doing their work.)
b. **Ana** *tusi ia*. (These are his books.)
c. **Lota** *mana'o lena*. (That is my desire.)
d. *Le finagalo lea o* **lo tatou** *malo*. (This is the will/desire of our government.)

Agglutinative Language Expansion

There is a process in which a language develops through "gluing" or stringing together base root words (morphemes) without changing them in spelling or phonetics. An explanation of this can be found in the Oxford Dictionaries.

The application of particles, verb particles, and phrasal verb particles, and of conjugated verbs and nouns, are among the various ways Samoans exploited, in order to create new and longer words. This is the basis for "reduplication" in Samoan verbs. The expanding development of the Samoan language came through extensive use of verbal particles including the following:

1. Particles of limitation **ona, tau, na 'o**
2. Optative particles **e fia**
3. Particles expressing disgust **ta** or **se'i**
4. Euphonic particles **na**
5. Particles of negation **e, le'i, e leai se lelei**, *le*, **aua, ne'i**

6. Causative particles **aua**, as in *aua ua e faatau 'oe ia te oe fai mea leaga*.
7. Conditional particles **afai, ana, 'a, pe a** as in *Pe a 'e faatau se au'auna*
8. Particles of sequence **aua** as in *aua ua 'ou le lavalava*
9. Emphatic particles **lava, la** as in *Ua oti lava 'o ia*
10. Interrogative particles **ea** as in *O a'u 'ea le leoleo o lo'u uso?*

In order to meet the demands of modern speech, compound words are constantly being formed. The "Samoanization" of foreign words on products and services, as well as ideas— psychology, physiology, medical, philosophy, etc.—is accomplished by the use of compound words. As Rev. George Pratt said in 1876, "The possibilities of the language in this direction are unlimited."

Words and Expressions

Words to give direction

The Samoan concept of direction is not North, South, East, and West. As we saw earlier (see What the Master Sailor must Know on page 285) it is related to the direction where the sun rises and sets, and the direction toward the mountains versus the ocean. So Samoans would say:

a. *sisifo* (west)
b. *sasa'e* (east)
c. *gauta* (always point to the mountain)
d. *gatai* (always point to the ocean)
e. *gag'ifo* (westward)
f. *gaga'e* (eastward)
g. *saute* (south)
h. *matu* (north)

Further directions were derived by association with heavenly bodies—such as the sun, moon, and stars—including, also, the wind direction in different seasons of the year:

a. *Fuaoletoelau* refers to a dry wind from the direction of the Island of Tokelau.

b. *Matagi mai Toga* refers to the wind from the direction of the Island of Toga.

c. *E afua mai Sauā, se i pai, a le fafa o sauali'i* which means "the sun rises from the village east of Manu'a called Sauā in Fitiuta and sets in the west in the village of Falealupo in the Island of Savai'i, where the ocean path to the underworld of the deceased souls of the ancestors is located." It is also a figure of speech acknowledging that the original birth settlement in these island chains is Sauā village in the Fitiuta district of the Kingdom of Manu'a. Manu'an orators often use this to remind other orators from Samoa of who is the older, as evidenced by the birthplace or origin of all Samoa.

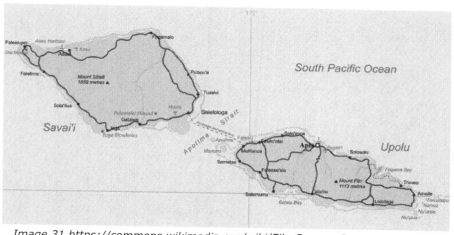

Image 31 https://commons.wikimedia.org/wiki/File:Samoa_Country_map.png
Falealupo at top left CloudSurfer at the English-language Wikipedia, CC BY-SA 3.0
<http://creativecommons.org/licenses/by-sa/3.0/>, via Wikimedia Commons

So, when a Samoan would ask where you just came from, the answer might be "I came from *sisifo* (the west)," with answers such as, "I came from Apia town," representing a relatively new development in language and culture.

Words to tell time

Time is determined by the position of the sun in the morning, noon, afternoon, and evening. At night, time is also determined by the position of the moon relative to its size, such as full, half, quarter, or no moon, or the position of certain stars such as the Southern Cross, evening stars, and midnight stars.

There are specific chieftain words for salutation at different times of day and night. For example:

a. *malu taeao, sautia,* for the morning
b. *laina* for and during the hot noon time
c. *paologia* for late afternoon
d. *pouligia* for the evening and
e. *sautia* for early morning

So, the welcoming salutation would be: *Sautia mail lau Sūsūga le Fa'afeagaiga* or *Ia, pouligia mail lau Tofā a le Mātua Fetalai*, meaning "Good morning your Hon. Reverend Faleula," or "Good evening your paramount elder orator."

The use of Proverbial Expressions

In compiling his well-received and very necessary work on *Samoan Proverbial Expressions*, Dr. E. Schultz consulted the works of Dr. Krämer, Pratt, Buelow, Sierich, Stair, Stuebel, and Turner, the missionaries who documented Samoan and Manu'an history, language, and culture, and the demographics of the people of these islands.[cxxxvii] The compilation of 560 proverbial expressions is broken down into the following everyday activities: fishing, hunting, manual work inside and outside the house, food and its preparation, games, dances and feasts, land and sea travel, and miscellaneous.

While the usage of these proverbial expressions is the domain of the chiefs, they are also widely used by the church ministry and by culturally educated people. The usage of these proverbial expressions and storytelling techniques easily gets the main point of a message across while using fewer words.

Proverbs encourage storytelling in oratory and presentation. They reinforce cultural development and practices and, ultimately, survival in isolation. The creative usage of these expressions, taken from legends, mythology, history, and everyday life, frequently rendered in elliptically mutilated forms, gives richness to the growth of the Samoan language. For *Usiusi a va'a savili*—"Obedient is the sail to the wind."

Equivalently elliptical forms, using an inverted relationship between the syntactic elements of parallel phrases, lead to the familiar phrases in English: "To stop too fearful, and too faint to go," by Oliver Goldsmith[cxxxviii]; and "Ask not what your country can do for you but what you can do for your country" by J.F. Kennedy.[cxxxix]

Where did it Drift from?

The word "drift" in the Samoan language is *tafea*. *Ta fea* means "strike where" where *fea* means "where."

Na tafea mai means "something came floating from somewhere." And *Na fea* means "floating from where?"

'O fea na sau ai? means "Where did it drift from?"

The Samoan language is very precise when using *tafea* or "drift"—it is clear that what drifts must have drifted "from" somewhere. And so *tafea* becomes a navigational term meaning "control-drifting," to obey the wind and current. But *tafea* (or *tafefea,* plural) is also often used sarcastically to refer to a family that "drifted in" from somewhere. *Na tafefea mai fea?* "They drifted from where?"

The word "drift" is different from the word "journey"—*malaga*. *Malaga* means well-planned journeying, which is a different thing. It takes a deliberate action to plan a long journey.

I mention this "drifting" process because, in the discussion of a matrilineal and matrilocal society, we've looked at the concept of drifting from island to island. "Drift" can also refer to how language and cultural traditions "drift" to nearby islands. So Samoans know that, throughout Samoan history, the idea of drifting is not a new concept. It is a reality of life in the Pacific Ocean.

The Language of Mythology

The land is full of mythology, legends and folklore said Reverend Ellis, referring to the Samoan Islands during his tenure as a missionary in the Pacific from 1832 to 1844. These assets— mythology, legends, and folklore—are foundational to the development of the Samoan language. Folklore and mythology provide clarity of thought, philosophy, ethics, and customs for

Samoans. They provide the metaphors and, in many cases, the proverbial expressions that illustrate the moral of a story relating to a particular type of occasion, situation, mood, purpose, or objective. Observed over thousands of years of everyday life-experiences, the mythology is full of learning lessons that are incorporated into the culture, leading to the processes and protocols used in carrying out Samoans' everyday responsibilities.

This incorporation of proverbial expressions, sayings, metaphors, and parables into the language helps subsidize the limited vocabulary. The usage of proverbs and sayings or metaphors acts as a multiplier on the vocabulary used by a speaker in a speech. For example, the use of N proverbs in speech means the same words convey PxN additional meanings, allowing much more information to be conveyed, without the use of additional vocabulary.

It should be noted that the effective use of proverbs and metaphors is also dependent on how creatively and cleverly the speaker uses the proverbial expression. But the impact of proverbs and sayings or metaphors on the embellishment and development of the Samoan language is tremendous.

Epilogue: The Future of Samoan and Manu'an Culture

We started this book with a matriarchal culture, with respect for women woven into the fabric of the culture. Now we shall end by looking at how modern culture has changed or stayed the same in its attitude to women.

Margaret Mead's Peaceful Culture

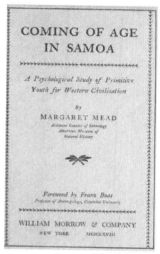

Image 32
https://en.wikipedia.org/wiki/Coming_of_Age_in_Samoa#/media/File:Coming_of _age_in_Samoa_title_page.jpg Margaret Mead, Public domain, via Wikimedia Commons

Margaret Mead's famous study, which resulted in her book *The Coming of Age in Samoa*,[cxl] was conducted on the Island of Manu'a in 1923. The focus of her study was to observe how young girls in this remote, primitive, closed, and isolated cultural society would navigate through adolescence, a critical stage in their lives. The important reason young Margaret Mead selected Manu'a was that it offered a closed and isolated ancient culture which had been fully indoctrinated in the dogma of Christianity for almost 100 years. For the advent of Christianity added and reinforced layers of Samoan culture, incorporating Christian values and practices so they became integral to the culture. This gave Margaret Mead a perfect laboratory environment in which to conduct her field work.

Professor Mead's book, *The Coming of Age in Samoa*, became a very successful work in the field of anthropology. And Professor Mead became very famous, even an American icon. She was also credited for the work she did in Papua New Guinea, studying malnutrition in the population's children. So between her expertise in adolescent behavior and in childhood malnutrition, it is no wonder that she became the head of the United Nations World Food Program targeting childhood malnutrition, with the aim of ridding the world of this severe problem.

There are regulations and legislation governing child-rearing, mandatory education of children, and school lunch programs in the United States, which trace back to Dr. Mead's teachings and philosophical views on how we should deal with adolescents in America today. One of the major elements of this is that we learn, early on in life, to work together as a team or make a collective effort.

But Professor Mead's conclusion, that Samoan culture offered an easy and free style of life, free from the pressure and anxiety of everyday lives found in industrialized society, was soon challenged by Dr. Freedman in his studies of violence and crime.

Dr. Freedman's Culture of Violence

Foundational to Dr. Freedman's argument in refutation of Dr. Mead's *Coming of Age in Samoa* are the empiric observations he made on the rate of crime and violence in the independent Island of Samoa. The data included some breakdowns of the types of violent crimes, but what stood out in the data was that these crimes were, for the most part, considered crimes of passionate aggression. And for years now, domestic violence and abuse of women has been a growing plague in society and in Samoan families.

The crimes Dr. Freedman recorded were often crimes caused by, or originating from, violations of the sacred boundary of the women in the family, e.g. rape or the taking of women by force, both constituting acts of violence or conflict. Also, land disputes can flare into immediate acts of aggression, and sudden argument and heated debate can trigger an act of violent aggression. However, insulting the women of the family or the family chief will always invite a violent aggressive act.

Throughout the history of Samoa, as we have seen, warring conflicts are most often caused by some form of insult directed to the women or toward the paramount chief(s) of the family or clan. Even Dr. Freeman's own data, when sorted, concluded that the data on deliberate and premeditated murder crimes not provoked by "insults" was not statistically significant.

But his conclusion, in contrast to Dr. Mead's, was clear, that Samoan culture was one of violence and conflict.

Violence in Society

Crimes of Passion

Two incidents resulted in guilty judgements and hanging in Dr. Freedman's data—only two, and this was never again allowed. They were judged to be crimes of premeditated murder. The first case was that of *Tualauipopotunu* of Palauli, a descendant of Tafa'ifa *Galumalemana* and son of Le'iatauaLesā *Aololoa* or *Moaulua* of Manono Island, born around 1800. This Le'iatauaLesā *Moaulua* was the father of Le'iatauaLesā *Lelologa*, who married *Lo'alo'a*, daughter of *Tuailemafua* of Samauga, Savai'i, and fathered the infamous Le'iatauaLesā *Tamafaigā*. *Tualauipopotunu* was charged with slaying numerous vagrant white men, escaped convicts from Sydney or sailors "jumping ship" from whaling boats. These men were not in good standing; they were not Christian, and they were scammers, taking advantage of the people with land, and coercing women under false pretenses and promises of marriage.

The other hanging of a criminal took place in the mid-1950s. The criminal was found guilty of murdering his wife and her lover while they were sleeping in the lover's house on the water at the beach shore.

I should also mention that many of the prisoners found guilty of severe crimes and serving lifetime sentences were not held behind bars, but rather they became housekeepers and gardeners of many paramount chief members of parliament. I know several who served the Malietoa monarch at the Head of State residence until they passed away. The point that I am emphasizing in this is that it was understood that some of these prisoners' crimes were driven by emotion and passion. They were not premeditated crimes, not examples of severe sociological and psychological problems such as the planning out of an execution or mass murder. The aiga, the family kin, is much too close to an individual to not detect this kind of horrible plan. And the fact is, everyone is aiga.

But there is no question that domestic violence is prevalent in the Island Nation. And facing it head on is critical.

Violence against Women

Looking at Dr. Freedman's data, significant numbers of crimes would be classified today as relating to or directly involving domestic violence against women. This assisted Dr. Freedman in building his case and counterargument, presenting Samoans as being of violent dispositions, as opposed to Dr. Mead's proposition of an easy and free style of life, free from the pressure and anxiety of everyday lives found in industrialized society. The implication and emphasis of Dr. Freedman's data is that violence, or domestic violence, has existed in Samoan society for some time from 1940-1970 (though the paucity of his sketchy data, manually collected, suggests it needs further scrubbing).

I do not want to focus on statistical arguments about problem definition, but I do want to remind readers that there is historical and current data to suggest we're far from solving the problem of violence and reducing the trend. This disease, of domestic violence against women, does not discriminate according to culture, race, color, religion, economics, or demographics. But I confine my discussion here to Samoan culture, because it is a growing problem.

While I am not a physician, or a psychologist, or a medical professional—I'm not qualified to render a medical, psychiatric, or sociological definition and diagnosis of this problematical disease—as a family leader and a member of the cultural custodian group, I am impelled to utilize this opportunity to help "sound the pandemonium" and call our people each to do their part. To borrow a phrase from Homeland Security: "If you see something, say something."

This medical and healthcare problem is a sign of the fragmentation of the overall healthcare situation of the country. And the healthcare issue is highly correlated to income levels or, more precisely, to the level of poverty.

The situation is straightforward: money or knowhow acquires food, nutritional types of food, and that provides energy and good health. But the opposite, of course, is equally true—that is, "bad foods" cause unhealthy bodies. A plethora of medical and healthcare studies have enumerated this fact of the human lifestyle cycle. I'm not going to belabor the problem's magnitude, for the causes and effects of domestic violence have long been articulated by studies in the field. But a summary is appropriate, to anchor my simple voice:

- The health of a country is evidenced in the health of its citizens.
- The wealth of the community is dependent on the health of its citizens.

The unhealthy disease of violence against women can not be ignored.

Is violence inherited?

The United Nations Population Fund Survey concludes the rates of intimate-partner domestic violence with Pacific Islanders are 64% of women in Fiji, 40% of women in Tonga, and 46% of women in Samoa. The definition of the problem is well-known and well-established, with a preponderance of statistical evidence, so dwelling on the obvious merely deflects attention from the salient point, which is: What can we do to aggressively reduce this disease?

Are Samoans prone to some inherited streak of violence from their past. Is the "Warrior" cultural identity somehow promoting violent behavior? No. It turns out that there is no such thing as an inherited streak of violence. There is, however, a tendency toward emotional and passion-driven violence that seems to be common among closed, family-oriented cultures. Thus, violating cultural boundaries and failing to show respect causes those savage emotional outbursts that tend to be satisfied through acts of violence.

There are plenty of studies examining the evolutionary development of the role of the male warrior species. To protect, acquire, conquer, demonstrate fertility, and lead are the attributes that have long been associated with the role of the warrior male, throughout the evolutionary process during the Neolithic period. But this doesn't lead to any permanent, exclusively Polynesian acquisition of violent, aggressive behavior. For every society, all across the globe, has gone through this same evolutionary process during the Neolithic period. So Samoans do not have a monopoly on violence.

But when that savage, primitive wrath explodes, it's fearful.

Knowing Ourselves

What can we learn from these two sages, Dr. Mead and Dr. Freedman? Is our human anatomy made up of both capabilities—of peaceful humility as well as that core of primitive, savage anger and violence? Samoans would tell you that, when a Samoan loves you, they love you to death. On the other hand, if they hate you, they hate you to death.

It's not scientific but we all seem to understand ourselves better than those who want to study us. It's this commonsense knowledge of ourselves that allows us to better understand each other. It begins with an understanding of ourselves and our behaviors, an understanding that is important to reshaping our narrative.

If we know, just from common sense, that education is the key to a better way of life, through the learning of skills leading to better employment opportunities, then what do we need to do? If education allows people to search out ways for better farming, cultivating the land for planting crops and providing sustainable food for the family, what do we to do? Likewise, if we know that domestic violence between intimate partners originates from anxiety, anger, depression, low self-esteem, bad health, unemployment, and a low level of education, what should we do?

Underreporting violence

According to the *Journal of Medical Internet Research*, those suffering from mental illnesses, such as psychotic disorders, are two to eight times more likely to experience some form of abuse or domestic violence and suffer poor health outcomes than the general population. Examples include suicide attempts and substance abuse. Also, women who have experienced domestic violence are at a significantly higher risk of experiencing a range of mental health conditions, including PTSD, anxiety disorders, depression, and thoughts of committing suicide.[cxli]

Victims of domestic violence, such as the physical abuse of wife and children, are more likely report incidents to authority and speak to mental health experts than are victims of intimate-partner violence. Victims of intimate-partner violence are very reluctant to report incidents, let alone to talk to mental health professionals. So underreporting is a significant issue with victims of rape or intimate-partner violence.

A 2003 Center for Disease Control report shows that, in the U.S., more than 25% of domestic (family) violence victims reported registering to speak with a mental health professional, as compared to victims of intimate-partner violence or abuse such as rape. This underlines the problem of underreporting in these cases. Underreporting is an area that is a major problem with Pacific Islanders. For Samoans, this issue of underreporting is exacerbated by cultural norms and protecting family reputation. But it doesn't have to be this way.

The Illness of Violence

The literature points to the problem of violence being sourced from biological, psychological, and situational factors: biological in the sense that violence is a physical health issue; psychological because it's a product of mental, emotional, and behavioral issues; and situational because of cultural norms and society, and of environmental surroundings.

These highly overlapping categories are parts of the definition of the problem. Scientists use the term "socialization" to describe the process by which a child learns the "scripts" for specific social behaviors, along with rules, attitudes, values, and norms that guide interactions with others. The other subcategory here is "cognitive." This refers to ideas, beliefs, and patterns of thinking that emerge as a result of interactions with the world, during a person's lifetime.

The literature continues, listing the common causes of violence, such as extreme aggression, assault, rape, and murder, which might be induced by frustration, exposure to violent media, violence in the home or neighborhood, and by seeing other people's hostile or violent acts.

So, understanding the risk factors that drive this illness of violent behavior becomes fundamental to helping these people. Clearly, the history of violent victimization, attention deficit disorders, hyperactivity, or learning disorders are only a few things that we must have a profound understanding of, if we are to help in education and rehabilitation.

So we see, this is deeply rooted in the upbringing in early life. This illness is not like catching a cold or the flu. It's acquired over time, through emulation and mimicking observed behaviors, particularly behaviors emanating from those that are admired, like parents and adult siblings. In other words, it's culturally influenced, and that's the challenge, because we have to re-examine our cultural narrative, if we are to seek long-term, sustainable solutions for this illness.

Cultural Norms and Violence

It's well-known, by health professionals and laymen, that Samoans practice a "keep it behind closed doors" attitude to incidents of domestic or intimate-partner violence. Airing your domestic problems out to the general public is highly discouraged. It brings shame to the family and the clan. It's a sign of losing control.

Gross violations, in overstepping the boundaries in so many ways, are shameful. And so, committing suicide is seen as the next best thing, if you have the courage to perform such a severe act resulting from depression or a feeling of defeat. But this is contrary to the proverb that "it takes a village to raise a child or build a family." There is no cultural norm that prevents family members from getting professional medical help.

The issue is knowledge, and knowledge comes from education. Through education, we can learn to ask for help without feeling that we are falling short of family expectations.

I remember one coach being interviewed on TV about an outstanding Samoan football player in his team. The coach asked the young player who or what he was playing for, to motivate himself, and he answered, "I play for my family, my village, my clan, my church, my island, my team, my teammates, my school, my coach." The coach said, "Young man, it's just a football game." And the young Samoan said, "For you it's just a game of football, but for me it's the whole culture and island country."

This kind of patriotism and loyalty is not exclusive to Pacific Islanders; it's common in many close-knit societies. And Samoan culture is "family first and individual second." Thus, if a family huddles together to help save lives, we should not view it as an alien concept. As pointed out in this section, the overlapping of all these healthcare and medical issues, combined with the constraints of cultural norms, helps fuel the disease of violence. So we will discuss what we can do about helping address the disease of domestic and intimate-partner violence from a cultural perspective.

Cultural Causes of Violence

The patriarchal nature of the current Samoan cultural emphasis promotes male-dominated chauvinism in attitudes and behavior. This perpetuates men keeping women down and "in the background," while it promotes male egoism and allows domestic violence to exist in the family. This fosters an environment and atmosphere that implies such treatment of women is integral to the Samoan culture. Wisdom and common sense tell us this is wrong, but we are creatures of habit—the more we see something, the more likely we are to participate in it, learning by emulation.

Do not underestimate the influence of learning by emulation. We start at childbirth and continue throughout adulthood. For example, the sage Noam Chomsky has promoted a theory that even grammar is innate in human nature; he points out how a child mimics sounds and words just by listening to the parents and people around them; that's how we learn words and language—by emulation. And so the domineering behavior of males in Samoan culture is an important aspect of a culture where women nurture the warrior characteristics of the Samoan male. It started early in the evolutionary development of the culture. It is a natural part of the norms of matriarchal organization. The women support and nurture the male for the tasks and responsibilities expected of them.

In a paper titled, "Why is the Human Primitive Warrior Virtually Always the Male of the Species?" J. M. G. van der Dennen[cxlii] points out that, from the way of life of hunter-gatherers until the paradigm shift to agriculture, women were supportive and nurturing toward their men. In the process of agricultural transformation, women took on more and more responsibility, and their position evolved into participation in the decision-making process. In the seafaring culture, from which the Polynesian Navigators originated, this evolved into a matriarchal structure of society.

The deep-rooted evolutionary practice of nurturing the male ego has, from long ago, become so woven into Samoan culture that we grow up accepting it as normal practice. The real issue, however, is that we have allowed the erosion of the demarcation of "boundaries" in our cultural norms. We don't have to unweave the "fine mat" of our precious culture, but we do need to "reshape" the weaves.

I will discuss this more in the section where I ask what we can do about this. My purpose here is to give clarity to the problem, and to do the necessary self-examination, cultural examination, examination of faith-based beliefs, reexamination of our educational system, and reexamination of our governance policy.

We know in our hearts how much we honor and love our princesses, but when those angry outbursts come out, we lose our sense of dignity. We practice humility and reticent behavior, but anger and emotional outbursts come out from us, and we become "over-the-top" aggressive.

In a PTSD therapy group, we discussed how, in a split second, we can go from the most humble and reticent person to the scariest person on earth. If this resonates with you, you are not alone. It's a disease, prevalent with all PTSD patients.

My Post Traumatic Stress Disorder (PTSD)

I had not planned to share my PTSD story until I realized that, if I don't, I would be less than honest, and thus I would betray the theme of this book. So, after thinking about it, wisdom kicked in, and here we go.

I was diagnosed with PTSD in 2002. This was after coming back from Vietnam and getting out of the Army in September 1970.

The Vietnam war did not invent PTSD. It was first observed in veterans of WWI, then followed up in all subsequent wars—it's an "infectious disease" of war. But PTSD not exclusive to war veterans; it can happen to anyone going through some kind of traumatic experience in life. Many PTSD sufferers are victims of severe accidents and domestic or intimate-partner violence. However, it was Vietnam veterans who fought to bring the problem to light, seeking its definition and eventual classification as a mental illness.

This "mental illness" classification is a double-edged sword in the sense that, while veterans were finally getting help medically and financially, the label "mental illness" was equivalent to the "kiss of death" in one's professional career. No management would promote a known PTSD sufferer to any senior management position, let alone even hire one in many cases. So, when I was examined for PTSD, when the doctors saw my biography and noticed I had been a senior manager at Bank of America and had already founded and taken a company public on NASDAQ, they would eventually get around to asking me: how did I manage to stay "cool and collected" in order to achieve my goals? I would answer that it was a personal struggle.

Keep in mind, it was over 30 years after I started with Bank of America that I was finally diagnosed with PTSD. So, during that 30-year career, I didn't know I was ill. And I don't want to go back; I could say it's water under the bridge, but what is important is that I got clarity and treatment. And, while I am here in this page, I want to acknowledge all my veteran buddies out there who are going through this illness: God be with you and your efforts.

I took advantage of the GI (Government Issued) Bill for education, and that's how I earned a couple of college degrees. So for over 30 years, I went along with my life, trying to make a living and raising a family. Life, for the most part, was moving fairly well, but I knew, early on, you have to make your own opportunities. Still, with a little bit of luck, I was able to achieve some of the things that I wanted to achieve. I had a good career in banking with one of the premier banks, at the Bank of America headquarters in San Francisco where it had been since its founding in1906. In the United States, at the time, Bank of America was either number one or number two in their on-going "horse race" with New York's Citibank.

I saw an opportunity to get educated and get hands-on experience with information technology—a technology that would forever change the banking landscape, and thus I obtained a competitive edge. But, before leaving Bank of America, I had never discussed anything about my military experience, let alone experience in Vietnam, with anyone. In fact, in our whole Treasury or Cashier's division of about 280 employees, there were only two of us that were Vietnam veterans. Actually, I met the other veteran in the men's room, when we exchanged greetings in a Vietnam GI slang, "Hey homie." The term "homie" originated back during the Mexican American, Spanish period in the early 1900s. But we used it likewise in the Vietnam era. Anyway, this is how we discovered we might be the only two Vietnam veterans in this division at the bank's world headquarters.

About 90% of the staff were Ivy League graduates, with Stanford, UCLA, Berkeley, and University of Chicago graduates included. They belonged to the generation that didn't really think going to war (to Vietnam) was a bright thing to do. So I just kept my narrative to myself and concentrated on getting my job done well and nothing more. And in fact, very few close friends knew that I was Vietnam veteran.

When I was finally recruited out of the bank, to do banking software consulting and development, it was a deliberate move on my part to get involved with information technology. And now, thirteen years later, I went into the VA hospital to get my wounded leg reexamined for my disability compensation. It was here that I got my surprise diagnosis of PTSD. I had never thought about filing for PTSD treatment or compensation until that day.

The amazing thing was that the veteran employee who was processing my appointment, in the course of getting all the paperwork done, went through a series of routine questions to fill in the form. He said, "Have you ever been tested for PTSD?" And I answered, "No," with a follow-up, "What the hell is that?"— familiar GI language. He said, "This is a test for people that are struggling with war memories and can't get control of themselves." And he immediately shifted his tactic to "Let's fill in a few questions and answers here, before you see your doctor." I said okay.

"Here we go, my friend. Let's start with, are you married?" I said no. "Were you ever been married?" I said yes. "How many times?" I said twice. "Do you have a girlfriend?" I said, yes. "How many girlfriends in last few years?" I said two or maybe three. "Did you ever raise your voice to your ex-wife." I said yes. "Do you ever have an angry outbursts?" I said yes. "Do you sometimes want to be alone?" I said yes. "Do you feel lonely at times?" I said yes. "Do you think this behavior might be the cause of your marriage breaking up?" I said maybe.

It is here that he stopped and looked dead into my eyes and said, "Dude, you have the disease. I will put it down that you need to be tested for PTSD."

The long-story-short is that I was tested, and I was enlightened. It explained everything, and more, of my past behavior or demons. I discovered that I managed my anger and aggression by going away from the confrontation. I would rather walk away than confront the situation. And it seemed to speak to me exactly of how I had gotten divorced twice.

This is not an excuse, but it is my reality. It's the way I navigate through my professional career, by avoiding confrontation. I began, early after I came home from service, to

343

practice ways to mediate my own aggression. And yes, I went through therapy and anger-management periodically, when I felt I needed it. I often remember how my dear first wife, mother of our only daughter Manaia, said to me, early on after my return home, that she saw a change in my mannerisms. But I took that to mean we were growing apart.

My first wife was correct; I had changed. I would say I have a mild case of PTSD and it's under control, but I can remember times when I struggle through it all. It never goes too far away. It's a state of mind, because it is the mind that is ill, but I am conscious of it always.

I also suffer from type 2 diabetes, and a new study from Kings College London in the United Kingdom is finding that people who are lonely may be more likely to develop type 2 diabetes.[cxliii]

Poverty and unequal economic opportunities

We have drilled down now to understand the social sources of this illness of violence, but we likewise need to address the culprit in the environment that fertilizes this way of life. The chasm between the economic haves and have-nots is severe, and this must be dealt with, as it is integral to finding a sustainable treatment for this disease.

The health of a community is dependent on the wealth of the community. The community's ability to earn a living is fundamental to wealth creation and sustainability. The collective income and income-producing assets of the community determine the wealth or poverty status of the community. And the basic mantra of economics is to determine how people make or earn their livings: everything else is a corollary to that premise.

This is where statistics have failed us. Because a small percentage looks like a small number, especially when compared to other big countries, one might imagine it implies a small problem. But, for example, if 18.8% of the population lives below the national poverty line, this is a highly significant number, even in a population of less than half a million people. The majority of the poor are those are living in rural areas and villages, and the problem is they can't farm the land; they don't have access to clean drinking water and healthcare; and also of significance, they have been granted only a low level of education.

Government workers involved with data-gathering note that the lack of knowledge and skills to cultivate the land for agricultural production is an issue of concern. They see that there is plenty of family land available for cultivation, but without initiative, ambition, and motivation to work the land, little can be done to solve the problem of poverty and lack of food production capabilities.

The history of economic development of the family in Samoa has been one of cash crops for export—bananas, corpora, cocoa chocolate beans, coconut, etc. Farming was the cornerstone of building a decent income for the family.

The issue of poverty is a worldwide problem, not unique to the Pacific Island countries, but having 19% of the population below the national poverty level is still a big problem. This shines a spotlight on the Island Nation. So it has to be addressed in a sustainable manner.

Food and Diet

If the prevalence of diabetes among Pacific Islanders is a sign of malnutrition in the diet, then the foods they consume must be outright bad. Diet derives from food production. Bad food equals bad diet equals bad health. With a bad diet, body parts deteriorate, and the functions of the body become susceptible to infection from viruses causing illness. Weakening of the immune system causes deterioration of both physical and psychological functions.

Diet and exercise are key elements in attacking the spread of diabetes. But a prerequisite is education about the illness and about diet management. The problem arises from the type of food consumed and from the amount. When bad food is consumed in high quantities, then we have a recipe for disaster. (I speak from experience.) Diabetes induces high blood pressure, high cholesterol, and poor circulation. Then comes weight gain, and then it gets uncontrollable. So now we have obesity as a disease.

Medical and healthcare literature notes that diabetes affects all three factors of health—physical, psychological, and the way you live your life. Diabetes has effects on depression, anxiety, emotional outbursts, anger, and uncontrollable physical expressions of emotions that induce violence. The more this happens, the more it's likely to become habit, or a pattern of violent behavior.

So we have a pattern of problems, all working together toward violent behavior:

- Diabetes
- Obesity
- High blood pressure
- Depression
- Mental health
- Observation of violent behavior
- Angry outbursts
- PTSD prevalence

So where do we start to unwind these bad habits and behaviors? We have all the bad habits moving in unison, all down the cliff. But we know the problem, and we also know what to do to eradicate it. But we are struggling with a lack of initiative, motivation, purpose, or energy to take action.

Proposed Solution

Perhaps I can propose an approach with which we can deliberate to find some answers and thus a sustainable cultural approach to this severe human illness. Melinda Gates' post on LinkedIn, on April 15, 2021, suggested that if we want to live in a society where women are seen and valued equally, we must address those disparities concerning whose stories get told, and we must be mindful of who's doing the telling.

So the narrative must be reshaped to effectively address these critical problems—justice for women, domestic and intimate-partner violence, health, education, and poverty. It starts with the following:

The Chiefs Council

The village Chiefs Council must play a critical role in enforcing laws and ordinances protecting the safety of domestic violence victims. The detection and advisory roles, as well as the reporting of cases, are very important tasks that can be performed at the village level.

Reporting incidents of domestic and intimate-partner violence is crucial to getting help and finding a resolution to the situation. The prerequisite is basic education and training for the chiefs, so they can do an effective job in helping victims and, more importantly, in reporting incidents immediately to the authorities.

Perhaps the government administration of village mayors can provide incentives for mayors to arrange training and implement procedures for handling domestic violence incidents at the village level. The organizational structure of the village Chiefs Council is already well-established as part of the culture. Incorporating these added procedures should be straightforward.

The Ministry

Education about domestic violence should become a part of the curriculum of all seminary colleges and teacher-training programs on the island. The current curriculum does not have specific courses or classes covering the disease of domestic and intimate-partner violence. The study of domestic violence in social studies should not simply be a family sociology course. The problem is more complex than it looks, as I have already highlighted. The ministry has a very significant role and impact on teaching the population. It's a leadership role that can really provide a paradigm in its approach to our attitudes toward women, as well as toward domestic and intimate-partner violence.

The ministry must step up to their responsibilities to care for their flocks. Ignoring this problem is to hide behind the pulpit or the cloth. The leadership authority residing in a Samoan minister is very powerful, and we should apply it to saving these victims' lives. This has to be on the agenda in the ministry's message. This can be very effective in explaining the narrative and bringing the subject into the open. We should not hide it anymore, but we should see it and treat it as part of our everyday lives, as part of the trials and tribulations of life that need to be healed.

Education System

Currently there is no specific curriculum, nor are their healthcare courses on domestic and intimate-partner violence, available in any school or community college or university. I've pointed out the multidimensional nature of domestic violence, that it is an issue of physical and mental healthcare and of way of life. It's a disease that is psychological and sociological and driven by income level.

These are academic subjects that must be offered and studied within the education system. This type of information is not intuitive. You don't learn about it from internet. It must be taught to the general population and particularly to the students

Reshaping the Cultural Narrative

It all begins in the family. Any solution to this problem of violence will take an "all hands on deck" commitment from all members of the family. If we catch the problem at this level, then the village Chiefs Council would become the support group to the family. If we talk about it in the family, church, and school, then we can achieve open-mindedness and understanding.

We have to shape a new cultural narrative. We have to openly recognize that our culture was and still is a matriarchal society. We all know how much we love our princesses, but we don't make a point of recognizing them in our speeches and literature, at home or in the family. We don't have to wait for a wedding or funeral ceremony to mention and acknowledge the family princess. There is nothing wrong with acknowledging the princess, much like we acknowledge the chief's or the pastor's wife in our discourse.

Justice for women starts at home, with showing and practicing the giving of respect to women, and with adherence to the customs and norms about honoring boundaries covering men vis-a-vis women. These norms are not new; they are as old as the culture. They just have to be reaffirmed.

This why I did not use the word "change." We do not need to "change" the cultural narrative, but rather "reshape" it, because it is not new or hard, like metal that you can't bend. The culture, as we have seen, is elastic and has a fluidity that promotes creativity, to shape it based on life's demands.

The new generation of men and women in chieftain leadership is more formally educated than our parents were—here I'm talking about my baby-boomer generation. Recognizing women in leadership roles, in guiding the family as a chief, is an excellent start. But violence directed toward women is often caused by jealousy of the male partner, due to the woman's success and achievement. So again, we come back to the education dialog. No matter how verbose I can be, it comes down to education in cultural norms: to boundaries, respect, humility, and practicing these norms.

We must start with the children. That way, they can practice this behavior as they grow up. It has to be an integral part of our everyday language and mannerisms.

Income and Poverty

As well as all this, we must recognize that there is a poverty problem. We cannot advance this discussion if we're not in agreement that there is a poverty problem. 19% of the nation's population lives at the poverty level, based on the national demographics on income levels. That means one out of five is in poverty in Samoa. Ignorance of the data-driven science on income disparity illustrating poverty level is the same as being intelligence-impoverished.

The data on economic demographics suggest that limited access to education and clean water, and a lack of knowledge of agricultural methods and practices, are two things plaguing the rural or outlier villages. We have to revive the "cash crops" agricultural approach in rural areas. We have to teach this simple way of earning a living and feeding the family.

There is an agriculture department that should be spearheading the educational initiative to reach these people. This has to be a hands-on approach. People have conquered this before in the past. But somehow we've lost the battle again. Reports show that the United Nations, World Bank, and the IMF have given funds to this cause, and that they have been waiting for some good news on the situation concerning the rate of poverty. But unfortunately, no such luck.

I know that the government is working through the village Chiefs Council organization to encourage agricultural development at the village level. There are incentives designed to promote planting and cultivation of the land for food and cash crops. But it needs a laser focus on the part of the government, and a concerted initiative, to tackle this problem. It has to be a multi-level, comprehensive initiative—that is, one that combines culture and science with agriculture, education, water-resource management, leadership, and incentive programs available at all levels (individual, family, village, and district).

How to move Forward

Again, as Melinda Gates said in her March 29th 2021 blogpost, it makes a difference who shapes the stories we hear and the stories we see, because those stories shape our lives. It's important that culture shapes our narrative, because the culture and narrative are more overarching and profound than any one person's attempt to solve a problem. So I challenge the following organizations to take on the task, to use their leadership, skills, and resources to fight these causes:

- o The family
- o The chiefs
- o The ministry
- o The educators
- o The village authority
- o The district authority
- o The Ministry seminary
- o The schools and universities
- o The government legislative authorities
- o The government administration departments
- o The nongovernment nonprofit organizations
- o The citizen volunteer corps

Conclusion

After reading the honorable High Llama's book *How to Expand Love: Widening the Circle of Loving Relationships*,[cxliv] I cannot help but conclude that love requires two or more persons to fulfill it. We have plenty of terminology for self-love, if that makes sense, but to find reciprocal love you need another person, and this is really the love we are all searching for, at all levels of life. Thus, collective love is what a family strives for in a happy cohesive family, and likewise, with extended family, clan, village, and community.

This is the key differential with Samoan culture—collective love of siblings, family, village, district, culture, and country. And it is practiced starting at birth. This is how Samoans survived for thousands of years. It's a matter of human bonding. Man was not created to love himself, by himself. The whole (Biblical) premise of creating woman was to love and be a partner, to explore and be passionate about and appreciate the rest of God's creation. It's caring for one another that reinforces the weave and the knots of the metaphorical fishing net that is the family network.

In the same way, military soldiers bond to create esprit-de-corps and cohesiveness, the camaraderie that binds military units together. It automatically instills caring and protection among soldiers as a cohesive unit. Thus it allows the unit to function efficiently and as a single unit.[cxlv]

Many studies have been directed toward identifying any and all correlation in relationships between soldiers with their pre-war home background—for example, a peaceful, happy, close family with loving siblings, vis-a-vis a dysfunctional family life—and relating this to their personal attitudes and management of their PTSD illnesses. In short, the studies have found lower levels of impact of PTSD on the health and wellbeing of soldiers who came from close family bonding, as opposed to from dysfunctional families.[cxlvi] Collective behavior, such as that in a loving family, siblings, and community, begins at home and at an early age.

351

The studies show that the power of collective actions to induce cohesiveness, in a military unit or in community organizations, is critical to survival in a diverse and multicultural society.

The greatest asset of Samoans and Manu'ans is their collective love for each other and family and country. This gives them the cohesiveness and unity to weather any storms that befall them. It is self-evident. And it is seen throughout their history and culture, from the beginnings of that matriarchal culture, with which I started this book, to the present day.

Look out for Volume II of this book, *Navigators Founding a Nation,* to see how our future as a nation depends also on the ocean ecology and economy, and to learn how the history of Samoa and Manu'a fits into the history of the world we live in.

Notes

[i] By this author. Navigators Quest for a Kingdom in Polynesia, p. 218

[ii] Campbell, Joseph. *The Masks of God: Primitive Mythology*, Penguin Books Ltd, London, England 1959, 1969 Edition, p. 55, referencing the 1921 Nobel Prize winner in literature author Gerhardt Hauptmann

[iii] Encyclopedia Britannica Online, Jan 27 2009 in its entry on Adolf Adolf Bastian; also Deacon, Terrence. *The Symbolic Species: The Co-evolution of Language and Brain.* WW Norton & Co, 1997

[iv] Poznik, G.D. Science (2013); Francalacci, P. Science (2013); Mendez, F.L American Journal of Human Genetics (2013)

[v] Gilson, R.P. *Samoa 1830 to 1900. The Politics of a Multi-Cultural Community.* Oxford University Press, Melbourne 1970. p. 68

[vi] Ioannidis, A.G., Blanco-Portillo, J., Sandoval, K. et.al. "Paths and timings of the peopling of Polynesia inferred from genomic networks." Nature 597, 5222-526 (2021). https://doi.org/10.1038/s41586-021-03902-8 9/22 2021

[vii] Campbell, Joseph. *The Masks of God: Primitive Mythology*, Penguin Books Ltd, London, England 1959, 1969 Edition, pp. 177-8

[viii] A.R. Radcliffe-Brown, see *Navigators Quest for a Kingdom in Polynesia*, p. 235-236

[ix] Wikipedia contributors. "Matrilineality." Wikipedia, The Free Encyclopedia. Wikipedia, The Free Encyclopedia, 6 Nov. 2020. Web. 17 Nov. 2020.

[x] Marck, Jeff. "Proto Oceanic Society was Matrilineal." The Journal of the Polynesian Society. 1986

[xi] W.H.R. Rivers, see *Navigators Quest for a Kingdom in Polynesia*, pp. 134-35

[xii] Ali'i Felela Fred Henry: *Talafa'asolopitoo Samoa*, Commercial Printers Ltd, Apia, Samoa, 1945-59, p. 104

[xiii] Krämer, Dr. Augustin. *The Samoa Islands: An Outline of a Monograph with Particular Consideration of German Samoa*: Vol 1. 1902. trans. Theodore Verhaaren. Auckland. Polynesian Press Samoa House. 1994, pp. 121-125

[xiv] Lafai- Sauoāiga, *O le mavaega i le tai / [Lafai- Sauoāiga]*, Vasa I Faletea. 1949. Genealogy of the Samoan people and stories of the ancestors collected and transcribed by Lafai- Sauoāiga. The Malua Printing Press, Apia, Western Samoa, 1988, pp.60-62

[xv] Mead, Margaret. *The Coming of Age in Samoa.* US. William Morrow and Company 1928

[xvi] Cosma, Sorinel. "Ibn Khaldun's Economic Thinking." Ovidius University Annals of Economics. Ovidius University Press 2009. XIV:52–57

[xvii] The MUQADDIMAH, AN INTRODUCTION TO HISTORY THE CLASSIC ISLAMIC HISTORY OF THE WORLD: IBN KHALDÛ, Translated and introduced by Franz Rosenthal Abridged and edited by N.J.Dawood. London Rutledge and Kegan Paul in association with Secker and Warburg in 1967. The current Princeton Classics is with an introduction by Bruce B. Lawrence. Princeton University Press. The first complete English translation, by the eminent Islamicist and interpreter of Arabic literature Franz Rosenthal, was published in three volumes in 1958 as part of the Bollingen Series and received immediate acclaim in the United States and abroad. A one-volume abridged version of

Rosenthal's masterful translation first appeared in 1969. The Princeton Classics of the abridged version includes Rosenthal's original introduction as well as a contemporary introduction by Bruce B. Lawrence. This volume makes available a seminal work of Islam and medieval and ancient history to twenty-first century audiences. Paperback published: April 27, 2015

[xviii] Khaldun, Ibn. *The Muqaddimah: An Introduction to History* - Abridged Edition translated by Franz Rosenthal. Princeton University 1981

[xix] Kirch, P.V. "Peopling of the Pacific: A holistic anthropological perspective." Annual Review of Anthropology 2010, pp. 39, 131-148

[xx] Kirch, P.V. *How chiefs became Kings: Divine kingship and the rise of archaic states in ancient Hawai'i*. University of California Press, 1st edition. Dec 2 2010

[xxi] Kayser, M; Brauer, S. "Melanesian and Asian Origins of Polynesians: MtDNA and Y-Chromosome Gradients Across the Pacific." Molecular Biology and Evolution. 2006

[xxii] Skoglund, Pontus. "Genomic insights into the peopling of Southwest Pacific" Nature. Oct 2016

[xxiii] *Concise History of the World an Illustrated Timeline*. eds Neil Kagan, Jerry H. Bently, Director Board of Advisers. National Geographic. 2006

[xxiv] Referencing the authors lectures and notes: 2013 January Workbook pp. 29-34

[xxv] Fofo I. F. Sunia, *Lupe o le Foaga* (the lead pigeon of the flock), Self Published by Fofo Sunia, Fagatogo, American Samoa, 1997, 2nd edition 2000, pg.35-53. My translation

[xxvi] Wikipedia contributors. "Fish locomotion." Wikipedia, The Free Encyclopedia. Wikipedia, The Free Encyclopedia, 18 Aug. 2020. Web. 23 Nov. 2020.

[xxvii] Pratt G. *Samoan Dictionary: English and Samoan, and Samoan and English, with a Short Grammar of the Samoan Dialect*, London Missionary Soc., 1862 p. 210

[xxviii] Pratt G. *Samoan Dictionary: English and Samoan, and Samoan and English, with a Short Grammar of the Samoan Dialect*, London Missionary Soc., 1862, p. 196

[xxix] Pratt G. *Samoan Dictionary: English and Samoan, and Samoan and English, with a Short Grammar of the Samoan Dialect*, London Missionary Soc., 1862 p.195

[xxx] Fuimaono Na'oia, *O Le Suaga A Le Va'atele*. (The findings of the big canoe). The Samoa Observer Co Ltd. 1996, pp. 273-274

[xxxi] Fuimaono Na'oia, *O Le Suaga A Le Va'atele*. (The findings of the big canoe). The Samoa Observer Co Ltd. 1996, p. 236

[xxxii] *O le tusi fa'alupega o Samoa atoa* (Book of Salutations of all of Samoa), Methodist Church in Samoa; Tusi Faalupega Committee. Apia [Samoa]: Methodist Church in Samoa, 1985, Methodist Church, Apia, Samoa,1985

[xxxiii] Pratt G. *Samoan Dictionary: English and Samoan, and Samoan and English, with a Short Grammar of the Samoan Dialect*, London Missionary Soc., 1862 pg.286

[xxxiv] Krämer, Dr. Augustin. *The Samoa Islands: An Outline of a Monograph with Particular Consideration of German Samoa*: Vol 1. 1902. trans. Theodore Verhaaren. Auckland. Polynesian Press Samoa House. 1994, p. 316

[xxxv] Krämer, Dr. Augustin. *The Samoa Islands: An Outline of a Monograph with Particular Consideration of German Samoa*: Vol 1. 1902. trans. Theodore Verhaaren. Auckland. Polynesian Press Samoa House. 1994

[xxxvi] Krämer, Dr. Augustin. *The Samoa Islands: An Outline of a Monograph with Particular Consideration of German Samoa*: Vol 1. 1902. trans. Theodore Verhaaren. Auckland. Polynesian Press Samoa House. 1994, p. 314

[xxxvii] *O le tusi fa'alupega o Samoa atoa* (Book of Salutations of all of Samoa), Methodist Church in Samoa; Tusi Faalupega Committee. Apia [Samoa]: Methodist Church in Samoa, 1985, Methodist Church, Apia, Samoa,1985, p.265

[xxxviii] Reference the author's lectures: 2013 January Booklet Page 91

[xxxix] Fuimaono Na'oia, *O Le Suaga A Le Va'atele*. (The findings of the big canoe). The Samoa Observer Co Ltd. 1996

[xl] Oral history from Moliga, Leasau, and Nua, The Pupuali'i, family, Tau, Manu'a.

[xli] Krämer, Dr. Augustin. *The Samoa Islands: An Outline of a Monograph with Particular Consideration of German Samoa*: Vol 1. 1902. trans. Theodore Verhaaren. Auckland. Polynesian Press Samoa House. 1994 p. 537

[xlii] *Navigators Quest for a Kingdom in Polynesia*, p.150

[xliii] Fuimaono Na'oia, *O Le Suaga A Le Va'atele*. (The findings of the big canoe). The Samoa Observer Co Ltd. 1996, p. 258-9

[xliv] Lafai-Sauoāiga, *O le mavaega i le tai / [Lafai-Sauoāiga]*, Vasa I Faletea. 1949. Genealogy of the Samoan people and stories of the ancestors collected and transcribed by Lafai-Sauoāiga. The Malua Printing Press, Apia, Western Samoa, 1988, p. 82

[xlv] Lafai-Sauoāiga, *O le mavaega i le tai / [Lafai-Sauoāiga]*, Vasa I Faletea. 1949. Genealogy of the Samoan people and stories of the ancestors collected and transcribed by Lafai-Sauoāiga. The Malua Printing Press, Apia, Western Samoa, 1988, pp. 82-86

[xlvi] Krämer, Dr. Augustin. *The Samoa Islands: An Outline of a Monograph with Particular Consideration of German Samoa*: Vol 1; trans. Theodore Verhaaren. Auckland. Polynesian Press Samoa House. 1994, pp. 556-8, 562.

[xlvii] Schultz, Dr. E. *Samoan Proverbial Expression Alagā'upu Fa'a-Samoa*. 1953. Translated into English by Brother Herman, Polynesian Press Samoa House, 1994 Edition. Aotearoa, New Zealand

[xlviii] Krämer, Dr. Augustin. *The Samoa Islands: An Outline of a Monograph with Particular Consideration of German Samoa*: Vol 1; trans. Theodore Verhaaren. Auckland. Polynesian Press Samoa House. 1994. pp.118-9.

[xlviii] Krämer, Dr. Augustin. *The Samoa Islands: An Outline of a Monograph with Particular Consideration of German Samoa*: Vol 1. 1902. trans. Theodore Verhaaren. Auckland. Polynesian Press Samoa House. 1994 p.534

[xlix] Krämer, Dr. Augustin. *The Samoa Islands: An Outline of a Monograph with Particular Consideration of German Samoa*: Vol 1. 1902. trans. Theodore Verhaaren. Auckland. Polynesian Press Samoa House. 1994, p. 539

[l] Schultz, Dr. E. *Samoan Proverbial Expression Alagā'upu Fa'a-Samoa*. 1953. Translated into English by Brother Herman, Polynesian Press Samoa House, 1994 Edition. Aotearoa, New Zealand, p 69

[li] Lameko Hon. Pule. *Samoa Lest We Forget*. Apia, Western Samoa by Malua Printing Press, Tamaligi 1994

lii Lameko Hon. Pule. *Samoa Lest We Forget*. Apia, Western Samoa by Malua Printing Press, Tamaligi 1994; also v. Bülow, Turner, Stuebel, and Dr. Krämer

liii Schultz, Dr. E. *Samoan Proverbial Expression Alagā'upu Fa'a-Samoa*. 1953. Translated into English by Brother Herman, Polynesian Press Samoa House, 1994 Edition. Aotearoa, New Zealand, p. 108

liv Schultz, Dr. E. *Samoan Proverbial Expression Alagā'upu Fa'a-Samoa*. 1953. Translated into English by Brother Herman, Polynesian Press Samoa House, 1994 Edition. Aotearoa, New Zealand, p. 64

lv Krämer, Dr. Augustin. *The Samoa Islands: An Outline of a Monograph with Particular Consideration of German Samoa*: Vol 1. 1902. trans. Theodore Verhaaren. Auckland. Polynesian Press Samoa House. 1994, p. 333-335

lvi Krämer, Dr. Augustin. *The Samoa Islands: An Outline of a Monograph with Particular Consideration of German Samoa*: Vol 1. 1902. trans. Theodore Verhaaren. Auckland. Polynesian Press Samoa House. 1994, p. 321-2, citing: v. Bülow #9, p. 10, Turner p. 238-240, Stuebel p. 72, 86, and Stair p.240.

lvii Reference the author's lecture series: 2013 January Workbook p. 73-74

lviii Krämer, Dr. Augustin. *The Samoa Islands: An Outline of a Monograph with Particular Consideration of German Samoa*: Vol 1. 1902. trans. Theodore Verhaaren. Auckland. Polynesian Press Samoa House. 1994, pp. 383-4

lix Krämer, Dr. Augustin. *The Samoa Islands: An Outline of a Monograph with Particular Consideration of German Samoa*: Vol 1. 1902. trans. Theodore Verhaaren. Auckland. Polynesian Press Samoa House. 1994, p. 115

lx Fuimaono Na'oia, *O Le Suaga A Le Va'atele*. (The findings of the big canoe). The Samoa Observer Co Ltd. 1996, pg.238

lxi Fuimaono Na'oia, *O Le Suaga A Le Va'atele*. (The findings of the big canoe). The Samoa Observer Co Ltd. 1996 p.194

lxii Lambert, Tim. "A Timeline of Houses in History." www.localhistories.org

lxiii *Concise History of the World an Illustrated Timeline*. eds Neil Kagan, Jerry H. Bently, Director Board of Advisers. National Geographic. 2006

lxiv Roach, John. "Science and Innovation, in Mohenjo Daro 101 Faceless Indus Valley City Puzzles Archaeologists," National Geographic.com

lxv INSIDE: Austronesian Houses-Perspectives on Domestic Designs For Living. Ed. Fox, James J. Canberra: Australian National University. 1993

lxvi Referencing the author's lecture presentation and personal experience: 2012 November Booklet p. 10

lxvii Referencing the author's lecture presentation and personal experience (39:51-42:15, Reference to the Maota slide that includes the labels of each title post) (The Lutu clan was an example)

lxviii Aiono Dr. Fanaafi LeTagaloa: *O le Faasinomaga*. Lamepa Press, Alafua, Samoa, 1997. *O le tusi fa'alupega o Samoa atoa* (Book of Salutations of all of Samoa), Methodist Church in Samoa; Tusi Faalupega Committee. Apia [Samoa]: Methodist Church in Samoa, 1985, Methodist Church, Apia, Samoa,1985, pg. 265-67.

lxix Krämer, Dr. Augustin. *The Samoa Islands: An Outline of a Monograph with Particular Consideration of German Samoa*: Vol 1. 1902. trans. Theodore Verhaaren. Auckland. Polynesian Press Samoa House. 1994, p. 482

lxx from Paramount Chief Fuimaono, the genealogy of Tapumanaia I, II, & III

[lxxi] Krämer, Dr. Augustin. *The Samoa Islands: An Outline of a Monograph with Particular Consideration of German Samoa*: Vol 1. 1902. trans. Theodore Verhaaren. Auckland. Polynesian Press Samoa House. 1994, p. 324

[lxxii] Krämer, Dr. Augustin. *The Samoa Islands: An Outline of a Monograph with Particular Consideration of German Samoa*: Vol 1. 1902. trans. Theodore Verhaaren. Auckland. Polynesian Press Samoa House. 1994, p. 229, 236

[lxxiii] Fofo I. F. Sunia, *Lupe o le Foaga* (the lead pigeon of the flock), Self Published by Fofo Sunia, Fagatogo, American Samoa, 1997, 2nd edition 2000, pg. 86-106. My translation

[lxxiv] Fofo I. F. Sunia, *Lupe o le Foaga* (the lead pigeon of the flock), Self Published by Fofo Sunia, Fagatogo, American Samoa, 1997, 2nd edition 2000, pg. 120-144. My translation

[lxxv] Fuimaono Na'oia, *O Le Suaga A Le Va'atele*. (The findings of the big canoe). The Samoa Observer Co Ltd. 1996, p.120

[lxxvi] Palefuiono, S. P. Mailo, prepublished manuscript printed at Fanuatanu, American Samoa, January 14, 1972, p.18

[lxxvii] *Fa'amatuainu Fa'afetai Tu'i, Lāuga: Samoan Oratory*, Published by the Institute of Pacific Studies and the Western Samoa Extension Center of the University of the South Pacific and the National University of Samoa, 1987, pp. 83-98

[lxxviii] Krämer, Dr. Augustin. *The Samoa Islands: An Outline of a Monograph with Particular Consideration of German Samoa*: Vol 1. 1902. trans. Theodore Verhaaren. Auckland. Polynesian Press Samoa House. 1994, p.533

[lxxix] Krämer, Dr. Augustin. *The Samoa Islands: An Outline of a Monograph with Particular Consideration of German Samoa*: Vol 1. 1902. trans. Theodore Verhaaren. Auckland. Polynesian Press Samoa House. 1994, p. 29, quoting Stuebel

[lxxx] Lebot, Vincent; Merlin, Mark; Lindstrom, Lamont. *Kava The Pacific Elixir The Definitive Guide to its Ethnobotany*, History & Chemistry Healing Arts Press, 1997

[lxxxi] Wikipedia contributors. "Kava." Wikipedia, The Free Encyclopedia. Wikipedia, The Free Encyclopedia, 6 Nov. 2020. Web. 25 Nov. 2020.

[lxxxii] Pittler, Max H; Ernst, Edzard. "Kava extract versus placebo for treating anxiety." The Cochrane Database of Systematic Reviews vol. 2003,1 CD003383. 20 Jan. 2003, doi:10.1002/14651858.CD003383

[lxxxiii] https://kava.com/articles/botany-of-kava/

[lxxxiv] Cook, James; Forster, George. *The Three Voyages of Captain Cook Round the World, Vol. III (of VII) Being the First of the Second Voyage*

[lxxxv] Forster, George. *A Voyage Round the World*. October 1773

[lxxxvi] *1915 International Standard Bible Encyclopedia* (public domain)

[lxxxvii] Wikipedia contributors. "Cup-bearer." Wikipedia, The Free Encyclopedia. Wikipedia, The Free Encyclopedia, 8 Nov. 2020. Web. 25 Nov. 2020.

[lxxxviii] Wikipedia contributors. "Cup-bearer." Wikipedia, The Free Encyclopedia. Wikipedia, The Free Encyclopedia, 8 Nov. 2020. Web. 25 Nov. 2020.

[lxxxix] Wikipedia contributors. "Cup-bearer." Wikipedia, The Free Encyclopedia. Wikipedia, The Free Encyclopedia, 8 Nov. 2020. Web. 25 Nov. 2020.

[xc] Referencing the author's power point presentation, Liliu Chapter 3

[xci] Original Manuscript pre-publication of the Palefuiono by S. P. Mailo. Published at Fanuatanu, AmericanSamoa. January 14, 1972

[xcii] Malinowski, Bronisław. *Argonauts of the Western Pacific*. London, G. Routledge & Sons; New York, E.P. Dutton & Co. 1922

[xciii] Joost-Gaugier L. (2006), *Measuring Heaven: Pythagoras and his Influence on Thought and Art in Antiquity and the Middle Ages*. Ithaca, New York: Cornell University Press, pp. 79-116

[xciv] Fowler, Michael. *Early Greek Science: Thales to Plato*, University of Virginia Physics, 07.23.2015. (http://galileoandeinstein.phys.virgina.edu.thales to plato/)

[xcv] Internet Encyclopedia of Philosophy

[xcvi] Mehta N. "Mind-body Dualism: A Critique from Health Perspective" (2011), Brain, Mind and Consciousness: A International, Interdisciplinary Perspective (A.R. Singh and S.A. Singh eds.), MSM, 9(1), pp 202-209

[xcvii] McClure, Michael; Scott, Leonard A. *Myth and Knowing: An Introduction to World Mythology*, New York: McGraw-Hill, 2004, Print, pg. 63-65.

[xcviii] McClure, Michael; Scott, Leonard A. *Myth and Knowing: An Introduction to World Mythology*, New York: McGraw-Hill, 2004, Print, pg. 65

[xcix] Huffman, Carl, "Pythagoras," The Stanford Encyclopedia of Philosophy (Winter 2018 Edition), Edward N. Zalta (ed.), URL =https://plato.stanford.edu/archives/win2018/entries/pythagoras/>

[c] The Internet Encyclopedia of Philosophy (IEP) (ISSN 2161-0002) https://iep.utm.edu/aristotl/

[ci] The Internet Encyclopedia of Philosophy (IEP) (ISSN 2161-0002) https://iep.utm.edu/soc-cont/

[cii] Durkheim, Emile. *The Division of Labour in Society*. Trans. Halls, W.D. intro. Coser. Lewis A. New York: Free Press, 1997

[ciii] Drucker, Peter F. *Management: Tasks, Responsibilities, Practices*. Harper Business Reprint Apr 14 1993

[civ] Muldoon, Jeffrey. "The Hawthorne legacy: A reassessment of the impact of the Hawthorne studies on management scholarship, 1930-1958" January 2012 Journal of Management History 18(1): 105-119 DOI: 10.1108/17511341211188682

[cv] Locke, John. *Second Treatise of Government*. Ed. Macpherson, C.B. Hackett Publishing Company, Inc. Jun 1 1980

[cvi] Fingarette, Herbert. *Confucius: The Secular As Sacred*. Harper and Row 1972

[cvii] Locke, John. *Second Treatise of Government*. Ed. Macpherson, C.B. Hackett Publishing Company, Inc. Jun 1 1980

[cviii] Dr. Krämer, *Samoa Islands* Volume I, pg. 615 references: Pratt, George. No.1. *Grammar and Dictionary of the Samoan Language*. 3rd Edition. London,1891 and Stair, J.B. No.7. *The names and movements of the heavenly bodies as looked at from a Samoan point of view*. J.P.S. VI.1895.

[cix] Krämer, Dr. Augustin. *The Samoa Islands: An Outline of a Monograph with Particular Consideration of German Samoa*: Vol 1. 1902. trans. Theodore Verhaaren. Auckland. Polynesian Press Samoa House. 1994, p.574

[cx] Krämer, Dr. Augustin. *The Samoa Islands: An Outline of a Monograph with Particular Consideration of German Samoa*: Vol 1. 1902. trans. Theodore Verhaaren. Auckland. Polynesian Press Samoa House. 1994 p 145,

referencing Fraser, John. No. 3. V. The history of Tagaloaaui; a tala (P.-F. No. XV) and Stuebel, O. Samoanische Texte. Herausgegeben von F.W.K. Müller Veröffentlichungen aus dem königlichen Museum für Völkerkunde. IV. Bd. 2-4 Heft.

[cxi] Krämer, Dr. Augustin. *The Samoa Islands: An Outline of a Monograph with Particular Consideration of German Samoa*: Vol 1. 1902. trans. Theodore Verhaaren. Auckland. Polynesian Press Samoa House. 1994, p.285.

[cxii] Krämer, Dr. Augustin. *The Samoa Islands: An Outline of a Monograph with Particular Consideration of German Samoa*: Vol 2 *Material Culture*. 1902. trans. Theodore Verhaaren. Auckland. Polynesian Press Samoa House. 1994, p 284

[cxiii] Pratt G. *Samoan Dictionary: English and Samoan, and Samoan and English, with a Short Grammar of the Samoan Dialect*, London Missionary Soc., 1862 pg. 322

[cxiv] Pratt G. *Samoan Dictionary: English and Samoan, and Samoan and English, with a Short Grammar of the Samoan Dialect*, London Missionary Soc., 1862, pg.290

[cxv] Krämer, Dr. Augustin. *The Samoa Islands: An Outline of a Monograph with Particular Consideration of German Samoa*: Vol 2 *Material Culture*. 1902. trans. Theodore Verhaaren. Auckland. Polynesian Press Samoa House. 1994. pp. 284-5

[cxvi] Krämer, Dr. Augustin. *The Samoa Islands: An Outline of a Monograph with Particular Consideration of German Samoa*: Vol 2 *Material Culture*. 1902. trans. Theodore Verhaaren. Auckland. Polynesian Press Samoa House. 1995, p. 31, 467

[cxvii] Krämer, Dr. Augustin. *The Samoa Islands: An Outline of a Monograph with Particular Consideration of German Samoa*: Vol 1. 1902. trans. Theodore Verhaaren. Auckland. Polynesian Press Samoa House. 1994, p.33

[cxviii] Krämer, Dr. Augustin. *The Samoa Islands: An Outline of a Monograph with Particular Consideration of German Samoa*: Vol 1. 1902. trans. Theodore Verhaaren. Auckland. Polynesian Press Samoa House. 1994pp.528.

[cxix] Krämer, Dr. Augustin. *The Samoa Islands: An Outline of a Monograph with Particular Consideration of German Samoa*: Vol 1. 1902. trans. Theodore Verhaaren. Auckland. Polynesian Press Samoa House. 1994; also Pratt G. *Samoan Dictionary: English and Samoan, and Samoan and English, with a Short Grammar of the Samoan Dialect*, London Missionary Soc., 1862

[cxx] Krämer, Dr. Augustin. *The Samoa Islands: An Outline of a Monograph with Particular Consideration of German Samoa*: Vol 2 *Material Culture*. 1902. trans. Theodore Verhaaren. Auckland. Polynesian Press Samoa House. 1995.

[cxxi] Krämer, Dr. Augustin. *The Samoa Islands: An Outline of a Monograph with Particular Consideration of German Samoa*: Vol 2 *Material Culture*. 1902. trans. Theodore Verhaaren. Auckland. Polynesian Press Samoa House. 1995, p. 261

[cxxii] Krämer, Dr. Augustin. *The Samoa Islands: An Outline of a Monograph with Particular Consideration of German Samoa*: Vol 2 *Material Culture*. 1902. trans. Theodore Verhaaren. Auckland. Polynesian Press Samoa House. 1995. p.264

cxxiii Campbell, Joseph. *The Masks of God: Primitive Mythology*, Penguin Books Ltd, London, England 1959, 1969 Edition

cxxiv Clarke et al.,2006; Fitzpatrick & Callaghan, 2009; Thomson et al., 2014; and Zhangel et at., 2004

cxxv Pratt G. *Samoan Dictionary: English and Samoan, and Samoan and English, with a Short Grammar of the Samoan Dialect*, London Missionary Soc., 1862

cxxvi Zerega et al., 2004, 2006; Chang et al., 2015; Gonzalez-Lorca et al., 2015; and Seelenfreund et al., 2011

cxxvii Campbell, Joseph. *The Masks of God: Primitive Mythology*, Penguin Books Ltd, London, England 1959, 1969 Edition, referencing Carl O. Sauer "Cultivated Plants in South and Central America," *Handbook of South American Indians*, Vol. VI (1950), pp 499-500, 502-503, 506, 510, 513.

cxxviii Ali'i Felela Fred Henry: *Talafa'asolopitoo Samoa*, Commercial Printers Ltd, Apia, Samoa, 1945-59, p 11-2),

cxxix Campbell, Joseph. *The Masks of God: Primitive Mythology*, Penguin Books Ltd, London, England 1959, 1969 Edition, pg. 183-186

cxxx Lafai-Sauoāiga, *O le mavaega i le tai / [Lafai-Sauoāiga]*, Vasa I Faletea. 1949. Genealogy of the Samoan people and stories of the ancestors collected and transcribed by Lafai-Sauoāiga. The Malua Printing Press, Apia, Western Samoa, 1988, p. 82

cxxxi Wuttke, Heinrich. *History of Script and Writing* 1972. Samoan Tattoo

cxxxii Mark, Joshua J. "Writing." Ancient History Encyclopedia. Last modified April 28, 2011. https://www.ancient.eu/writing/

cxxxiii Everett, Daniel L. *Dark Matter of the Mind: The Culturally Articulated Unconscious*. University of Chicago press. 1st Edition. Nov 15 2016; also Everett, Daniel L. *How Language Began: The Story of Humanity's Greatest Invention*. Liveright. 1st Edition. Nov 7 2017

cxxxiv Tuitele and Kneubuhl. *Upu Samoa: Samoan Words*. the Department of Education, American Samoa. 1978

cxxxv Pratt G. *Samoan Dictionary: English and Samoan, and Samoan and English, with a Short Grammar of the Samoan Dialect*, London Missionary Soc., 1862, p 20

cxxxvi *Journal of Henry Nisbet, Samoa, 1875, 16 Aug 1875 - 23 Oct 1875*. Council for World Mission Archive. School of Oriental and African Studies (SOAS) Archives, University of London. GB 102 CWM/LMS/02/05/173

cxxxvii Schultz, Dr. E. *Samoan Proverbial Expression Alagā'upu Fa'a-Samoa*. 1953. Translated into English by Brother Herman, Polynesian Press Samoa House, 1994 Edition. Aotearoa, New Zealand

cxxxviii Goldsmith, Oliver, The Traveller. poem originally published Dec 19, 1764

cxxxix John F. Kennedy's Inaugural Address, January 20, 1961

cxl Mead, Margaret. *The Coming of Age in Samoa*. US. William Morrow and Company 1928

cxli "Prevalence of Mental Illnesses in Domestic Violence Police Records": Text Mining Study Published on 24.12.2020 in Vol22, No 12 (2020): December

cxlii van der Dennen, J.M.G. "Why is the Human Primitive Warrior Virtually Always the Male of the Species?" Center for Peace and Conflict Studies, University Groningen, the Netherlands [cxliii] Bird, Eleanor M.S. "Loneliness associated with diabetes risk" MedicalNewsToday.com, September18, 2020

[cxliv] His Holiness the Dalai Lama, *How to Expand Love: Widening the Circle of Loving Relationships Atria Books; Reprint edition* 14 June, 2005

[cxlv] Nevarez, Michael D; Yee, Hannah M; and Waldinger, Robert J. "Friendship in War: Camaraderie and PTSD Prevention," Journal of Traumatic Stress, October 12, 2017. Online: October 12, 2018. www.ncbi.nlm.nih.gov

[cxlvi] Oliver, L. W., Harman, J., Hoover, E., Hayes, S. M., & Pandhi, N. A. (1999). "A quantitative integration of the military cohesion literature." Military Psychology, 11(1), 57–83. https://doi.org/10.1207/s15327876mp1101_4, Also, King, LA; King, DW; Vogt, DS; Knight, J; Samper, RE. "Deployment Risk and Resilience Inventory: A collection of measures for studying deployment-related experiences of military personnel and veterans" - Military Psychology, 2006. Online: 2016 Author. International Society for Traumatic Stress Studies published by International Society for Traumatic Stress Studies. View online at wileyonlinelibrary.com DOI: 10.1002/jts.22135)

Made in the USA
Columbia, SC
15 January 2022

53818356R10209